Voegelin, Schelling,
and the Philosophy of Historical Existence

Eric Voegelin Institute Series
in Political Philosophy

Other Books in the Series

Augustine and Politics as Longing in the World,
by John von Heyking

Eros, Wisdom, and Silence: Plato's Erotic Dialogues,
by James M. Rhodes

*A Government of Laws: Political Theory, Religion,
and the American Founding,*
by Ellis Sandoz

Hans Jonas: The Integrity of Thinking,
by David J. Levy

Lonergan and the Philosophy of Historical Existence,
by Thomas J. McPartland

The Narrow Path of Freedom and Other Essays,
by Eugene Davidson

*Transcendence and History: The Search for
Ultimacy from Ancient Societies to Postmodernity,*
by Glenn Hughes

Voegelin, Schelling,

and the Philosophy of Historical Existence

Jerry Day

University of Missouri Press   Columbia and London

Copyright © 2003 by
The Curators of the University of Missouri
University of Missouri Press, Columbia, Missouri 65201
Printed and bound in the United States of America
All rights reserved
5 4 3 2 1   07 06 05 04 03

Library of Congress Cataloging-in-Publication Data

Day, Jerry, 1964–
    Voegelin, Schelling, and the philosophy of historical
existence / Jerry Day.
        p.   cm. — (Eric Voegelin Institute series in
political philosophy)
    Includes bibliographical references and index.
    ISBN 0-8262-1493-2 (alk. paper)
    1. Voegelin, Eric, 1901–   2. Schelling, Friedrich
Wilhelm Joseph von, 1775–1854.   3. History—
Philosophy.   I. Title.   II. Series.
B3354.V884 D39   2003
193—dc22   2003016072

♾ ™ This paper meets the requirements of the
American National Standard for Permanence of Paper
for Printed Library Materials, z39.48, 1984.

Designer: Kristie Lee
Typesetter: Phoenix Type, Inc.
Printer and Binder: Thomson-Shore, Inc.
Typefaces: Adobe Garamond and Gill Sans

Publication of this book has been assisted by generous
contributions from Eugene Davidson and the Eric
Voegelin Institute.

CONTENTS

ACKNOWLEDGMENTS

I shall begin with the pleasant task of thanking the people most responsible for improving my understanding of the specific themes discussed in this book. Zdravko Planinc originally suggested that I examine Voegelin's unpublished work on Schelling, specifically the "Last Orientation" part of the *History of Political Ideas,* during a visit to the Voegelin archives at Stanford University. He then supervised the doctoral dissertation on Voegelin's use of Schelling that grew out of my initial engagement with the unpublished material. Barry Cooper responded to an early paper I presented on the subject of my dissertation at the 1997 meeting of the American Political Science Association, raised several questions and problems for the interpretation of Schelling and Voegelin, and later shared with me part of his own research on Voegelin's use of Schelling. Ron Srigley spent countless hours with me discussing my accounts of Voegelin's central texts and proved himself to be an invaluable friend at every stage of my work and personal life. Oona Ajzenstat and I had thoughtful discussions about Voegelin's philosophy of consciousness, based on her work on Emmanuel Levinas. Geoffrey Price improved my understanding of Schelling's reception by continental thinkers in the early twentieth century and respectfully challenged my understanding of Christian eschatology within and beyond Voegelin's thought. Ellis Sandoz provided me with several opportunities to present my research to the Eric Voegelin Society meetings of the American Political Science Association, one of which included the organization of an international panel on Voegelin's understanding of the Germanic spiritual sciences *(Geisteswissenschaften).* Fred Lawrence kindly took on the responsibilities of an external examiner for my dissertation and provided me with an extensive and thoughtful review of my work. P. T. Kroeker, D. Clark, P. Widdicombe, and H. Stover read my dissertation carefully and improved my understanding of various matters with thoughtful questions and comments. Daniel Shapiro kindly provided stylistic guidance during the transition of this manuscript from dissertation to book, as did two anonymous readers for the University of Missouri Press. Beverly Jarrett, Jane Lago, Karen Renner, and Annette Wenda—each acting with or for the University of Missouri Press—took on various duties with a professional and cordial manner that I greatly appreciated throughout the publication process.

Kathleen Austin courageously bore our first child, Aidan, during the publication stage of this book. She also made my scholarly tasks a great deal more pleasant with her cheerfulness, perpetual interest in noble things, and critical eye for suspect turns of phrase, all of which help to keep me good-spirited in our daily life together.

Finally, I wish to dedicate this book to the memory of my father, Gerald Q. Day, and the honor of my mother, Betty N. Day, without whose care and support over the years nothing achieved here would have been possible.

⌒

I am grateful for the permission to reprint from the following works:

Reprinted from *Anamnesis,* translated and edited by Gerhart Niemeyer, by permission of the University of Missouri Press. Copyright © 1978 by the Curators of the University of Missouri.

Reprinted from *The Collected Works of Eric Voegelin, Volume 14: Order and History, Volume I, Israel and Revelation,* edited by Maurice P. Hogan, by permission of the University of Missouri Press. Copyright © 2001 by the Curators of the University of Missouri.

Reprinted from *The Collected Works of Eric Voegelin, Volume 15: Order and History, Volume II, The World of the Polis,* edited by Athanasios Moulakis, by permission of the University of Missouri Press. Copyright © 2000 by the Curators of the University of Missouri.

Reprinted from *The Collected Works of Eric Voegelin, Volume 16: Order and History, Volume III, Plato and Aristotle,* edited by Dante Germino, by permission of the University of Missouri Press. Copyright © 2000 by the Curators of the University of Missouri.

Reprinted from *The Collected Works of Eric Voegelin, Volume 17: Order and History, Volume IV, The Ecumenic Age,* edited by Michael Franz, by permission of the University of Missouri Press. Copyright © 2000 by the Curators of the University of Missouri.

Reprinted from *The Collected Works of Eric Voegelin, Volume 18: Order and History, Volume V, In Search of Order,* edited by Ellis Sandoz, by permission of the University of Missouri Press. Copyright © 2000 by the Curators of the University of Missouri.

Reprinted from *The Collected Works of Eric Voegelin, Volume 25: History of Political Ideas, Volume VII, The New Order and Last Orientation,* edited by Jürgen Gebhardt and Thomas A. Hollweck, by permission of the University of Missouri Press. Copyright © 1999 by the Curators of the University of Missouri.

ABBREVIATIONS

Works by F. W. J. von Schelling

Werke   Schelling's *Sämmtliche Werke,* Manfred Schröter edition
with page numbers from the original K. F. A. Schelling
edition. The pagination from the original edition is still
retained by most other editions and scholarly studies. There
are fourteen volumes in this work, divided into two parts
(Abtheilungen). A typical reference might read 1.6.152, where
the respective numbers account for part, volume, and page.

Works by Eric Voegelin

Anam.   *Anamnesis.* Ed. and trans. Gerhart Niemeyer. Columbia:
University of Missouri Press, 1990.

Anam. Ger.   *Anamnesis: Zur Theorie der Geschichte und Politik.* Munich:
R. Piper and Co. Verlag, 1966.

AR   *Autobiographical Reflections.* Ed. Ellis Sandoz. Baton
Rouge: Louisiana State University Press, 1989.

Conversations *Conversations with Eric Voegelin.* Ed. E. O'Connor.
Montreal: Thomas More Institute, 1980.

CW   *The Collected Works of Eric Voegelin.* Ed. Paul Caringella,
Jürgen Gebhardt, Thomas A. Hollweck, and Ellis Sandoz.
34 vols. Columbia: University of Missouri Press, 1990–
2000. A typical reference might read *CW,* 25:222, where
the respective numbers indicate volume and page.

"EESH"   "Equivalences of Experience and Symbolization in
                History." In *CW,* 12:115–33.
FER   *From Enlightenment to Revolution.* Ed. John H. Hallowell.
                Durham: Duke University Press, 1975.
"Immortality"   "Immortality: Experience and Symbol." In *CW,* 12:52–94.
"LO"   "Last Orientation," title of the last completed part of the
                History of Political Ideas, which Voegelin never published
                during his lifetime; typescript located in the Hoover
                Institution Archives (Stanford University), Voegelin
                Papers, box 59, folder 7, pp. 126–244; now published in
                CW, 25:173–250.
NSP   *The New Science of Politics.* Chicago: University of
                Chicago Press, 1952.
OH   *Order and History.* Columbia: University of Missouri Press,
                2000–2001. A typical reference might read *OH,* 5:22,
                where the respective numbers indicate volume and page:
                Vol. 1, *Israel and Revelation* (1956).
                Vol. 2, *The World of the Polis* (1957).
                Vol. 3, *Plato and Aristotle* (1957).
                Vol. 4, *The Ecumenic Age* (1974).
                Vol. 5, *In Search of Order* (1987).

Voegelin, Schelling,
and the Philosophy of Historical Existence

INTRODUCTION

Eric Voegelin was an Austro-American political philosopher and historian. This book examines the extent to which he drew upon a number of relatively unknown writings by F. W. J. Schelling in the formation of his mature philosophy of consciousness and historiography.

Voegelin was born in Cologne, Germany, in 1901, to a German father and a Viennese mother. His family lived in Cologne and Königswinter for most of his early youth, but moved to Vienna in 1910, then capital of the Austro-Hungarian Empire. Shortly after the First World War and the decomposition of the empire that followed, Voegelin began to study at the Law School of the University of Vienna, where he received a doctorate in political science *(Doctor rerum politicarum)* in 1922. The years following his graduation were not immediately filled with professorial employment. Instead, they were composed of more study and the beginnings of significant travel. Voegelin won numerous fellowships with which to pursue postdoctoral studies in England, Germany, the United States, and France. He met colleagues in some of these places who would later prove themselves to be friends in a time of crisis. Six years of further study and travel brought Voegelin back to Vienna and a relatively secure teaching position (as *Privatdozent*) in general political science and sociology at the university from which he had graduated. Voegelin married Lissy Onken a few years later, in 1932, and by 1935 received a promotion to associate professor of political science *(a.o. Universitätsprofessor)*. All seemed well for Voegelin. A first-rank education in the social sciences undertaken with some of the world's most influential scholars, extensive travel to broaden the existential reaches of his book learning, the promising beginning of a new family, an attractive teaching position with stimulating colleagues, and the potential for financial stability all pointed the way to a fruitful life of study and scientific discovery. Not long after the start of this promising career in Vienna, however, Voegelin and his wife were forced to flee their homeland in the middle of July 1938. Their flight was necessitated by the Nazis' recent occupation of Austria, during the so-called *Anschluss,* the invasion and forcible incorporation of the country into the German Reich. Voegelin had been specifically marked by the Gestapo for his publication of several books in the early thirties that, among other things, highlighted the impossibility of justifying Nazi race propaganda on grounds of sociopolitical science.[1] A few months later, he managed to secure a temporary teaching position at Harvard University, drawing on the resources of friends and colleagues he met while traveling. This position allowed him and his wife to emigrate to the United States, where they eventually became citizens, in 1944, retaining this citizenship until their deaths but never having children.

Voegelin's work began to attract serious attention from American conservatives in the early 1950s. The book that created his initial celebrity was *The New Science of Politics* (1952). It became a best-seller by academic standards and won him the distinction of being chosen as the political philosopher whose work could guide the editorial policies of *Time* magazine. The editors of *Time* were interested in Voegelin because his work provided them, they supposed, with a responsible guide for critical journalism during the cold war. They praised Voegelin's thought by distinguishing it from what they called the lamentable state of "intellectuality" in the modern West. They specified their understanding of the central problem with sociopolitical science at the time as follows: "[T]he idea of an objective, unchanging moral law is hotly denied by many social scientists, defended by other intellectuals and by a lot of non-intellectuals. The resulting confusion, the lack of a common ground, may explain why the man in the street today has no poet and the popular lecture hall no philosopher."[2] In Voegelin, the editors of *Time* found someone who could offer them a compelling intellectual basis for recovering the "common ground" of their disintegrating civilization. More to the point, they found his work offered a historical science of myth and poetry that, as the editorial itself demonstrates, could be translated into common-

---

1. Barry Cooper tells the story of the Voegelins' narrow escape from the Gestapo in *Eric Voegelin and the Foundations of Modern Political Science,* chap. 1. Much of the foregoing biographical material has been derived from a series of letters, published by Cooper, that Voegelin wrote in application for teaching positions in the United States, describing his curriculum vitae and the circumstances leading to his particular need for emigration papers and employment.

2. Review article on Voegelin's *New Science of Politics,* "Journalism and Joachim's Children."

sense terms for the "man in the street." They also found that Voegelin could elaborate an attractive theoretical philosophy of order for the lecture hall, one that was capable of making great strides in transcending problems associated with the modus operandi of contemporary social science, that is to say, the methodic separation of public or objective facts and private or subjective values. The editors were able, it appears, to sense something more to life than the fact/value distinction allowed them to address—precisely the common ground of their humanity—and they looked to Voegelin to help them with the articulation of its nature and scope.

Voegelin was ultimately of little help to conservative journalists, however. Aside from two relatively short studies directed to problems associated with positivism, he did not choose to dwell on what he considered to be the decay of political philosophy in the social sciences.[3] Instead, he turned to focus on the recovery of philosophy per se, of which he held political philosophy to be an important part. The editors of *Time* were correct to say that Voegelin wanted, in part, to regain a philosophically defensible understanding of the common ground of humanity. But they were quite wrong to imply that he would do so by appeals to "the idea of an objective, unchanging moral law." Voegelin was not a moralist. He was a philosopher who found it necessary, through argumentation based on the history of experience and symbolization, to discard much of what he considered to be no more than the social-scientific jargon of his time—the language of "facts and values," "conservatives and liberals," "subjects and objects," and the division of humanity into "worldviews," "belief systems," "perspectives," and the like—an abstract language that he considered to be part of the self-understanding of modern intellectuals with little or no genuine understanding of the life experiences of their predecessors. Thus, instead of entering into the corruption of language and the confusion of experiences he found in many of his contemporaries, Voegelin increasingly focused his critical works on the attempt to reformulate a classical or at least premodern understanding of philosophy, one that could account for the transcultural origin of human life without leaning on the works of dogmatic or even systematic theologians, nor on their reactionary equivalents in the self-styled, secular practitioners of the natural sciences. This focus on premodern philosophers contributed much to

---

3. See "Positivism and Its Antecedents" (*FER*, 74–109) and the discussion of Max Weber's unsuccessful attempt to make the fact-value distinction scientifically respectable (*NSP*, 1–26). For further discussion, see Dante Germino, *Beyond Ideology,* chaps. 4, 8; and Cooper, *Voegelin and Foundations,* chap. 3.

his eventual description of modernity as an "incredible spectaculum," replete with conflicting tensions of a disturbing though insubstantial nature. Voegelin summarized what may rightly be considered his lifelong assessment of modernity in a later essay. He calls it

> both fascinating and nauseating, grandiose and vulgar, exhilarating and depressing, tragic and grotesque—with its apocalyptic enthusiasm for building new worlds that will be old tomorrow, at the expense of old worlds that were new yesterday; with its destructive wars and revolutions spaced by temporary stabilizations on ever lower levels of spiritual and intellectual order through natural law, enlightened self-interest, a balance of powers, a balance of profits, the survival of the fittest, and the fear of atomic annihilation in a fit of fitness; with its ideological dogmas piled on top of the ecclesiastic and sectarian ones and its resistant skepticism that throws them all equally on the garbage heap of opinion; with its great systems built on untenable premises and its shrewd suspicions that the premises are indeed untenable and therefore must never be rationally discussed; with the result, in our time, of having unified mankind into a global madhouse bursting with stupendous vitality. ("Immortality," 55)

This catalog of miseries may indeed touch upon several distinctively modern problems in political reality, but its production is not the focus nor the great achievement of Voegelin's work. Its importance to scholarship lies in its ability to suggest the magnitude of confusions from which Voegelin sought to free himself. Dismissed from his university post due to his inability to find anything within the order of reality supporting Nazi race policies, forced to flee his homeland due to the same, Voegelin eventually sought to escape a madhouse of global proportions by searching for order in history.

After the initial celebration of his *New Science of Politics,* popular interest in Voegelin began to change as his work appeared to change disciplines. He became better known as a philosophical historian when the first three volumes of his great work, *Order and History,* were first published—all within one year of each other (from 1956 to 1957). These volumes, the majority of what would eventually be a five-volume work, could be published so closely together because they were based on more than a decade of unpublished writing: a four thousand–page typescript on major figures in the *History of Political Ideas.* Voegelin began writing this *History* in 1939, only one year after his emigration. By the early 1950s, however, he had decided that it was unpublishable, due to the discovery of apparently insuperable problems with his assumptions about the nature of historical research and truth. One of the central motivations of this work was an attempt to understand how the common ground of Western political and religious civilizations had been lost and how, if possible, it could be recovered. In his *Autobiographical Reflections* (1973), Voegelin says that his early *History* "started from the conventional assumptions that there are ideas, that they have a history, and that a history of political ideas would have to work its way from Classical politics up to the present. Under these assumptions, [he] humbly worked through the sources, and eventually a manuscript of several thousand pages was in existence" (*AR,* 78). The great size of the manuscript presented a problem. Voegelin initially undertook this project as a textbook of moderate size for McGraw-Hill. He began by taking works such as George H. Sabine's *History of Political Theory* (1937) as a model for such a project, determining what should be included or excluded in his own work. But the standard textbooks ultimately proved to be of limited value when Voegelin found it necessary for his *History of Political Ideas* to include interpretive work on an unlikely candidate for a book on political philosophy, namely, Friedrich Wilhelm Joseph von Schelling.

The decision to include a chapter on Schelling in the last part of the study that Voegelin would ever complete proved fatal for the entire project as initially conceived. Voegelin reflects: "While working on the chapter on Schelling, it dawned on me that the conception of a history of ideas was an ideological deformation of reality. There were no ideas [in history] unless there were symbols of immediate *experiences*" (*AR,* 63; emphasis in original).[4] In a later autobiographical comment, made in 1983, Voegelin specifies that it was one of Schelling's last works, his *Philosophy of Mythology,* that produced the decisive change in his understanding of the initial project: "[W]hen I studied the philosophy of the myth, I understood that ideas are nonsense: there are no ideas as such and there is no history of ideas; but there is a history of experiences which can express themselves in various forms, as myths of various types, as philosophical development, theological development, and so on." Voegelin realized that he was still too much of a conventional social scientist, having presupposed that "ideas" are empty abstractions, perhaps even arbitrary constructions or values, without taking into consideration the concrete experiences that motivated their expression in language symbols throughout history. This realization brought a "crash" to the *History* project: "I cashiered that history of ideas, which was practically finished in four or five

---

4. Throughout this book, unless indicated otherwise, I do not add typographical emphases to quoted texts. All emphases belong to their authors.

volumes, and started reworking it from the standpoint of the problem of the experiences. That is how *Order and History* started."[5]

An important point has begun to emerge from these remarks: the reworking of Voegelin's history of ideas into his great work, *Order and History*, began with his studies of Schelling in the early 1940s. Schelling appears to have helped Voegelin's thinking to become more concrete. But this point is itself cause for wonder, since it is still common for Schelling to be interpreted as a German idealist, hardly a concrete or realistic thinker. Schelling is best known as one of the founders, along with G. W. F. Hegel, of a school in German philosophy known as absolute idealism. Schelling eventually broke with the "Hegelian" philosophy he helped to found, but not in any writings published during his lifetime. The publication of these works was hampered by some unfortunate events. In 1811, for example, F. H. Jacobi became perhaps the most notable of several intellectuals to bring charges of pantheism against Schelling, forcing him to defend his previous works.[6] The frustration that Schelling expressed over these charges seems to have been the major reason behind his decision to abandon publishing, for he confined his publications thereafter to a few minor articles. Despite appearances, he continued to write prolifically, but his important break with idealism became known only to a few of his students in a series of public lectures shortly after the death of Hegel. To complicate matters further, these lectures were poorly received and perhaps even misunderstood. They were quickly discounted as a confused mixture of the idealism for which Schelling had once been famous and the Christian dogmatism into which the allegedly resentful rival to Hegel's greater fame had fallen. At the time of his return to public lecturing, Schelling's Hegelian students wanted another Hegel, which they did not get. And some of his Christian students wanted an anti-Hegelian apology for the faith, which they did not get.[7] Instead of trying to please the majority of his students, Schelling attempted to remain true to his central concern: to articu-

---

5. Voegelin, "Autobiographical Statement at Age Eighty-two," 119.

6. Schelling could draw attention to one text in particular where the charge was anticipated and (to his mind) refuted. See his *Philosophische Untersuchungen über das Wesen der menschlichen Freiheit* (1809), in *Werke*, 1.7.338–50. Schelling also addressed this problem in an earlier work, which was published only posthumously. See his *System der gesamten Philosophie und der Naturphilosophie insbesondere* (1804, published posthumously), in *Werke*, 1.6.177–81.

7. Schelling began lecturing to 800 students and finished the year with only 29; Kierkegaard became one of the most famous of the 771 to leave. See Jean-François Marquet's introduction to his French translation of Schelling's *Philosophie der Offenbarung*, as *Philosophie de la Révélation, Livre Premier: Introduction à la Philosophie de la Révélation*, 7.

late a defensibly philosophical science of nature and the history of its spirit
(Geist). In doing so, he neither embraced nor criticized completely the Christian tradition from which his thought had developed, and his attempt to
steer a middle course disappointed nearly everyone. Consequently, he died
relatively unknown and dejected.[8]

Schelling was too late, and perhaps insufficiently clear, to be successful in
his attempt to regain the warm reception he once received as a public lecturer.
Scholarly opinions were fixed. His reputation as an idealist had already been
firmly established on the basis of his earlier publications. And so he continues
generally to be known to this day, namely, as a transitional figure between
the ahistorical idealism of J. G. Fichte and Hegel's more celebrated attempts
to make philosophy an essentially historical science.[9] This account of Schelling's position in the history of philosophy began to change only in the early
decades of the twentieth century, as the voluminous works of his post-
Hegelian philosophy began to be published and studied by subsequent generations after his death. A more comprehensive understanding of Schelling's
late thought *(Spätphilosophie)* has begun to emerge, but more work remains
to be done.[10] One indication of his relative neglect by English-speaking scholars is seen in the fact that the most substantial parts of his late work, his
voluminous *Philosophy of Mythology* and *Philosophy of Revelation,* have yet to
be translated into English.

Although most knew of Schelling only from his idealistic writings prior to
1809, Voegelin was one of few American scholars able to draw upon his complete works and find in Schelling one of the most philosophically compelling

---

8. These comments follow a standard account of Schelling's reputation. See Emil L. Fackenheim, *The God Within: Kant, Schelling, and Historicity,* 50–53, 92–93.

9. See Victor C. Hayes, "Schelling: Persistent Legends, Improving Image."

10. Schelling scholars have not been able to reach a consensus on when his "later" philosophy begins. This situation has been caused by difficulties pertaining to the assignment of
periods to his thought. Some think, as Hegel once said, that Schelling published his drafts,
thus creating a situation in which each new book marks a new period in his ephemeral thought.
Schelling has often been dismissed as a philosophical Proteus on account of this quip. Others
see substantial lines of continuity in all of Schelling's thought. They replace strict periodiza-
tions with accounts of the development of earlier notions in his later works (see Fackenheim,
God Within; Edward Allen Beach, *The Potencies of God(s): Schelling's Philosophy of Mythology;*
and A. Bowie, *Schelling and Modern European Philosophy*). Because Voegelin would have
agreed more with the latter group, I shall use the term *Spätphilosophie* to indicate Schelling's
posthumously published writings. This division works best for the purposes of this study, for
these are the works in which Schelling develops his critique of Hegel and the positive philosophy of history so important to Voegelin.

"spiritual realists" ever to have achieved notoriety. Indeed, in the concluding chapter of his *History of Political Ideas,* Voegelin praises Schelling as "one of the greatest philosophers of all times." He credits him with developing "perhaps the profoundest piece of philosophical thought ever elaborated," and thereby with establishing "a new level of consciousness in Western intellectual history in general and in the history of political thought in particular" ("LO," 198, 208, 236). It is no exaggeration to say that this is the highest praise Voegelin ever bestows upon anyone in any of his writings. But it remains relatively unknown, because it was not published during his lifetime. The chapter on Schelling in question is found at the end of Voegelin's *History of Political Ideas,* and the part of which it forms the centerpiece bears the title "Last Orientation." To the early Voegelin, Schelling was—like Plato, Augustine, and Thomas Aquinas—a thinker who articulated a final point of orientation as his civilization entered a decisive crisis of spiritual and political meaning. The crisis of modernity was clearly evident in the political events of the late nineteenth and early twentieth centuries. But following these events, Voegelin also found evidence of a renaissance of classical philosophy through the works of Schelling. In the mid-1940s, he found a number of distinctively Schellingian elements in the thought of several relatively contemporaneous intellectuals; this discovery led him to characterize the early decades of the twentieth century as a "Schelling Renaissance."[11] To be sure, one may never have heard of such a renaissance. This situation is due, in part, to an emerging association of Schelling with some form of existentialism or another, whether of a Kierkegaardian or Heideggerian stripe. But the Schelling of Voegelin's "Last Orientation" is a "spiritual realist," not an existentialist.

In his "Last Orientation," Voegelin describes the early decades of the twentieth century as being characterized by an "undercurrent influence" of Schellingian "realism," arising in opposition to the "spiritually decadent" forces of "economic materialism, Darwinism, liberal economic theory, neo-Kantian epistemology, historicism, empirical sociology and psychology"—in short, the dominant social and intellectual movements that defined the age. Voegelin criticizes these movements as decadent because of their characteristically modern attempt to replace philosophical inquiry into the meaning and substance of reality with biological, economic, and psychological analyses of the phenomenal aspects of reality alone. For Voegelin, the decadence of modernity is best evident in its "phenomenalism." He notes:

11. Voegelin borrows this phrase from Frederick de Wolfe Bolman Jr.'s introduction to his translation of Schelling's *Ages of the World* (cf. "LO," 199 n. 2).

Parochialization of thought according to communities and fragmentiza-
tion of thought according to partial perspectives of contemporary interest,
with the concomitant inevitable decay of philosophical technique, are the
great mass trends of the eighteenth century and after. We enter a period of
confusion in which anybody can easily be right because almost everybody
else is wrong to the extent that it is sufficient to stress the opposite of what
somebody else says in order to be at least as partially right as the opponent.
("LO," 197)

This statement is an excellent summary of Voegelin's frustration with the poor
state of theoretical science at the time. However, it does not reveal the extent
to which Schelling's works helped him to understand the precise nature of
the crisis and pointed the way to its possible solution.

Voegelin found Schelling to have been extraordinarily successful in his
personal attempts to rise above the din of parochial confusions and to bring
philosophy back to its principal task: the exploration of the substance of
reality, within and beyond its phenomena, as this becomes manifest in the
symbolic history of human experiences of order. At the same time, however,
Voegelin also knew that Schelling failed to become socially effective in his
regenerative efforts. Schelling suffered the common plight of a philosophical
realist in an age of cultural and intellectual crisis:

[T]he realist finds himself in an intellectual and social environment that is
no longer receptive to the rational, technically competent thought of a
spiritually well-ordered personality. In the disorder of irrationalisms pitted
against each other, he will frequently find the continuity of problems broken. Questions that have long been settled will be resumed as if nobody
had treated them before. Elementary philosophical mistakes can be advanced
with success and dominate a public scene that has lost the rational standards of critique. ("LO," 198)

Despite the clear signs of decadence in modern society, however, Voegelin
remains confident that such spiritual decay has its limits:

[A] philosopher of the stature of Schelling can be relegated from the public scene when the movements occupying it are spiritually decadent, but he
cannot be prevented from exerting an undercurrent influence that will
swell in importance with time. The very tension between the realist and
his age that precludes an immediate effectiveness will be dissolved in a
delayed effect when the spiritually blind forces have run their course into
helpless confusion. ("LO," 199)

Voegelin claims to find Schelling's "undercurrent influence" in the works of Schopenhauer and Kierkegaard, von Hartmann and Lotze, Bergson and Tillich, Jaspers and Heidegger, Ortega y Gasset and Berdyaev. But he also finds that many of these thinkers based their accounts of reality on no more than individual parts of the total complex of experiences discussed in Schelling's thought. Consequently, the extraordinary quality of Schelling's singular effort became lost in a dispersion; his analyses of many experiences became *disjecta membra,* scattered throughout the writings of the better-known names and movements of several generations:

> the experiences of the will and the nirvana in Schopenhauer; the craving for the inner return in Kierkegaard; the psychology of the unconscious in Freud; the experiences of Dionysus and of immanent grace in Nietzsche; the social critique of the age and the longing for the Third Realm in the mass movements of Communism and National Socialism; the ominous orgiastic experiences with their anxiety in Nietzsche, in Freud, and in the orgasms of destruction and self-destruction of the General Wars. This scattering of the elements is the signature of the crisis, as their balance was the signature of Schelling's greatness. ("LO," 241)

Voegelin acknowledges only the beginning of a Schelling Renaissance at the turn of the century and its early decades. The greatness of Schelling had started to become a regenerative force in the philosophical exploration of substance, beyond the "phenomenalisms" of the day, but a philosopher equal to his breadth of vision had yet to arise.

I shall argue throughout the developing course of this book that the general character and orientation of Voegelin's lifework is best understood as an attempt to become *the* philosopher of the "Schelling Renaissance." Voegelin sought to reunite the *disjecta membra* of Schelling's thought in a properly "tensional" balance by attempting to develop a comprehensive philosophy of consciousness, symbolization, and its history. More specifically, after writing his early chapter "On Schelling," he began to recast his work in Schellingian form by taking materials from his abandoned *History of Political Ideas* and representing them under the rubrics by which his great work is named: "order" and "history." These are the twin pillars of a characteristically Schellingian understanding of philosophy, specifically in its "negative" philosophy of order and its "positive" philosophy of historical existence. Voegelin's attempt to develop the scattered elements of Schelling's thought in his own philosophy of consciousness and history is still far from obvious to his best-known interpreters, despite the evidence of Schellingian elements throughout his writings. This situation holds true for two reasons. First, as previously mentioned, Schelling's later works are still relatively unknown to the English-speaking scholars for whom Voegelin's major studies are most immediately accessible. Second, and more important, most of Voegelin's published references to Schelling are depreciatory. Schelling is criticized more than he is praised in almost all of Voegelin's publications. Accordingly, one is not likely to suspect that Voegelin ever learned anything transformative from Schelling. On the basis of the published writings alone, it would seem that Voegelin found Schelling to have been little more than a Hegelian idealist, an assessment much in keeping with conventional accounts of his place in the history of modern philosophy.

In light of this situation, one might justifiably wonder why a study of Voegelin's indebtedness to Schelling is needed at all. There seems to be an obvious solution to the question of the relationship. At most, it might be argued, Voegelin appears to have had some interest in Schelling's philosophy during the earliest part of his career, but he never published the fruits of this interest—his "Last Orientation" chapter on Schelling—and was openly critical of him in the vast majority of his publications, all of which may indicate that he simply changed his mind about Schelling and turned in a new direction of his own. This argument could stand were it not for a few decisive facts. First, near the end of his life, in his autobiographical reflections, Voegelin himself provided his interpreters with the means to assess Schelling's formative importance to his own thought. Second, Voegelin never destroyed his early work on Schelling but considered publishing it, also near the end of his life, as part of the last volume of *Order and History*.[12] Finally, and surprisingly, Voegelin's late autobiographical reflections agree substantially with his early assessment of Schelling's greatness. These points have prompted my research to question what elements of Schelling's thought may have continued to play significant roles in the formation of Voegelin's mature philosophy of consciousness and history, even in the works where he is explicitly critical of Schelling. This question has not been sufficiently examined by other scholars. To be sure, most books on Voegelin have at least one reference to Schelling

---

12. In 1969 and 1971, Voegelin sent two letters to his publisher concerning the contents proposed for *In Search of Order*, the last volume of *Order and History* (see *CW*, 28:239–43). The "Schelling" chapter from the *History of Political Ideas* is planned for publication in both letters.

in their indexes. But the reference is, generally speaking, a reproduction without further discussion of one of the autobiographical comments where an elderly Voegelin recalls his early encounter with Schelling. There are, however, a few notable exceptions in the scholarship.

Review of Scholarship

Voegelin's "Last Orientation" chapter on Schelling has been known to a few scholars for several decades, and some began to address the question of Voegelin's indebtedness to Schelling even before its publication. Jürgen Gebhardt, an editor of Voegelin's *Collected Works,* was perhaps the first to publish quotes from Voegelin's "Last Orientation." He did so in two articles from the early 1980s: one examining Voegelin's notion of "spiritual realism," and the other his own account of how the symbol of "universal humanity" develops throughout history.[13] However, Gebhardt is not primarily concerned with the relationship between Voegelin and Schelling's thought in either of these articles, perhaps because he reads the "spiritual realist" discussed in the "Last Orientation" as a reference to Voegelin himself, rather than as Voegelin's reference to Schelling. Consequently, neither article provides a detailed analysis of how Voegelin's early appreciation for particular elements in Schelling's thought may have continued in his later explicitly critical works. In the final analysis, Gebhardt appears to think that Schelling had little to do with the development of Voegelin's mature philosophy.

The "Last Orientation" has recently come to light as volume 25 of Voegelin's posthumously published *Collected Works.* Gebhardt is the volume's editor, but his introduction says nothing substantially new about the question of Voegelin's relationship to Schelling. Gebhardt acknowledges:

> Schelling had figured prominently throughout Voegelin's early work [of the 1930s]. In the unpublished "Herrschaftslehre" and in *Race and State* Voegelin refers to Schelling as an intellectual authority. In particular [Voegelin's] analysis of the myth-making function of the political idea had drawn on Schelling's theory of myths. Thus, the ["Last Orientation"] chapter on Schelling presents a reinterpretation and is linked immediately with the incipient work on a theory of consciousness. (*CW,* 25:29)

13. See Gebhardt, "Erfahrung und Wirklichkeit—Amerkungen zur Politischen Wissenschaft des spirituellen Realismus" and "Toward the Process of Universal Mankind: The Formation of Voegelin's Philosophy of History."

Gebhardt touches upon a number of significant points in this passage, all of which will be discussed in due course, but he does not attempt to follow up this suggested link between Voegelin's studies of Schelling and the development of his philosophy of consciousness. Instead, he drops all discussion of Schelling in favor of Max Scheler as the most important guide to Voegelin's understanding of philosophical anthropology.[14] Gebhardt's turn to Scheler is occasioned by his acceptance of Voegelin's later critical remarks against Schelling.[15] Consequently, his work leaves the central question of my study essentially unexamined.

Paul Gottfried has also discussed the matter briefly. He read Gebhardt's work from the early 1980s and developed a brief discussion of the extent to which Voegelin's thought may be in general agreement with Schelling's. Gottfried's account relies heavily upon a few salutary references to Schelling's process theology in Voegelin's early essay "On the Theory of Consciousness" (1943), and on the publication of several quotes from the "Last Orientation" in Gebhardt's articles. Gottfried also refers occasionally to volume 4 of *Order and History* (1974), ostensibly to reveal Voegelin's—at times Schellingian, at others Hegelian—understanding of order and truth in the developing process of world history. Unfortunately, Gottfried leaves his readers with a somewhat confused account of Voegelin's actual conception of truth in history. On the one hand, he argues:

> In exploring the history of consciousness, Voegelin applies a Schellingian, and even Hegelian, criterion of progress. He undertakes to classify the experiences of [divine] transcendence in terms of the growing openness to being.... Thus Voegelin, while interpreting Christian revelation as being one of many "symbolic" expressions of religious encounter, asserts that St. Paul's "experience of the God of the beyond" was a fuller one than that of Isaiah and Plato.[16]

14. The discussion of Scheler's importance to Voegelin's thinking is at present speculative, as Voegelin had less to say about him than about Schelling. William Petropulos has begun to address the issue in "Eric Voegelin and German Sociology" and "Social Science and Salvation: Notes on One Branch of German Sociology."

15. Gebhardt refers his readers to one place where the later Voegelin dismisses Schelling as a "Gnostic" intellectual who confuses humanity with divinity (*OH*, 4:21). But then he jumps to the conclusion that "Voegelin never again referred to Schelling with such enthusiasm as in this ['Last Orientation'] presentation of his philosophy, because his evocation of a divine image in which blend the features of Dionysus and Christ fell under the verdict of modern Gnosticism" (*CW*, 25:31). As the rest of this book attempts to prove, this statement is a premature closure of what turns out to be a complex matter.

16. Gottfried, *The Search for Historical Meaning: Hegel and the Postwar American Right*, 100.

Although the relationship in Voegelin's later thought between Saint Paul's "pneumatic" and Plato's "noetic" experiences of revelation is more complex than Gottfried suggests, there are aspects of Voegelin's mature philosophy of history that are developmental or providentially historicist in nature, and thus perhaps Schellingian or Hegelian. On the other hand, Gottfried claims that Voegelin's conception of "the possibility, and even probability, of backsliding from a higher to a lower level of religious consciousness within the same civilization, [makes Voegelin's] view of cumulative spiritual advance . . . less mechanistic than Hegel's." Ultimately, Gottfried does not decide the issue of whether Voegelin's thought was more consistent with the mature thought of Hegel or the later Schelling. This confusion may stem from ambiguities in Voegelin's changing assessments of Schelling, or it may be rooted in Gottfried's own failure to address the complexity of Voegelin's historiography. Despite this difficulty, Gottfried does manage to suggest, albeit without supporting textual evidence, several points of agreement between Voegelin and Schelling: both men, as "philosopher-mystics," deplored the divorce between theology and philosophy; both criticized rationalists "who tried to imprison the divine substance within all-encompassing systems," that is, both were critical of idealism; their philosophical explorations of the history of consciousness comprised in large part attempts to understand the truth of religious mythology; and both sought a middle position between Kant and Hegel with regard to how the divine ground of being can be understood as "present and operative in consciousness." Some of these points will prove to have merit. Yet the manner in which Gottfried advances them results in an unconvincing estimation of Schelling's importance to Voegelin. Gottfried makes his claims without mentioning any of Voegelin's critical remarks against Schelling—by far the majority of his published references. This is a remarkable oversight. As a result, Gottfried leaves his readers with the strong impression that Voegelin's use of Schelling, characterized ostensibly by "a spirit of indulgence born of admiration," resulted in something akin to the famous case of Samuel Taylor Coleridge's plagiarism of Schelling.[17] It is relatively easy for Gottfried to give his readers this impression, because he neglects to comment on Voegelin's published attestations to Schelling's role in the guidance of his own thought.[18] Finally, and least persuasively, Gottfried's readers

17. Ibid., 154 n. 62, 96–97, 98. For an account of Coleridge's plagiarism, see the appendix in Thomas Pfau, trans. and ed., *Idealism and the Endgame of Theory: Three Essays by F. W. J. Schelling*, 271–78.

18. For example, see Voegelin's works "Plato's Egyptian Myth" (1947), *Anamnesis* (1966), and relevant autobiographical statements available at the time of Gottfried's publication,

are led to assume that Voegelin's narrow miss with plagiarism occurred unconsciously, that Voegelin "may have been to Tübingen," the first intellectual
home of Hegel and Schelling, "without even knowing it."[19] This conclusion
cannot be supported by a thorough analysis of the textual evidence, as I
shall argue, even though some of Gottfried's less extreme suggestions accurately touch upon the general character of Voegelin's use of Schelling.

Eugene Webb also comments on the possibility that Voegelin's mature
thought may have been guided by Schelling. He does so briefly in his influential book *Philosophers of Consciousness.* This volume brings together six
modern authors to discuss the general theme of the nature of consciousness.
It produces a discussion that turns out to be heavily guided by Webb's concern for what each thinker may contribute to "any Christian thought of the
future that wishes to be taken seriously." Webb argues that all of his subjects
of study were Christians of one sort or another—"unchurched" though Polanyi
and Voegelin were—or at least sympathetic to the functional replacement of
Christian orthodoxy by "various schools of psychoanalysis." Voegelin is read,
among the other five, for his ability to serve as a transitional figure between
Lonergan's desire for objectivity in the philosophy of consciousness and the
increasingly subjective existentialism of Ricoeur, Girard, and Kierkegaard.
Schelling factors into Webb's heuristic presentation of the experience of "absolute mystery in 'inwardness' or subjectivity"—what is also taken to be
Kierkegaard's "'faith in the eminent sense'"—by being the source of Voegelin's
ostensible "romanticism."[20] At the conclusion of his chapter on Voegelin,
Webb advances a number of suggestions, but little more than that, pertaining to what Voegelin may have learned from Schelling. These include:

- Schelling's understanding of what Webb calls the "spontaneous generation"
of symbols, and the "revelatory" character of mythic symbols in particular;

- Schelling's claim that genuine mythic symbols precede the formation of
distinct peoples;

---

including Ellis Sandoz, *The Voegelinian Revolution: A Biographical Introduction;* and Voegelin,
"Autobiographical Statement." Sandoz's book appears in Gottfried's bibliography, but he
neglects to comment on the significance of the autobiographical remarks about Schelling,
namely, that Voegelin himself led his interpreters to take up the discussion of Schellingian elements in his thought.

19. Gottfried, *Search for Historical Meaning,* 103.

20. Webb, *Philosophers of Consciousness: Polanyi, Lonergan, Voegelin, Ricoeur, Girard, Kierkegaard,* 24, 19–21, 24, 110, 135–36.

• Schelling's claim that changes in mythic symbols reveal a discernable order in history;

• Schelling's notion that history is a story told by God through mythic symbols engendered in human consciousness; and

• Schelling's claim that the best place to look for this story of God is not in the consciousness of Hegel.[21]

My study finds that all of these suggestions have some merit, but they turn out to be more misleading than revealing in Webb's presentation of them. The central reason for this problem is found in Webb's attempt to place Voegelin (and Schelling for that matter) squarely within the romantic tradition, always with a view toward *using* what he calls Voegelin's "assumptions" about the indispensable character of mythic symbols in philosophy as a rhetorical transition between Lonergan's relative disregard for myth and Ricoeur's hermeneutical appreciation therefor. This placement and subsequent use of Voegelin's thought result in a number of misleading claims about Voegelin's philosophy of consciousness, and obscure the extent to which Schelling helped Voegelin to refine his understanding of consciousness, in particular, to the level of a philosophical science of order. First, Voegelin does not assume that myth is indispensable for philosophy; he argues the point at length in various portions of texts that Webb overlooks in the relatively sparse exegesis he uses to support his claims. Second, Voegelin does not say that Schelling was an existentialist but specifically calls him a "spiritual realist." Webb's contrary reading does not take into account the specific problems that this discrepancy may entail. Third, the appeal to Voegelin's Schellingian romanticism makes it relatively easy for Webb to import a number of analytical terms (especially found in his frequent references to "objective" and "subjective" poles of experience), which, though commonly accepted by his social-scientific contemporaries, obscure the precision of Voegelin's terminology and lose sight of his attempts to articulate a critical science of order—indeed, one that is largely in opposition to contemporary assumptions and beliefs about the nature of human consciousness and the comprehending order of reality. Webb's specific complaint that Voegelin's distinction between "primary," "secondary," and "tertiary" types of mythic symbols reveals little more than a subjective preference on Voegelin's part for some traditions over others is especially troubling as a case in point.[22] It readily

21. Ibid., 130–36.
22. Ibid., 123–24, 126–30.

leads one to believe that Voegelin is least impartial or scientific (and most arbitrary) in his philosophy of consciousness—precisely the place where, as I shall argue, his thought comes closest to breaking free from the bygone era of positivistic assumptions about subjects of cognition and their objects of study.

These problems and others of a more specific nature will be taken up at greater length in a more appropriate context, Chapter 1 of this study, where the focus turns specifically to consider Schellingian elements in Voegelin's philosophy of consciousness. Suffice it to say, at present, that Webb has failed to appreciate the impartial character of Voegelin's scientific investigation of structures in human consciousness. His reading makes Voegelin seem more conventional than he was, presumably in an attempt to make him more accessible to contemporaries, and overlooks the central point of my chapter on the same theme: that Voegelin developed his philosophy of consciousness with help from an unlikely area of Schelling's thought, one hitherto escaping the notice of Voegelin scholars, namely, Schelling's philosophy of absolute identity.

Barry Cooper has provided the most complete discussion of the Voegelin-Schelling question to date. Cooper is a sound interpreter of Voegelin's thought. His book *Eric Voegelin and the Foundations of Modern Political Science* argues that Voegelin was "the most important political scientist of the [twentieth] century" and concludes with a chapter devoted to Voegelin's interpretation of Schelling in the "Last Orientation." Cooper makes a convincing case that Voegelin's mature work is also indebted to Giordano Bruno and Giambattista Vico, among others, but the point with which his chapter and book end—the claim that Voegelin "built his political science on the foundation Schelling had left"—begins to suggest that Schelling was not simply one foundation among others but of decisive importance to the development of Voegelin's mature thought. This is a good beginning, but it comes at the end of Cooper's chapter and book, and it is not further developed because of programmatic reasons: Cooper's focus on the foundations of Voegelin's thought causes him to restrict most of his discussions to reports on what Voegelin had to say about Schelling in the 1940s. This focus does not allow him to discuss the central question of my study—namely, how a Schellingian legacy may have endured or been transformed in Voegelin's later works—but limits his analysis to relatively early comments about Schelling. Of course, there is nothing wrong with the need for programmatic restrictions when interpreting a large and disparate body of writings; my point is simply to call attention to the difference in scope between our studies. Where Cooper cites foundations of the "intellectual mansion Voegelin erected," my work argues for the centrality of one of these and submits it to critical analysis over the course of Voegelin's entire career.[23]

The past two decades of Voegelin scholarship have yielded a number of interpreters who touched upon the possibility of Schellingian elements in Voegelin's mature thought. But these same interpreters have all turned to other pursuits, prematurely it would seem, each leaving aside a thorough assessment of how Voegelin may indeed have been guided by Schelling. It is not difficult to find the reasons. The following section reveals one of these, namely, the great ambiguity that surfaces when one considers what Voegelin himself had to say about the man who was possibly his greatest mentor.

Chronological Overview of Voegelin's Published Remarks on Schelling

Voegelin publishes considerable praise for Schelling at the beginning of his career and in the last four years of his life. But he criticizes him severely in the intervening decades, a period yielding the majority of the published remarks in question. In this period, from 1951 to 1981, Voegelin often criticizes Schelling's thought for its "Gnosticism," usually by appealing to its Hegelian character. In Voegelin's use of the term, "Gnostic" thinkers either claim to have achieved or assume that it is possible to achieve complete knowledge of the intractable mysteries of life, death, the nature of the divine, and the meaning of world history. Gnostics claim either to possess or to have the method for eventually possessing the saving knowledge that results from the eradication of these mysteries—the knowledge that others have attributed to God alone. More specifically, Gnostics attempt to replace knowledge based on religious faith or philosophical hypothesis with even more questionable claims to certainty based on esoteric doctrines, and their alleged overcoming of uncertainty is often announced as an apotheosis.[24] Voegelin consistently argues that knowledge of divine essence cannot be attained by human beings. Thus, one would not readily suspect that Schelling,

---

23. Cooper, *Voegelin and Foundations*, xi, 432, 435.

24. Voegelin's most sustained discussions of modern Gnosticism are to be found in *The New Science of Politics* (1952), *Science, Politics, and Gnosticism* (1968), and *From Enlightenment to Revolution* (1975). Hegel, Comte, Saint-Simon, Marx, and Nietzsche are the most common targets for his critique of Gnosticism.

if he were a Gnostic intellectual, could have provided any significant guidance for Voegelin's own understanding of philosophy, the nature of human consciousness, and the broader sense of order that the latter manifests in history. But the published praise of Schelling at the beginning and end of Voegelin's career indicates otherwise. It allows for three periods to be distinguished in Voegelin's attempts to assess Schelling as a philosopher: the period of moderate praise and acknowledged dependency, from 1933 to 1947; the period of general criticism, from 1951 to 1981; and the period when Voegelin reacknowledges the importance of Schelling, during the last four years of his life (from 1981 to 1985), offering high praise of Schelling in public and private conversations, while reproducing the critique of his ostensible Gnosticism in published writings. This classification indicates the complexity of the subject matter with which my study has to deal. The specific point of this study becomes especially acute, however, when one considers the fact that Voegelin's praise of Schelling at the beginning and end of his career allows one to question the depth of the apparent change governing the middle period. By way of introduction to the discussions that follow, therefore, it will be of considerable help for us to examine in greater detail the specific nature of Voegelin's changing estimation of Schelling throughout each of the periods indicated.

The Period of Moderate Praise (1933–1947)

Voegelin first encountered the works of Schelling in graduate school, at the University of Vienna, while working under the supervision of Othmar Spann (cf. *AR*, 1–4).[25] It is clear that Spann held Schelling's thought in high esteem. In several of his works from the early 1920s, Spann drew upon Schelling—along with Augustine, Thomas Aquinas, and Meister Eckhart— to develop an account of the "inner" unity and "religiousness" that he considered a prerequisite for understanding the philosophical history of all religions. Several decades later, Spann published a work on the philosophy of religion, inspired by Schelling's *Philosophy of Mythology* and *Philosophy of Revelation,* which Manfred Schröter, the editor of one collection of Schelling's *Works,* considered to be the fulfillment of Schelling's entire program.[26]

---

25. See also Barry Cooper, introduction to *Political Religions,* by Voegelin, vi.

26. See Spann, *Religionsphilosophie: Auf geschichtlicher Grundlage.* For other important works by Spann and Schröter's assessment of the religion philosophy, see Petropulos, "Voegelin and German Sociology," 3, nn. 9–14.

Race and State

There are no references to Schelling, nor any clear indication of his distinctive guidance, in Voegelin's first book, *On the Form of the American Mind* (1928). Voegelin begins to discuss Schelling only in his 1933 book, *Race and State*. In the context of an attempt to reach a critical understanding of the emergence of race consciousness in "particularist communities," Voegelin says that "Schelling's doctrine of myth as the ground of being of all peoples or nations seems to us the first profound insight into the religious nature, in the broadest sense, of all community formation" (*CW*, 2:150–51). Schelling argues that a people does not create its mythology. Rather, the reverse is true: a people emerges when a common, inner movement of the spirit creates the basis for a shared mythology. This mythology, in turn, is what yields the consciousness that a particular people has come to stand apart from humanity, presupposed as an original unity.

> A people's or nation's ground of being *[Seinsgrund]* and its unity is its myth. Simply living together in an area does not unite individuals into a people; nor do they become a people by virtue of their shared pursuit of agriculture and trade or by a common legal order. What makes a people and sets it apart is "community of consciousness," "a common world perspective," a shared "mythology." A people or nation is not given its mythology in the course of its history; instead, its mythology determines its history. In fact, for Schelling . . . mythology *is* history itself. (*CW*, 2:149)[27]

The impulse that eventually creates a people or nation "does not come from outside." It is a common movement in the consciousness of individuals who eventually declare themselves to be a distinct people. Thus, Voegelin also credits Schelling with making "the first contribution to the psychology of particularist communities separating themselves from humanity. [Schelling] speaks of the barb of internal unrest, the feeling of being no longer all of mankind but only a part of it, of no longer belonging to the absolute One but to have fallen prey to a particular god." In order to account for the impetus to divide, Schelling speaks of a "spiritual crisis" that breaks the consciousness of human unity and drives apart individuals and their groups, eventually to form nations. In remotest antiquity, he imagines, the absolute

---

27. Voegelin is interpreting one of Schelling's latest works, the "Historical-Critical Introduction" to his *Philosophie der Mythologie*, in *Werke*, 2.1.65 (Manfred Schröter ed. with page numbers from the original K. F. A. Schelling ed.).

unity of humanity "was effected by a spiritual power," and all later separations from this original unity were "caused by new spiritual powers springing up. The principle binding people into unity was *one* God." The original religion of humanity was monotheistic, according to Schelling's speculation, and "the means of separating [peoples] is polytheism" (*CW,* 2:149, 151, 150).[28] These points bear significantly on Voegelin's broader examination of race consciousness. Even in the early 1930s, he considers National Socialist attempts at community formation to be far worse than what was once an acceptable, genuinely spiritual, though historically contingent form of polytheism. Schelling's focus on the "inner," divine motivation for the development of mythical symbols in history likely plays a considerable role in persuading Voegelin to discount the reasons usually given by social scientists—for example, natural disasters, trading practices, and other types of cross-fertilization between cultures—in order to account for the formation of new peoples and their myths (cf. *OH,* 1:14, 126, 409, 412, 2:1–14, 186–87, 4:3, 5).[29] Schelling's elaborate account of divine "potencies" or powers, which actualize themselves throughout various epochs of human consciousness, seems to have been especially important for persuading Voegelin, as it did his teacher Othmar Spann, that the primary motivation behind community formations in history is spiritual, not pragmatic. He concludes his 1933 remarks on Schelling by noting that "[t]he significance of Schelling's philosophy of mythology for the theory of community is gradually becoming clear"—for example, in Ernst Cassirer's *Philosophy of Symbolic Forms* (1925) and Gerbrand Dekker's work on Schelling's return to myth in *Die Rückwendung zum Mythos: Schellings letzte Wandlung* (1930) (*CW,* 2:113, 150, 153 n. 17).

Political Religions

Voegelin commends Schelling briefly in his 1938 study of *Political Religions.* He credits him with raising the "radical metaphysical question: Why is there Something; why is there not Nothing?" The ability to raise this question, which Voegelin laments as the "concern of few," indicates to him that

---

28. Ibid., 2.1.207. Schelling's notion of "spiritual crisis" as a catalyst for epochal advances in history is discussed in Chapter 2. The functional equivalence of this notion and Voegelin's understanding of historical "leaps in being" is discussed in Chapters 3 and 4.

29. In these passages, Voegelin emphasizes the "inner" origin of mythical symbolization and the impossibility of certain cultures influencing each other's symbols across vast distances. In doing so, he leaves behind a common practice among social scientists, which attempts to find socioeconomic causes for all hierophantic symbols.

Schelling is beyond the purely temporal and scientistic understanding of the world as mere "content" or sheer fact. Schelling has transcended the understanding of reality that is shared by "the large masses" who engage in little more than "political religiosity." He has attempted to understand the world in its spiritual "existence."[30] The point of this reference is clear enough, but it is odd that Voegelin should attribute this "radical metaphysical question" to Schelling. In his later works, Voegelin more frequently attributes it to Gottfried Wilhelm Leibniz. There is at least one important consequence to the later change. Schelling asked this question in the context of his thoughts on God's transcendent freedom from the necessary powers *(Potenzen)* of nature. And his thoughts on divine freedom in existence, beyond the essence of divine necessity in nature, contributed greatly to his critique of Hegel.[31] By shifting attention away from Schelling in later references, Voegelin avoids discussion, perhaps unintentionally, of a potentially serious problem with his critique of Schelling's Gnosticism. Schelling, like Voegelin himself, became a staunch critic of Hegel. But Voegelin never mentions in print that he is aware of Schelling's existential critique of Hegel's idealism. His awareness of this critique is to be found only in his unpublished "Last Orientation."

"Plato's Egyptian Myth"

The period in which Voegelin publishes moderate praise for Schelling draws to a close in his 1947 article, "Plato's Egyptian Myth." By this time, Voegelin has emigrated to the United States and has become an American citizen. His understanding of Schelling begins to show some changes. He clearly draws on Schelling's philosophy of consciousness and mythology in his interpretation of a section from Plato's *Timaeus* (17–27b). But Schelling is mentioned only in a general way in the concluding note to this article. This point, in addition to an odd claim made in the note itself, may reveal the beginning of Voegelin's reticence to be associated with Schelling in his interpretation of Platonic myth, philosophy, and its historical significance. The article's concluding note begins with the following statement: "We have conducted the analysis of the Egyptian myth on the basis of Plato's work

---

30. Voegelin, *Political Religions,* 58.

31. Schelling's most concentrated critique occurs in the Hegel chapter of *On the History of Modern Philosophy.* For summary discussions of this critique, see Bernard M. G. Reardon, "Schelling's Critique of Hegel"; Andrew Bowie, introduction to *On the History of Modern Philosophy,* 23–37; and "LO," 213–14.

only." This claim is peculiar, because it is only partly true. In the third section of his article, Voegelin contends: "[W]e have to remember that the *Timaeus* is not the report of a historic event but the work of a poet and philosopher; we have to take our position outside the dialogue and to inquire into the meaning which the work has as a creation of Plato." Indeed, Voegelin seeks ultimately to interpret the entire dialogue as a historic event, as "a drama within the soul of Plato." He speaks of Plato's poetic ability to "find Atlantis" through a recollective (anamnetic) investigation of "the collective unconscious which is also living in him." But Plato's text is not the only basis for Voegelin's interpretation. Plato does not tell us in any of his dialogues about dramas in his soul—not to mention investigations of a "collective unconscious." He simply does not write in this way. Thus, readers are left to wonder what informs Voegelin's particular reading of the *Timaeus* and *Critias.* The second sentence of the concluding note provides an answer: "The problem of the idea [of a novel myth] and of its relations to the unconscious could be clarified considerably through a comparison with the work of the other great philosopher who struggled with it, that is through a comparison with the work of Schelling." Voegelin admits that a comprehensive account of how Plato and Schelling struggled to understand the same phenomenon, experiencing the need for new myths, "would require an extensive, preliminary presentation of Schelling's philosophy" that, in turn, "would burst the framework of this article."[32] He is likely thinking of his own research on Schelling, which would soon lead to the writing of his "Last Orientation," the text in which he provides the suggested presentation of Schelling's philosophy required for understanding the experiential origin of mythic symbols.

In his "Last Orientation" manuscript, if not in the article, Voegelin reveals the extent of his knowledge of Schelling's account of the birth of mythical symbols through what he calls "protodialectic experiences" and "anamnetic" explorations of the "unconscious." These terms refer simply to the claim that genuine symbols arise beyond the conscious control of their symbol makers. They arise from powerful experiences in the human soul and, so to speak, call out for names of their own. A symbol maker then "recollects" these experiences and gives them names—for example, Prometheus, Sisyphus, Oedipus, and so on. Such is the account of symbol formation that Voegelin takes to be thematic in Schelling's work. Thus, it may turn out to be that Schelling, not Plato, is the principal guide to Voegelin's understanding of "recollection" (anamnesis), both in its personal and in its historical

32. Voegelin, "Plato's Egyptian Myth," 323, 315, 316, 323.

dimensions.[33] At this point in his career, Voegelin considers Schelling to be a "great philosopher," and key elements from the *Philosophy of Mythology* have already started to play important roles in Voegelin's "dramatic" and historical reading of Plato, points later to develop into cornerstones of his own philosophy. Yet, when compared to his earlier work, it is difficult to ignore that Voegelin has relegated public recognition of Schelling's pioneering work on the interpretation of myth to a concluding note, claiming in the main text to be interpreting the Atlantis myth "on the basis of Plato's work only." It seems, among other things, that Voegelin has become more concerned with striking out on his own.

The Period of General Criticism (1951–1981)

The New Science of Politics

In 1951, Voegelin gave the prestigious Walgreen Lectures at the University of Chicago. These lectures were published the following year as *The New Science of Politics*. At this point in his thought, criticism begins to outweigh praise in his published remarks on Schelling. Both the tone and substance of these remarks change greatly in *The New Science*. Schelling is mentioned only twice: once in relation to Hitler and a second time in relation to Hegel. The two citations are related by the general theme of Gnosticism, for *The New Science* is where Voegelin presents most forcefully his innovative critique of modern Western society as a collection of mass movements based on Gnosticism. The fact that Schelling is not exempted from Voegelin's criticism should now come as a surprise, given the appreciative character of remarks found in the previous period. Moreover, the fact that he begins to criticize Schelling for Gnosticism may also appear as a perplexing development for readers already familiar with Voegelin's later works, where Schelling is eventually credited with coining one of the central terms—namely, *pneumopathology*—with which Voegelin interprets Gnosticism as a "spiritual disease." In *The New Science*, Voegelin criticizes Gnostic thinkers as "pneumopathological," but he does not call attention to Schelling as the one responsible for coining this term.[34] He classifies Schelling only among the ranks of the spiritually sick. Later readers are left to wonder how Schelling could have been a Gnostic intellectual when he was also the one who coined the term

---

33. See, for example, Voegelin's sections on "The Anamnetic Dialogue" and "Anamnesis and History" in "LO," 211–13.

34. For Voegelin's further uses of the term *pneumopathological*, see *NSP*, 139, 169, 186.

central to Voegelin's critique of Gnosticism. This ambiguity first appears in *The New Science of Politics,* and it remains throughout the rest of Voegelin's published works.

Given the appreciation of Schelling evident in earlier writings, the portrayal given in *The New Science* is shocking. First, Schelling is related to Hitler. In the context of his discussion of Gnosticism as the nature of modernity, Voegelin asserts: "Hitler's millennial prophecy [concerning the Third Reich] authentically derives from Joachitic speculation." This remark refers to the historical speculation of Joachim of Fiore (1135–1202), for whom the order of history was understood as a progression along three distinct ages, each governed successively by the Father, Son, and Holy Spirit of Christian Trinitarian symbolism. Voegelin suggests that Hitler's progressivism derives from a distinctively Christian type of historiography, albeit one that has been "mediated in Germany through the Anabaptist wing of the Reformation and through the Johannine Christianity of Fichte, Hegel, and Schelling." Note well that Schelling is now placed in a direct line of progressivist historical speculation that leads right to the comparatively "flat and provincial" self-understanding of National Socialists. The latter simply replace the Third Age of Christian speculation with the *Dritte Reich,* a symbol that propagandists are said to have acquired through "dubious literary transfers" from Moeller van den Bruck's tract of the same name (*NSP,* 113). Voegelin does not explain this provocative link in further detail. Instead, he leaves one to wonder how these "dubious literary transfers" relate to Hitler's "authentic" derivation of a millennial prophecy from a twelfth-century Italian monk. More to the point, it is odd that Schelling should be placed in this lineage, as scholars are now in a better position to know what Voegelin already knew then: it is possible to make explicit distinctions between the historiographies of Schelling and Joachim, distinctions based on solid exegetical grounds. Voegelin made them himself in his "Last Orientation" (cf. "LO," 231, 233–34, 237).

The particular character of Schelling's alleged Gnosticism is described further in *The New Science.* Gnostic experiences are said to be characterized by "an expansion of the soul to the point where God is drawn into the existence of man." People who "fall into these experiences" tend to "divinize themselves by substituting more massive modes of participation in divinity for faith in the Christian sense." It is possible to distinguish "a range of Gnostic varieties according to the faculty [of the human soul] which predominates in the operation of getting this grip on God." Schelling's particular variety of gnosis is described as "primarily intellectual" and "contemplative." He is joined explicitly in this regard by the company of Hegel (*NSP,* 124). Voegelin's brief dismissal of Schelling raised no objections from any of his contemporaries. It was well in keeping with the conventional understanding of Schelling as a "Hegelian" idealist. But it is odd nonetheless for Voegelin to equate Schelling's thought with Hegelian gnosis. Unlike many of his American contemporaries, Voegelin knew and appreciated the works in which Schelling was most critical of Hegel. Indeed, they provided significant grounds for the celebration of Schelling's philosophical achievements in his "Last Orientation." But the attempt to dismiss Schelling as a Gnostic intellectual in *The New Science* would seem to indicate that Voegelin has changed his mind considerably about Schelling. Such is the strong implication, at least, though it is one that would be extremely difficult to substantiate further on textual grounds, for Voegelin's comments are impressionistic and vague, rather than openly exegetical. At most, one can say that he now seems content to dismiss Schelling in a conventional way, despite his apparently novel remarks on Gnosticism.

Order and History, Volumes 1–3

Voegelin reproduces this impression of Schelling's Gnosticism throughout most of *Order and History.* Schelling is not mentioned in the first volume, *Israel and Revelation* (1956), but is said to be a Gnostic intellectual in the second, *The World of the Polis* (1957). Schelling's *Ages of the World,* a relatively early work, is said to contain mythic speculation that resembles cabalistic and theosophic forms of gnosis. Voegelin makes this suggestion in a footnote located in the broader context of his distinction between polytheistic and monotheistic types of myth in history. "While this is not the place to develop the problem further," he says, "the suggestion may be thrown out that gnostic speculation, when it appears as demythization of the world is not an unbroken process; there may break through again, in the monotheistic phase of religiousness, a desire for remythization on the highest level of intellectual speculation. This certainly was the case of Schelling's *Weltalter*" (*OH,* 2:136 n. 22).[35] Voegelin does not dwell on this suggestion, at least with

---

35. Schelling develops his own critique of theosophy, which nonetheless retains a measured respect for its manifestation in Jakob Böhme. Schelling describes Böhme as "a miraculous apparition in the history of humanity," words that remind us of Voegelin's own summary of Schelling in his "Last Orientation," but Schelling distinguishes the historical and scientific nature of his own "positive philosophy" from the thoroughly mystical speculation of Böhme. See Schelling, *Philosophie der Offenbarung,* in *Werke,* 2.3.119–26; and the chapter on Böhme and theosophy in *On Modern Philosophy,* 164–85.

respect to Schelling's own "remythization" of philosophy. We are told only that Schelling's turn to myth is a "reversion" in contrast to Hesiod's comparatively free invention of mythic symbols. Within the larger context of Voegelin's study, this remark suggests that Schelling's turn to myth is historically regressive. Hesiod was free to write myths about the presence of divinities in the world, without being criticized as a Gnostic, because he lived before the first experience and symbolization of God's radical transcendence from the world, which, according to Voegelin at this time, occurs only with the historical advent of Judeo-Christian revelation. But Schelling lived in the Christian era, a time when myth was ultimately subordinate to philosophy and revelation as the highest expressions of existential truth. Accordingly, Schelling's high regard for myth in his *Ages of the World* could appear to Voegelin as a nostalgic fall into natural theology, albeit one "on the highest level of intellectual speculation," which tends to leave Schelling's thought open to the charge of being historically pedestrian.

The question of a philosopher's freedom to create mythic symbols resurfaces in the third volume of *Order and History* (1957). Voegelin writes of Plato's "freedom toward the myth" and Schelling's relative lack in this regard. "[Plato] evokes the new myth of the soul; but he preserves an ironic tolerance toward the old myth, even in those instances where quite probably it has become unintelligible to him, because there is a truth in it even if it is no longer quite understood" (*OH,* 3:191).[36] Like Hesiod, as one who lived before Judeo-Christian experiences of divine revelation, Plato was free to create mythical symbols for human experiences of the divine. Yet, unlike Hesiod, Plato is said to have lived during a transitional time in history, when philosophy flourished as a symbolic form between myth and revelatory theology. Due to his historical position, therefore, Plato's approach to myth is considered to be free in two respects: he is free to make myths in a traditional way, but he is also free not to remain bound to myth as the exclusive symbolism for expressing human experiences of the divine. Unlike Hesiod, Plato also has recourse to philosophy as a symbolic form to depict such experiences. His philosophical consciousness of the perpetual difference between myths and the experiences they symbolize is especially important; it allows him to appreciate the intractable mysteries symbolized by myths, without accepting them in an improperly literal way:

36. Voegelin takes the notion that every myth has its truth from Plato's *Epinomis* (cf. *OH,* 1:11, 3:191; and *CW,* 12:93).

> Plato knows that one myth can and must supersede the other, but he also
> knows that no other human function, for instance "reason" or "science,"
> can supersede the myth itself. The myth remains the legitimate expression
> of the fundamental movements of the soul. Only in the shelter of the myth
> can the sectors of the personality that are closer to the waking conscious-
> ness unfold their potentiality; and without the ordering of the whole per-
> sonality by the truth of the myth the secondary intellectual and moral
> powers would lose their direction. (*OH*, 3:186)[37]

What may be true of Plato in this summary is certainly true of Schelling.
Voegelin's interpretation of Platonic myth is thoroughly oriented by Schellingian notions. It is Schelling, not Plato, for whom the historical succession
of myths becomes a thematic concern. It is Schelling who devotes, throughout
his *Philosophy of Mythology* and *Philosophy of Revelation,* explicit attention to
elucidating how the "sectors of the personality," or potencies *(Potenzen)* of
the soul, unfold their potentialities in historical succession. Plato does not
write in this way, at least in his own name. It is Schelling who explicates
what may have been implicit in Plato's understanding of mythology. Nonetheless, Voegelin has little more than criticism for Schelling in volume 3 of *Order
and History.* In contrast to Plato's "freedom toward the myth," he accuses
Schelling of the vain supposition that all mysteries of the divine may be
overcome one day through the perfection of dialectical philosophy:

> The coincidence that the creator of a myth is at the same time a great phi-
> losopher who knows what he is doing, as in the case of Plato, is unique in
> the history of mankind. Even in the case of Schelling, who ranks next to
> Plato as a philosopher of the myth, his achievement is marred by the gnos-
> tic inclination to intellectualize the unconscious and to reduce its move-
> ments to the formula of a dialectical process. Schelling cannot be quite
> absolved of the charge levelled by Irenaeus against the gnostics of the sec-
> ond century A.D.: "They open God like a book" and "They place salvation
> in the gnosis of that which is ineffable majesty." (*OH*, 3:193)[38]

37. Voegelin's account of Plato's historical position between cosmological myth and revelatory theology tacitly agrees with Schelling's account of the same. This thesis is argued in
Chapters 3 and 4.

38. This criticism, that Schelling tended to intellectualize the unconscious depth of the
soul, reappears in the 1970 essay "Equivalences of Experience and Symbolization in History"
(see *CW*, 12:130). Schelling himself appears to have sensed the potential for this criticism of
his philosophy of consciousness. At two points in his latest work he qualifies the formula used
in his historical discussion of tensions between unconscious and conscious dimensions of the
soul, saying that this language is merely hypothetical, a presupposition used to account for
the present order of consciousness. See Schelling, *Philosophie der Mythologie,* in *Werke,* 2.2.523;
and *Philosophie der Offenbarung,* in *Werke,* 2.4.8.

This is an odd charge to bring against Schelling. Throughout his *Philosophy of Mythology* and *Philosophy of Revelation,* he frequently makes a point of distinguishing between the types of knowledge that can be conveyed by mythical symbols and Christian revelation. He makes his case clearly: myths, which he tends to depreciate as pagan, cannot reveal God's "ineffable majesty." Mythic symbols can reveal, at most, how the powers or potencies of nature form the mysterious basis of human consciousness—nothing more and nothing less. In other words, a myth can open only the book of nature, partially divine though it is, and reveal how it is experienced in the human soul. But Schelling does not hold nature to be simply equivalent to God's "ineffable majesty." Rather, he maintains that God's freedom from the world is what constitutes the true essence of divinity, presupposes that freedom is more divine than necessity, and does not claim that any myth or philosophical system could ever lay bare the transcendental majesty of divine freedom.[39]

These points could not have escaped Voegelin, as his "Last Orientation" study of Schelling's thought reveals that he knew the *Philosophy of Mythology* and *Philosophy of Revelation* quite well. Nonetheless, without reference to either of these works, he continues his critical contrast of Plato and Schelling in another important passage:

> The difference in the attitudes of the two philosophers is perhaps most clearly revealed in Schelling's criticism that Plato had to use the myth for expressing the fundamental relations of soul and cosmos because dialectical speculation could not yet serve him as the instrument for sounding the abyss [that is, of the unconscious depth of consciousness]. The criticism characterizes as a shortcoming in Plato, though as one that was conditioned by his historical position, precisely what we consider his greatest merit, that is, the clear separation of the myth from all knowledge that is constituted in acts of consciousness intending their objects. (*OH,* 3:193–94)

Aside from being an amplification of the earlier point, it is interesting to note here that Voegelin takes no exception to Schelling's account of Plato's "historical position." This is because Voegelin, like Schelling, thinks that Plato's mythology only "prefigures" the superior distinction between divine transcendence and cosmological immanence, which is gained only with the advent of Judeo-Christian revelation (*OH,* 3:92–93, 96, 226–27). Yet, when all of these points are taken into consideration, Voegelin's interpreters are left to wonder how he can truly praise Plato's free use of myth as his "greatest

---

39. These points are discussed with reference to Schelling's texts in Chapter 2.

merit" when, in tacit agreement with Schelling and other Christian histori-
cists, he thinks that Plato's historical position left him no other choice but to
be free in this way. Voegelin offers no textual references pertaining to where
he thinks Schelling is guilty of interpreting myths in an improper way. In a
later essay, however, he makes a similar contrast—this time between Platonic
and Hegelian interpretations of myth—and provides textual references and
arguments in support of the claim that Hegel improperly transforms mythical symbols into the concepts of his objectifying reason.[40] This point may
help to explain Voegelin's peculiar treatment of Schelling in the earlier text.
It seems that, in the third volume of *Order and History,* he simply continues
to conflate the thought of Schelling and Hegel in a manner consistent with
the conventional understanding of these thinkers at the time.

Consider a final point from the text under consideration. As suggested
previously, Voegelin criticizes Schelling's understanding of the significance of
myth for philosophy, but he does so while continuing to use the distinguishing features of Schelling's philosophy of the unconscious. This point can be
supported by considering the broader context in which his critical remarks
on Schelling have been found. Immediately before his critique of Schelling,
for example, Voegelin conveys the principles of what appears to be his own
philosophy of mythology:

> [T]he conscious subject occupies only a small area in the soul. Beyond
> this area extends the reality of the soul, vast and darkening in depth, whose
> movements reach into the small area that is organized as the conscious
> subject. The movements of the depth reverberate in the conscious subject
> without becoming objects for it. Hence, the symbols of the myth, in which
> the reverberations are expressed, can be defined as the refraction of the
> unconscious in the medium of objectifying consciousness. . . . Before a phi-
> losopher can even start to develop a theory of the myth, he must have ac-
> cepted the reality of the unconscious as well as of the relation of every
> consciousness to its own unconscious ground; and he cannot accept it on
> any other terms than its own, that is, on the terms of the myth. Hence, a
> philosophy of the myth must itself be a myth of the soul. That ineluctable
> condition is the chief obstacle to an adequate philosophy of the myth in an
> age in which the anthropomorphic obsession has destroyed the reality of
> man. (*OH,* 3:192, 193)

This is an excellent summary of the principles guiding Schelling's philosophy
of mythology. Voegelin focuses on the unconscious origin of mythic sym-

---

40. See Voegelin, "On Hegel: A Study in Sorcery," in *CW,* 12:232–33. This essay was originally published in 1971 as an extended version of a conference paper that was given in 1969.

bols, the relation of consciousness to its unconscious depth, and the critique of anthropomorphism that are distinctive features of Schelling's philosophical interpretation of myth. In his "Last Orientation," Voegelin reveals that he is clearly aware that these points are thematic concerns in Schelling's thought, but he neglects to relate them to Schelling in the third volume of *Order and History*. Instead, the Schellingian interpretation of myth published in "Plato's Egyptian Myth" (1947) is reproduced almost verbatim in the pages immediately preceding the critical remarks just considered (cf. *OH*, 3:171–80). In volume 3 of *Order and History*, however, Voegelin drops the concluding note in which he formerly alluded to the Schellingian presuppositions guiding his reading of Plato. Criticism replaces the acknowledgment of dependency from the earlier article, but Voegelin's interpretation of Platonic myth and its historical position remains the same—that is, Schellingian. Thus, critical remarks notwithstanding, it is clear that Voegelin continues to draw upon Schelling's philosophy of mythology in his interpretation of Platonic myth. But why he does so without reference to Schelling in *Order and History* remains, at present, unclear.

Wissenschaft, Politik, und Gnosis

In 1958, Voegelin left his position at Louisiana State University and accepted an offer to establish the new Institute for Political Science at Ludwig-Maximilian University (Munich). The first major publication resulting from this move—*Wissenschaft, Politik, und Gnosis*—appeared a year later. This text is an expanded version of Voegelin's inaugural lecture to the university. It refers to Schelling only once, in a passing remark on the Gnostic character of his "philosophy of nature" *(Naturphilosophie)*. The comment is important, however, because it reveals one of Voegelin's principal sources for his understanding of Schelling's Gnosticism: what he calls the "monumental" work of Ferdinand Christian Baur, *Die christliche Gnosis, oder die Religions-philosophie in ihrer geschichtlichen Entwicklung* (1835). In Baur's work, Voegelin finds that "[t]he speculation of German idealism is correctly placed in its context in the gnostic movement since antiquity."[41] Following Baur, Voegelin includes a surprisingly broad range of movements and thinkers under the heading of "German idealism": Böhme's theosophy, Schelling's nature-philosophy, Schleiermacher's doctrine of faith, and Hegel's philosophy of religion. Yet

---

41. Voegelin, *Wissenschaft, Politik, und Gnosis*, 9. The English edition quoted is *Science, Politics, and Gnosticism*, 3.

Voegelin's reliance on Baur is surprising in another respect.[42] Baur published in 1835, roughly seven years before Schelling had completed his *Philosophy of Mythology* and *Philosophy of Revelation* and publicized these studies in his famous Berlin lectures. In these lectures, Schelling delivers a strong criticism against idealistic speculation in philosophy, precisely the type of thinking he once shared with Fichte and Hegel. Baur knew of and discussed only the earliest of Schelling's writings, those in which he is indeed more easily classified with "speculative Gnostics." Accordingly, it is not surprising that Baur's portrayal of Schelling drew no criticism from contemporaries to whom only the early works were known. But Voegelin's reliance on Baur is surprising because he knew Schelling's later writings, and even profited from Schelling's critique of idealism in his "Last Orientation." To be sure, not much can be drawn from this observation. But it can be noted that Voegelin's decision to use an outdated secondary source to support his public dismissal of Schelling is a peculiar feature of the increasingly odd way that he presents Schelling's thought in print.

By this point in his career, the frequency of Voegelin's critical remarks against Schelling may suggest that he has left his guidance well behind. But such is not the case. Voegelin continues to use the Schellingian adjective *pneumopathischen* (pneumopathological) in his interpretations of Gnosticism, and he continues to do so without reference to Schelling.[43] Despite the confusion that stems from this practice, however, one point has started to become clear. Voegelin's conflicting accounts of Schelling may have much to do with the tension that arises between his own sympathetic reading of Schelling's later works (in "Last Orientation") and the portrayal of him that he is partially compelled to accept from the most respected secondary interpreters at the time.

"Religionsersatz: Die gnostischen Massenbewegungen unserer Zeit"

In 1960, Voegelin published a short essay, "Religionsersatz," in which he contends that the Gnostic mass movements of his time are pseudoreligions.[44]

---

42. This reliance is not simply occasional. It resurfaces in Voegelin's later writing for a similar purpose (see *OH*, 5:53). Voegelin also credits Baur, not Schelling, with helping him to understand Hegel as a Gnostic intellectual (see "Response to Professor Altizer" [1975], in *CW*, 12:296).

43. Voegelin, *Wissenschaft, Politik, und Gnosis*, 47, 69; *Science, Politics and Gnosticism*, 36, 57.

44. This essay has been translated as "Ersatz Religion: The Gnostic Mass Movements of Our Time" and appended to the English edition of *Science, Politics, and Gnosticism*, 81–114.

He refers to Schelling twice in this essay. First, in his discussion of "Gnostic ideas" that divide history into three progressive phases, he says that "Schelling, in his speculation on history, distinguished three great phases of Christianity: first the Petrine, followed by the Pauline, which will be sealed by the Johannine phase of perfect Christianity."[45] This brief remark immediately follows an equally brief list of three-phase historiographies in writings by Biondo, Turgot and Comte, Hegel, Marx, and Engels—with no discussion of differences between any of these intellectuals and their systems. This practice is by now typical of the casual manner in which Voegelin places Schelling in the company of such dubious thinkers as Hitler. A few pages later, however, he acknowledges for the first time in print that it was Schelling who coined the term *pneumopathology* in order to interpret the spiritual disease that he calls Gnosticism. The remark in question occurs in the context where Voegelin wonders about Thomas More's writing of *Utopia:*

> [More's *Utopia*] opens up the problem of the strange, abnormal spiritual condition of gnostic thinkers, for which we have not as yet developed an adequate terminology in our time. In order, therefore, to be able to speak of this phenomenon, it will be advisable to use the term "pneumopathology," which Schelling coined for this purpose. In a case like More's, we may speak, then, of the pneumopathological condition of a thinker who, in his revolt against the world as it has been created by God, arbitrarily omits an element of reality in order to create the fantasy of a new world.[46]

Pneumopathological thinkers arbitrarily deny one aspect or another of reality in order to fantasize about new and perfect worlds, which they occasionally attempt to build. They are not "realists," to use a term that Voegelin employs elsewhere to describe Schelling (cf. "LO," 199).

The Problem of "Pneumopathology"

Voegelin's first reference to Schelling's coinage of the term *pneumopathology* should have caused him, at least, to question Schelling's Gnosticism. Clearly, Schelling could not have been so much at variance with reality's order if he was able to criticize spiritual sickness in much the same way as Voegelin criticizes Gnosticism. So how are we to explain this tension in Voegelin's reading of Schelling? The task of finding a satisfactory answer to this question is

45. Voegelin, *Science, Politics, and Gnosticism,* 95.
46. Ibid., 101.

greatly complicated by the fact that Voegelin does not provide any textual references to any of Schelling's works in any of his published writings. This means that he provides no references to where Schelling allegedly coined the term *pneumopathology*.[47] It is clear that Voegelin first used this term in his *History of Political Ideas* (1945), as it appears several times in the chapters published from this work under the title *From Enlightenment to Revolution* (1975) (cf. *FER*, 117, 259, 263, 276). Schelling is not mentioned as the term's author in any of these early references. Then, in 1976, Theo Broerson wondered about Voegelin's use of *pneumopathology* and asked him where he had found it. Voegelin replied by letter, saying that he could not remember exactly where he had found it. He recalled first encountering the term some thirty years earlier, during his intensive studies of Schelling for the "Last Orientation," but he said that he was now unable to locate it in Schelling's works: "I refer to it only, because I do not want to be accused by some Schelling scholar of having pinched the term without acknowledging its authorship."[48] Voegelin's concern to avoid "pinching" Schelling is interesting. By 1976, he had revealed more of his appreciation for Schelling than has come to light thus far in my exegeses, but his enduring concern suggests a certain uneasiness, perhaps even an awareness that he could have revealed more than the occasional references one finds scattered throughout his writings.

Working from these references, it is possible to determine that the specific term *pneumopathology* was of more importance to Voegelin than it was to Schelling. This is not to say that what the term signifies was unimportant to Schelling. On the contrary, there are several places in his *Works* where he discusses the problem of "spiritual sickness"—essentially a revolt against God's ordering of reality—which Voegelin calls pneumopathology. But Schelling seems to have preferred other terms for his description of this condition. For example, as early as 1797 he notes: "*Mere* reflection is . . . a spiritual sickness [*Geisteskrankheit*] of man."[49] These words foreshadow his later preoccupation with criticizing German idealism, what he calls "negative" or purely "rational" philosophy. In his later critique, Schelling elaborates a philosophy

---

47. Neither are there any references to this term in the following standard referencing sources: the analytical table of contents to Schelling's *Werke,* the secondary sources listed in my bibliography, the *Historisches Wörterbuch der Philosophie* (Basel: Schwabe, 1971–), and the *Encyclopedia of Philosophy* (New York: Macmillan and Free Press, 1967–1972).

48. Voegelin to Broerson, February 24, 1976 (Eric Voegelin Papers, Hoover Institution Archives, box 8, file 44). Voegelin's comments to Broerson have been reproduced by the editors of volume 31 of his *Collected Works* (101 n. 35).

49. Schelling, *Ideen zu einer Philosophie der Natur,* in *Werke,* 1.2.13.

of consciousness that seeks to remind his readers that life experience always presents more to its interpreters than they can account for with rational systems of philosophy based exclusively upon reflective consciousness—what Voegelin eventually calls intentionality. Schelling also maintains that consciousness is always grounded by an unconscious depth over which reflective consciousness can exercise no ultimate control. He even wins great acclaim from Voegelin, at least in the unpublished "Last Orientation," for his account of how consciousness is related to its transcendent depth.

In 1810, only three years after the publication of Hegel's *Phänomenologie des Geistes,* Schelling begins to develop his critique of purely reflective systems of philosophy. He contends that an "illness of the temperament *[Gemüthskrankheit]*" will emerge if a proper understanding of relations between human beings and God breaks down: "For it is the soul [namely, something broader than the conscious mind] through which man establishes a rapport with God, and no creature, especially no human being, can ever exist without this rapport."[50] Schelling speaks of a "rapport" here, not of a constructed or reflective identity with the divine. According to the philosophical anthropology developed in his *Stuttgart Seminars,* he would have thought it incorrect to speak of psychopathologies *(Seelenkrankheiten).* He takes the soul to be what is most "impersonal" in humanity, and thus closest to the divine. Only the spirit or conscious mind *(Geist)* can become ill, he says, because it occupies a potentially confusing and volitional middle position between the soul and its passions. When the human spirit turns properly toward the divine ordination of the soul, it becomes virtuous; when it turns toward the passions, especially nostalgia, it becomes vicious or corrupt. Thus, Schelling understands "spiritual sickness" as a perversion of the human spirit. In one instance, he describes this condition as a "consumption of the spirit *[Verzehrung des Geistes].*" This condition may result, for example, from excessive reflection on the idea of infinite progress, "the most distressing and empty thought of all." This "consumption" may be closest to what Voegelin has in mind when he says that Schelling coined the term *pneumopathology* in critical opposition to "the progressivism of his time."[51] But what of the specific term? Because Voegelin could not remember where he found it, it has not been discovered by any of the secondary sources listed in my bibliography, and Schelling discusses equivalent states of spirit with the terms *Geisteskrankheit,*

50. Schelling, *Stuttgarter Privatvorlesungen,* in *Werke,* 1.7.469 (Pfau translation, 232).
51. Schelling, *Philosophie der Offenbarung,* in *Werke,* 2.4.13; Voegelin, "Reason: The Classic Experience," in *CW,* 12:278 (also *Anam.,* 102).

Gemüthskrankheit, and *Verzehrung des Geistes,* it is likely the case that "pneumopathology" is Voegelin's own coinage for this range of critical terms used by Schelling.

Anamnesis

In the original publication of *Anamnesis: Zur Theorie der Geschichte und Politik* (1966), Voegelin's German readers learn for the first time of his general agreement with Schelling's process theology. Schelling's theology attempts to describe how the same God is experienced differently by human beings at different times in history. Voegelin's understanding of this theology is found in passing comments in a letter (dated November 1943) to his friend Alfred Schütz, the phenomenologist. The letter has been published in *Anamnesis* under the title "On the Theory of Consciousness." Even though the references to Schelling are brief, they reveal how he helped Voegelin to balance conflicting aspects of Hegelian and Kantian thought. More specifically, Schelling helped Voegelin to appreciate the enduring legitimacy of "ontological speculation" *(Die ontologische Spekulation),* while continuing to accept the basic restrictions on human knowledge of divine transcendence developed in Kant's critical philosophy. The fact that Schelling raised and addressed the fundamental question about the universe—"Why is Something, why is there not rather Nothing?"—is once again mentioned by Voegelin. Schelling's freedom to ask this question indicates to him that something in the human soul is always capable of transcending the logical determinations of thought that lead to the Kantian antinomies. Voegelin explains:

> Ontological speculation is a legitimate philosophical undertaking, founded in precisely describable experiences, which it interprets with the means of "understandable" *[verstehbarer]* categories of process. The formalized Something as an alternative to Nothing is a correctly formed ontological concept. It is antinomic in Kant's sense, but the idealization of reason that leads to the antinomies is not "nonsense" *[Unsinn],* its problems are not "false problems" *[Scheinproblem].* Schelling's "Something" is a symbol as much as is a logical or cosmological "infinite," a symbol justified inasmuch as it renders transparent the meditatively experienced real ground of being in finite language.... Schelling's question is significant insofar as it refers to the problem of process in the ground of being, the assumption of which seems to me to be an unavoidable requirement of system in a consistent interpretation of the ontological experience complex. (*Anam.,* 29–30; *Anam. Ger.,* 53–54)

Voegelin makes the further claim that process theology *(Prozeßtheologie)*, which he finds particularly in Schelling's *Potenzenlehre,* is the "only meaningful systematic philosophy." He understands process theology as "a matter of developing a symbolic system that seeks to express the relations between consciousness, the transcending intraworldly classes of being [Schelling's divine potencies *(Potenzen)* of nature], and the world-transcending ground of being [what Schelling refers to as God's transcendent freedom from the world]." Process theology expresses these relations "in the language of a process constructed as an immanent one." As such, it resembles the theological language that Thomas Aquinas called the *analogia entis.* Voegelin commends Schelling's process theology for attempting, successfully it would seem, to describe experiences of divine transcendence with a "comprehensible" language of consciousness accessible "from within"—that is, from the concrete experiences of a human soul *(Anam.,* 26–27; *Anam. Ger.,* 50–51).[52] These statements indicate that, already in the early 1940s, Voegelin thought of Schelling as a helpful guide beyond certain perceived extremes in the thought of Kant and Hegel. The "negative" (rational-essential) and "positive" (historical-existential) aspects of Schelling's philosophy allow Voegelin to appreciate the insights gained by Kant's *Critique of Pure Reason,* while avoiding its alleged inability to account for the historical aspects of human existence. Schelling's *Potenzenlehre* also allows Voegelin to avoid the obfuscation of boundaries between the human and the divine—for example, in Hegel's appeals to "absolute knowledge"—precisely because of Schelling's greater ability to provide a reasonable account of God's transcendent freedom from the world.

Schelling elaborated the *Potenzenlehre,* his doctrine of divine potencies, over several decades in several works, the most important being his *Ages of the World, Philosophy of Mythology,* and *Philosophy of Revelation.* Summarized briefly, the *Potenzenlehre* describes all of reality in terms of a tensional process of divine powers or potencies, consisting of divine immanence (natural necessity) and divine transcendence (freedom) as its fundamental poles. This process, according to Schelling, can never be abolished by human will or thought. What is more, because reality is experienced as a process, it is always said to remain mysterious. God's freedom always transcends human understanding and control, Schelling maintains, and is properly approached by

---

52. I have added the bracketed comments in order to reflect the understanding of Schelling's *Potenzenlehre* found in Voegelin's "Last Orientation" (*CW,* 25:208–9).

the interpretation of grace experiences rooted in "faith."[53] All of these points return in Voegelin's criticisms of Hegel, who allegedly attempted to destroy the intractable mystery of the divine in human consciousness. Against Hegel, and in agreement with Schelling, Voegelin argues that human beings are akin to the divine, but nothing more. He maintains that the knowledge of how we are both alike and unlike the divine is gained in a historical process of divine revelations, but he sees no humanly willed end to the process of history.

These points of Schellingian realism become consistent features in Voegelin's later thought, but it takes the better part of two decades before he again refers favorably to Schelling—and, then, only in relatively informal public talks. The publication of *Anamnesis* marks the last time that Voegelin reveals anything significantly new in his appreciation of Schelling's thought.

Order and History, Volume 4

In volume 4 of *Order and History* (1974), Voegelin returns to writing primarily for an English audience. His standard criticism of Schelling also returns. He reproduces the claim that Schelling was a Johannine Gnostic, the point first suggested in *The New Science of Politics*. By this time, however, Voegelin has encountered some resistance to his claim that German idealism, in particular, should be understood as a form of gnosis, making claims to perfection similar to those found in the ancient gnosis of, say, Valentinus. Accordingly, he finds it necessary to distinguish between "the essential core and the variable part of a Gnostic system. The essential core," he continues, "is the enterprise of returning the pneuma [spirit] of the Beyond through action based on knowledge. Moreover, the god of the Beyond to whom the Gnostic speculator wants to return must be identical, not with the creator-god but with the god of the creative tension 'before there was a cosmos.'" Voegelin warns that in order to exclude German idealism from this essential core of Gnosticism, one "must ignore the fact that the modern Gnostics do not appeal to Valentinus or Basilides as their ancestors but to the Gospel of John. One must ignore, for instance, that Schelling has developed a law of three phases for Christian history: The Petrine Christianity was followed by the Pauline of the Reformation; and the Pauline will now be followed by the Johannine Christianity of the German speculative systems" (*OH*, 4:20, 21). Once again, this summary seems to be accurate, and certainly in keeping with generally accepted notions of how some German intellectuals carved

53. These points will be elaborated with reference to Schelling's texts in Chapters 2–4.

up history's order, but the matter becomes slightly more complicated once we return to the texts in which Schelling himself presents his thoughts on the historical development of Christianity.

Schelling's discussion of the three phases of Christianity occurs in lecture 37 of his *Philosophy of Revelation*. He says nothing about his teaching as a "law" of Christian history that is "now" to be fulfilled by "German speculative systems." Rather, he appeals to a Johannine phase of Christianity, not as something to be forced into existence by the will of a human speculator, but as a bona fide eschatological symbol, much like Voegelin's own account of the historical emergence of "universal humanity," found in the conclusion of the fourth volume of *Order and History*. According to Schelling, Johannine Christianity is equivalent to "philosophical religion." It is the type of religion that will come about when God brings history as we know it to an end, a time when humans will no longer feel the need to distinguish between the real and the ideal, the inner and the outer, and other such dichotomies. Human consciousness will be reconciled to God. Schelling maintains clearly that this type of religion does not yet exist. His appeals to philosophical religion describe his hope of being reunited with God beyond history as we know it, nothing more and nothing less. He does not say that speculative philosophy can bring about this transfigured state of human existence, but maintains that such transfiguration will need to have a divine cause, thus completing God's work in creation. Schelling links the Johannine phase of Christianity with a biblical vision of the "new Jerusalem" (Rev. 21): "John is the apostle of the Church to come, the only truly universal Church; he is the apostle of this second and new Jerusalem, which he himself saw descending from the heavens."[54] Schelling even wonders if *Church* is still the right word for a divinely transfigured "city of God *[Stadt Gottes]*" in which Jews, Pagans, and Christians all live united in the presence of the divine, that is to say, without needing to distinguish among themselves along the lines of their former religions. But he is clear about when this phase of Christianity is supposed to ensue: "[T]he Apostle [John] poses this time as being the end *[das Ende]*, and even this ultimate being-all-in-all of God *[dieses letzte alles in allem Seyn Gottes]* will not be in the manner of a pure *theism,* in the sense of our theists and rationalists; on the contrary, it will be a theism which presupposes and contains in itself all the path [that is, the history and natural unfolding] of God." The "function of saint John," in other words, the period of Johannine Christianity, "begins with the time of Christ's return, therefore

54. Schelling, *Philosophie der Offenbarung*, in *Werke,* 2.4.328.

with the last time of the Church." Schelling realizes that this time has not yet come. "This Church is, to speak truthfully, yet still to come *[noch immer zukünftig],* since until now the two elements [Jewish and Pagan] are still discernable."[55]

These passages indicate that any attempt to find the end of history in Schelling's positive philosophy will be questionable at best. I have emphasized the time and transcendent manner in which Schelling expects history to end because these and similar points are clearly known by Voegelin in his unpublished "Last Orientation," ignored in his published remarks, and speak against his treatment of Schelling as a modern Gnostic comparable to Hegel. But what of the God with whom Schelling longs to be reunited? Perhaps his understanding of God is consistent with the theology that Voegelin ascribes to Gnostics, specifically with regard to their search for a God who is "identical, not with the creator-god but with the god of the creative tension 'before there was a cosmos.'" This claim recalls the well-known point that ancient Gnostics despised nature and its god; they sought perfection in a God who had nothing to do with the creation of this world. But a fundamental point speaks against the inclusion of Schelling in such company. We recall that Schelling's early fame arose from his Nature-philosophy *(Naturphilosophie),* precisely the style of thinking that contributed to charges that he was a pantheist. But the Gnostics alluded to by Voegelin were not pantheists in any sense of the term. They acknowledged only the divinity who completely transcends the world. Schelling held nature itself to be divine, not an aberration created by a pseudodivinity. And he maintained this understanding of nature throughout all of his mature works, despite the fact that the focus of his thought changed with the 1809 publication of his philosophical investigations into the nature of freedom. It is true that the later Schelling accepted various accounts of nature as fallen, but a closer look at his account of the Fall reveals that his thought was closer to orthodox Christianity than to Gnosticism.

Schelling's account of the Fall is found in lectures 16 and 17 of his *Philosophy of Revelation.* Unlike ancient Gnostics, he says that God's creation is essentially good; the tensional powers of nature (matter, spirit, and self-consciousness) are unified at the beginning of the universe and at rest in a divine Sabbath. In these claims, he is attempting to follow traditional Christian readings of the seventh day of Creation in Genesis. He says that God ordained "original man" to preserve the unity of divinity and nature, while

---

55. Ibid., 2.4.321, 328, 333, 331, 327.

giving us the freedom to accept nature's harmonious tensions, with God as their cause, or to rebel against the divine ordination of nature by attempting to proclaim humanity as the ultimate cause of all things. In accordance with traditional readings of Genesis, Schelling accepts the notion that humans eventually fall. They do so by attempting to arrogate God's freely creative powers exclusively to themselves. But their fall does not occur all at once. It occurs as a process in which they increasingly posit the world "outside God, not simply *praeter,* but *extra Deum,*" and ultimately begin to think that God's world is the creation of their own wills.[56] When humanity revolts against God's world in this way, it sets in motion a new tensional process, one that causes the original unity of God and Creation to be divided into divine transcendence (the God of Judeo-Christian theology) and divine immanence (the divinities of nature in pagan theologies). Schelling explains the consequences of this divide as follows:

> [B]etween this new tension, which survives in human consciousness, and the original one, which was in the Creation, there is a great difference: the original tension was created by the will of God; the second is created by man; man has therefore put himself in the place of God and, to speak truthfully, in place of the God who was the *cause* of the tension and whom we have called the *Father.* Man usurps in this way the rightful majesty of God *[das Majestätsrecht Gottes].*[57]

As his account develops, the specifically Christian elements in Schelling's thought increasingly reveal themselves. He claims that "[t]he tension caused by man has separated the Son [the demiurgic Creator of the world] from the Father [the substance of Creation]." And herein one finds a circumscript version of the basic presupposition behind Schelling's account of the entire history of the world: true progress in history is spiritual; it amounts to the gradual overcoming of the Fall, the Son's return to the Father. In other words, history is Christ writ large, a drama of salvation in which all of Creation shall eventually be restored to the Father.[58] Thus, it would seem that Schelling's Gnosticism is not beyond dispute. Schelling understands all of Creation as an order of divine tensions. The God with whom he longs to be reunited is the Creator of the originally harmonious tensions of nature, the "Son" of

56. Ibid., 2.4.365, 357, 349, 352. Schelling has Fichte's ego-based dialectics in mind here.
57. Ibid., 2.4.366.
58. Ibid., 2.4.371, 375–80. Voegelin eventually makes the same claim about history (see "Immortality," 78), but he does so in the context of a discussion of how Thomas Aquinas came to understand the historical Christ as the Lord of all humanity.

Christian theology who suffers from human rebellion, not the Gnostic god "before there was a cosmos." Schelling does not strive to be reunited only with a transcendental divinity. He does not indulge in the fantastic desire to be anything more than a creature, either now or in the transfigured reality toward which he directs his eschatological hopes. This much, at least, can be stated by way of reopening the question of his Gnosticism, while reserving further treatment of the texts in which he interprets the general order of history for Chapter 2.

From Enlightenment to Revolution

In 1975, Voegelin allowed John Hallowell to edit and publish considerable portions of his abandoned *History of Political Ideas* under the title *From Enlightenment to Revolution*. Schelling is mentioned several times in this volume, always in a favorable light, and is specifically credited with solving the problem of phenomenalistic science. With his "*Potenzenlehre* and the philosophy of the unconscious" (*FER*, 115), teachings that interpret both matter and spirit as substantial aspects of one reality, Schelling exposes the superficiality of scientific communities that attempt to limit themselves to the discussion of phenomena alone, as though they were appearances of nothing substantial. Voegelin also mentions the problem of the three-stage philosophies of history, but this time he says that they developed "in the wake of Schelling" and became "an increasingly important strand in the fabric of modern political ideas." In contrast to his criticism of modern thinkers, he distinguishes Schelling's historiography from deterministic accounts of history as a perpetual march toward the human perfection of humanity:

> The construction of Turgot-Comte was defective because in the concept of the third stage [of history] the problem of [natural] substance was not shown in a further phase of development, but was simply excluded from consideration. If we do not exclude it, but conscientiously continue the line of thought initiated in the description of the first phase, the question will arise: what becomes of the problem of substance once it has passed beyond the stage of anthropomorphic symbolism? We know the answer given by Schelling in his philosophy of the theogonic process and in the new roles assigned to the protodialectic experiences and their dialectical elaboration. But we also know Schelling's ultimate dissatisfaction with a type of philosophical speculation that is a poor substitute for the forceful imagery of mythology, a dissatisfaction that leads him to expound the necessity for a new myth of nature. When it comes to the symbolization of substances, the myth is a more adequate mode of expression than a critical

concept which can only clarify our experience but cannot incarnate the substance itself. (*FER,* 116)

This passage, written in the early 1940s, reveals the general tone of Voegelin's "Last Orientation." It reveals his early contention that Schelling's critical philosophy properly addresses the problem of substantial speculation ignored by positivism. Second, and in direct contrast to the claims made in *Order and History's* third volume, it reveals Voegelin's understanding of Schelling's sensitivity to myth. We are given no sense from the preceding passage that Schelling suffered from an inclination to "intellectualize the unconscious" and reduced its manifestations in consciousness to the machinations of a dialectical formula. To be sure, Voegelin's willingness to publish these comments in 1975 hardly amounts to a retraction of his former criticisms of Schelling. But it does reveal that he may have known better than to dismiss him simply in accordance with conventional accounts of his idealism.

A philosopher's response to "the destruction of the myth, to the dedivinization *(Entgötterung)* of the world," can take either "contemplative or activist" forms, Voegelin argues, and he praises Schelling for his contemplative response to the destruction of myth by modern science. He also finds a similar effort in the thought of Henri Bergson, whose *Deux sources de la morale et de la religion* is described as having been written "strongly under the influence of Schelling." These contemplative responses to the destruction of myth are praised in sharp contrast to the "pneumopathology" of activist responses in Saint-Simon and Comte (*FER,* 117).[59] Voegelin suggests that the contemplative response can best be found "in Schelling's *Philosophie der Mythologie und der Offenbarung,*" that is to say, his *Philosophy of Mythology* and *Philosophy of Revelation.* No specific references are given to these texts, but Voegelin summarizes his understanding of their content as follows:

> The spiritual process in which the symbols of myth and dogma are created is recovered [by Schelling] from the unconscious through *anamnesis* (recollection), and the symbols actually created in the course of human history are interpreted as meaningful phases of the theogonic process [that is, process theology], manifesting itself in history on rising levels of spiritual consciousness. In this contemplative attitude the myth of the past need not be

59. There are several other references to "pneumopathology" and "spiritual disease" in this volume (see *FER,* 259, 263, 276). These references indicate that Voegelin knew of the term already in his *History of Political Ideas*—though, curiously, it does not appear in the Schelling chapter of this work.

abandoned as the aberration of an undeveloped intellect but can be understood as a necessary step in the expression of spiritual reality. It can be superseded historically but not invalidated in its own place by subsequent fuller and more differentiated symbolic expressions. (*FER,* 116–17)

This passage is an excellent summary, both of Schelling's latest historiography and of Voegelin's own. It indicates how each thinker attempts to balance the discovery of permanent truths in historical experience with the considerable changes that also emerge in their symbolic expressions. To be more specific, one finds herein the Schellingian seeds of Voegelin's notion of experiential and symbolic "equivalents" in history, a notion that first appears in *Anamnesis* (1966) and is further elaborated in the article "Equivalences of Experience and Symbolization in History" (1970).

Finally, in *From Enlightenment to Revolution,* Voegelin defends both Schelling and Hegel against Mikhail Bakunin's suggestion that German idealists have brought about the same revolution in the intellectual world that Napoléon brought about in the sociopolitical world (cf. *FER,* 197). Voegelin draws a clear line between the "derivative Christianity of Hegel and Schelling," on the one hand, and the "revolutionary speculation of Bakunin," on the other:

> Hegel's and Schelling's interpretations of history were contemplative in the sense that the understanding of history was for them the most important cathartic exercise in clarifying and solidifying their own existence. However far their ideas diverged from orthodox, dogmatic Christianity, however far they went in the direction of Gnosis, they still remained substantially Christian thinkers and were concerned about the order of their souls. (*FER,* 199)

Voegelin's later appraisal of Hegel, as previously suggested, diverges widely from these relatively charitable remarks. He eventually characterizes Hegelian thought, using his favorite Schellingian term of critique, as a "pneumopathological" flight from the actual world of experience toward the "Second Reality" constructed by an extremely selective imagination.[60] However, he never develops the same type of critique against Schelling. Instead, some of his work begins to reveal greater signs of the importance of Schelling to his own philosophical development.

---

60. See Voegelin, "On Hegel," in *CW,* 12:236.

Reacknowledging the Importance of Schelling (1981–1985)

Autobiographical Remarks

In the last four years of his life, Voegelin begins to reacknowledge the considerable extent of Schelling's guidance to his own philosophical development. He does so in the context of autobiographical reflections on his decision, several decades earlier, to abandon his projected *History of Political Ideas.* Schelling was not mentioned in Voegelin's first published account of this decision, in the 1966 Memorial to Alfred Schütz (*Anam. Ger.,* 19–20). However, in 1973, Voegelin discussed Schelling's significance for his own work, during the course of a two-week series of interviews granted to a former student, Ellis Sandoz. Most of the comments from these talks were then published at various places throughout Sandoz's book *The Voegelinian Revolution* (1981). Voegelin recalls the time when he was engaged in the research and writing of his *History of Political Ideas:* "While working on the chapter on Schelling, it dawned on me that the conception of a history of ideas was an ideological deformation of reality. There were no ideas [in history] unless there were symbols of immediate *experiences.*"[61] Schelling's role in this insight is somewhat unclear from this remark. Was Voegelin's realization brought on by insights conveyed through Schelling's works or through his discovery of their fundamental errors? In 1983, Voegelin offered further public remarks that begin to clarify this ambiguity. In his "Autobiographical Statement at Age Eighty-two," he says that his history of ideas "crashed" when he studied Schelling's philosophy of mythology. He describes Schelling as "an intelligent philosopher"—no longer as a Gnostic intellectual—and recalls how he was affected by his studies of Schelling in the mid-1940s:

> [W]hen I studied the philosophy of the myth, I understood that ideas are nonsense: there are no ideas as such and there is no history of ideas; but there is a history of experiences which can express themselves in various forms, as myths of various types, as philosophical development, theological development, and so on. . . . So I cashiered that history of ideas, which was practically finished in four or five volumes, and started reworking it from

61. Voegelin quoted in Sandoz, *Voegelinian Revolution,* 77. This remark is reproduced in *AR,* 63. Here Voegelin adds that the original project for a small textbook also "exploded" due to his studies of the ancient Israelite and ancient Near Eastern texts that would have to be interpreted in a comprehensive study of political order in Western history. Despite these other technical reasons for the collapse of his original project, Schelling is increasingly singled out as the major theoretical catalyst for the change in program.

the standpoint of the problem of the experiences. That is how *Order and History* started.[62]

This remark indicates clearly that Voegelin's rereading of Schelling had much to do with his decision to rework the structure of the largest part of the project that eventually became his great work. However, because Schelling is only criticized in *Order and History,* it remains unclear how Voegelin was able to rework his *History of Political Ideas* on Schellingian grounds, while consistently criticizing the man whose thought served as the major catalyst for his reorientation. Fortunately, there are more autobiographical comments that help to clarify this problem.

After mentioning to Sandoz the role that Schelling played in the reorientation of his thought, Voegelin relates that it took some time before *Order and History* began to emerge as we know it: "I would characterize the five years between 1945 and 1950 as a period of indecision, if not paralysis, in handling the problems that I saw but could not intellectually penetrate to my satisfaction. . . . [O]n the whole it was a period of theoretical paralysis with mounting problems for which I saw no immediate solutions." His work did not stop during this five-year period. Specifically, he recalls being elected by his department at Louisiana State University to teach courses in Chinese government, which meant that he had to begin learning Chinese and to study Chinese history (*AR,* 64). These studies may well have helped him to overcome his period of theoretical paralysis, as they provided him with an opportunity to reflect on one of the central problems encountered by Schelling's philosophy of history: what Schelling takes to be the relative lack of historical development in Chinese symbols.

The cornerstone of Schelling's historiography, as discussed at length in Chapter 2, is his attempt to argue that human consciousness differentiates, or "unfolds," in a relatively homogeneous pattern throughout all civilizations in world history. He goes to great lengths to find similar patterns of emerging self-consciousness in the West, the ancient Near East, and India. He is able to show, with varying degrees of plausibility, that mythological consciousness begins in all of these civilizations with the symbolization of the Sky, the Earth, and the Sea—the principal gods who exercise a considerable measure of control over human life. He also finds that roughly contemporaneous "spiritual crises" occur on civilization-wide bases, leading their mem-

---

62. Voegelin, "Autobiographical Statement," 119.

bers to the next phase of historical differentiation. Ancient mythologists gradually become aware of the role played by their own consciousness in the symbolization of various divinities. Their symbols "unfold," or show greater signs of self-consciousness, as they begin to reflect on the precise nature of differences between humanity and divinity. But Schelling is unable to demonstrate that Chinese symbols unfold in accordance with the pattern he finds in other civilizations. Chinese symbolists seem to retain a compact way of thinking, specifically because they do not attain consciousness of world-transcendent divinity on their own. This notion is brought to them only much later, he argues, by people from the West. Schelling acknowledges the problem that this difference in the nature of Chinese symbolism presents to his universal account of emerging consciousness in world history, and he attempts to resolve it by using Chinese symbolism as a countermeasure against which the unfolding civilizations can be understood as having attained higher levels of consciousness. But this solution seems to have persuaded no one completely, at times not even Schelling himself. What is more, it creates and leaves unresolved the problem of what appears to be a Eurocentric bias in his historiographic thought.

These problems were certainly encountered by Voegelin when he set out to recast his philosophy of history on Schellingian grounds, and they likely contributed to his period of theoretical paralysis. But the full extent to which he might have struggled with such problems, because he found them in Schelling, cannot be determined with great precision; he remains silent about many of the details concerning his use of Schelling. It has been left to scholarship to investigate these details—a task that will be taken up at proper length in Chapters 3 and 4, where we examine the unmistakable echoes of Schellingian problems (and even some of the solutions) in Voegelin's response to Eurocentric bias in world-historical constructions and the "static" nature of symbols from the "Chinese Ecumene."

Order and History, Volume 5

On two occasions, in 1969 and 1971, Voegelin sent outlines to his publisher for the manuscript of the fifth volume of *Order and History.* Both of these outlines reveal a surprising plan that ultimately did not materialize: the "Last Orientation" chapter on Schelling from the abandoned *History of Political Ideas* was to be included in the last volume of *Order and History.* This is a most interesting point, for Voegelin also says that only stylistic revisions were necessary before the chapter could be published.[63] Had he published this chapter substantially intact, he would have decisively overturned the estimation of Schelling given in the preceding volumes of *Order and History.* The reasons he ultimately decided not to include it remain unknown. But this much is clear: Voegelin concludes *Order and History* with one of his most perplexing estimations of Schelling's significance to the history of modern philosophy.

Schelling is mentioned only once in the fifth volume of *Order and History.* Voegelin says: "As we know from numerous statements by Reinhold, Fichte, Schelling, Hegel, Friedrich Schlegel, and Schiller," the actors who played out the transcendental revolution in consciousness "interpreted it as the German variant of the general revolution that was taking place on the pragmatic level in America, France, and the Netherlands (Batavian Republic of 1795). [These men] derived the intenseness of their fervor from the sense of participating in a world-historic revolution of consciousness" (*OH,* 5:50–51). This is the last of Voegelin's published references to Schelling, now placing him in the company of German idealists and blurring the lines more than ever between some thinkers who were and continue to be distinguished by scholarship.[64] Once again, Voegelin's comment implies that he accepts the once conventional account of Schelling as a Hegelian idealist. This impression is reinforced by the volume's editor, Paul Caringella, Voegelin's personal secretary at the time. Caringella adds a footnote to Voegelin's remark, citing M. H. Abrams's *Natural Supernaturalism* for "representative statements" by Schelling and others (*OH,* 5:51 n. 2). Yet Abrams's work provides no new grounds for thinking that Schelling remained an idealist. It reproduces the conventional account of Schelling by focusing its discussion almost exclusively on his earliest, most idealistic writings, when he was closely associated with Fichte and Hegel. Abrams, like Voegelin in *Order and History,* does not distinguish between periods in Schelling's philosophical development. Consequently, he neglects to mention that Schelling became a strong critic of both Fichte and Hegel. As one may learn from detailed references in the "Last Orientation,"

---

63. See *CW,* 28:241, 243, 239 (for Voegelin's comment on the merely stylistic revisions needed for this chapter). The editors of volume 28 of the *Collected Works* confirm that the proposed chapter on Schelling for the last volume of *Order and History* was indeed the same one from the *History of Political Ideas* (xxiv n. 11).

64. For example, see my bibliographic references to works by Tillich, Spann, Bolman, Gutman, Heidegger, Schulz, Tilliette, Hayes, Reardon, and Fackenheim. In recent years, the ability of these earlier authors to distinguish Schelling's thought from German idealism has been confirmed by Bowie, Beach, Danz, Žižek, and Pfau.

Voegelin knew better than Abrams about Schelling's critique of Hegel, even if his reasons for not calling attention to it remain, for the moment, unclear. What can be said at this point is that Voegelin may have had much more in common with the later Schelling than any of his critical remarks suggest.

Despite the confusing mix of opinions expressed by Voegelin's published remarks on Schelling, one point has become quite clear: Voegelin consistently criticizes Schelling only in *Order and History,* a project written primarily for an English-speaking audience, whereas he offers increasingly sympathetic references to him in German publications, articles, and public talks. Why is this so? Furthermore, how can one understand Schelling as the Gnostic thinker targeted by Voegelin's critical remarks when he also appears to have been one of the principal guides for Voegelin's critique of Gnosticism as a "pneumopathological" disorder? In light of this critique, can one sustain the argument that Voegelin's philosophical anthropology differs significantly from Schelling's own? Given that both philosophers attempt to recover a Platonic understanding of human existence and a mythological sense of order, does Voegelin's understanding of anamnesis and the way in which mythological symbols rise to articulate speech differ significantly from Schelling's? Finally, given Plato's relative lack of concern for what has come to be known as the historicity of consciousness, what role might Schelling's philosophy of history have played in helping Voegelin to understand the historical dimension of philosophical truth?

These questions have arisen from conflicts in Voegelin's published remarks on Schelling. In order to gain a better understanding of the conflicts and their broader theoretical implications, an extensive reinterpretation of Voegelin's mature philosophy is in order. There are three parts to the study I offer in partial fulfillment of this need. Part 1 is devoted to the theme of order. It comprises one chapter, which highlights the essential features in Schelling's negative philosophy of rational order and its equivalent in Voegelin's philosophy of consciousness. Part 2 is devoted to the theme of historiography. It comprises three chapters. Chapter 2 is devoted exclusively to an account of Schelling's historiography, as developed in the writings that were most important to Voegelin. Chapters 3 and 4 assess the extent to which Voegelin's historiographies, of which he says there are two, continue to draw upon Schelling's work. Part 3 is my conclusion. It summarizes key points of the Schellingian orientation in Voegelin's later work, the aspects of his mature thought that make *him* one of the most important philosophers, if not *the* philosopher of the "Schelling Renaissance."

PART ONE

Order

Historiography

Conclusion

CHAPTER ONE

The Order of Human Consciousness

[D]er Mensch zwischen dem Nichtseyenden der Natur und
dem absolut Seyenden = Gott in der Mitte steht.
—F. W. J. von Schelling, *Werke*, 1.7.458

F. W. J. Schelling and Eric Voegelin eventually devote the majority of their writings to the study of psychological and cosmological order in history. But their historical turn itself has a history, one precipitated by extensive investigations in the area of philosophical anthropology or, as they sometimes prefer to call it, the philosophy of consciousness. Their work is complex and ambitious. It often begins with what appears to be an epistemology, because both thinkers devote much attention to what can be known and how it is known. However, they also attempt to surpass many of the characteristic restrictions placed on the philosophy of consciousness by post-Kantian epistemologists. They seek to elaborate a philosophy of order that gives primary place to reflections on the entire order of reality as that which constitutes the particular order of human consciousness. In other words, they attempt to philosophize in the manner of critical realists for whom ontology (in the broadest sense of the term) is the first science to which epistemology is properly subordinate. Schelling summarizes this thesis in the following proposition: "[I]t is not because of thinking that there is being, but because

of being that there is thinking."[1] Voegelin's philosophical anthropology is
structured by a similar orientation. He claims that "ontological problems . . .
constitute the *premise* of epistemology" and, like Schelling, argues that it is
possible to make such claims without returning to the relatively uncritical
speculation of pre-Kantian metaphysics (*Anam.,* 32). Both philosophers find
it necessary to describe the ground of human consciousness without recourse
to metaphysical notions of God, being, reality, or the transcendental Ego of
phenomenology. The guiding thread in their anthropologies is a critical
focus on the nature of experience. This focus helps them to articulate a philosophy of order that falls between the epistemological skepticism of Immanuel
Kant and the reflective Gnosticism of Georg Hegel. But Schelling is truly
the pioneer. His work grounds the philosophy of consciousness in mythic
symbols that reflect concrete experiences, symbols that arise beyond the intentional control or arbitrary manipulation of genuine symbolists. Then,
once he is able to determine which symbols are primary manifestations of
the divine ground in human consciousness, his subsequent turn to historiography helps Voegelin to chart meaningful advances in the clarity of equivalent symbols—finally to realize that the most comprehensive way to find
order is in the study of its history.

Before each thinker turns to the broader perspective of historical study, he
addresses the interests of his contemporaries. For both Schelling and Voegelin
this means that each finds it necessary to become a critic of modernity, that
is, to criticize the nearly exclusive preoccupation among modern intellectuals
with:

- the division of reality into *subjects* of cognition and *objects* known;
- the corresponding focus on the "intentionality" of consciousness (which,
  to scientific "realists," allows subjects to focus on their objects of study
  and, to speculative "idealists," creates merely the questionable appearance
  of external objects for study);
- the corresponding supposition that thinking subjects are completely in
  control of reason (or that consciousness is thoroughly imbued with intentionality);
- the corresponding prejudice that science yields objective truth, while
  philosophy (or even religious thinking) yields only subjective opining;
- the prejudice against myth as a vehicle for expressing philosophical truths;
  and

---

1. Schelling, *Philosophie der Offenbarung,* in *Werke,* 2.3.161 n. c: *"Denn nicht weil es ein
Denken gibt, gibt es ein Seyn, sondern weil ein Seyn ist, gibt es ein Denken."*

- the assumption that science and philosophy, respectively, may be comfortably divided into practical and theoretical pursuits.

These points indicate some habits of thought that were present in other ages, to be sure, but that crystallize with a remarkable intensity of focus that allows them to be cited as distinctive features of modern thought.

Schelling and Voegelin developed their critiques of modernity along similar lines. Schelling tried to balance the interests of neo-Kantian rationalists (and the thought of both religious and romantic reactionaries thereto) with his positive philosophy of mythology and revelation. His attempt was only partly successful. Thus, Voegelin found that it fell to him, as well as to other participants in the "Schelling Renaissance," to try to moderate the thought of those indebted to the traditions of neo-Kantian rationalism—phenomenologists in the wake of Edmund Husserl (as well as religious and ideological reactionaries thereto)—with his own philosophy of order in history. My analysis in the following chapter follows the development of Schelling's and Voegelin's respective critiques of modernity, the philosophy of consciousness that emerges therefrom, and the extent to which Voegelin drew on Schelling as his principal guide to the *science* of order in human consciousness.

Schelling's Anthropological Critique of Modern Subjectivity

The greatest transformations in thought paradigms often have simple premises: Copernicus replaces the geocentric cosmos of Ptolemy with his relatively abstract notion of a heliocentric universe. This move, then, opens the way to further abstractions, eventually leading to the claim that no discernible center can be established anywhere in an infinite universe.[2] In a similar way, modern epistemology has tended to follow cosmology. The premodern notion that the human soul's primary contact with visible reality is what constitutes the common ground of knowledge for all is replaced by Kant's self-proclaimed Copernican revolution in thought, where an a priori structure of the human mind becomes the center and relatively private ground of knowledge with respect to the natural world.[3] Kant expands a line of thought

2. For discussion of how Copernicans and Newtonians opened the way to thoughts of a decentered universe, see Thomas S. Kuhn, *The Copernican Revolution,* chap. 7.
3. Kant, *Critique of Pure Reason,* Bxvi, Bxxii n. a.

previously developed by René Descartes, among others, and prepares the way for Johann Fichte to complete this inward turn, ultimately by declaring that each human Ego is the self-positing creator of all that it experiences in itself and in the so-called natural world. Like Kant, it is true, Fichte attempts to account for the unity of human experience in his practical philosophy. He argues that a moral imperative can be discerned in nature that is equally binding upon all. But his theoretical anthropology leaves this claim open to question. It allows one to suspect that even moral imperatives are colored by the subjectivity of the Ego that posits everything else in its willful construction of an essentially private reality.[4] As a result, it appears that no common ground or center of knowledge, whether theoretical or practical, can be discerned in the wake of German idealists. The center of what was once thought to be the reality in which all humans live has become relative to the individual maker of idiosyncratic "worldviews," "value systems," and the like.

This is the central problem with which Schelling's philosophy of consciousness contends: the increasingly solipsistic character of German idealism and its failure to account for the reality of a natural world common to all. Schelling observes that this problem has led to the "subjectivization *[Subjektiviren]*" of all rational knowledge *(Vernunfterkenntniß)*.[5] Reality, it seems, can be fashioned in different ways by different people without significant consequences in a real world common to all. Although some have attempted to defend this notion as the precondition of human freedom, or as reason to celebrate the diversity of human cultures, Schelling dismisses it as the manifestation of a spiritual sickness, a willful refusal to perceive the substantial order of reality that has nothing to do with human making or willing. He argues that the subjectivization of reason is caused by a fundamental error in thinking: the presupposition that the human mind and the rest of reality are *substantially* different, or, otherwise said, that the difference between "subjects" of cognition and "objects" of knowledge is a substantial one. He calls this error the *proton pseudos*—a term with a variety of meanings, depending on the context, including first or premier falsehood, error, or even lie. The type of thinking circumscribed by this term is so common that it has become habitual. Each appeal to the "subjectivity" or "objectivity" of an opinion or scientific claim, for example, tends to presuppose the substantial difference between

---

4. For a brief account of this matter, see Schelling's *Immanuel Kant* (1804), in *Werke*, 1.6. 1–10; and his *Darlegung des wahren Verhältnisses der Naturphilosophie zur verbesserten Fichteschen Lehre* (1806), in *Werke*, 1.7.42.

5. Schelling, *System der gesamten Philosophie*, in *Werke*, 1.6.142.

subjects and objects as its premise. And this is the premise isolated for criticism: "In our first reflection on knowledge," Schelling notes, "we believe to have distinguished in it a subject of knowledge (or knowledge when conceived of as an act) and the object of knowledge, that which is known. I purposely say: we *believe* to have discriminated, for precisely the reality of this distinction is at issue here."[6] Schelling throws relativistic thinking back on itself and begins to suggest that it is not a substantial basis for anyone who seeks to articulate a serious philosophy of order. The exclusively temporal and spatial type of thinking that follows from the subjectivization of reason tends to yield, with respect to one's knowledge of the external world, the antinomies of Kant's pure reason. One may expend great effort in the attempt to make subjects and objects "correspond" within a system of reflective dialectics. But to follow this path to its end will eventually compel one to admit that this divide cannot be bridged by discursive reasoning. Schelling grants that a "noumenal" dimension of reality will always be found to elude the grasp of synthetic dialectics. At worst, this repetition of the *proton pseudos* yields a semirational form of skepticism that may become dogmatic, yielding an attitude that Schelling found to be characteristic of the majority of his contemporaries. At best, to discover the error in the *proton pseudos* may help one to philosophize beyond the contentions of would-be philosophers who have reduced themselves to the status of professional epistemologists.

Schelling's solution to the subjectivization of reason is found in his philosophy of absolute identity, his identity philosophy *(Identitätsphilosophie)*. Although present in earlier works, the culmination of Schelling's identity philosophy is formulated in the 1804 *System of Philosophy in General and of Nature-Philosophy in Particular*. This work is highly critical of major trends in the history of philosophy and attempts to restore some premodern solutions to the problems it discusses. Schelling opens this text by formulating a proposition that is intended to reverse the effects of the *proton pseudos*. He proposes that all knowledge worthy of the name can begin only as follows: "The first presupposition of all knowledge *[Wissen]* is that the knower and that which is known are the same." By formulating this counterproposition, Schelling begins to question the especially modern habit of dividing the world into subjects and objects. Although his counterhypothesis can be stated clearly, its consequences are extensive and perhaps initially difficult to understand. He attempts to describe no less than the absolute, substantial identity

6. Schelling, *System der gesamten Philosophie*, in *Werke*, 1.6.137 (Pfau translation, *Idealism and the Endgame*, 141).

of all things.[7] At first glance, his identity premise seems to yield some amusing consequences. Without further explanation, it suggests that I am identical to my toaster, my car, elephants, and everything else in the universe. Indeed, these consequences appear to be what led Hegel to make the now-famous joke about Schelling's identity philosophy: the claim that it leads one into the worst of all possible obscurities, into "the night, in which, as people say, all cows are black." The identity philosophy does not rest on the knowledge it claims to secure, Hegel maintains, but on "the naïvety of the lack of knowledge."[8] The joke leaves one to assume that only a private or subjective individual—an idiot *(idiotēs)* in Schelling's sense of the term—could take the identity philosophy seriously.

Schelling was no idiot.[9] The people who make this joke, and even those who initially laugh at it, reveal that they have not understood one of the cardinal points of the identity philosophy: Schelling maintains that the absolute identity of all things *precedes* discursive or reflective thought; it is the *Prius* to which all reflection stands in formal opposition.[10] The joke is initially amusing only because those who laugh at it tacitly continue, by force of habit or in sophisticated resistance to his central claim, to smuggle reflective differences into the prereflective identity of the absolute. One laughs because one habitually presupposes the *substantial* reality of polarities such as "night and day," "cows and noncows," and "black and white." But in Schelling's symbolization of the absolute, such antitheses are not conceivable as indications of *substantial* differences between things. There is no night opposed to day, no cows opposed to noncows, no black opposed to white. Rather, Schelling attempts to call attention to the substantial identity of absolutely everything. He knows that a number of paradoxes will arise from this presupposition.

7. Schelling, *Werke,* 1.6.137, 156.

8. Hegel, *Phänomenologie des Geistes* (Frankfurt: Suhrkamp, 1970), 22. It was Schelling who thought that Hegel was directly attacking his identity philosophy by making this joke. However, the case has been made recently that Hegel was sincere in his 1807 reply to Schelling, which states that he was criticizing only some of the excesses of Schelling's followers, not Schelling himself. H. S. Harris contends that Hegel had Reinhold and Bardili in mind when he relayed this joke. See Dale E. Snow, *Schelling and the End of Idealism,* 187f.

9. Schelling criticizes the notion of an *idiotēs,* due to its implication that the human soul, or even divine being, is an indivisible unity *(Eigenheit)* upon which a purely reflective philosophy of being could be constructed (see *Philosophie der Offenbarung,* in *Werke,* 2.2.230); Voegelin also dismisses the "egophanic" ground of "idiots" (see *Anam.,* 179).

10. Schelling, *System der gesamten Philosophie,* in *Werke,* 1.6.170. For discussion, see Thomas Pfau, "Identity *before* Subjectivity: Schelling's Critique of Transcendentalism, 1794–1810," in *Idealism and the Endgame,* trans. and ed. Pfau, 24–57.

But he is willing to confront them, it seems, in order to accomplish two fundamental goals: to criticize rationalists of his time by suggesting that the fundamental reality sought by modern epistemologists is always already beyond rational control, and to point up the contemplative aspect of reason, beyond its instrumental use of the subject-object distinction.[11] In order to avoid a host of possible misunderstandings at this point, one must pay close attention to Schelling's claim that the absolute is not *produced* by reason or even the human will; it is immediately encountered as that which produces reason and will per se. This claim attempts to reverse much of the thinking that Schelling encountered in the intellectual climate of his time. But is it truly the basis for a persuasive alternative to modern systems of philosophy founded on egological reflection?

Modern epistemology typically begins by presupposing substantial differences between the self and the world, the self and the divine, the self and other selves. This presupposition leaves the search for knowledge to focus on how to effect a union, if possible, between these substantially different things. This union, it is initially supposed, is what would be required to yield knowledge of the other by the self. Kant, Fichte, and Hegel are best known for their attempts to establish this type of knowledge in the productive or synthetic union of opposites by pure thought. Kant and Fichte concluded, however, that synthetic unions could yield only phenomenal knowledge of objects within the synthesizing mind of particular subjects, because the substantial or noumenal reality of objects was found to lie beyond the grasp of *essentially different* subjects of cognition. Even when the subject of cognition and the object known were the same, as in the self-consciousness proposed by Fichte, one could never be certain that the concept of Ego was not itself derived from the categories of reason used in the transcendental construction of external objects.[12] The conclusions of transcendental idealism disappointed Schelling and Hegel alike, both of whom wanted to obtain direct knowledge of the substance of reality. Their respective attempts to provide a better account of the matter, however, eventually took dissimilar paths.

Hegel attempted to find mistakes in what he took to be the essentially correct reflective philosophy of Kant and Fichte. He sought to overcome

---

11. On the notion that the absolute *Prius* is beheld in "contemplative *[contemplative]*" experiences or "intellectual intuition *[intellektuelle Anschauung]*," see Schelling, *Werke*, 1.6.153–55.

12. This summary account of fundamental developments and concerns in modern thought paraphrases a number of Schelling's analyses (cf. *Werke*, 1.6.144–45, 154–55, 186–87; *Zur Geschichte der neueren Philosophie*, in *Werke*, 1.10.73–98; and *Philosophie der Offenbarung*, in *Werke*, 2.3.passim).

their logical mistakes in order to attain the knowledge of noumenal reality that avoided their grasp, likewise presupposing differences in order to bring about the identity of subjective cognition and objects known, including the self, at the end of his system. But Schelling realized, one might say, that reflection is always already distancing. It is reflective consciousness itself that creates what are, in fact, only apparent differences between "subjects" of cognition and the "objects," including the self, that they attempt to know. Consequently, it is the divisive nature of reflective consciousness itself that will never be able to effect the union it seeks to accomplish. Schelling argues:

> [I]f reflection is expected to restore the finite particular to the All *[dem All]* from which it has been derived, it recognizes the nature of its task, though it does not know how [to bring it about]; it does not comprehend that in this renewed dissolution what is being restored will lose precisely what reflection had obtained only through and in the process of disjunction. For reflection, then, this identity of the finite *[des Endlichen]* with the infinite *[dem Unendlichen]* remains a mere *synthesis* and no genuine dissolution *[kein wirkliche Auflosung]* of one into the other.[13]

This realization leads Schelling to perceive considerable limitations in the methods of rationalists and to search for a different way to the substantial knowledge of reality. But it also poses certain problems for his own attempts to articulate a different approach. Specifically, it forces him to give formal logic a penultimate place in his thought. He cannot begin his philosophy of consciousness with a logical proof for the ground of his knowledge, for such a proof would have to be presented in the language of discursive reasoning itself, thus making his work appear to be no less of a subjective construction than that of anyone else. To avoid this problem, he returns to a pre-Cartesian understanding of how philosophical study must begin: it must begin with an unprovable hypothesis, a presupposition, which is then tested for its ability to clarify the broadest range of human experiences. Accordingly, Schelling claims that the notion of absolute identity is intelligible only as that which precedes all reflective or differentiating thought. It is intelligible only when "[t]he absolute light *[absolute Licht]* . . . strikes reason like a flash of lightning, so to speak, and remains luminous in reason as an eternal affirmation of knowledge *[und leuchtet in ihr fort als eine ewige Affirmation von Erkenntniß]*."[14]

13. Schelling, *System der gesamten Philosophie*, in *Werke*, 1.6.182 (I have modified Pfau's translation slightly).
    14. Ibid., 1.6.155.

This luminosity of consciousness does not become thematic in Schelling's theory of consciousness. However, it is always presupposed when he stresses the prereflective or immediate way in which the absolute comes, so to speak, to enlighten the mind.

The following aspects of consciousness have emerged thus far in Schelling's philosophical anthropology: the intentionality of reflection, the distancing quality of reflection, and the nonreflective luminosity of consciousness. Schelling drew no significant resistance from rationalists to his description of the first and second aspects of consciousness. The third was the chief source of contention for contemporary critics of the identity philosophy, as noted specifically in Hegel's dismissal. Schelling's appeal to the luminous or contemplative dimension of consciousness allowed some to think that his philosophy remained naive or mystical, and his references to the absolute as "God" led others to suspect that his thinking amounted to little more than a sophisticated attempt to have Christian theology appear to be compatible with philosophical science. The general claim that thought and being are absolutely identical before reflection may indeed raise concerns that Schelling is engaged in a dubious attempt to achieve objective knowledge. After all, is it not true that a highly reflective mode of consciousness is evident when he articulates his central claim about the absolute? But Schelling would insist that the reflection involved here governs only the articulation of the absolute in speech, wherein he attempts to use language in its highest and most easily misunderstood aspect: to point beyond itself, back to the fundamentally inarticulate nature of experience. At one point, for example, he complains that "if someone should demand that we communicate the intellectual intuition [of the absolute identity] to him, this would be the same as to demand that reason be communicated to him. The absence of the intellectual intuition proves only that in him reason has not yet reached the transparency of self-knowledge. Intellectual intuition is never anything particular, but is precisely and unconditionally universal."[15] Any attempt to refute the identity philosophy with discursive logic alone will reveal only logical problems, rather than ontological ones, he suggests. To substantiate this point, he would have us consider how the absolute comes to be intuited and symbolized in the first place.

In its use of the subject-object distinction, reflective consciousness is an exclusively temporal and spatial type of thinking. Its logical truths are structured around "moments" and "steps" of differentiated thought processes.

15. Ibid., 1.6.154.

But Schelling argues that there is more to human consciousness than its capacity for perceiving objects in space and time. For example, it is also possible for one to come to know that the reality of experience reveals an eternal and nonspatial quality to life, where eternity is not to be misunderstood as an extremely long *time* but, properly speaking, as the absence of time per se. Schelling occasionally describes this capacity of the soul with the Platonic term for recollection: *anamnesis.*[16] He says that Plato understood well that the ideas, in his particular sense of the term, are not constructed by the human mind; rather, they are the instructors of the mind. These instructors structure (the human) mind, making it what it is. According to Schelling, Kant was unable to understand this point due to his unquestioned belief in the substantial difference between noumena and phenomena. Kant's "entire philosophy is guided by reflection," Schelling claims, and this feature of Kant's thought causes him to misunderstand the Platonic conception of ideas as "but a mystical exaggeration for which Plato begs our indulgence." Kant hopes that Plato's fall into mysticism will be "replaced by humbler terms that will prove more adequate to the nature of the matter." But this expressed desire for humility results, according to Schelling, in the arrogant suspicion that all but moral ideas are constructs of the subjective ego. Even worse, again in Schelling's account of the matter, Kant is unable to substantiate his choice of moral ideas as the sole constituents of the mind's essential structure. His choice must appear to be completely arbitrary to minds dominated by reflective consciousness. To correct these problems, Schelling argues against the presupposition that the human ego is the substantial ground of knowledge. He refers to this presupposition as that "vain habit of selfhood *[eitlen Trieb der Selbstheit],* which converts everything into *its* product" and emphasizes that all true differentiation must presuppose the absolute and substantial

16. Schelling typically uses the term *Erinnerung* for Platonic remembrance (see *Werke,* 1.6.186). However, in his 1827 lectures *Zur Geschichte der neueren Philosophie,* he summarizes the fundamental practice of philosophy, contrasting his own way to that of Fichte, by writing the following: "The individual I finds in its consciousness only, as it were, the monuments, the memorials of that path [the path to self-consciousness], not the path itself. But for that very reason it is the task of science, indeed of the primal science, philosophy, to make that I of consciousness come to itself, i.e., into consciousness, *with consciousness.* Or: it is the task of philosophy that the I of consciousness should *itself* cover the whole path from the beginning of its being-outside-itself [in the unconscious dimension of nature] to the highest consciousness—with consciousness. Philosophy is, as such, nothing but an anamnesis *[Anamnese],* a remembrance for the I of what it has done and suffered in its general (its pre-individual [or substantial]) being, a result which is in agreement with familiar Platonic views" (*Werke,* 1.10.94–95; I have followed Bowie's translation, *On Modern Philosophy,* 110).

identity of what has been divided by thought. The identity of the absolute must be understood both formally (perceived by the mind alone) and really (pertaining to "objects" of sense perception).[17]

In effect, Schelling is asking his readers to recall the following points from experience: Every human being lives in a meaningful and mysterious world *before* he or she begins to interpret or differentiate the "world" and its many "things." All consciously human life begins without reflective self-consciousness. Stated positively, consciousness precedes self-consciousness. Accordingly, the latter is no ground upon which an absolute system of knowledge could ever be built: "In truth, there does not ever nor anywhere exist a subject, a self, or any object or nonself. To say; 'I' know or 'I' am knowing is already the *proton pseudos.* 'I' know nothing, or *my* knowledge, to the extent that it is *mine,* is no true knowledge at all. Not 'I' know, but only the *All [das All]* knows in me, if the knowledge that I consider my own is to be a true knowledge."[18] In its failure to bridge the (arbitrarily imposed) gap between appearances and reality, Schelling argues that synthetic reflection does not attain the status of what is properly called reason. He has little regard for the "natural reason" of Enlightenment philosophers and traditional theologians alike. Instead, when he speaks of reason he emphasizes the self-affirmation of the absolute in human consciousness, a primordial *(ursprünglich)* state of mind in which the affirmed and that which affirms are one. "Hence," he concludes, "the fundamental law of reason and of all knowledge, to the extent that it is rational knowledge, is the law of identity or the proposition A = A."[19]

Schelling uses many words as synonyms for the absolute. One word he does not use in this way is *nonbeing,* or *Nichtseyn.* He points out that it is quite impossible to think of a negation as though it were the differentiating force in reality.[20] Nothing does nothing, least of all can it allow one to understand the order of apparent differences between things. That is to say,

17. Schelling, *System der gesamten Philosophie,* in *Werke,* 1.6.185–87, 146.

18. Ibid., 1.6.140. In his later work, Schelling occasionally uses the Platonic term *to pan* as an equivalent symbol to his *All* (see *Philosophie der Offenbarung,* in *Werke,* 2.3.174).

19. Schelling, *System der gesamten Philosophie,* in *Werke,* 1.6.142–43, 148, 145.

20. An especially ambitious attempt to use negation as the primary differentiating force in reality may be found in Jacques Derrida's "inscription" of the term *"la différance."* Derrida coins this term in an attempt to maintain that no knowledge can ever become present or firmly established in human consciousness, because consciousness is always already different/deferred (spatially and temporally) from the transcendent ground (egological or ontological) upon which it would have to base its cognitive claims. Because no such ground is ever present to human consciousness, Derrida maintains, no knowledge is possible—only opinion and belief. See Derrida, "Différance," in *Margins of Philosophy,* 1–27.

the concept of nothing cannot be used to account for anything *primary* in philosophy. Any attempt to describe the absolute as nonbeing reveals only that the thinker is still trapped—notwithstanding recent appeals to the "postmodern" character of this move—in a Kantian-Hegelian, distinctively modern, and strictly reflective mode of thinking.[21] Schelling explains why the absolute cannot be conceived as a negation:

> If the opposition of the subjective and the objective was the point of departure and the absolute merely the product, to be posited only after the fact by way of an annihilation of the opposition, the absolute itself would be a mere negation, namely, the negation of a difference of which we would not know whence it comes and why precisely this should serve, by way of its negation, to demonstrate the absolute [as nonbeing]. The absolute, then, would not be a *position* but merely a negative idea, a product of synthetic thought, or as some people still believe, of the synthesizing imagination, and quite clearly a mediate *[mittelbarer]* rather than the immediate *[unmittelbarer]* object of cognition.[22]

To underscore the immediacy of the absolute, Schelling uses the term *Being (Seyn)* as one of its synonyms. The concept of nonbeing is understood only as a reflective *product* of analytical thought, one that can have meaning only when conceived as relative to the Being of the absolute. Such, perhaps, is one of the distinctive limitations of having a human mind, where "[p]recisely this Being and this relative nonbeing of the particular in the universe constitute the seed of all finitude."[23]

This fundamental point about negations is not relinquished in Schelling's later work. He consistently accepts the language of the ancient Greeks, specifically that of Aristotle, for its ability to distinguish between contradictory and contrary types of negation by means of "appropriate particles." When speaking of nonbeing as one of the potencies, for example, he still retains an awareness of its tension to being. Thus, he explains, "non-being *[nicht Seyn] (mē einai)* does not signify nothing at all *[Nichtseyn] (ouk einai)....*

---

21. Careful consideration of the contemplative origin of Schelling's identity philosophy makes it possible to draw a sharper line between Schelling's absolute and Derrida's *différance* than others have been prone to do. In an otherwise excellent account of this discussion, Andrew Bowie tends to see too many similarities between Schelling and Derrida, due to the fact that the *function* of the absolute and *différance* is similar in both thinkers. See Bowie, *Modern European Philosophy,* 67–75.

22. Schelling, *System der gesamten Philosophie,* in *Werke,* 1.6.163–64. I have modified Pfau's translation slightly.

23. Ibid., 1.6.181.

The mere privation of being *[Veraubung des Seyns]* does not exclude the ability to be *[seynkönnen]*. Pure ability to be *[Reines können]*, as we have defined the simple subject, does not signify *Nichtseyn*."[24] X. Tilliette has offered a conflicting interpretation of Schelling's use of negation. He contends that Schelling's *Prius* is described in contradictory terms (as *ouk on*), so that Schelling can convey the sense that "the creation does not proceed simply from the concept of God, but from his will."[25] This claim may indeed provide an accurate summary of Schelling's ultimate descriptive aims. But Tilliette's philological point breaks unnecessarily with Schelling's Aristotelian language at this stage in his writings. Schelling himself says that the *Prius* can be understood only as a contrary type of negation, thus *Dynamei on = mē on.*[26]

Schelling's use of the word *Being* does not make him an "essentialist" in the now-common sense of the term, as postmodern criticisms of essentialism tend to be based on the assumption that being has been *constructed* by acts of *reflective* consciousness. We have already found clear indications that his use of the term *Being* cannot fall legitimately within the scope of this critique, provided that one remembers his point about the prereflective constitution of all reflective constructions. But further support for this point must be rejoined in the next chapter, where his account of how the potency of being emerges in world history will be taken up in proper detail. For now it must suffice briefly to address a related problem. Once the substantial identity preceding phenomenal differences has come to light in the anamnesis of Schelling's theoretical science, the question may arise as to how this objectivity of reason may be used, given that reflective thinking tends to dominate practical and political matters. In other words, does (or could) Schelling's attempt to reestablish the universality of reason yield a threatening political "totality," as criticized by Emmanuel Levinas and others?[27] Could it result

---

24. Schelling, *Philosophie der Mythologie,* in *Werke,* 2.1.288–89; see also 2.2.32–33. (God is the "subject" of these passages.) Schelling's use of negations remains contrary, rather than the contradictory type that Derrida has attempted to use in his appeals to *différance* as the *Prius* of all reality and experience.

25. Tilliette, *Schelling: Une philosophie en devenir,* 89.

26. See Schelling, *Philosophie der Mythologie,* in *Werke,* 2.1.289 n. 1. The reference Schelling gives for this identification is Aristotle, *Metaphysics* (4.4). Tilliette's point is also unnecessary when considered in light of the logic of Schelling's potencies. What might be described as his potentialization of being already accounts for the dynamics of a divine will, resulting in Creation, and for equivocal experiences of human willing in consciousness.

27. See Levinas, *Totality and Infinity: An Essay on Exteriority.*

perhaps even in the formation of a totalitarian State that could devise practical applications for the oppression of minorities based on the homogeneity of its Reason?

Schelling would insist that his description of the All *(das All)* could not truly form the basis for such a State. But on what grounds? According to the logic of his identity philosophy, only one thing can be known objectively by human beings, that is to say, with complete impartiality: "God, or the absolute, is the only immediate object of knowledge *[der einzige unmittelbare Gegenstand der Erkenntniß]*."[28] Because the absolute or God is not a human construct, it is impossible for any individual to bring the central teaching of the identity philosophy into service for parochial ends. Once "I" reflectively disassociate "myself" from the All, "my" thinking and speaking become subjective in the pejorative sense. At best, "I" could speak for the All. But this could not be done rationally, according to Schelling. "My" prophecy would yield an inadmissible type of subjectivity, one that approaches tyranny. For the same reason, the absolute "in" human consciousness cannot become an Archimedean point from which "I" could turn to survey the expanse of reality objectively laid out beneath "my" feet. The knowledge of finite things in the natural world is based, Schelling argues, only on partial or "finite representation *[endliche Vorstellen]*." It yields "no absolute affirmation of what is known." This point is true, he maintains, even though "nothing is *outside* of God." But it can be substantiated only by the experience of theoretical intelligence or contemplation. It has no practical application beyond itself. And, finally, what is true for "myself" is also true for any other human being, he claims. No one can truly put words into the mouth of God, Being, the *Geist,* or any other supposedly absolute agent in historical and political reality. The attempt to do so reveals that one has not properly understood the unconditional nature of the absolute to which Schelling's language attempts to point. All use or control of another person or thing results in a mediated, subjective break from the substantial immediacy of the absolute, so the objectivity of reason cannot be used for anything beyond the reorientation of individual souls to their common divine ground. This reorientation results only in personal felicity, once the notion of absolute identity is correctly understood, and "the subject can rejoice in the divine to the extent that it has espoused the universal."[29]

28. Schelling, *System der gesamten Philosophie,* in *Werke,* 1.6.151; see also 162.
29. Ibid., 1.6.170, 169, 154, 152.

The central teaching of the identity philosophy would have public significance, therefore, only if a considerable number of people could successfully make what he calls the felicitous "inner return" and begin to understand the commonality of their humanity. If this were to occur, then the demos that rules in a democracy, for example, would know itself to be substantial. It would be a republic (res publica), a truly public and impartial polity beyond the partisan concerns of its private members. But Schelling did not hold out any great hopes that this state would ever occur in political reality. At best, he conceded, a good political order can do no more than approximate the like-mindedness of its members—or *homonoia,* as Voegelin often describes it—that may stem from contemplative experiences of the objectivity of reason. And it is relatively easy to understand why. Political leaders, as with anyone else, can know only one thing objectively: God is God (A = A). Political leaders can say only two things objectively: God is God, and all people need to realize the truth of this point for themselves. Clearly, nothing follows immediately from these points that could inform the daily need to solve problems caused by too much reflective differentiation of things in the world, on the one hand, and too little contemplation of that from which they have been separated, on the other. Thus, once again, it becomes clear that any attempt to use the identity philosophy for ulterior motives will bring about its destruction and therewith any chance for it to effect potentially desirable changes in political reality.

The analysis of consciousness thus far attained may be summarized in four points: first, Schelling understands consciousness to be structured by the immediate "light" of the absolute and mediated or reflective responses to this contemplative experience of order; second, the fundamental error in reflective attempts to attain knowledge of the substantial order of reality is the presupposition that subjects and objects are substantially different; third, the only true presupposition yielding universal ("objective") knowledge is that subjects and objects are *substantially* identical before reflection, and this is all that the human mind can know objectively (A = A); and, finally, objective knowledge cannot be used for partisan purposes—theory has no practical application beyond the felicitous order it brings to the contemplative soul.

Schelling never abandoned these central features of his identity philosophy, although he did qualify them significantly in later works. In his work *On the Essence of Human Freedom* (1809), he begins to give the concept of freedom a central place in his thought. One of the apparent limitations of the identity philosophy is that it does not account for how an actual human being tends to experience life as a mixture of necessary and contingent events. Schelling himself perceived this to be a limitation. To take one example, in his lectures *On the History of Modern Philosophy,* he clarifies his earlier work on the philosophy of absolute identity: "This philosophy... should have acknowledged that it is a science wherein there is no mention of *existence* or of what *actually exists,* or of knowledge in this sense either. It treated only the relations its object takes on in mere thought."[30] Despite this qualification, the principles of the identity philosophy remain in Schelling's later works. His critique of the attempt to reduce consciousness to its reflective capacity alone remains the basic presupposition of his "negative" philosophy.[31] This feature distinguishes Schelling's rational philosophy from that of Kant, Fichte, and Hegel, among others.

Beyond the identity philosophy of 1804, Schelling describes the absolute as "eternal freedom," the purest God, that freely differentiates itself in the divine forces of nature and produces a discernable order in the history of human consciousness.[32] Eternal freedom forms the basis or hypothetical *Prius* for Schelling's "positive philosophy" of existence, his philosophy of historical revelation. It allows him to describe the concrete particulars of natural (mythic)

30. Schelling, *Zur Geschichte der neueren Philosophie,* in *Werke,* 1.10.125. This quote is specifically in reference to an earlier version of the identity philosophy, one that posited substantial identity at the end of a lengthy treatment of nature philosophy *(Naturphilosophie)* and the philosophy of spirit. But it applies equally well to the 1804 philosophy of absolute identity, in which the notion of substantial identity comes first. Either way, Schelling eventually decides that this type of thinking yields only a "negative" form of rationalism, which cannot account for the world in its existence.

31. This claim is in agreement with Manfred Frank's isolation of the "fundamental thought" that unifies Schelling's entire philosophical project, namely, that "being or absolute identity is irreducible to the happening of reflection." See Frank, *Eine Einführung in Schellings Philosophie,* 8. Frank is important among German scholars as one whose interpretive work has persuaded many that a reassessment of Schelling's later philosophy is in order.

32. By mentioning the principled continuity of the identity philosophy in Schelling's later works, I do not wish to diminish the profound change that came over Schelling's thinking when he started to bring freedom more directly into the scope of his analyses. In his redescription of the absolute as eternal freedom, Schelling allows that the divine life is at least capable of substantial change or development. This forms the basis of his process theology of history. The notion of a process in the divine life itself—its tensional freedom to conceal and reveal itself—is what substantiates the claim that history is marked by essentially different epochs (of which more in the next chapter). The notion of a process in the divine ground itself is something Schelling flatly denied in earlier works (cf. *Bruno oder über das göttliche und natürliche Prinzip der Dinge. Ein Gespräch* [1802], in *Werke,* 1.4.303; and *System der gesamten Philosophie* [1804], in *Werke,* 1.6.170).

and historical (revelatory) types of experience as actualizations of the divine forces of nature, or "potencies." His positive philosophy attempts to account for the universe in its dynamic existence, whereas his negative philosophy accounts for the static and formal essence that comes to light in purely rational thought. Both types of philosophy are needed, he maintains, in order to address the entire range of experiences afforded to humanity by its distinctive awareness of the tensions between essence and existence. One senses that any attempt to specialize in but one type of philosophy will reveal, at best, the earnest pursuit of an intellectual, but not the serious breadth of a philosopher worthy of the name. All true philosophy must be able to account for both essential order and existential history. And Schelling takes philosophy per se to be the unified science of order and history, essence and existence. This much can be advanced, even though the accent in his later thought falls on the positive philosophy of historical existence, wherein the philosopher attempts to understand God not simply as a self-identical essence or regulative idea, but as an expressed or effective existence.

The division of labor in Schelling's philosophical enterprise is clear enough. But where, one might ask, does a real human being fall within his vision of the All? Schelling's answer to this question is clear: in the middle. At least, this is how he describes the human soul's place within the order of reality to the lay audience of his *Stuttgart Private Lectures:* "Man stands in the middle *[in der Mitte]* between the nonbeing of nature and the absolute being = God."[33] This middle position indicates that one aspect of human consciousness appears to be free from God and nature, speaking colloquially, thus a mixture of freedom and necessity. It also implies that humanity has a definite share in both, that "[e]verything divine is human, and everything human divine. This phrase of the ancient Hippocrates, taken from the depths of life, was and still is the key to the greatest discoveries in the realm of God and nature." Schelling says that nature, more specifically, is that which "unfolds itself more and more into a substance which is not merely corporeal and not merely spiritual but is between the two." This substance "between" body and spirit is the self-reflective aspect of human consciousness. "Man is really the connection point of the entire universe, and one can thus far indeed say that really everything was envisaged in him." More specifically, it is the human will that holds the position of the between, because "the will operates only as with an alien intelligence, of which it is not itself master, an

33. Schelling, *Stuttgarter Privatvorlesungen,* in *Werke,* 1.7.458.

intermediate state between the complete night of consciousness and reflective mind."[34]

The middle position of the human soul does not become thematic in
Schelling's writings. He uses this terminology in public only when addressing
the lay audience at Stuttgart. But a similar notion is presupposed throughout his later writings, where the concrete reality of human existence is always
said to be caused by a tensional play, a mixture of divine potencies.[35] It is
relatively clear why Schelling did not conceptualize human consciousness as
restricted to the "middle" ground between God and nature. This conceptualization could easily obscure the identity of the soul's unconscious depth
with its divine ground. It could force one to speak only in *relational* terms
about the soul's "contact" with the fundamental substance of the universe.[36]
Once substance is understood only as a relation, the reflective divisions between soul and soul, soul and world, soul and God would easily return, taking philosophical discussion back to the total ignorance of noumenal reality
proclaimed by Kant and the reflective philosophy proposed for bridging this
divide by Hegel, among others. Once the language of relation is used as
though it were substantially true, and the notion of substantial identity is lost,
the way is prepared for a return to the predominance of reflective thought.
This problem does not arise in Schelling's later anthropology. He retains the
notion of substantial identity in his descriptions of God as the absolute *Prius*
of immediate experience.[37] But he also limits this identity by describing it as
always already beyond consciousness.[38] Hence no "Gnosticism," in Voegelin's

34. Schelling, *Die Weltalter,* in *Werke,* 1.8.291, 282, 297, 337 (Bolman translation).

35. For example, Schelling raises the issue of human freedom from God and nature briefly
in his *Philosophie der Offenbarung.* He says that the ability to distinguish ourselves from both
God and nature is a result of the Fall (see *Werke,* 2.3.353–54). Schelling's account of the Fall,
the condition of the possibility for God's self-revelation in history, will be discussed at length
in the next chapter.

36. I do not wish to imply that Schelling had no use for relational language in his later
anthropology. He frequently speaks of the soul's "participation" in the divine potencies and of
relations between the potencies themselves. But his relational language, as part of his positive
philosophy of existence, is always related to his particular understanding of substantial identity,
which forms the basis of his negative philosophy.

37. Much later in his life, one still finds Schelling defending his particular philosophy of
identity in contrast to the "negative" rationality of Fichte and Hegel. See lectures 3–5 of his
Philosophie der Offenbarung, in *Werke,* 2.3.51–93. The prereflective *(ursprünglich)* constitution
of identity "in" human consciousness is also defended in the *Philosophie der Mythologie,* in
Werke, 2.2.118–19.

38. Specifically, the divine *Prius* is redescribed as "the immediate potential to be," which is
"before being or *that which will be"* (*Philosophie der Offenbarung,* in *Werke,* 2.3.207).

sense of the term, can be ascribed to Schelling's later anthropology. His work attempts to acknowledge an impartial order of reality that can be grasped in philosophical contemplation alone, but not used for partisan purposes by any individual as a private possession of absolute truth. All of these qualities appealed to Voegelin in ways that have yet to be fully appreciated.

Voegelin's Later Anthropology: Consciousness and Its Ground

In addition to the explicit payments of debts to Schelling already considered in the Introduction, a further indication of the Schellingian orientation in Voegelin's mature thought may be found in the self-interpretation of his work provided by a frequently overlooked autobiographical remark. Near the end of his life, Voegelin reflected on the course of his philosophical development and described the interpretive principle underlying all of his "later" work with the following statement: *"[T]he reality of experience is self-interpretive"* (*AR*, 80). This curious remark is made in one of the contexts where Voegelin reflects on his decision to abandon his *History of Political Ideas*. The period of time recalled by this reflection, the mid-1940s, suggests that Voegelin understands his "later" work to begin with his decision to abandon the *History* as originally conceived. The fact that Schelling's thought played a significant role in this decision suggests that the interpretive principle underlying all of Voegelin's later work may be Schellingian. But so does something in the substance of the remark. Voegelin's formulation of this interpretive principle bears a great resemblance to the way in which Schelling describes reason as the self-manifestation of the divine in human consciousness. It also resembles, contrary to the claims made in *Order and History*, Schelling's account of how philosophers should interpret the experiences that give rise to mythic symbols. And here we find an initial key to interpreting the Schellingian orientation in Voegelin's later thought beyond the obvious appeals to his greatness already considered elsewhere.

At one point in Schelling's *Philosophy of Mythology*, the work that Voegelin claims brought the "crash" to his *History*,[39] one finds the following claim: "[I]t is not *we* who have placed mythology, but mythology has placed *us* in the perspective from which, at present, we shall consider it. The content of this conference is henceforth no longer mythology explained by us; it is mythology

---

39. Cf. *supra*, 5–6; and Voegelin, "Autobiographical Statement," 119.

as it explains itself *[die sich selbst erklärende Mythologie]*."[40] This comment occurs after a lengthy discussion of deficient approaches to the interpretation of myth. Schelling begins to argue that mythological experience and the symbols it engenders are self-interpretive. Genuine mythic symbols do not arise as reflective signs that a clever person has intentionally fashioned in order to construct an arbitrary "reality" of his or her own making. They arise from the human soul's prereflective immersion in the divine substance of the cosmos. Accordingly, Schelling continues, mythical symbols are not properly interpreted as merely "allegorical."[41] Such interpretation mistakenly assumes that symbols are best understood with reference to other symbols, perhaps even within an essentially closed system of meaning. Considered linguistically, allegorical interpretation suggests that words interpret only other words—a point, we might add, that makes allegorical interpretation closely related to the structuralist account of language.

Schelling argues, to the contrary, that the origin of symbols cannot be understood with reference only to other symbols. His particular understanding of the self-establishing character of symbols leads him to contend that they are best interpreted as "tautegorical."[42] It was Samuel Taylor Coleridge who was first led to formulate the specific term *tautegorical* after reading one of Schelling's previous works, *Die Gottheiten von Samothrake,* which dealt in part with the proper interpretation of myth. Schelling commends Coleridge as "the first of his English compatriots to have understood and put to intelligent use German poetry, scholarship *[Wissenschaft],* and especially philosophy." Schelling defends Coleridge against being "too severely criticized" by his fellow countrymen for his "unacknowledged borrowings *[Entlehnungen]*" from Schelling himself. He states: "Because of this excellent term that I borrow from him, I voluntarily pardon him for all of the borrowings which he himself has made from my works, without mentioning my name." But Schelling also notes that his use of the term *tautegorical* may be more radical than that which he finds in Coleridge. For Coleridge, according to Schelling, the term appears to be synonymous with *"philosopheme,"* which may still convey the sense that mythic symbols are signs for other phenomena (natural or euhemeristic), thus leaving open the possibility of allegorical interpretations. In his use of the term *tautegorical,* Schelling wishes to suggest a most intimate connection between mythic symbols and the

40. Schelling, *Philosophie der Mythologie,* in *Werke,* 2.2.139.
41. Cf. ibid., 2.1.lectures 2–3, 2.2.139–40.
42. Ibid., 2.1.195–96.

experiences that give rise to them.[43] Indeed, it would be no exaggeration to say that mythic symbols *are* what they symbolize. They arise beyond conscious control and are, in some sense, identical to the experiences that have engendered them. For example, he contends that the "Prometheus" of Æschylus is "not a human thought." It is one of the "primordial thoughts which pushes itself into existence."[44] This point suggests that not all words simply interpret other words; some break loose from linguistic conventions and effectively call attention, at least, to what remain essentially inarticulate experiences of natural order, or what Schelling calls "primordial thoughts" *(Urgedanken)*. What is more, when such thoughts arise in human consciousness, they are said to create a meaningful historical divide before and after the symbol came into existence. For Schelling, this divide has an objective quality about it, giving the history of symbolization a discernible order. Consequently, his *Philosophy of Mythology* and *Philosophy of Revelation* undertake an extraordinarily complex effort to interpret this general history of order as it emerges in the specific order of human experience. Precisely with this historical aspect of symbolization in mind, he is able to claim that "mythology has placed *us* in the perspective from which, at present, we shall consider it."

Voegelin's tacit agreement with Schelling's "tautegorical" interpretation of myth is found in the third volume of *Order and History* (1957), only a few pages before Schelling's philosophy of myth is explicitly dismissed for its allegedly "gnostic inclination to intellectualize the unconscious." Voegelin says that "the 'truth' of the myth will arise from the unconscious, stratified in depth into the collective unconscious of the people, the generic unconscious of mankind, and the deepest level where it is in communication with the primordial forces of the cosmos." Mythic truth is self-authenticating, Voegelin argues, "because the forces which animate its imagery are at the same time its subject matter." The truth of mythic symbols is therefore tautegorical. "A myth can never be 'untrue,'" he continues, "because it would not exist unless it had its experiential basis in the movements of the soul which it

43. Cf. ibid., 2.1.196 n. 1, 2.2.139–40; see also Pfau, *Idealism and the Endgame*, 275, 278. Beach has noted, following Tilliette, that *tautegorical* was used before Coleridge by Karl Philipp Moritz, in his *Götterlehre oder mythologische Dichtungen der Alten* (Berlin: Unger, 1795), 2–3. See Beach, *Potencies of God(s)*, 261 n. 38. Voegelin's later criticism of the allegorical interpretation of symbols resembles Schelling's (cf. *OH*, 4:33–36). Both Voegelin and Schelling find what the former calls "allegoresis" to result in an inadmissible type of reductionism.

44. Schelling, *Philosophie der Mythologie*, in *Werke*, 2.1.482. In Schelling's words: *"Prometheus ist kein Gedanke, den ein Mensch erfunden, er ist einer der Urgedanken, die sich selbst ins Daseyn drängen."*

symbolizes" (*OH,* 3:184; see also 190).[45] Clearly, Voegelin and Schelling agree that mythic symbols arise from the soul's unconscious depth and break forth into the conscious articulation of experiences. But they also agree that what holds true for mythic symbols is true of linguistic symbolization in general.

Consider Schelling's remarks on the formation of language. He contends that the development of language cannot be understood in a "piecemeal or atomistic" way. An atomistic account of the origin of language could easily lead one to believe that the soul is fundamentally in conscious control of the symbols it makes. This notion is declared to be patently false when Schelling reflects on how nascent symbols come into existence. Language must have developed as a whole, he argues, in an "organic" *(organisch)* way. It must have originated, like mythic symbols in particular, from the soul's unconscious depth. "Since neither philosophical nor even generally human consciousness is possible without language," Schelling maintains, "it is inconceivable that consciousness can be the ground of language; and so the more we penetrate its nature, the more we acquire the certitude that it transcends by its profundity any conscious creation."[46] This realization leads Schelling to discern an objective *(objectiv)* quality in language itself *(Sprache selbst),* a point that allows him to argue, in effect, that nascent symbols must be understood as self-generating and self-interpretive, when properly traced back to their engendering experiences.

Of course, Schelling is speaking here only about bona fide symbols. At this point, he does not address the problem that reality can be intentionally misrepresented when a would-be symbolist chooses not to accept the rela-

---

45. Clearly, Webb's claim that Voegelin "never presented an explicit account of his conception of the generation of mythic symbols" is factually mistaken (*Philosophers of Consciousness,* 130). This oversight has important consequences. By overlooking Voegelin's *arguments* attempting to explain the priority of some symbols, Webb is led to declare that Voegelin's interpretive focus in history reveals merely a "subjective" preference on his part for some authors—usually Plato—to the exclusion of others. But Voegelin also speaks of the self-generating character of Hesiodian symbols. And, like Schelling, he argues that Hesiod's works reveal the first transitionary steps in history from mythic to philosophical consciousness (cf. *OH,* 2:126–31; cf. Schelling on the same point in *Philosophie der Mythologie,* in *Werke,* 2.2.595–96). Voegelin does not mention that Schelling also notes the transitional character of Hesiod's writings. He credits Aristotle with this observation.

46. Schelling, *Philosophie der Mythologie,* in *Werke,* 2.1.51, 52. In Schelling's words: *"Da sich ohne Sprache nicht nur kein philosophisches, sondern überhaupt kein menschliches Bewußtseyn denken läßt, so konnte der Grund der Sprache nicht mit Bewußtseyn gelegt werden, und dennoch, je tiefer wir in sie eindringen, desto bestimmter entdeckt sich, daß ihre Tiefe die des bewußtvollsten Erzeugnisses noch bei meitem übertrifft."*

tively humble status of human consciousness in the symbol-making process. However, as previously noted, he does discuss such rebellion and even expands his thoughts to include the range of problems addressed by Voegelin's work on "pneumopathological" disorders, in addition to the terminological variants of this problem that I have referenced in Schelling's works.[47] The problem of sophisticated symbolization may be set aside for the moment in order not to lose sight of the specific point that Schelling sets out to make: The conscious "self" that interprets a symbol cannot be understood as the *cause* of the experience that constitutes its origin. All conscious interpretation of symbols, in order to be true, must not forget the fact that it comes relatively late in the order of events and, therefore, needs always to respect the tension between consciousness and the unconscious dimension of human existence through which the symbols have come to exist.

Voegelin has precisely this tension in mind in two of his latest essays, when he claims that "[t]he truth of . . . symbols is not informative; it is evocative," and that symbols "do not refer to structures in the external world but to the existential movement [that is, the experiences] . . . from which they mysteriously emerge as the exegesis of the movement in intelligibly expressive language."[48] Given the preceding, Voegelin says elsewhere, one cannot "prove reality by a syllogism," as though its truth were only a matter of coordinating the right words within an essentially closed linguistic system; "one can only point to [reality] and invite the doubter to look."[49] The "depth" of the soul from which symbols are said to arise is not a datum of sense perception. It is a word symbolizing the unconscious origin of symbols in consciousness. In his latest works, Voegelin tends to replace references to the "unconscious" with references to the soul's "depth," presumably in order to avoid the practice of some psychoanalysts who mystify the unconscious then claim the ability to explore its topography with a method that, in effect, disregards the limits of empirical science. Voegelin seems to have Sigmund Freud and Carl Jung in mind as the subjects of his later critique, for he criticizes the practice of populating the soul's depth with "libidinous dynamics" and the "archetypes" of a "collective unconscious." This practice is said to misconstrue the

47. Cf. *supra*, 33–36.
48. Voegelin, "Wisdom and the Magic of the Extreme" (1977), in *CW*, 12:344.
49. Voegelin, "Quod Deus Dicitur" (1985), in *CW*, 12:388. It should be emphasized that the "look" mentioned here is not strictly in reference to sensory perception. Part of the "look" of reality is only intelligible. For example, when Voegelin turns his attention to look for the origin of symbols, he discovers this origin—following Heraclitus, Æschylus, and Plato—in a "depth" of the psyche that is "beyond articulate experience."

essentially elusive character of the unconscious in an attempt to gain "by *for-nicatio fantastica* an absolute which a critical analysis of experience will not deliver" ("EESH," 124). The unconscious remains in its unfathomable depth beyond consciousness, Voegelin maintains. It may have libidinous dynamics all its own, but these cannot be exhaustively exposed or controlled by systems of reflective psychoanalysis or philosophy, systems that seek to eradicate the depth qua depth. All of this is to say, despite the change in terminology, that Voegelin retains his earlier understanding of the unconscious origin of symbols even in his latest essays.[50] He also remains an *empiricist,* following Schelling, according to a premodern sense of what this term has symbolized.

Both Schelling and Voegelin rely on a broad notion of experience in the development of their philosophical anthropologies. To put the matter bluntly, they both attempt to remind modern empiricists that even ideas have discernible, experiential content. In lecture 7 of his *Philosophy of Revelation,* for example, Schelling distinguishes between two types of empiricism. He asserts: "The lowest degree of empiricism is that in which all knowledge is restricted to experience obtained by the mediation of the senses, and in which everything supra sensible must be denied, either generally, or at least as a possible object of knowledge." This sensual type of empiricism does not exhaust the meaning of experience for philosophy, according to Schelling. Instead, he calls attention to "a more elevated degree of philosophical empiricism," one in which "we affirm that the supra sensible can become an effective object of experience." This type of philosophy is based on something that Schelling calls "mystical empiricism."[51] Whether he succeeds in persuading others of

50. This claim is not contradicted by Voegelin's brief remarks on the origin of language in the last volume of *Order and History.* To be sure, he says that one cannot decide between an essentially natural or conventional account of how words relate to reality because no one was "present when language originated." The people who were present, at least, "left no record of the event but language itself. . . . [T]he epiphany of structures in reality—be they atoms, molecules, genes, biological species, races, human consciousness, or language—is a mystery inaccessible to explanation" (*OH,* 5:17). But the conclusion to this comment is overstated, for Voegelin himself offers an explanation in the same sentence where such explanations are denied: he claims that "structures" in reality emerge in an "epiphanic" way. The theory of consciousness Voegelin develops in this work attempts to explain how the epiphany of structures is experienced concretely by human beings. What is more, the claim that no one was present when language originated is simply equivalent to saying that no one was reflectively conscious at the origin of a language symbol. And this is the substantial point in Schelling's theory of symbolization.

51. Schelling, *Philosophie der Offenbarung,* in *Werke,* 2.3.115–16; *Philosophie der Mythologie,* in *Werke,* 2.1.326, 386.

the need for recognizing two types of empiricism, the "mystical empiricism" in Schelling's philosophy of mythology and revelation seems to have persuaded Voegelin that his history-of-ideas approach to philosophy—the interpretation of ideas-as-opinions without critical reference to empirical control— yields an inadmissible distortion of both human existence and its history, or, to cite his technical language, "an ideological deformation of reality" (*AR*, 63). More to the point, however, Schelling's mystical empiricism, his appeals to the unconscious depth of conscious experience and, consequently, to the historical character of truth appear to have been important factors in the process of thought that eventually brought Voegelin to the realization that his *History of Political Ideas* needed to be reworked. Such, at least, are the initial appearances that need to be put to the test in the pages that follow.

Beyond this general agreement between Voegelin and Schelling, a more detailed account of the relation can be brought to light by comparing two texts that Voegelin published explicitly on the theory of consciousness: one preceding his American publishing career, "On the Theory of Consciousness" (1943), and the other from the end of his life, chapter 1 from *In Search of Order* (1985). These texts frame Voegelin's mature discussions in the philosophy of consciousness. Interpreting them, in addition to relevant comments from intervening works, will reveal that there are no substantial changes in his theory of consciousness throughout this entire period, including the extent to which his thought continues to bear traces of Schelling's philosophy of absolute identity.

"On the Theory of Consciousness"

In 1943, Voegelin wrote an extended letter to Alfred Schütz, concerning the phenomenology of Edmund Husserl, in which he included some thoughts on what is required for a theory of consciousness to address aspects of experience unaccounted for by phenomenology.[52] This letter is important, among other reasons, for its ability to reveal how Voegelin's thought was oriented by

52. For discussion of Schütz's critical yet sympathetic reception of Voegelin during their long-standing correspondence, see Helmut R. Wagner, *Alfred Schütz: An Intellectual Biography*, chap. 12. German readers will also benefit from consulting the detailed study of Voegelin and Schütz by Gilbert Weiss, *Theorie, Relevanz, und Wahrheit: Eine Rekonstruktion des Briefwechsels zwischen Eric Voegelin und Alfred Schütz (1938–1959)*. A summary of the main themes in this work is also available in English. See Weiss, "Political Reality and the Life-World: The Correspondence between Eric Voegelin and Alfred Schütz, 1938–59."

Schelling shortly before the publication of the major books that won him critical acclaim in America. That is to say, it allows one to understand the theory of consciousness presupposed in *The New Science of Politics* (1952) and the first three volumes of *Order and History* (1956–1957).[53] The letter comprises three parts, written in the following order: a critical discussion of Husserl's phenomenology, based on his *Krisis der Europaeischen Wissenschaften* (1936) and *Méditations Cartésiennes* (1931); an account of "anamnetic experiments," recollections of formative experiences from Voegelin's childhood; and "On the Theory of Consciousness," Voegelin's specific attempt to develop a theory of consciousness that corrects problems left unaccounted for by phenomenology.[54] The last part of the letter bears directly on the central theme of this chapter. It was written at the same time that Voegelin was researching and writing his "Last Orientation" for the *History of Political Ideas.* As such, its interpretation may be clarified by comparison with relevant sections from the unpublished work. More to the point, however, it mentions Schelling's *Potenzenlehre,* which Voegelin calls a "process theology *[Prozeßtheologie],*" for its ability to address problems in the theory of consciousness with which Voegelin had struggled in his first book, *On the Form of the American Mind* (1928).

In the prefatory remarks to the second part of the letter, the section that now bears the title "Anamnetic Experiments," Voegelin gives a helpful summary of the presuppositions that he will develop in the theory of consciousness that follows:

---

53. Voegelin says that the 1943 correspondence with Schütz articulates the theoretical presuppositions governing these works (cf. *Anam. Ger.,* 8).

54. These parts of the letter were first published in *Anamnesis: Zur Theorie der Geschichte und Politik* (1966), 21–76. I have determined the order in which they were written by comparing the German and English versions of *Anamnesis.* The first part of the letter, which directly concerns the thought of Husserl, is dated September 20, 1943. The second part, on "Anamnetic Experiments," is dated October 25 to November 7, 1943 (cf. *Anam. Ger.,* 36, 76). In the English translation of *Anamnesis* (1978), Voegelin says that the third part of the letter, "On the Theory of Consciousness," was written immediately after the second part, thus in November 1943 (cf. *Anam.,* 13). Reestablishing the order in which these texts were written suggests how the letter is to be interpreted as a whole. First, Voegelin calls attention to problems for a theory of consciousness that arise from a textual analysis of Husserl's writings. Second, he calls attention to problems for phenomenology with reference to the "history" of an actual human life—his own. Finally, he attempts to formulate a theory of consciousness that addresses the problems of history, both personal and social, for which he found that phenomenology had not provided a sufficient account.

1. Consciousness "is not constituted as a stream within the I."

2. Consciousness—in its finite, "intentional function"—transcends into the world, but "this type of transcendence is only one among several and must not be made the central theme of a theory of consciousness."

3. "[T]he experiences of the transcendence of consciousness into the body, the external world, the community, history, and the ground of being are givens in the biography of consciousness and thus antecede the systematic reflection on consciousness."

4. "[S]ystematic reflection operates with these experiences or, at least, in its operations sets out from these experiences."

5. "[R]eflection is a further event in the biography of consciousness that may lead to clarification about its problems and, when reflection is turned in the direction of meditation, to the ascertainment of existence; but . . . it never is a radical beginning of philosophizing or can lead to such a beginning." (*Anam.*, 36)

These propositions suggest two themes that we already know to be central to Schelling's philosophy of consciousness: the derivative nature of the ego, and the secondary importance of reflective consciousness in philosophical accounts of order. Furthermore, in all of his later work, Voegelin frequently uses the term *anamnesis* to describe the primary function of consciousness with respect to its knowledge of reality and itself. His use of the term implies, as it did in Schelling, that reality is not *constructed* by a completely self-transparent ego in reflective modes of consciousness but is *remembered* when formative experiences of an individual's consciousness are re-collected, thus revealing the order (and disorder) of its discreet existence. The formative experiences to which Voegelin appeals do not originate in self-conscious reflection. They occur spontaneously, in the immediacy of an actual life. The formative experiences become "objects" of consciousness only upon subsequent reflection, when they are intentionally brought into memory or, as it were, assert themselves as memories. Thus, Voegelin is led to speak of a dual aspect of anamnesis: one in which a memory is brought to mind, the other in which a memory comes to mind (see *Anam.*, 37). This dual aspect of anamnesis plays an important part in his later distinction between two modes of the "meditative complex" that is consciousness.

In "On the Theory of Consciousness," Voegelin's remarks contain "biographical materials" that "report on the results of anamnetic experiences," the experiences set out in the second part of the letter. The motive for interpreting these experiences is said to have come "from a feeling of discontent with the results of those philosophical investigations that have as their object an analysis of the inner consciousness of time." This focus became central in the nineteenth century and "today occupies the place that was held by meditation before thinking in Christian categories dissolved." Voegelin's discontent is occasioned specifically by the perceived failures of Shadworth Hodgson, Franz Brentano, Edmund Husserl, Charles Peirce, William James, and George Santayana to deliver a phenomenological description of perception and consciousness with the categories of "thatness and whatness, pure experience, act and reflection, etc." Upon closer inspection, Voegelin says that he found these attempts to be based not on a completely empirical theory of consciousness, but on the "speculative construction of an experience that obviously could not be grasped with the conceptual apparatus of description."[55] Even Husserl's later terminological refinements, the added notions of *retention* and *protention,* "did not get beyond the construction of a subtle apparatus of equivocations" (*Anam.,* 14). They helped only to reveal that the central problem in phenomenology lay in its attempt to interpret the entire order of consciousness with an exclusive focus on the experience of a temporal flow. The flow of consciousness was described by phenomenologists only with partial correctness when they analyzed the auditory perception of a tone. Voegelin certainly does not deny "a phenomenon of 'flow.'" But he claims that it amounts only to the "limit experience *[Grenzerfahrung]*" that comes to light "under the specific conditions of giving oneself to a simple sensuous perception." The flow is "a phenomenon of limit *[Grenzphänomen],*" but "consciousness as a whole does not flow" (*Anam.,* 18, 19; *Anam. Ger.,* 42). "[I]t is the function of human consciousness *not* to flow but rather to constitute the spaceless and timeless world of meaning, sense, and the soul's order" (*Anam.,* 16).

To gain a better sense of Voegelin's critical point, consider what occurs when we listen to the ringing of a bell. After being struck, the initial intensity of the bell's tone is heard to dissipate gradually. To the phenomenologists mentioned by Voegelin, experiences such as this reveal that consciousness is structured only by the temporal flow of successive moments.[56] Voegelin points out, however, that different consequences follow from a more com-

---

55. Voegelin conducted his analysis of these attempts in his chapter "Time and Existence," in *On the Form of the American Mind,* in *CW,* 1:23–63.

56. In Husserl's words, time is "the universal form of all egological genesis." The universe of one's subjective processes "is a universe of compossibilities only in the universal *unity-form of the flux,* in which all particulars have their respective places as processes that flow within

prehensive analysis of this experience. First, he says, the perception of a tone does not reveal the consciousness of time: "[T]hat which is described on the occasion of an auditory perception is not the consciousness of time but precisely the consciousness of the perception of a tone, a tone that has an objective structure determined in turn by the structure of man's faculty of perception, the noetic structure in Husserl's sense" (*Anam.*, 15). Second, the perception of a tone does reveal that in order to arrive at an adequate conception of time consciousness, one must have recourse to another dimension of consciousness to describe the event, which, at a given point, transcends the temporal flow perceived by intentionality. This other dimension of consciousness is the one for which phenomenology had not provided an account. Voegelin describes it, in this relatively early text, with what may appear to be some equivocations of his own. Before Schelling's name is mentioned explicitly, he alludes to a dimension of consciousness based on limit experiences of "meditation" and "illumination." These experiences, he says, are conducive to experiences of "transcendence." The type of transcendence Voegelin has in mind is not restricted to experiences of a characteristically religious nature. He says that even phenomenological analysis may serve to illustrate the point that consciousness is more than the conscious flow perceived by its capacity for intentional reflection:

> A speculation about the stream of consciousness may serve as a substitute for meditation because it, too, conduces to transcendence; both processes have the function to transcend consciousness, one into the body, the other into the ground of being; both processes lead to a "vanishing point," in that the transcendence itself cannot be a datum of consciousness. The processes carry one only to the limit and make possible an instantaneous experience of the limit, which empirically may last only a few seconds. (*Anam.*, 18)

Perhaps the best way to bring this other dimension of consciousness to light is to recollect and reexamine the example of the bell, paying greater attention to what actually grounds consciousness and serves as the condition of the possibility for the experience of a temporal flow.

---

it." Husserl says that consciousness is structured entirely by what he calls "intentionality," a word that "signifies nothing else than this universal fundamental property of consciousness: to be consciousness *of* something; as a *cogito*, to bear within itself its *cogitatum*." See Husserl, *Cartesian Meditations*, 75, 33 (Cairns trans.)

The bell is struck. The tone is perceived in consciousness and appears to flow. The initial intensity of the bell's tone is heard to slide into the "past," but only when changes in its pitch and volume are compared with the memory of its initial intensity (cf. *Anam.*, 15). In order to experience this "flow" at all, therefore, one must continually relate the reflectively isolated "moments" of the tone's dissipation back to previous present "instances" when it was comparatively more intense. One must mark time and compare differences between particular moments in the experience. But here is the problem. What can mark time in a consciousness thoroughly immersed in a temporal flow? The comparison of "present moments" definitely occurs, producing the experience of a flow, but where there is no difference—that is, in a consciousness structured only by time—it becomes impossible to understand how this comparison itself can take place. During the actual experience, the continual comparison of the bell's initial intensity and subsequent dissipation occurs only unconsciously. This unconscious function is intimately connected with what might be described as an unintentional or involuntary aspect of memory. Thus, one aspect of the memory—that which unintentionally marks time and compares differences between times—is always immediately unconscious in each of the "present" moments of the actual experience. This aspect of memory has and uses the ability, as it were, to jump between remembered "moments" in order to make the comparisons, so it cannot be understood as completely bound by time. Voegelin observes:

> [T]he *ordering* of the momentary image, in the dimension created by illumination, into the succession of a process requires experiences of processes transcending consciousness. The "present," thus, seems to be indeed not directly experienceable; rather, it is the result of the interpretation of the momentary image as we resort to the knowledge of the history [that is, the memory] of our bodily existence and the dating of this history through references to events in the external spatio-temporal world. (*Anam.*, 31)

Of course, memory is partially structured by intentionality. One can intentionally remember something. But intentionality does not exhaust the whole of memory; some memories arise unintentionally. Thus, Voegelin is led to speak of a dual aspect of memory when he brings the temporal categories of past and future into consideration: "I do not remember something that lies 'in the past,' but I have a past because I can make present a completed process of consciousness—either through a deliberate effort of my attention or in less transparent processes of so-called 'free associations.' Past and future are the present illuminatory dimensions of the process in which the energy center [of consciousness] is engaged" (*Anam.*, 20).[57] The present immediacy of an experience is described as both "luminous" and a process "transcending consciousness," namely, by virtue of the unconscious. This dimension of "the soul's order" comes to light only in "anamnetic" experiences. When, therefore, Voegelin says that it is the function of consciousness "*not to flow but rather to constitute the spaceless and timeless world of meaning, sense, and the soul's order,*" he is referring to this luminous, unconscious principle of order in consciousness. In other words, it is the unconscious eternity of the present that must intersect and constitute each of the conscious "points" on what can be only a *derivative* line of temporal succession. The "present" is therefore not a temporal category itself, but eternally different from time. It eludes the grasp of reflective or intentional consciousness during the immediacy of an actual experience and can be brought to consciousness only in subsequent acts of reflection. In these reflective acts, all that comes to light is the limit experience of a tension between conscious acts intending objects and the unconscious constitution of intentionality. This is why terms such as *eternity* and the *unconscious* can appear to be little more than mystical fancies to minds dominated by the conventions of reflective or strictly intentional thought.

Voegelin argues that reflection cannot bring the conscious self completely into self-transparency. The unconscious present always remains immediately unconscious. That is to say, reflection does not allow consciousness to jump over its own shadow.

> No "human" in his reflection on consciousness and its nature can make consciousness an "object" over against him; the reflection rather is an orientation within the space of consciousness by which he can push to the limit of consciousness but never cross those limits. Consciousness is given in the elemental sense that the systematic reflection on consciousness is a late event in the biography of the philosopher. The philosopher always lives in the context of his own history, the history of a human existence in the community and in the world. (*Anam.*, 33)

In other words, as discussed in the works of Schelling, consciousness always precedes self-conscious reflection. The unconscious and eternal present is the condition of the possibility for the experience of a temporal "flow."

---

57. This notion recalls the distinction made by Thomas Aquinas between "active" and "passive" aspects of the "memorative power": the syllogistic apprehension of a memory, and the sudden recollection of a past event (cf. *Summa Theologica*, 1a.78.4).

The sensuous perception of a tone "does not conduce to a better under-standing of the problem of consciousness and time as a whole but only to an understanding of the roots of consciousness in the sphere of the body." The body comes to light as a "bottleneck . . . through which the world is forced as it enters the order of consciousness." The natural constitution of the body structures some experiences of the world, but the meaning of these experi-ences can be discerned only when sensual images enter into a "spiritual realm, which has, at least directly, nothing to do with the flow of time." If one's awareness of body-based consciousness "hypertrophies into the causation of consciousness by the body, then the radicalization and hyperbolization re-veals *[sic]* an attitude that is to be characterized as morbid in the pneumato-pathological sense of Plato's *nosos*" (*Anam.*, 16, 17, 15, 17).

Phenomenology does not suffer from the problems of vulgar materialism. Its problems are different. Specifically, its attempt to explain time conscious-ness only with the dimension of intentionality results, for Voegelin, in a denial of the plurality of experienced structures in consciousness, one that notably fails to take into account the constant presence of the unconscious ground.[58] Voegelin explains:

> Narrowing down the problem of consciousness to the flow and its [con-scious] constitution is untenable if only because of its incompatibility with the phenomena of sleep, dreams, and the subconscious psychic processes. But even apart from this complex of problems, the reduction remains symp-tomatic of a doubtful hypertrophy of a correctly observed experience. . . . This hypertrophy implies a radical perversion of the facts as given in expe-rience. In experience, consciousness with its structures, whatever they may be, is an antecedent given. The limit experience of "flowing," as demon-strated through the model of the perception of a tone, is possible only in a specific act of turning attention to that limit. It is not the consciousness of time that is constituted by the flow but rather the experience of the flow is constituted by consciousness, which itself is not flowing. (*Anam.*, 17–18)

Voegelin is aware that phenomenology, in its attempt to supplant the un-conscious through reflective acts of consciousness, tends to appeal to an unconditional or transcendental "I," chiefly as the agent responsible for constructing "reality." However, once again, when he turns to reflect on a

---

58. To speak of "structures" in consciousness is Voegelin's way of classifying different types of experiences. This classification is made possible by at least one of the structures, which comes to light in the discussion that follows.

specific experience, he discovers that no "I" is ever discernible as the primary agent in the constitution of consciousness and its ground:

> I "will" to get up from my chair and observe how the "willing" and the "getting up" proceed. I can clearly recognize the project of my "getting up," but what occurs between my decision and my actual getting up remains quite obscure. I do not know why I get up just at this moment and not a second later. Closely though I may observe the process, I can find only that at the actual getting up something, from a source inaccessible to me, makes me get up and that nothing of an "I" is discoverable in the act. This observation does not tell me anything about the determination or indetermination of acting; it merely indicates that the actual getting up does not occur in the form of "I." The "I" seems to me to be no given at all but rather a highly complex symbol for certain perspectives in consciousness. (*Anam.,* 19)

The "I" is discovered to be a derivative phenomenon, constituted in the same way as the experience of a temporal flow, for the conscious "I" rests upon an otherwise "inaccessible" ground of unconscious activity. In Schelling's words, we recall, the "I" is little more than a "vain habit."[59]

Voegelin does not wish to give the impression that phenomenology needs to be dismissed *tout court*. He acknowledges that the transcendental turn has had certain merits. Specifically, it has gained "magnificent successes in the clarifications of consciousness-structures in which the objective order of the world is constituted." But he also notes that phenomenology emerged as part of "a 'reaction' against a crisis of the spirit" in the West, that is, the

---

59. Voegelin's anamnetic account of the "present"—a meaningful symbol that, nonetheless, cannot be brought into complete self-presence by reflection—avoids the problems of presence in the "ontotheological determination of Being" criticized by Heidegger and Derrida, among others. See Derrida, "Différance," in *Margins of Philosophy*, 16–27. Derrida also attempts to criticize the theory of consciousness in Husserlian phenomenology. But his criticism suffers from an inability to account for the range of experiences based in recollection. His thinking tends to perpetuate the *proton pseudos,* presupposing substantial differences between human consciousness and the reality of which it is a part. By failing to question this presupposition, he also continues in the rationalistic methods of the transcendental critique of consciousness and reality, precisely what he intends to oppose. This much can be suggested at present without further detracting from the main focus of this chapter. For further discussion of how Voegelin's philosophy of consciousness may be read as a response to Derrida and like-minded thinkers, see Ronald D. Srigley, *Eric Voegelin's Platonic Theology: Philosophy of Consciousness and Symbolization in a New Perspective*, esp. chap. 2; and Steven Shankman, *In Search of the Classic: Reconsidering the Greco-Roman Tradition, Homer to Valery and Beyond.*

breakdown of Christian civilization and its long history of metaphysics. The reactionary beginnings of phenomenology do not immediately discount its ability to clarify problems of consciousness during a time of spiritual crisis: "In such a situation, an attempt to begin anew is not only legitimate in the sense that an old symbolism cannot be honestly used when its value of communication has declined, but it is also the indispensable requirement for the development of a new, more adequate symbolism. Protesting against such a new beginning in the name of a tradition is nothing more than a symptom of spiritual sterility." Even so, Voegelin notes that some reactions are better than others, "and sometimes the reaction is worse than the tradition against which it critically reacts" (*Anam.*, 35, 34). Such is the case in Voegelin's final analysis of phenomenology:

> The development of the transcendental critique down to Husserl is characterized by the dissolution not only of traditional symbolic systems but also by the exclusion of the underlying areas of experiences and problems from the orbit of philosophical reflection. It is the fate of symbols in the history of the mind that transparence turns to "appearance." But that the reality that they illuminated comes to be, if not downrightly denied, at any rate rejected as a motive of philosophizing, is a desperate move, a bankruptcy of philosophy. (*Anam.*, 35)

The relative successes of phenomenology have been marred by its inability to account for the experiences of transcendence to which Voegelin's own analyses have begun to point. To summarize: Consciousness cannot be understood as being structured completely by time; it is grounded by something that transcends time. The "I" cannot be turned into a thoroughly conscious creator of reality, for this concept is always derived from an order of reality over which "I" have no ultimate control. And consciousness is able to transcend itself not only into the body, but also into the "ground of being," something that is categorically ignored by phenomenology. "The creation of the transcendental I as the central symbol of philosophy implies the destruction of the cosmic whole within which philosophizing becomes at all possible. The basic subjectivity of the egological sphere, Husserl's philosophical and nondiscussable ultimatum, is the symptom of a spiritual nihilism that still has merit as a reaction, but no more than that" (*Anam.*, 35).

Two structures in Voegelin's theory of consciousness have begun to emerge: consciousness and its unconscious ground. Voegelin begins to clarify these structures when he turns to consider what he understands to be a better protest against the spiritual crisis of the modern West: the process theology, or *Potenzenlehre,* of Schelling.[60] Process theology is concerned, Voegelin observes, with "developing a symbolic system that seeks to express the relations between consciousness, the transcending intraworldly classes of being, and the world-transcending ground of being, in the language of a process constructed as an immanent one." He has high praise for this aspect of Schelling's thought, saying that he is "incline[d] to believe *[zu glauben]*" that "the process-theological attempt and its expansion, a metaphysics that interprets the transcendence system of the world as the immanent process of a divine substance, is *[sic]* the only meaningful systematic philosophy" (*Anam.,* 26–27; *Anam. Ger.,* 50–51). The distinctive feature of Schelling's process theology is its ability to account for experiences of "transcendence in immanence" with a "comprehensible" language. Voegelin isolates the systematic starting point of this theology in Schelling's formulation of this question: "Why is Something, why is there not rather Nothing?" By asking this question, Schelling calls attention to the fact that "[e]very being implies the mystery of its existence over the abyss of a possible nonexistence." Voegelin knows his audience and realizes that some will try to dismiss this notion as though it were based on meaningless speculation, "because the 'Something' in Schelling's question is a formalized or idealized formula for the only finite something that can be experienced." Once the idealized formula is discounted, finite things will be explained with recourse to the causalities of nature, and the objectors will contend that "[p]hilosophy is supposed to confine itself to the framework of finite, critical cognition. . . . Consciousness that is attentive to the content of the world including the givens of consciousness, can lift itself above finite experience only to a transcendental reflection on the structure of subjectivity, in which the objective order of things in the world is constituted" (*Anam.,* 27). In a way that recalls Schelling's partial acceptance of the objectivity gained in "negative philosophy," Voegelin grants that this position is "immanently irrefutable." However, in a manner consistent with the theme of Schelling's "positive philosophy," he also notes that the restriction of consciousness to the subjectivity of immanent experience does not hold true "in the general course of history." When considered in light of historical experiences and their symbolic differentiations of reality, it becomes clear to Voegelin that human consciousness has developed to the point where the denial of transcendent reality is presently inadmissible, that is, in a sound philosophy of human existence. The *experiential* discoveries of divine transcendence have occurred, in

60. Voegelin uses the terms *process theology* and *Potenzenlehre* synonymously (cf. *Anam. Ger.,* 50).

Greek philosophy and Judeo-Christian revelation, so it is no longer possible for philosophers worthy of the name to speak only in terms of a purely immanent or "cosmological" understanding of reality.

Resistance is now possible to the anachronistic type of thinking that would deny transcendence; it comes from "various sources, but ultimately... issues from two experiential complexes." The first is given "through man's experience of his own ontic structure and its relation to the world-immanent order of being." This is the intentional mode of consciousness that reflects on "objects" in the world and the objective concepts of pure reason. But human consciousness "is not a process that occurs in the world side by side with other processes without contact with these processes other than [reflective] cognition; rather, it is based on animalic, vegetative, and inorganic being, and only on this basis is it consciousness of a human being" (*Anam.*, 27). It is possible to realize, through reflections on biological order, that most of one's life is lived as an unconscious participant in all of the realms of immanent being previously mentioned: "Speaking ontologically, consciousness finds in the order of being of the world no level which it does not also experience as its own foundation. In the 'basis-experience' of consciousness man presents himself as an epitome of the cosmos, as a microcosm."[61] In this reflective mode of consciousness, it must be admitted that "we do not know in what this basis 'really' consists; all our finite experience is experience of levels of being in their differentiation; the nature of the cosmos is inexperienceable, whether the nexus of basis be the foundation of the vegetative on the inorganic, of the animalic on the vegetative, or of human consciousness on the animal body." All that can be known by reflection is that "this basis exists," and "there must be something common which makes possible the continuum of all of [the other strata] in human existence." To account for what is common in the "intimate interrelationships" of immanent being, Voegelin introduces a second structure of consciousness: "The second experiential complex is the experience of meditation, at the climax of which the intention of consciousness is directed toward the contents of the world, not objectively, through the *cogitata,* but rather nonobjectively toward the transcendent ground of being" (*Anam.*, 28–29).

The "considerations which lead to process-theology" arise when conscious-

---

61. This point is restated in *The New Science of Politics:* "Science starts from the prescientific existence of man, from his participation in the world with his body, soul, intellect, and spirit, from his primary grip on all the realms of being that is assured to him because his own nature is their epitome" (5).

ness is understood to have these two structures: the capacity for intentional reflection on objects in the world, and the capacity for being drawn beyond the partiality of an egological science toward the impartial view of the All, gained in experiences of "meditation." These structures in consciousness are not understood to be autonomous entities. They are understood to be partial manifestations of a substantial whole, a "meditative complex" of consciousness and the comprehensive reality of which it can know itself to be a part. Voegelin attempts to describe the intimacy of these structures in what might be called a process-theological anthropology:

> If the levels of being in human existence are based on each other, if there is a parallelism of processes, if human existence is incorporated in the world spatio-temporally and causally, if finally there is in consciousness a reflection of the world, then the ontologist infers a background of substantive identity of the levels of being. The differentiation of the experienced levels of being can be made understandable only by interpreting it through the category of process as a series of phases in the unfolding of the identical substance that attains its illumination phase in human consciousness. The meditative complex of experiences in which the reality of the ground of being reveals itself then leads to the necessity of seeing the world-immanent process of being conditioned by a process in the ground of being. (*Anam.*, 29)

Both aspects of Schellingian philosophy are reproduced here: the substantial identity of all things, gained in the meditative aspect of the identity philosophy; and the unfolding of the identical substance in the positive philosophy of history. Where Schelling speaks of substantial identity as the only "presupposition *[Voraussetzung]*" for philosophy,[62] Voegelin speaks of it as the necessary "hypothesis *[Hypothese]*" upon which a comprehensible philosophy of human existence must be based. Also like Schelling, Voegelin maintains that the knowledge of this unity can be obtained only by presupposing a constitutive force operative in consciousness but beyond reflective consciousness itself:

> The substantive unity *[substantielle Einheit]* of human existence, which must be accepted as ontological hypothesis *[ontologische Hypothese]* for the understanding of consciousness's basis in body and matter, is objectively inexperienceable. That does not mean, however, that there is no such thing. At any rate, the hypothesis is indispensable for grasping the "ensemble" *[»Zusammen«]* of consciousness and bodily process in the total process of human existence. (*Anam.*, 31; *Anam. Ger.*, 55)

62. Schelling, *System der gesamten Philosophie*, in *Werke*, 1.6.137.

The substantive unity is inexperienceable when considered in the objectifying light of reflection. But it is experienced in recollections based on philosophical meditation.

Voegelin does not have much to say about meditation in this relatively
early work. But he says a great deal about the anamnetic results of meditative experiences. It is from within this complex of problems that "Schelling's
basic question *[Grundfrage]* appears in a different light." In brief, Schelling's
philosophical orientation is found effectively to transcend the narrow restrictions placed on philosophy by post-Kantian epistemologists, without nonetheless relinquishing appeals to empirical control:

> Ontological speculation is a legitimate philosophical undertaking, founded
> in precisely describable experiences, which it interprets with the means of
> "understandable" categories of process. The formalized Something as an
> alternative to Nothing is a correctly formed ontological concept. It is anti-
> nomic in Kant's sense, but the idealization of reason that leads to the
> antinomies is not "nonsense," its problems are not "false problems *[»Schein-
> problem«]*." Schelling's "Something" is a symbol as much as is a logical or
> cosmological "infinite," a symbol justified inasmuch as it renders transpar-
> ent the meditatively experienced real ground of being in finite language.
> The idealizations lead to "insoluble" problems only within the framework
> of world-immanent experience [that is, in reflective consciousness]; they
> are, however, "significant" in the framework of ontological experiences.
> Schelling's question is significant insofar as it refers to the problem of process
> in the ground of being, the assumption of which seems to me to be an un-
> avoidable requirement of system in a consistent interpretation of the onto-
> logical experience complex. (*Anam.*, 29–30; *Anam. Ger.*, 53–54)

Voegelin's appreciation for Schelling is clear enough from these remarks,
but does it really help him to surmount the basic problems identified previously in his discussion of the temporal dimension and apparent flow of consciousness? The problem remains that Voegelin is speaking of consciousness
and its ground in terms of a "process." He notes that "[a] follower of the
theory of a 'stream of consciousness,' and its constitution through the I, can
object that the problem of the 'flowing' has simply been shifted to the 'process'
and that introducing this word has not contributed anything to the compre-
hension of consciousness and its processive character." To address this problem, Voegelin returns to consider how time consciousness is constituted,
now in light of the insights gained by Schelling's identity philosophy and
Potenzenlehre. Once again, the central problem concerns the concept of the
"present." The objection can be raised that the present is "no fixed point

from which the directions of a process [that is, past and future] would become visible." This objection has some merit, Voegelin grants. It forces a "radical philosophy of the moment" to do without the concept of the present and "to adopt a solipsism of the moment, the moment in which images become visible of which we cannot say with certainty that some of them precede others in a succession" (*Anam.*, 30–31). There is only one way out of the solipsism of the moment, Voegelin contends: to grant that "[c]onsciousness is not a monad that exists in the form of the momentary image but rather human consciousness, *i.e.,* consciousness based on the body and on the external world." By hypothesizing the substantial identity of consciousness-body-world-ground, it becomes possible to find the present in a meaningful way: through recollection of past presents that have determined themselves as recognizable dates in personal and generally human dimensions of history. In so doing, "[t]he illuminated, but really flat momentary image acquires the depth of a process, and thereby becomes presence, as the elements of the image, the memories, and projects are incorporated into the experiential nexus of the body's history and the external history." By inferring substantial identity, one's personal history becomes meaningful as the field in which insights have erupted into consciousness, thereby providing memory with discernible dates and a progressive order leading up to the experience of one's own present: "The phenomenon of dates for consciousness and the dating of consciousness are closely connected. In this dependence [on] the order of the natural process[,] of its relatedness to consciousness, I see the root for the epistemological theory of the ideality and categoriality of time in the experience of nature." Genuine insights, the kind that allow one to mark dates in consciousness, are not constructions of a self-transparent ego. Rather, the climax of an insight is said to break forth as the involuntary experience of "illumination," and the depth of consciousness presupposed to allow for this experience is thought to be well suited to indicate the substance of reality itself, as it cannot be manipulated by the intentionality of the human will. These are important points; they allow Voegelin to suppose that the meaning of one's personal history, at least, does not have to be contingent upon arbitrary constructions of one's "own" making but can be interpreted with an impressive degree of impartiality that gives primary attention to the memories and events that have established themselves. Thus, Voegelin is led to understand the order of his own consciousness by examining the "anamnetic experiences" that continue to present themselves to his memory (*Anam.*, 31–32, 36–51). In his work "On the Theory of Consciousness," he only implies that the method used to determine the order of one's personal history can be extended to help one understand the constitution of order in human history per se. However, this extension becomes the methodical basis for his lifelong project, *Order and History,* a work marked by the constant search for the origin of "new" symbolic accounts of reality's order in an attempt to understand the order and disorder of consciousness leading up to Voegelin's contemporary circumstances (cf. *Anam.,* 32–33).

But what of the problem of the "flow" or "process" in consciousness? Specifically, how can Voegelin mean to say that not all of consciousness is "flowing" when it is embedded in the "processive" or historical nature of reality itself? Voegelin does not address this problem clearly in this text. However, the outlines for its solution have already become apparent. Consciousness can be said to flow, in part, only when its attention is focused on what is moving, that is, on physical objects. The "illuminated" dimension of consciousness, however, does not flow during these experiences but constitutes the stable measure, the nontemporal difference, by which a "flow" can be distinguished in the first place. During the conscious experience of movement or change, the illumined dimension of consciousness is firmly embedded, albeit unconsciously, in the ground of being. Voegelin presupposes that it is not typical for the ground of being to change. In this sense, his thought partially agrees with the static, ontotheological account of being that forms the basis of Western metaphysics. But it must be emphasized that this agreement is only partial. His broader understanding of philosophy is not simply that of a traditional metaphysician. Schelling's process theology, in particular, helps Voegelin to understand how the *relatively* stable ground of being can be thought to change, albeit infrequently, at various points in the course of world history. It also allows him to contend that historical differences in the experience and symbolization of divinity—evident, for example, in Greek philosophy and Judeo-Christian Revelation—can be explained only as effects caused by changes in God's self-revelation to humanity. Summarized theologically, it must be said that God is not always eternal, but has the freedom to enter, change, and withdraw from time. When such changes occur, "new" experiences and symbols are said to erupt into the consciousness of particular people who, for reasons unknown, become aware of them. Concrete experiences are thus thought to antecede claims of divine revelation, but they also allow historians to differentiate epochs—when revelations to one or few become accepted by many. The conclusion to this line of thought is clear. Different historical epochs must be constituted in much the same way as important changes in one's personal life can give one the sense of a personal history (cf. *Anam.,* 34). All of these points are perfectly in accord with

Schelling's positive philosophy. History, for Schelling, is only "human" in a secondary way. Primarily speaking, he thinks that history is an account of how eternal being acts in time.[63]

Intervening Works on the Philosophy of Consciousness (1945–1966)

Between "On the Theory of Consciousness" (1943) and *In Search of Order* (1985), Voegelin wrote three texts in which major sections are devoted to the philosophy of consciousness: "Last Orientation" (1945), *Order and History*, volume 1 (1956), and *Anamnesis* (1966). The following section interprets relevant passages from these texts in order to assess what changes, if any, were introduced before Voegelin returned to address the philosophy of consciousness in the last years of his life.

The discussion in the preceding section is based only on relatively sparse references to Schelling's thought in the 1943 letter from Voegelin to Schütz. Schelling is not the primary subject of discussion in this letter, but a contemporary text—the "Last Orientation" part of Voegelin's *History of Political Ideas*—helps to clarify more of what Voegelin knows and appreciates in Schelling's philosophy of consciousness. Voegelin praises Schelling for making anthropology "the key to speculation" in serious philosophical meditations. Schelling allows nothing to "enter into the content of speculation that cannot be found in human nature, in its depths as well as in its heights, in the limitation of its existence as well as in its openness to transcendent reality." Although surrounded by intellectual Christians from various schools, Schelling "does not return to a Christian ontology, nor to the pneumatocentric anthropology." Rather, he returns to the distinctive task of philosophy: symbolizing the universe "as an intelligible whole with the means that can be found in the nature of man" ("LO," 210, 205).[64] Schelling's return to empirical philosophy begins to correct what Voegelin refers to as the "philosophical

---

63. For Schelling's discussion of a notion of eternity that includes movement, see *Philosophie der Mythologie*, in *Werke*, 2.1.304–6; for Voegelin's discussion, see "Eternal Being in Time" (*Anam.*, 116–40).

64. My analysis of the "Last Orientation" throughout this book follows the precise understanding of Schelling's thought that Voegelin was able to develop from Schelling's German works. I consistently cite all of Voegelin's own translations, place these in triple quotation marks, and indicate the text by Schelling in footnotes. All German terms placed in parentheses within quotations have been inserted by Voegelin. And everything said of Schelling reflects my attempt to represent Voegelin's understanding of his thought, rather than my own.

dilettantism" of his age. The dilettantes to whom Voegelin alludes were famous thinkers with followers—especially Voltaire, Charles Darwin, Karl Marx, and Sigmund Freud. These men all tended to confuse phenomenal and substantial aspects of reality, usually by pitting dogmatic forms of religion and natural science against one another. The popular success of their polemical stances against spiritual matters is well known. However, Voegelin's study of Schelling's ontology, in particular, is greatly responsible for his ability to dismiss the mass creeds associated with these names as instances of "phenomenalism." This term refers to the preoccupation with "the phenomenal aspects of the world, as they appear in [modern] science, and the atrophy of awareness of the substantiality of man and the universe." The critical term *phenomenalism* is not developed in opposition to science per se.[65] Rather, it designates "sentiments, imaginations, beliefs, ideas, speculations, as well as patterns of conduct determined by them, which originate *on occasion* of the [modern] advancement of mathematized science" ("LO," 178–79). To be sure, Voegelin knows that the study of phenomena—the noetic (intellectual) and aesthetic (perceptual) appearances of things—is nothing new or inherently problematic. However, that which gives phenomenalism its distinctively modern and problematic twist is its systematic attempt to exclude from the scope of rational inquiry any questions pertaining to the substantial ground of reality.

What results from the spread of phenomenalism is the breakdown of a common philosophical language and, indeed, the inherently public nature of reason itself. The civilization where humans once attempted to live with their differences in a common world becomes fragmented as charismatic leaders break away from rational scrutiny in attempts to create their own

---

65. Voegelin tends to use the term *science* in three ways: with reference to the natural and human sciences of essences and appearances, a favorable and broad use of the term, recalling the Aristotelian *epistamai;* with reference to modern "scientism," a pejorative term, indicating the restriction of knowledge to quantifiable aspects of experience; and with reference to the science of substance and appearances, indicating a critical clarification of classical realms of knowledge in the Germanic *Wissenschaften,* which Schelling and Voegelin, among others, attempt to defend. Voegelin borrows the term *scientism* from F. A. von Hayek's "Scientism and the Study of Society," parts 1–3, in *Economica* 9:32 (1942), 10:37 (1943), 11:41 (1944). His praise of the German spiritual sciences *(Geisteswissenschaften)* of politics, philosophy, and historiography resembles Hans-Georg Gadamer's appreciation for the same. For more on the nineteenth-century character and development of the spiritual sciences in Germany, see Gadamer, *Truth and Method,* 3–42, 551–79. For more discussion of Voegelin's understanding of the spiritual sciences, see the introduction to his first book, *On the Form of the American Mind* (*CW,* 1:ix–xxxv).

"creed communities." This situation is unnecessary, Voegelin contends, where reason holds sway over public debate. He stresses that people may "differ profoundly in their sentiments and attitudes and still live in the same universe of discourse." But when philosophers give up their vocation and allow public debates to degenerate into uncritical opining,

> [t]he common philosophical language begins to break down, and with it the possibility of men understanding each other across the differences of sentiments and attitudes. Moreover, with the difficulties of understanding increases the unwillingness to discuss rationally at all, and the various creed communities begin to move each in its own vacuum of discourse. The breakdown of the common language has various causes, and the cause that we are isolating in this context is only one of them, but it is a highly important one: we mean the increasing philosophical dilettantism. . . . A not inconsiderable part of the intellectual confusion of our time . . . is due to the fact that the philosophical dilettantes run amok. ("LO," 194–95)[66]

Beyond the creed communities of his day, each focusing exclusively on a preferred stratum of reality, Voegelin praises Schelling for attempting to let the various strata of reality be what they are, regardless of how this may offend members of the different communities. As part of this effort, he also praises Schelling for recovering a properly spiritual understanding of reason. First, Schelling recovers what Voegelin calls a "sound ontology."[67] His ontological thought attempts to allow matter and spirit to be what they are, substantially considered and publicly defended. It successfully transcends the dilettantish character of phenomenalism by effectively criticizing all reflective attempts to conflate either matter or spirit into its opposite, thus clarifying the basis of all reasonable discussion in the process.

> If the realms of being are not distinguished properly, if they are not recognized each in its peculiar substance and structure, if spirit is construed as an epiphenomenon of matter, or matter of spirit, if the operations of the

66. For an insightful study of problems associated with technological phenomenalism, one that relies directly on Voegelin's use of the term in "Last Orientation," see Barry Cooper, *Action into Nature: An Essay on the Meaning of Technology,* esp. chap. 3, "Phenomenalism."

67. *Ontology* is not the best term for what might be described as Schelling's gradational pantheism, because his ontological thought also describes *non-being* at the heart of divine nature and *eternal freedom beyond being* as two of its key terms. As long as these points are kept in mind, Voegelin's conventional use of the term *ontology* will not create the mistaken impression that Schelling was an "essentialist."

spirit are reduced to psychological relations or explained as the sublimation of instincts, or as the effects of an economic or social situation or of racial determinants, discourse ceases to be rational, because by the principle of epiphenomenal construction the various ontic realms are distorted in their own structure as well as in their relations to each other, and because consequently things are not called by their names but by the names of things of another realm. ("LO," 195)

The solution to this confusion is to be found in "the representation of reality by language symbols that follow the stratification of being, without any attempts at applying the symbols for the phenomena in one realm of being to the phenomena of another realm." An important example of this solution is found in Schelling's *Potenzenlehre,* the "sound ontology" to which Voegelin refers. It seems that no superlative was too great for him to use in describing this teaching. Voegelin calls it "perhaps the profoundest piece of philosophical thought ever elaborated" ("LO," 195, 208). But his account of it is remarkably brief, constituting only one and a half typescript pages in the "Last Orientation."[68] He says that the details of the *Potenzenlehre* are not his primary concern. Rather, he is more concerned with clarifying how it allows Schelling to be distinguished in the history of philosophy.

Schelling's thought is distinguished, first, by its attempt to reformulate Giordano Bruno's questionable appropriation of Christian and Hellenic philosophical symbols—one that still allows debate today over whether Bruno was a common pantheist. Those who continue to think of him in this way tend to do so by isolating his account of the universe as a "world-soul," taking this alone to be what he acknowledged as God. It is true, Voegelin notes, Bruno wrote of the *anima mundi* as a divine being. Yet, following Schelling, Voegelin also maintains that Bruno acknowledged an aspect of divinity that transcends the world and animates it. This point was not unknown to the Inquisition that persecuted Bruno, but it was not enough to keep him from being burned at the stake. The Inquisition suspected that Bruno was a unitarian deist, that his theology supported the notion of creation as a "world-machine which after creation runs according to its own laws." And if God is limited by the creation, the Inquisition decided, Bruno was not acknowledging the God of Christian orthodoxy. Despite the debatable ambiguity in Bruno's terminology, Voegelin rules against the Inquisition's decision to kill him and accepts Schelling's account of his probable intent. Schelling returns to Bruno in full view of the need for clarification of his theological philosophy.

68. I undertake further discussion of the *Potenzenlehre* in Chapter 2.

He realizes, according to Voegelin, that Bruno's inconclusiveness was due to "the lack of an adequate terminology for distinguishing the substantial identity of God and the realms of being from their static morphological differentiation" ("LO," 207–8).[69]

In his attempt to distinguish points that Bruno left unclear, Schelling uses the "much misunderstood term 'potency' *(Potenz)*" for the stages or degrees of the one substantially divine process of reality. Among other things, the German term *Potenz* "designates the degree of a member in a series of mathematical powers (for instance $2, 2^2, 2^3 \ldots 2^n$)." Schelling uses this terminology to designate degrees in the substantially unified process of the "One," differentiating its strata as the formal potencies A^1, A^2, A^3. The first potency (A^1) is "nature." This is the potency "that resists revelation and articulation," the unknown whatness of Kant's noumenal *Ding an sich,* and the unconscious dimension of the human psyche. The second potency (A^2) represents "spirit" or "consciousness." It is substantially identical to the first, though its activity is different. It is found always to be "blossoming out of nature into the articulated world from inorganic forms to man." Humanity does not remain completely blind to the substance of nature, as Kant thought. Rather, its substance is partially revealed to us by virtue of the activity of the second potency, this "'savior and liberator'" ("LO," 208).[70]

It is important to stress that spirit (A^2) is shared by humans and the rest of nature, albeit to different degrees. The implication here is that one's mind (spirit) is always already substantially identical to anything one attempts to know; it is created not through dialectical reflection but by something that precedes all conscious differentiation. Voegelin accepts this notion of identity with a favorable description of its main consequence: "[T]his identity is not comprehensible empirically [that is, in the temporal flow of reflective dialec-

---

69. Schelling was not burned at the stake, but he was accused of pantheism by some of his contemporaries. He dismissed them in a characteristic way for him, namely, by suggesting that they return to school for some lessons in ancient Greek logic (cf. "LO," 198–99). The central point of contention was the meaning of the copula in Schelling's claim that "God is nature." To some, this claim suggested a vulgar identification of nature and God. But Schelling maintained, following the "profound logic of the ancients," that the copula was meant to indicate a relationship between *antecedens et consequens.* Accordingly, he intended to convey that God is superior to nature, though nature is within God. Schelling argues that it is also possible to defend Spinoza along similar lines: Spinoza's real error is found in the deterministic nature of his theology, that it did not rise to account sufficiently for freedom. See Schelling, *Philosophische Untersuchungen über das Wesen der menschlichen Freiheit,* in *Werke,* 1.7.340–49 (Gutman trans., *Of Human Freedom,* 11–22).

70. Voegelin citing Schelling, *Die Weltalter,* in *Werke,* 1.8.244.

tic]. The experience of identity abolishes all time and puts right into the middle of time absolute eternity." The eternal "in" humanity is symbolized as unconscious nature (A^1). The human soul becomes conscious (A^2) of the eternal, however, by virtue of the actualization of a third potency. This is the activity of a higher spirit, lifting nature into "freedom" (A^3). By symbolizing this potency, Schelling attempts to account for the experience of a free relation between nature and spirit. The third potency is "the world-soul" or "the connecting link between the universe (the *All*) and the purest God (the *lauterste Gott*)." With this introduction of the "purest God" we find the central reason used by Voegelin to disagree with F. H. Jacobi's charge that Schelling was a common pantheist. "The articulation of the necessity in God into the universe and the consequent articulation of the freedom in God into a transcendent 'purest God,' show perhaps most clearly Schelling's solution of the theological problem that had remained in suspense with Bruno" ("LO," 219, 208, 209).

Schelling does not say that nature is identical to God. Rather, nature is thought to belong only to what is "necessary" in God, a point that allows the experienced order of nature to be understood as divine necessity, or God's nature. That which is most properly called the divine essence is God's transcendent freedom from the necessary order of nature. Thus, Schelling occasionally refers to this aspect of divine freedom as potency A^0. This symbol allows him to account for the purest divinity's "rank outside the struggle of the potencies." Even so, it is interesting to note that both the immanent and the transcendent poles of reality are said to be divine: "'Only the whole can be called God, and not even the whole, after it has grown out of the One into the All and thus has issued, as it were, from the Godhead'" ("LO," 209).[71] Voegelin raises no objections to this grandiose, pantheistic language. Instead, he emphasizes passages in Schelling's thought where divine transcendence is said to be radical, apparently in an attempt to dismiss the charges of vulgar pantheism, identifying God and matter, brought against Schelling by his contemporaries.

Voegelin acknowledges several advantages to Schelling's "ontology." First, it resolves certain ambiguities in Bruno's accounts of nature and God. Sec-

---

71. Ibid. Voegelin's account of the *Potenzenlehre* follows Schelling's relatively early development of this line of thought in *Die Weltalter* (1811–   ). Voegelin knows that Schelling continued to develop his *Potenzenlehre* throughout the rest of his life, eventually stressing the dynamic over the formal aspect of the potencies in his works after 1847 (cf. "LO," 209 n. 9). Voegelin attempts to account for the more dynamic aspect of the potencies later in his text, but this section reveals the extent of his formal understanding of Schelling's teaching.

ond, it allows Voegelin to correct "grave difficulties" in Friedrich Nietzsche's thought, whose "philosophy of existence is always in danger of sliding into a cheap naturalism because the distinction between nature as the 'ground' of existence—Schelling's first potency—and nature as the articulated realm of being [Schelling's second potency, A^2] is never drawn clearly." More specifically, the "'will to power' as the will of the universe to self-realization and the *libido dominandi* as the biological urge of a particular human existence to self-assertion are with Nietzsche in a permanent state of confusion" ("LO," 209).[72] Finally, Voegelin grants that Schelling's ontology, his *Potenzenlehre*, allows him to escape "the difficulty of having to identify terminologically the fundamental substance [of the universe] with any of the partial phases [that is, the potencies] into which the process of the whole is articulated." Schelling does not have to choose arbitrarily between spirit or matter as the fundamental substance of the universe. He understands reality as an entirely living and divine process. "The fundamental substance is, therefore, neither matter nor spirit, neither a transcendent God nor an immanent nature, but the identity of the process in which the One becomes the articulated universe" ("LO," 208). Despite the mystical character of these words, Voegelin maintains that Schelling has not left behind the order of human experience to speculate about the nature of reality in an idiosyncratic way. Even the "experience of identity" that is "not comprehensible empirically" is found to make sense as an example of "protodialectic experience," a term coined by Voegelin to clarify Schelling's account of how inarticulate experiences become articulated insights.

To speak of protodialectic experience is to account for "the experience of the emergence of a content from the unconscious [A^1], still in the state of flux and vagueness before its solidification into language symbols [by virtue of A^3], together with the 'tones' of the soul [A^2] that accompany the emerging, such as anxiety, contraction, urge, pressure, striving, hesitation, unrest, disquietude, release, joy, etc." As such, protodialectic experience is akin to

---

72. Be that as it may, the matter is not clarified by Voegelin, nor perhaps even by Schelling's *Potenzenlehre*. Voegelin suggests that the "will of the universe to self-realization" would be in Schellingian terms the activity of the first potency (A^1). But here one encounters problems, for so is the *libido dominandi* of a particular human existence to self-assertion. Perhaps the ambiguity could be clarified by saying that the universal "will to power" is the activity of the third potency (A^3), while the particular manifestation of this will is due to the activity of the first potency. But this is not how Schelling describes the matter (of which more in Chapter 2). Furthermore, it still remains unclear how the universal and particular wills are to be distinguished from each other when they are said to be substantially identical.

the "wonder" that Plato's Socrates finds at the beginning of philosophy, perhaps even to the restlessness of the heart seeking God that Augustine mentions in the opening lines of his *Confessions*.[73] Voegelin finds protodialectic experiences described "all through Schelling's work, usually in the context of a dialectical elaboration that they serve to support." Rather than attempting to provide a full survey of these descriptions, he speaks generally about Schelling's analysis of experience, all with a view toward criticizing "the development of anthropology after Schelling" ("LO," 214, 215).

Protodialectic experience "is the experience of the creative process," rather than a creative *act,* the latter of which would imply too much intentional control over a phase of consciousness that is only nascent. "There is as much passion in this process as action. It is the process that links the conscious with the unconscious." In the words of Schelling, as translated and quoted by Voegelin, "'All conscious creation presupposes an unconscious and is only an unfolding, an explication of the latter.'"[74] The "moments" that phenomenologists commonly use to interpret stages of experience are replaced here by a description of "tones," suggesting that a more subtle account of experience is being developed: a variety of tones can exist simultaneously, either in harmony or in dissonance with one another, whereas "moments" cannot. The first set of tones described is said to have an "orgiastic tinge." In order to avoid breaking the rhythm of Voegelin's commentary, his description of the tones needs to be quoted in full:

> The active potency [A^1] does not manifest itself immediately in full power but rather as a *gentle contraction,* like that which precedes awakening from deep slumber. With increasing strength the powers of being [A^2 and A^3] are excited to *sluggish, blind, activity. Shapeless births* begin to rise. The being that exists in this strife *heaves as in heavy dreams* that rise from being, that is, from the past. With increasing conflict these births of the night pass like *wild fantasies* through the soul, and it experiences in them *all the terrors* of its own being. The predominant feeling in this conflict of tendencies, where it does not know which way to turn, is that of *anxiety* or *dread (Angst).* "Meanwhile the *orgasm of powers* increases more and more and makes the integrating power of the soul [A^3] fear a *complete dissociation,* or *total dissolution.*" At this juncture the integrating power *sets free* or *surrenders* its own life, by recognizing it as already past, and in this act of

73. Cf. Plato, *Theaetetus* 155d; Augustine, *Confessions,* 3. For Voegelin's discussion of "wonder" and "unrest" at the beginning of philosophy, see "Reason: The Classic Experience," in *Anam.,* 92–94; and *CW,* 12:268–70.

74. Voegelin citing Schelling, *Die Weltalter,* in *Werke,* 1.8.337.

release, the *higher form* of its own life and the *quiet purity* of the spirit appear before it as in a flash. ("LO," 215)[75]

This passage attempts to describe the origin of a conscious insight. Like childbirth, the experience is said to be extremely painful. A certain degree of "orgiastic suffering" is said to be inevitable, because "'pain is something general and necessary in all life; it is the inevitable passage to freedom. . . . Each being must learn to know its own depth; and that is impossible without suffering.'"[76] The suffering of the philosopher, it seems, is caused by the peculiar consciousness of potencies becoming actualized in the soul. This consciousness arises when the eternal dimension of the unconscious (A^1) provokes the world soul's freedom (A^3) to search out its own depth. This is a great burden to bear for human consciousness (A^2), the most tumultuous part of the world soul. It is a terrifying experience, indeed, for consciousness to realize that it is caught between, so to speak, the concupiscential relations of divine potencies. This terror is said to be universally present, though it comes to explicit consciousness only in humans. Voegelin takes particular notice of the fact that

> Schelling considers this experience as revealing the character of the universal process in general. "It is a futile endeavor to explain the manifoldness of nature as a peaceful interpenetration and harmonization of different powers. All that comes into being can do so only in restlessness and discontent *(Unmut),* and as anxiety is the fundamental feeling of every living creature, so is everything that lives conceived and born in violent strife." ("LO," 215, 216)[77]

This anxiety is experienced to some degree by everyone, perhaps even by everything. But it is known most acutely only to a few humans. There is an exponential relation suggested here: the more searching the conscious mind, the closer it comes to consciousness of the actual fray of potencies. But the people who cultivate this consciousness, though suffering greatly, are also best able to enjoy the extraordinary release that comes about when the relations between potencies occasionally give birth to substantial harmony and peace in the soul.

75. Ibid., 1.8.336.
76. Ibid., 1.8.335. This description of how spirit (A^3) painfully gains its freedom resembles Schelling's account of what occurs in Christ's Resurrection. This teaching is interpreted further in Chapter 2.
77. Ibid., 1.8.322.

Voegelin thinks that Schelling intends fully to describe the universal process in terms pertaining to sexual tension, release and procreation. He assumes that "the term *potency* was chosen with an awareness of its sexual implication. And, to the extent to which it rests on this aspect of the protodialectic experience, the *Potenzenlehre* would be a mathematizing speculation on the experience of the procreative act" ("LO," 217). Clearly, judging by Voegelin's high praise for this insight, Schelling persuades Voegelin of the need for a descriptive terminology that transcends contemporary standards in phenomenology. Schelling's return to Bruno allows for the critical clarification of a pantheism that does not simply equate God and the natural world, but attempts to account for divine freedom in the play of naturally divine potencies.

In the introduction to this section, it was noted that Voegelin finds Schelling to be a great philosopher, not least because his philosophical anthropology is able to transcend the Cartesian dualism of mind and matter. Thus far, however, it may appear that Schelling has not solved the problem of dualism. Rather, it might be argued, he has simply created a potentially confusing shell game of potencies. It seems that the substance of reality can move from matter to spirit, or back again, depending on the type of critique needed to refute a particular type of phenomenalist. But Voegelin would likely respond to this objection by calling attention to the apex of Schelling's anthropology, his recovery of a properly spiritual or contemplative understanding of "rationalism." Voegelin is careful to point out that Schelling understands substantial rationality and the type of thinking that dominated the Age of Reason to be fundamentally and historically opposed ("LO," 195). Enlightenment rationalism assumes Reason (capitalized) to be the immanent possession of human beings, who are considered to be substantially different from God or the substance of the universe. It assumes that reason is human, and Revelation is divine—hence irrational. Enlightenment rationalists thus remain essentially within the conceptual dichotomy of reason and Revelation produced by orthodox Christianity. They simply accentuate, in a reactionary way, the human pole of this dichotomy—while continuing to accept the Christian-theological description of human reason as *merely* natural. Once again, Schelling returns to Bruno as his principal guide beyond this problem, and finds that the reason-Revelation distinction lacks empirical substance.

Voegelin interprets Schelling's account of substantial reason in several aphorisms, all of which emphasize the human mind's "immersion" in the substance of the divine universe. This notion of immersion is the main point that Schelling takes from Bruno.

1. Not we, not you or I, know about God. For reason, insofar as it affirms God, can affirm *nothing* else, and in this act it annihilates itself as a particularity, as something that is *outside God.*[78]

Voegelin emphasizes the unity of all things "in" God conveyed by this aphorism. He calls attention to Schelling's implicit step beyond Fichte here, whose system stood on the strict or real difference between the ego and nonego (the knowing subject and the object known), and agrees with Schelling that these terms cannot be reified as strictly independent entities. This is the critical mistake of modern rationalists.

2. The "I think," "I am," is since Descartes the fundamental error of all knowledge *(Erkenntnis);* thinking is not my thinking, and being is not my being, for all is only of God, or of the All.

Schelling abandons the *ego cogitans* of Descartes, at least as the ground of consciousness, and rediscovers that "[t]he ego is not an ultimate entity with faculties of reasoning but a medium through which the substance of the universe [or God] is operating in its processes. In the knowledge of God, there is for Schelling no subject or object of knowledge; there is instead the life of the divine substance, animating the world and man as part of the world" ("LO," 206–7). Some important consequences, also cited as aphorisms, follow from these principles:

3. Reason is not a faculty, or tool, and it cannot be used: indeed there is no reason that we have, there is only a reason that has us.

4. Reason is not an affirmation of the One, that itself would be outside the One; it is a knowing of God that itself is in God.

5. Reason does not *have* the idea of God, it *is* this idea, and nothing else.

6. There is no ascent of knowledge to God, but only an immediate recognition; not an immediate recognition by man, but of the divine by the divine.

Both the theological and the anthropological significance of these remarks are appreciated by Voegelin: "In no way can God be an object of knowledge; we are never outside God so that we could posit him as an object. Equally reprehensible is an attitude in which the subject would assert itself as the subject." Theocentric theology and egocentric philosophy are equally under-

---

78. Voegelin quotes Schelling from his *Aphorismen zur Einleitung in die Naturphilosophie* (1806), in *Werke,* 1.7.148 ff. I have numbered Voegelin's quotations ("LO," 204).

mined by Schelling's rediscovery of the inability of reason to establish conventional distinctions between God and humanity, or even subjects and objects, with substantial force.

> 7. There is no belief in God as a quality in the subject. You only wanted to save the subject, you did not want to transfigure *(verklären)* the divine.
>
> 8. Hence the Absolute can be eternally preserved only as the absolute and indivisible identity of the subjective and the objective, which formula is equivalent to the infinite self-affirmation of God.

In these aphorisms, Voegelin finds "the full stop after the Age of Enlightenment and Reason" ("LO," 204). One might say, with due caution for an ambiguous term, that Schelling becomes Voegelin's guide to a *postmodern* understanding of reason and reality, albeit one that transcends the communitarian relativism often associated with postmodernism. Schelling's philosophical anthropology develops a broadly based empiricism, composed of a substantial though processive "ontology" (the *Potenzenlehre*) and an understanding of rationality grounded in meditation. In the ontology, relational differences among the strata of being are distinguished by the symbols for divine potencies (A^1, A^2, A^3, A^0). In the rationalism, the substantial identity of these terms is emphasized, and the particular strata in the order of being are contemplated for their immersion in "the All." The full extent to which Voegelin appreciates all of these insights will surface through consideration of his later works. For now, it is sufficient to note the relatively early and general manifestation of agreement among Schelling's identity philosophy, his rejection of the "subjectivization of reason," and Voegelin's critique of "phenomenalism."

By the early 1950s, Voegelin's anthropology began to emphasize the central claim that human being "participates" in all of the realms of being, from the divine ground to the relative nonbeing of nature. This claim governs all of his statements with respect to the symbolic position of humanity in the order of reality. The participatory nature of existence allows one to acknowledge and name the other participants in being: God, oneself, nature, and other humans. It also sets a limit to all possible knowledge of oneself and others. From this primary experience of all the realms of being, "from this primary cognitive participation, turgid with passion, rises the arduous way, the *methodos,* toward the dispassionate gaze on the order of being in the theoretical attitude" (*NSP,* 5). This "theoretical attitude" is the climax of "illumination" mentioned in the earlier text. Participatory knowledge is never complete or absolute knowledge, Voegelin claims, even with respect to the knowledge

that human participants may attain of themselves: "At the center of his existence man is unknown to himself and must remain so, for the part of being
that calls itself man could be known fully only if the community of being and
its drama in time were known as a whole.... Knowledge of the whole, however, is precluded by the identity of the knower with the partner, and ignorance of the whole precludes essential knowledge of the part" (*OH*, 1:2).
The potential extremity of this statement is qualified when Voegelin also
admits that ignorance cannot be turned into an absolute:

> The ultimate, essential ignorance is not complete ignorance. Man can
> achieve considerable knowledge about the order of being, and not the least
> part of that knowledge is the distinction between the knowable and the
> unknowable.... The concern of man about the meaning of his existence in
> the field of being does not remain pent up in the tortures of anxiety, but
> can vent itself in the creation of symbols purporting to render intelligible
> the relations and tensions between the distinguishable terms of the field.
> (*OH*, 1:2, 3)

Symbolic "differentiations" of this "compact" primordial field are, of course,
quite different between civilizations. But Voegelin's philosophical anthropology seeks to account for a common order of human lives in the broader context of reality.

> Participation in being . . . is not a partial involvement of man; he is engaged
> with the whole of his existence, for participation is existence itself. There is
> no vantage point outside existence from which its meaning can be viewed
> and a course of action charted according to a plan, nor is there a blessed
> island to which man can withdraw in order to recapture his self. The role
> of existence must be played in uncertainty of its meaning, as an adventure
> of decision on the edge of freedom and necessity. (*OH*, 1:1)[79]

Note that all of these passages are concerned primarily with "existence."
They are not statements pertaining to the substantial ground of being. Accordingly, Schelling would agree with all of these claims. Voegelin has articulated the central presuppositions of Schelling's positive philosophy of existence. The philosophical arguments in *Order and History* are not based upon
modern conceptions of the "self." They focus on the participatory nature of
individual souls in historical existence.

---

79. Voegelin's appeal to the "decision" between necessity and freedom resembles Schelling's
account of this decision in the order of being itself (cf. *Die Weltalter*, in *Werke*, 1.8.220–21, 241,
245, 261–62).

But what of essence? Does Voegelin's emphasis on the "participatory" nature of existence preclude his earlier acceptance of Schelling's account of the substantial identity of the partners in being? No, it does not. Where Schelling speaks of identity, Voegelin speaks of the "consubstantiality" of all the partners. If this were all he said, one might be left with the impression that the partners may be substantially different and only *related* by reflective thought. But Voegelin has more to say about the consubstantiality of the human soul and reality in general:

> The community of being is experienced with such intimacy that the consubstantiality of the partners will override the separateness of substances. We move in a charmed community where everything that meets us has force and will and feelings, where animals and plants can be men and gods, where men can be divine and gods are kings, . . . where the underground sameness of being is a conductor for magic currents of good or evil force that will subterraneously reach the superficially unreachable partner, where things are the same and not the same, and can change into each other. (*OH,* 1:3)

Despite his participatory language with respect to existential matters, Voegelin still presupposes the substantial identity or "underground sameness" of the partners in being—the central feature of Schelling's identity philosophy. Furthermore, as with Schelling's appeals to the unconscious as the site of this identity, so, too, Voegelin locates this sameness "underground." He does not retract these Schellingian presuppositions in any of his later works. They do, however, recede further and further underground.[80]

There are a number of changes in Voegelin's understanding of consciousness, reality, and history that develop between the writing of "On the Theory of Consciousness" (1943) and *In Search of Order,* the last volume of *Order and History* (1985). But these changes concern Voegelin's understanding of consciousness in *history.* They do not touch the Schellingian theory of consciousness with which he begins to philosophize in the 1943 text. The most

---

80. The theme of "consubstantiality" resurfaces in several of Voegelin's later writings (cf. "Theology Confronting World Religions?" [1967], in *Conversations,* 46–47; *OH,* 3:184, 4:72, 76 [1974]; "Reason: the Classic Experience" [1974], in *Anam.,* 95; and *CW,* 12:271). In the *Conversations* reference, Voegelin says he takes the term from work conducted on cosmological civilizations by the Oriental school at the University of Chicago. He is never as explicit with regard to the substantial identity of the "participants" in being, nor with regard to the specifically Schellingian theory of consciousness he formerly associated with this identity = consubstantiality.

notable change occurs in the German publication of *Anamnesis* (1966), in which Voegelin begins to suggest that the experiences and symbolizations of divine transcendence in the philosophy of Plato and Aristotle are equivalent to those normally associated with the subjects of Judeo-Christian Revelation. The details of this change and its implication for Voegelin's account of order in history will be discussed at length in Chapter 4. We turn now to consider an important terminological revision in Voegelin's anthropology.

Recall that Schelling occasionally summarized the perplexities of human life by saying that the soul exists in the "middle" between divine transcendence (eternal *freedom*) and divine immanence (the *necessary* order of the natural world). In 1964, Voegelin also began to write of the soul's middle position, in the essay "Eternal Being in Time." He does so, however, not with reference to Schelling but to Plato. He says that Plato understood human existence as that which occurs between *(metaxy)* the immortal gods and mortal nature, knowledge and ignorance, perfection and imperfection, and so on. The central text from which Voegelin takes the Greek term *metaxy* is Plato's *Symposium*. He refers to this text as the locus classicus for the mythical expression of the philosopher's awareness of existing in tension between time and eternity. For Plato, in Voegelin's account of the matter, it is true that "god and man do not mingle." But without some notion of a mediator, Voegelin argues, "it remains inscrutable how man, in temporal being (Plato's *thnetos* [mortal]), could experience eternal being." There must be a mediator that is not produced by reflective philosophy, for symbolic acknowledgments of the divine precede the historical advent of philosophy. Voegelin notes that Plato attributed the role of mediator to "'a very powerful spirit,' for the realm of the spiritual *(pan to daimonion)* lies between *(metaxy)* God and man." Although Plato's text alludes to several *daimones,* Voegelin cites only one, Eros (or Love), as "the symbol of the experienced tension between the poles of temporal and eternal being" (*Anam.,* 128).[81]

In the words of Plato, eros moves between the divine and human realms, "[i]nterpreting and transporting human things to the gods and divine things to humans; entreaties and sacrifices from below, and ordinances and requitals from above: being midway between, it makes each supplement the other, so that the whole is combined in one."[82] Voegelin says that the Platonic account "discreetly points up what is the core of the matter," namely, that man is not simply mortal or temporal "but experiences in himself the tension to divine

81. Cf. Plato, *Symposium* 203a, 202e.
82. Ibid., 202e.

being and thus stands between the human and the divine." Although this heightened state of tension may be experienced by humans generally, only people with "philosophical experience" are said to be *conscious* of existing in the erotic tension "in which the divine and the human partake of each other." The erotic nature of this experience can be liberating, for "[w]hoever has [philosophical] experience grows above the status of a mortal and becomes a 'spiritual man,' *daimonios aner.*" But the full breadth of eros can also be overlooked by "the complacent ignoramus." Voegelin explains that "the depressing fact of ignorance is that it is satisfied with what it is. The man who does not feel his condition of need does not desire what he is lacking. The philosopher, too, is *amathes* [ignorant], but his *amathia* [ignorance] is the one pole of the tension in which he experiences the other pole, *sophia* (wisdom). That *amathia* that is not a pole of philosophical experience characterizes the man without tension, who is spiritually dull." At this point, it seems as though there are fundamentally different constitutions of the human soul that may coexist in society: those who experience the erotic need for understanding, and others who do not. But Voegelin clarifies this matter. The difference is not primarily with respect to the presence or absence of erotic experience, but with respect to how one responds to this experience. The culpable "ignoramus" is one who "sinks down" into spiritual sterility because he "closes himself" to "the new order" proclaimed by the erotic philosophy of "Socrates-Plato" (*Anam.,* 128, 129, 154, 128, 129, 130).

The claim that spiritually dull people have closed themselves is an important one. It implies that all people experience the erotic tension to "philosophical experience" but simply respond to this experience differently. Those who ignore the impulse to understanding become, through this type of ignorance, "ignoramuses." This is a culpable state of existence. It forms the basis of Plato's judgment myths. Thus, in the *Gorgias,* Voegelin finds that Socrates was justified in his criticisms of Callicles and the Athenian resistance to philosophy he represented:

> The decision about the right order, which in time is made by the verdict of the Athenians about Socrates, is in eternity accomplished by the judgment of the dead. The poles of the psychic tension in the historical field become visible as those men who are beholden to "time" and the others who live with a view to "eternity"; or the "living ones" who through the splendor of time go toward death, and the "dead ones" who through their life in the tension of judgment go to eternity. Through the historical character of the philosophical experience other types of men become visible, in whose life and death contest the field of history is constituted. (*Anam.,* 130)

No plurality of human natures is implied in this analysis of the *Symposium,* only a plurality of responses to a nature that is common to all. Even so, the plurality of human responses to eros is rather pronounced in Voegelin's interpretation, because he does not attempt to describe humans who exist in society abstractly, but discusses the dispensations of psychological order that allegedly emerged only on the occasion of the birth of philosophy. Before Socrates-Plato, Voegelin suggests that Hellenes understood themselves only to be mortal *(thnetos).* The gods alone were thought to be immortal. The difference between gods and humans was symbolized in the mythical epics of Homer and Hesiod. Once Platonic philosophy clarifies the erotic nature of experience, however, suggesting it to be that which pulls human mortality into the immortality of the divine, two "new" dispensations of psychological order are said to emerge: the daimonic-erotic philosopher, exemplified by Socrates; and the resisting countermovement of the epic tradition. The latter response is then judged to be a spiritually sterile, conservative reaction—at least by Voegelin—when viewed against the standards of erotic philosophy.[83]

In close connection with the three types of responses to erotic experience, Voegelin finds three historical dispensations of psychological order to emerge from the Platonic account of eros: "the past world" of human mortality under the Homeric gods, "the new world" of Socratic philosophy, and "the resisting environment," where "the call of the new humanity is not heard at all or even rejected" by the *amathes.* The historical advance of philosophy is thought to be irreversible. "[O]nce the humanly representative level of differentiating experience has been attained, no way leads back to the more compact levels" of the preceding tradition (*Anam.,* 154, 129). One may attempt to resist the new order, of course, but only with conservative appeals to old myths, ignoring the "humanly representative" level of a newly differentiated anthropological truth in "Socrates-Plato." Voegelin does not wish to deny that the "erotic tension" toward the divine ground was present in human souls before its thematic differentiation in Platonic philosophy. What is new in the Platonic writings, he argues, is the *consciousness* of the soul's *metaxic* existence—where human consciousness is, as it were, promoted from the status of "mortal" to "spiritual." This point allows one to raise the question of similar promotions from discoveries in the future—say, of a Hegelian leap from spiritual philosophy to perfected knowledge. But Voegelin argues

---

83. Voegelin reproduces here a conventional account of Plato's understanding of poetry, especially that of Homer. For a counterargument, citing textual evidence for Plato's appreciation of Homer, see Zdravko Planinc, "Homeric Imagery in Plato's *Phaedrus.*"

throughout his writings that no further promotions of this magnitude have occurred. Even with the advent of Christian consciousness, with its "pneumatic" (spiritual) focus on the creative divinity beyond the world, human life remains structured by spiritual *tensions.* The truly and completely human existence is one that, since the time of Plato, remains consciously rooted in the tensional middle ground of the *metaxy.* In 1964, Voegelin began a long-standing practice of conceptualizing the term *metaxy.* It appears in nearly every text that he published until the end of his life. By 1974, it had become a technical term in the substantive, the capitalized *Metaxy* (cf. *OH,* 4:passim). But this word is not used as a technical term in Plato's dialogues.

The space restrictions of this chapter do not permit a thorough comparison of the dialogues and Voegelin's use of the term *metaxy.* But this much can be mentioned briefly. The term *metaxy* occurs ninety-nine times in the dialogues, usually as an adverb that often functions as a preposition taking the genitive case. The term is used only once as a substantive noun, in book 9 of the *Republic.* In this context, Socrates says that vulgar hedonists will be swept downward in their pursuits of bodily pleasures, back to the middle *(to metaxy)* in which they continue to roam about in helpless confusion, never experiencing the cathartic pleasure *(katharas hēdonēs)* that comes from setting one's sights on the reality above *(to alēthōs anō).*[84] Indeed, Socrates even refers to the middle ground as a place of confusion that any reasonable person ought to flee.[85] But Voegelin's conceptualization of the *metaxy* is a questionable use of the Platonic term for another reason. He later admits that Plato did not refer to this state of existence with the abstract noun *tension* (or *tasis* in Greek). It was the Stoics who first introduced the notion of "tension" to philosophy (cf. *Conversations,* 44). Thus, it might be argued that Voegelin's *"metaxy"* bears a greater resemblance to Schelling's tensional account of humanity's "middle" position in existence than it does to Plato's usage of the term. Schelling's writings are replete with the notion that human consciousness is a mixture of existential "tensions," and he occasionally summarizes this state of existence as occurring in the "middle" between divine immanence (the natural world) and divine transcendence (eternal freedom).[86] It would seem that Voegelin conceptualizes the *Metaxy* for heuristic purposes: to highlight his claim that human knowledge and ignorance always remain

---

84. Plato, *Republic* 586a.

85. Cf. Plato, *Theaetetus* 180e–181a.

86. For a comprehensive list of Plato's uses of the term *metaxy,* see William P. Simmons, "The Platonic *Metaxy* in the Writings of Eric Voegelin and Simone Weil," 32–34.

incomplete, tensional, or "in-between" their opposites. This move is directed primarily against attempts by German idealists in the nineteenth century—most notably Fichte and Hegel—to build comprehensive systems of logic seeking to eradicate the tensional nature of consciousness once and for all.

Voegelin's critique of idealism and simultaneous avoidance of phenomenalistic science are constant features of his later work on the philosophy of consciousness. They appear to have been helped considerably by his reliance upon the distinctive points of Schelling's thought encountered thus far:

- Schelling's tensional "ontology," his dynamic *Potenzenlehre,* helps Voegelin to avoid conflating real matter with ideal spirit. It also helps him to avoid making the opposite mistake, found in "vulgar materialists" who construe spirit as an epiphenomenon of matter.

- Schelling's psychological thought, specifically his account of symbol formation through "protodialectic experience," reminds Voegelin that reflection is always already distancing—hence no reliable means of *producing* the identity of human and divine "partners in being."

- Schelling's recovery of the meditative aspect of reason does the same. It allows Voegelin to acknowledge the "consubstantiality" of human and divine partners in being without falling prey to the suspicion that this symbolic language may be properly reduced to the product of a human mind divorced from the substance of reality.

- Finally, because Plato does not dwell on the middle position of the human soul in reality, but Voegelin does, Schelling's discussion of the same has been cited as a likely guide to Voegelin's conceptualization of the *Metaxy.* This instance would not be the first time that we have encountered Voegelin reading Plato with the help of a Schellingian theme: our introductory analysis of "Plato's Egyptian Myth" has already found Voegelin using and acknowledging several such themes in his interpretation of Platonic dialogues.

At least this much can be said by way of summarizing the previous section. But we have yet to reach the apex of Voegelin's philosophy of consciousness, formulated in the last volume of *Order and History.* It is to this volume that we must now turn in order to investigate the full extent of the Schellingian orientation in his mature thoughts on consciousness and its ground.

In Search of Order

As indicated by its title, Voegelin's last book focuses on the *order* of consciousness, rather than its development in world history. This text is more meditative than previous works. Yet, rather than breaking with them, it continues to build on an insight gained while writing "On the Theory of Consciousness" (1943). Voegelin describes this insight in the foreword to his 1966 edition of *Anamnesis:*

> The most important result of these [1943] efforts was the insight that a "theory" of consciousness in the sense of generically valid propositions concerning a pre-given structure was impossible. For consciousness is not a given to be deduced from outside but an experience of participation in the ground of being whose logos [that is, order] has to be brought to clarity through the meditative exegesis of itself. The illusion of a "theory" had to give way to the reality of the meditative process; and this process had to go through its phases of increasing experience and insight. (*Anam. Ger.,* 7)[87]

In the 1943 text recalled by Voegelin, the analysis of consciousness focused on an experience directly related to a sense perception, specifically that of the flow of a tone. In his last work, he continues the attempt to clarify the order of consciousness by meditating on actual experiences. This time, however, sensory perceptions fade to the background as he turns to consider experiences that arise during communication, specifically between a writer (Voegelin himself) and his readers.

In Search of Order opens with the chapter titled "The Beginning of the Beginning." Voegelin begins appropriately by searching for the beginning of his chapter: "As I am putting down these words on an empty page I have begun to write a sentence that, when it is finished, will be the beginning of a chapter on certain problems of Beginning." Voegelin wonders if this sentence is truly the beginning of his chapter and decides that he does not know, "for the chapter is yet unwritten; and, though I have a general idea of its construction, I know from experience that new ideas have a habit of emerging while the writing is going on, compelling changes in the construction and making the beginning unsuitable." This situation begins to reveal the paradoxical character of human consciousness itself, which, like the chapter Voegelin sets out to write, appears to have "no beginning before it has come to its end." It also causes Voegelin to realize that neither will the end of the chapter reveal the true beginning he seeks, thus increasing the paradox: The

---

87. Voegelin himself has translated these sentences from his foreword to the German *Anamnesis.* See "Consciousness and Order: Foreword to 'Anamnesis' (1966)," in *The Beginning and the Beyond: Papers from the Gadamer and Lonergan Conferences,* ed. Frederick Lawrence, 35–41. I have quoted Voegelin's translation (ibid., 35–36).

completed chapter will point beyond itself to the book of which it will be only a part, and the book will point beyond itself "to the intricate problems of communication between reader and writer. The book is meant to be read; it is an event in a vast social field of thought and language, of writing and reading about matters which the members of the field believe to be of concern for their existence in truth." The book will point beyond itself to a "communion of existential concern" that depends, furthermore, on a mutually comprehensible language: "Back we are referred, the reader and I, to the words, for they have begun before I have begun to put them down. Was the word in the beginning after all?" (*OH*, 5:13, 14).

Voegelin realizes that he is not simply writing in what is called "English." He is using a "philosophers' language," which has neither begun nor will end in his present work:

> [It] has been structured by a millennial history of the philosophers' quest for truth, a history that has not stopped at some point in the past but is continuing in the present effort between reader and writer. The social field constituted by the philosophers' language, thus, is not limited to communication through the spoken and written word among contemporaries, but extends historically from a distant past, through the present, into the future. (*OH*, 5:14)

Given this widening of the context in which meaningful experiences occur, when or where have the experiences begun that call for interpretation? There is "something peculiar" that Voegelin notices about the philosophers' language itself:

> In order to be intelligible, it had to be spoken in one of the several ethnic, imperial, and national languages that have developed ever since antiquity, though it does not seem to be identical with any one of them; and yet... they all have left, and are leaving, their specific traces of meaning in the language used, and expected to be understood, in the present chapter; but then again, in its millennial course the quest for truth has developed, and is still developing, a language of its own. (*OH*, 5:15)

The philosophers' language leaves the philosopher, Voegelin, somewhat at a distance from the words he uses in his chapter on the Beginning. The words he uses have been used by others before. He is conscious of this fact. But he also knows that the specific configuration in which he puts them down will stand apart as a symbolic work in its own right. The articulated thoughts are somewhat embedded in the history of communication, which Voegelin consciously continues, yet somewhat removed from the historical conventions of language serving him as the *means* of communication. Voegelin is faced with the problem of two languages, and his awareness of their difference, resulting in a complex situation that leads him to ask: "What is the structure in reality that will induce, when experienced, this equivocal use of the term 'language'?" The equivocation is induced, he decides, by "the paradoxical structure of consciousness and its relation to reality" (*OH*, 5:15). The three meanings of the term *language* correspond to three structures in the order of consciousness.

The first structure of consciousness is now explicitly named *intentionality:* "On the one hand, we speak of consciousness as a something located in human beings in their bodily existence. In relation to this concretely embodied consciousness, reality assumes the position of an object intended," and the corresponding reality acquires "a metaphorical touch of external thingness."[88] This "metaphor" of external thingness is found in common speech— for example, when one refers to being conscious of some*thing,* remembering or imagining some*thing,* and so on. The reality intended as the object of a subject's consciousness is habitually called a "thing" in English. This recollection leads Voegelin to describe the aspect of reality grasped by intentional consciousness as the "thingness" of "thing-reality." Intentionality is the mode of consciousness in which analytical concepts are formed about differentiated things in the world. But intentional states of consciousness do not exhaust the complete range of human experience, Voegelin argues. Thinking strictly within the subject-object distinction of intentional consciousness has its limitations. For example, it is always possible that during the course of one's thinking about such matters, the subject of cognition may recall that he or she is also part of the same reality that has been objectified by the intentionality of consciousness. When this realization occurs, reality no longer appears to be the relatively controlled, named, posited, or constructed object

88. Notice the description of intentional reality as "metaphorically" external. This point is clarified in a contemporary text in which Voegelin prepares the account of consciousness that ultimately appears in volume 5 of *Order and History.* He describes intentional reality as only "metaphorically" external in order to leave open the question as to whether there are external objects of *noemata* in a phenomenological sense. See Voegelin, "The Meditative Origin of the Philosophical Knowledge of Order" (1981), in *Beginning and the Beyond,* ed. Lawrence, 49. The "metaphorical" description of external reality also implies the substantive identity of subjects and objects of cognition.

of consciousness "but the something in which consciousness occurs as an event of participation between partners in the community of being." This realization has considerable consequences for how one is able to understand the "subject" of experiences: "[R]eality moves from the position of an intended object to that of a subject, while the consciousness of the human subject intending objects moves to the position of a predicative event in the subject 'reality' as it becomes luminous for its truth" (*OH*, 5:15). This type of experience induces awareness of the existential paradox of consciousness alluded to previously. It precludes the human subject from becoming a transcendental ego, effectively creating its "own" reality, and causes no necessary disorder in its wake. It opens the way for minds lost in the confusions of logical paradoxes to regain a sense of how the mind is always already a substantial part of anything it experiences.

This insight is made possible by virtue of what Voegelin now calls the *luminosity* of consciousness, the second structure named in his study. In contrast to the conceptual and narrative character of intentionality, luminosity is the symbolic and meditative aspect of consciousness. It allows one to understand the separated "parts" of reality as manifestations of the All. Luminosity has the passive character of "illumination," as mentioned in Voegelin's 1943 study of consciousness. It recalls to mind an unintentional type of experience in which the comprehending whole of reality, so to speak, *comes to mind.* Otherwise said, one cannot intentionally bring about a genuine experience of luminosity. It either occurs or fails to occur at the climax of one's meditative pursuits—or even during the course of daily life. Although the description of this class of experience has religious tones, luminosity is not limited to people with experiences or beliefs of a conventionally religious nature. It is a general structure of consciousness that everyone allegedly experiences on one level of clarity or another.

Voegelin wonders, returning to more conventional language, "where" the luminous experience of reality occurs. Because the subject-object distinction is meaningless in this mode of consciousness, he says that the experience

> has to be located, not in one of the partners, but in the comprehending reality; consciousness has a structural dimension by which it belongs, not to man in his bodily existence, but to the reality in which man, the other partners to the community of being, and the participatory relations among them occur. If the spatial metaphor be still permitted, the luminosity of consciousness is located somewhere "between" human consciousness in bodily existence and reality intended in its mode of thingness. (*OH*, 5:16)

Once again, the Greek word *metaxy* is used to suggest that luminous experiences occur between the comprehending reality and the consciousness that knows the body to be "located" in space and time. Luminous experiences have always preceded reflective differentiations of the "body" and "consciousness," even though one may have lost sight of this basic point due to the predominance of intentional concepts in phenomenology, other schools of modern thought, and the natural sciences. Voegelin's appeal to luminosity in a philosophical study of order recalls Schelling's account of how the "absolute light" of reality may come to strike reason "like a flash of lightning," thereby revealing the self-affirmation of the All in human consciousness. This discussion is a clear example of how Voegelin continues to develop his earlier account of "protodialectic experience," from his study of Schelling's anthropology, and helps to explain why "the reality of experience is self-interpretive."[89] Any genuine interpretation of a particular experience is always initially guided by the luminous order of consciousness. Such interpretation neither begins nor ends with a consciously constructed "human" or "social" reality. Thus, no genuine symbolization of ultimate reality can be explained as a groundless projection of a self-sufficient ego. The luminous interpretation of reality's order helps to keep Voegelin from perpetuating any manifestation of the *proton pseudos*. His empirical appeals to the luminosity of consciousness continue to imply, at least, that the human mind is substantially identical to the reality it attempts to represent—not arbitrarily project—with the formation of intentional concepts.

Voegelin searches for a word to name the comprehending reality in which luminous experiences occur. This reality is said to comprehend all of "the partners in being, *i.e.,* God and the world, man and society." He says that there is no technical term for it in common usage but notices that when philosophers "run into this structure incidentally in their exploration of other subject matters," they have "a habit of referring to it by a neutral 'it.' The It referred to is the mysterious 'it' that also occurs in everyday language in such phrases as 'it rains.'"[90] The comprehensive reality that comes to light in luminous experience is accordingly named the "It-reality," taking this term as an equivalent symbol for Plato's *to pan* (the All) (*OH,* 5:16; cf. 87–99)—not to mention Schelling's "All."

---

89. Cf. *supra,* 60–61 (for Schelling's "luminosity") and 99–101. (for Voegelin's "protodialectic experience").

90. One of the philosophers to whom Voegelin alludes here is Nietzsche; another is Karl Kraus (cf. Lawrence, *Beginning and the Beyond,* 49, 108).

Two structures of consciousness have come to light thus far. These may be summarized by listing the terms that Voegelin uses to distinguish them:

Intentionality	Luminosity
narrative	event, experience
concepts	symbols
intentional	expressive
thing-reality	It-reality

Voegelin knows that by casting this discussion in analytical language, he runs the risk of creating the mistaken impression that the terms he uses refer to essentially distinct or reified entities, so he argues explicitly against this problem. All structures of consciousness are always present, he contends. None can be studied to the exclusion of the others without creating an untenable anthropology. This point is summarized well in a contemporary essay: "There is . . . no luminosity as object of a special study about the 'It'; neither is there psychology or phenomenology as a special study about the intentionality of the subject. Human consciousness always manifests both structures."[91] There can be no strictly luminous theology, for example, without the corresponding witness to truth in the calculative reasoning (intentionality) that tends to predominate in the natural sciences, nor can the natural sciences and modern systems of philosophy in their wake do without the luminous dimension of consciousness. "Even when, in the climate of secularist epistemology, we believe ourselves to be safe from transcendence and to have immanent objects at hand, the humble object still is never god-forsaken but radiates transcendence in its immanent *actus essendi*."[92] Special studies invalidate themselves when they engage in "magic dreams of a truth that can be reached by concentrating exclusively on either the intentionality of conceptualizing science or the luminosity of mythic and revelatory symbols" (*OH*, 5:18). In Schellingian terms, all philosophy worthy of the name will recognize the "negative" concepts of a priori rationality and the "positive" symbols of a posteriori revelation. No reduction of consciousness to one or the other structure is permissible in a philosophical study of order, because the attempt will reveal itself to be an arbitrary preference for one type of symbolism over another.

These points are clear enough. But how is it possible to know that these structures of consciousness are distinct? Are they, after all, differentiated by

91. Ibid., 49.
92. Voegelin, "What Is History?" (1963), in *CW,* 28:6.

the intentionality of consciousness? The answer to this question must be no, according to Voegelin, because "structures in consciousness" are not objects with an external touch of thingness, thus belonging to the express purview of intentionality. Rather, it would seem that a third structure must be named to account for why the consciousness of difference can arise at all. Voegelin calls this structure *reflective distance*. Consciousness is structured "not only by the paradox of intentionality and luminosity, but also by an awareness of the paradox, by a dimension to be characterized as a reflectively distancing remembrance." The specific type of remembrance that Voegelin has in mind has become archaic. It refers to the art of reminding somebody "of who he is or what he is."[93] This is the notion of memory that was symbolized "compactly"—or incompletely—by Plato's anamnesis and Hesiod's *mnemosyne* (*OH,* 5:40–41; cf. 70–86). It is also the notion of anamnetic reflection differentiated by Schelling in his attempts to remind self-divinizing idealists that reflection is always already distancing, hence incapable of bringing about the desired synthesis of human and divine through rational reflection. Though building on classical notions of "reflectively distancing remembrance," Voegelin's appeal to the reflective *distance* of analytical consciousness bears a greater resemblance to Schelling's anamnesis than to Plato's: "The symbolism of reflective 'distance' . . . has been formulated in opposition to, and as a corrective of, the symbolism of reflective 'identity' developed by the German idealistic philosophers in their great attempt at differentiating the anamnetic structure of consciousness more adequately in its personal, social, and historical aspects" (*OH,* 5:48). Voegelin criticizes only the identity systems of Fichte and Hegel, which mistakenly attempt to reduce consciousness to its intentionality, and argues at length that this reduction is simply impossible to sustain in an empirical philosophy of consciousness. He says that both men were well aware of the luminosity of consciousness but for some reason chose to indulge in acts of "imaginative oblivion" with respect to its manifestation in experience (cf. *OH,* 5:39, 41–47, 61–62, 69).

Imaginative oblivion may be intentional or accidental. But any failure to recognize all of the structures of consciousness that this pejorative term implies will result in a host of errors. Phenomenologists, in Voegelin's estimation, tend to overlook the luminous dimension of consciousness, thereby causing an objectivist bias in their works. But the opposite problem is also common. For example, Eugene Webb overlooks the structure of reflective distance in his account of Voegelin's philosophy of consciousness and, consequently,

93. Lawrence, *Beginning and the Beyond,* 106–7.

neglects to appreciate the analytical and scientific character of Voegelin's thought. This problem leads him further to express agreement with a summary complaint that Bernard Lonergan once made about Voegelin: that he "doesn't get any objective truth" out of his existential philosophy; "it is just he knowing himself."[94] Many will undoubtedly share this complaint; many more will likely attempt to celebrate the subjectivity it implies in all knowledge. Webb takes the nobler route, at least for the sake of argument. He grants, briefly responding for Voegelin, that "the presence of the universal" might possibly be found "in the depths of individual existence" as one "pursues symbolic self-knowledge in the life of the spirit."[95] But Webb produces no textual evidence from Voegelin to back up this claim. Instead, his readers are left to assume that the qualification comes more from his own attempt to be charitable than from anything substantial in Voegelin's philosophy of consciousness. As such, the claim is unconvincing and, even worse, may lead one not to question his basic tendency to interpret Voegelin as a subjective existentialist—perhaps even a lover of myth-as-literature—who challenges the objectivity desired by Lonergan.

The case in point: Webb asserts that "luminosity" brings to light "the irreducibly subjective element one must recognize" at the "core" of intentionality.[96] This claim has far-reaching consequences. Voegelin does not say that luminosity produces a "subjective" view of reality—Eric Voegelin's private "worldview" or the like. Instead, he tends to limit his use of the distinction between subjects and objects to what may be discussed by virtue of the intentional mode of consciousness, precisely because intentionality is what allows for this distinction to be made in the first place. Luminosity is not, therefore, the private subjectivity of the individual life over and against the objectivity of reflective knowledge gained by virtue of intentionality. "Luminosity" is an anamnetic symbol that attempts to remind the thinking subject—in this case Voegelin himself *as a representative of the universal order of human consciousness*—that it is always already immersed in the comprehending whole of reality before the reflective aspect of consciousness differentiates subjects of cognition and objects known. Webb loses sight of this humanly representative type of knowledge that we saw Voegelin appreciating in

94. Webb, *Philosophers of Consciousness,* 95. Lonergan's comment may be found in *Caring about Meaning: Patterns in the Life of Bernard Lonergan,* in *Thomas More Institute Papers,* ed. Pierrot Lambert, Charlotte Tansey, and Cathleen Going (Montreal: Thomas More Institute, 1982), 82:117.

95. Webb, *Philosophers of Consciousness,* 105–6.

96. Ibid., 101–2.

"Socrates-Plato," Aristotle, and Schelling, and that Voegelin himself continues to pursue in his own thinking. Voegelin did not read symbolic accounts of
the soul's order to collect interesting perspectives or worldviews. He read the
works of thoughtful humans like himself in order to understand what is
arguably true about himself qua human. Thus, when he philosophizes about
the order of consciousness, one finds "he knowing himself," to be sure, but
Voegelin would have understood this to mean "he knowing himself" as a
human being substantially rooted in the same order of reality as others. One
may find reasons to question some of his results, but they cannot be dismissed
(or celebrated) merely as subjective opining without falling into further acts
of imaginative oblivion.

Voegelin balances his own criticism of deformative accounts of consciousness by calling attention to two cases in which all of the structures of consciousness emerge without suffering the effects of a programmatic reduction.
These cases are the Platonic dialogues and the myth of the Beginning in
Genesis 1. "When Plato writes a dialogue, then it is partially a matter of forming concepts analytically [by virtue of intentionality], partially of forming a
myth with symbols [by virtue of luminosity]; and the whole [remembered
by the distancing quality of reflection] offers us neither entirely an analysis
nor a symbolic myth entirely." Plato *writes* in the mode of reflective distance, where "the entire problem of luminosity and intentionality is now
transposed into a language of reflection, in which this problem is spoken
about as if there were a reality independent of reflection." Yet, unlike Hegel,
Plato keeps his "reflective I in the distance," separating it from "the participatory self" of concrete experience.[97] Plato understands better than Hegel
that the reflective activity of writing is always other than the life it attempts
to interpret; he is the better realist.

The same is true, Voegelin contends, of the unknown author of Genesis:

> The story that opens with Genesis 1 must not be construed hypostatically
> as a narrative told either by a revelatory God or by an intelligently imagi-
> native human being. It is both, because it is neither the one nor the other;
> and it has this paradoxic character inasmuch as it is not a plain narration
> of things, but at the same time a symbolism in which the human begin-
> ning of order becomes translucent for its meaning as an act of participa-
> tion in the divine Beginning. (*OH*, 5:26)

97. Lawrence, *Beginning and the Beyond*, 50.

Even though the story in Genesis cannot be understood simply as the declaration of a "revelatory God," Voegelin does grant that symbols are created, myths told, and dialogues written throughout history in which the It-reality tells its own story (cf. *OH*, 5:30, 35). In other words, luminous symbols are self-interpretive. This point can be known, however, only in the relative "distance" of reflective analysis. It cannot be used to grasp an absolute truth as though it were gained without any help from the remembrance of things past.

This much is clear from the interplay of the *three* structures in consciousness. But what has become of Voegelin's earlier willingness to write about the substantial identity of all the "partners" in being? One detects a greater reticence from Voegelin to speak of identity at this point, as much of his last book is concerned with criticizing the identity philosophy of German idealists. However, there are good reasons to suppose that his Schellingian orientation has not changed. Within his critique of idealism, for example, Voegelin passes over Schelling's philosophy of absolute identity in silence. He equates *Identitätsphilosophie* (or identity philosophy) with *Ichphilosophie* (or Ego philosophy) (cf. *OH*, 5:51), and the identity philosophy he criticizes is specifically the *Ichphilosophie* of Fichte and Hegel. This point speaks against including Schelling within the scope of Voegelin's critique. It is clear from his comments in "Last Orientation" and *Anamnesis* that Voegelin understood Schelling's identity philosophy not to be based on the reflective consciousness of a self-possessed "I," transcendental or otherwise. The human "I" was found to be a derivative construction produced by acts of reflective consciousness.[98] This much has been established. However, the possibility that Voegelin may continue to presuppose the validity of Schelling's prereflective notion of identity is obscured in his last book—and this for two reasons. First, again within his critique of identity philosophy, Voegelin does not call attention to the fact that not all identity philosophies are equal. Schelling's, at least, was not based on the questionable presuppositions of an *Ichphilosophie*. Second, Voegelin mentions Schelling's name in a list of young Germans who were all so impressed by the political revolutions in Europe and America, at the beginning of the nineteenth century, that they began to look for a dis-

---

98. Voegelin does not discuss the question of "self-consciousness" in *In Search of Order*. This matter is clarified, however, in the preparatory text for this volume, where he clearly thinks of self-consciousness as a derivative construct brought about by the reflective distancing mode of consciousness (cf. Lawrence, *Beginning and the Beyond*, 50, where the self-conscious "I" is distinguished from the more immediate "participatory self").

tinctively German revolution in consciousness (cf. *OH,* 5:50–51). This reference may imply that Schelling remained a youthful enthusiast for a German revolution in consciousness, one that would outshine the political revolutions of other nations. But this implication is false. Schelling matured, and Voegelin knew it. In his later works *(Spätphilosophie),* Schelling develops a process theology *(Potenzenlehre)* that prevents him from indulging in the vain hope for any transformation of consciousness that could neglect the divine cause of such a change.[99] When he does express eschatological hopes, he does so in a way that resembles Voegelin's own claims that the history of experience and symbolization has an "eschatological structure"—a point to be discussed at length in Chapter 4 of this study. Thus, when the conventional view of Schelling is set aside—in light of Voegelin's more comprehensive knowledge of his later works—it becomes clear that his own critique of reflective-identity systems does not touch the identity philosophy of Schelling. Rather, it borrows far more than it rejects—if, indeed, it ever rejects anything.

Conclusion

Voegelin's ability to transcend deformative accounts of the order of consciousness came mainly from two sources: his reading of Schelling's identity philosophy and his own meditations on structures in consciousness. In his meditations, Voegelin was able to corroborate the distinctive conclusions gained in Schelling's identity philosophy: the primacy of contemplative reason, the substantial identity of the unconscious mind or depth of the soul with all of the realms of being, the secondary role of reflective consciousness in philosophy, and the derivative nature or "middle position" of the ego. Nothing in Voegelin's thought perpetuates the *proton pseudos:* his work cannot be understood properly if we ascribe to its author the presupposition that thought and being are substantially different. Voegelin's description of the world as a "charmed community" in which all the "partners in being" are substantially identical ("consubstantial") suggests that the Schellingian identity philosophy he supports in his 1943 letter to Schütz continues to guide his anthropological thinking in later works. The majority of textual evidence has been found clearly to support this claim. But it is further supported by the facts that Voegelin never retracted his published support of Schelling's

99. Cf. Schelling, *Die Weltalter,* in *Werke,* 1.8.344; and *Philosophie der Offenbarung,* in *Werke,* 2.4.332–34.

"ontology" in the German *Anamnesis,* and his latest critique of ego-based *Identitätsphilosophie* cannot be said to have the mature Schelling in mind as one of its targets. What is more, other identity philosophies are clearly discounted by a contention that Voegelin shares with Schelling, namely, that the order of consciousness is constituted by its "luminous" dimension. Voegelin's philosophy of consciousness remains consistently indebted to Schelling's identity philosophy. This conclusion, it seems, is best able to account for his continued use of terms suggesting the prereflective, luminous, substantial identity of the "It-reality" and human consciousness in his latest work. As with Schelling, Voegelin's identity philosophy of order is the basis for his accounts of how "self-interpretive" meaning emerges in history.

PART TWO

Order

Historiography

Conclusion

CHAPTER TWO

Schelling's Historiography

"Die Geschichte selbst ist nichts anderes als die
Entwicklung dieser Versöhnung des Endlichen,
die in Gott ewig, ohne Zeit ist."
—F. W. J. Schelling, *Werke*, 1.6.567

The remaining chapters in this study turn to focus on Schelling's and Voegelin's accounts of order in history. This change in focus reflects a similar change in the path of their philosophical developments. Once they learn through studies in the philosophy of consciousness that the human ego is a derivative rather than an absolute ground of knowledge, they turn to historical studies in order to understand how the experienced structures in consciousness have emerged, revealing themselves to be what they are. Schelling and Voegelin both develop progressive accounts of how the order of consciousness has "unfolded" (Schelling) or "differentiated" (Voegelin) in history. Yet both are also critical of the historical relativism they find in modern progressivist accounts of history's order. Modern progressivists typically contend that epochal changes in the order of consciousness have been caused by relatively "immanent," human, or pragmatic factors—such as economic conditions, natural or genetic responses to environmental conditions, or the arbitrary desires of political and military leaders, to name but a few. They also tend to claim that progress amounts to the gradual mastery of what was once thought to be beyond the control of human will and artifice. Once the primitive thinking of mythological and theological times has been replaced by a thoroughly scientific understanding of human life, to put the matter bluntly, it will be possible for humans increasingly to fashion the order of their *own* history. Schelling and Voegelin argue, on the contrary, that the historical relativism of modern progressivists is superficial or phenomenalistic. To wit, it is unscientific. Philosophical study of the historical records of human experience and symbolization will reveal that epochal changes in the order of consciousness have not come about from purely immanent or pragmatic causes. Rather, they have arisen from divine causes that, according to Schelling and Voegelin, will come to light only in nonpartisan, scientific studies worthy of the name. What follows is an account of how Schelling understands this self-revelation of the divine, the ground of all science, to emerge in the history of human consciousness. In contrast to phenomenal historicism or progressivism, Schelling argues that historical studies should be able to reconcile in the soul of the historian the perceived division between infinite and finite worlds, because "[h]istory itself is none other than the development of this *reconciliation* of the finite *[des Endlichen],* which is eternal in God."[1] Schelling introduces his philosophy of history with an account of the need for a "positive" philosophy of existence in order to complement insights gained by the "negative" philosophy of pure reason.

Positive and Negative Aspects of Philosophy

In Schellingian terms, the passage from studies of order in consciousness to studies of order in history marks a transition from negative to positive types of philosophy. Put simply, negative philosophy is so named because it negates particular ("subjective") differences of experience in order to understand the a priori nature of the mind common to all human beings as such. Positive philosophy is so named because it interprets the particular aspects of existence as positive manifestations of the essential order glimpsed by negative philosophy; it proceeds, therefore, by granting that negative philosophy, the "rationalist" philosophy of "pure reason," is able to reach an impartial (or "objective") view of reality. Negative philosophy negates plurality (appearances) in order to understand unity (essence); positive philosophy presupposes the truth of essence in order to understand particular things and events as true appearances of this unity.

It was Immanuel Kant, according to Schelling, who unwittingly prepared the way for a clear distinction between negative and positive types of philosophy, specifically in his critique of metaphysics:

---

1. Schelling, *System der gesamten Philosophie,* in *Werke,* 1.6.567.

Whilst [Kant] believed that he had brought *all* knowledge of the super-sensuous to an end for all time by his critique, he really only caused the negative and positive in philosophy to have to separate, but precisely because of this the positive, now emerging in its complete independence *[in seiner ganzen Selbständigkeit]*, was able to oppose itself, as positive, to the merely negative philosophy as the second side of philosophy as a whole. Kant began this process of separation and the resultant process of clarification of philosophy in the positive. Kant's critique contributed to this all the more because it was in no way *hostile* towards the positive. While he demolishes the whole edifice of that metaphysics, he always makes his view clear that in the last analysis one must *want* what it wanted, and that its content would in fact finally be the *true* metaphysics, if only it were possible.[2]

What positive philosophy "wants" is to understand how finite things can be true appearances of the infinite All. Discursive reasoning is of some use in the attainment of this understanding. In agreement with Kant and other rationalists, Schelling admits that "[t]he whole world lies, so to speak, in the nets of the understanding or of reason." This situation is especially true of the human mind, in which he thinks an a priori structure has been correctly discerned by negative rationalists. But Schelling perceives a fundamental limitation in this type of thinking, despite its other gains: "Everything can be in the logical Idea without anything being *explained* thereby. For example, everything in the sensuous world is grasped in number and measure, but this does not mean therefore that geometry or arithmetic explain the sensuous world." A different aspect of philosophy is needed to account for the meaning of perceived structures in reality, a positive philosophy that seeks to understand "*how* exactly [reason] got into those nets, since there is obviously something other and something *more* than mere reason in the world, indeed there is something which strives beyond these barriers."[3]

2. Schelling, *Zur Geschichte der neueren Philosophie*, in *Werke*, 1.10.74–75 (Bowie's translation modified, in Schelling, *On Modern Philosophy*, 95).

3. Ibid., 143–44 (I have modified Bowie's translation). On the continuing importance of Kant's critical philosophy, see the introductory lectures of *Philosophie der Offenbarung*, in *Werke*, 2.3.31–93, esp. 82–84. Schelling became one of the first philosophers to call explicitly for a "return to Kant." As with other neo-Kantians, he made his return in order to surpass Kant. For more detailed accounts of the development of neo-Kantian thought, see Henri Dussort, *L'École de Marbourg;* and Judy Deane Saltzman, *Paul Natorp's Philosophy of Religion within the Marburg Neo-Kantian Tradition*. These works are of limited value with respect to the historical significance of Schelling; they retain the conventional view of him as a Hegelian idealist. But they are quite helpful with respect to understanding Voegelin's early training in the Marburg school (cf. *AR*, 1–7, 20–23; and "Autobiographical Statement," 112).

Schelling describes the transition from negative to positive philosophy in a number of places in his later work. Perhaps the clearest of these is located in his lectures *On the History of Modern Philosophy,* where the need for positive philosophy is clarified against the antithetical background of Georg Hegel's identity philosophy and F. H. Jacobi's romantic theosophy.[4] Schelling acknowledges that Hegel and Jacobi also perceived the need for a positive philosophy of existence, but they both failed to establish a convincing one— and this for similar reasons. In the first edition of his *Science of Logic* (1812), Hegel attempts to begin a presuppositionless science by positing the immediate concept of "pure being," taking this term to indicate that from which all things have come to be. This hypothesis is supposed to ensure him the objectivity of his beginning—seemingly a necessary departure for one seeking to develop a reflective science that leaves absolutely nothing outside of itself, a total explanation of the world of nature and spirit. Schelling, at least, understands Hegel's concept of pure being as that which indicates the negation of everything subjective. His pure being is not, therefore, the being of all determinate beings, but is equivalent to the concept of nothing. This point raises an initial difficulty. Hegel's science of logic begins with a negative abstraction without first giving an account of that from which this abstraction has been abstracted. Schelling explains:

> Concepts as such do in fact exist nowhere but in consciousness, they *are,* therefore, taken objectively, *after* nature, not *before* it; Hegel took them from their natural position by putting them at the beginning of philosophy. There he places the most abstract concepts first . . . ; but abstractions cannot be there, be taken for realities, before that from which they are abstracted; becoming cannot be there before something becomes, existence not before something exists.[5]

4. The date of Schelling's *On the History of Modern Philosophy* is a matter of some dispute. It is listed as 1827 in the compilation of Schelling's works by his son. However, Horst Fuhrmans and Bowie himself find that it was probably delivered in either 1833–1834 or 1836–1837 (cf. the preface in Bowie's edition, ix). Based on internal evidence pertaining to Schelling's discussion of Hegelian texts published after 1827 and the fact that these themes are strongly represented in the *Philosophie der Offenbarung*—initially delivered from 1831 to 1832 (cf. *Werke,* 2.4.231)— I shall assume the correctness of Bowie's account, which places the lectures in the mid-1830s.

5. Schelling, *Zur Geschichte der neueren Philosophie,* in *Werke,* 1.10.131, 140–41 (I have followed Bowie's translation, *On Modern Philosophy,* 145). Schelling thinks that this problem was caused by Hegel's mistaken attempt to begin his *Logic* with the absolutely pure being that Schelling himself had reached only at the end of his *Naturphilosophie.* In his nature philosophy, Schelling abstracted the purity of being gradually from nature and spirit and then posited it, in Kantian fashion, as that which is produced by the relations of mere thought. See Schelling's chapter *"Naturphilosophie"* in Bowie's translation of ibid.

There is a second problem with the premise of the *Logic*. Hegel grants to his concept of pure being "an inner restlessness which drives it on to further determinations" in the rest of the system. Yet he does not explain how motion can be attributed to pure being, not to mention nothing. Schelling objects by denying inherent movement to the concept of pure being and by noting the impossibility of the task for one who seeks to explain reality with an ideal beginning.[6] Hegel allegedly overlooks these problems and attempts to progress nonetheless. Schelling finds the basis for his attempt "only in the fact that thought is already accustomed to a more concrete being, a being more full of content, and thus cannot be satisfied with that meager diet of pure being in which ... no determinate content is thought." In the final analysis, that which prevents Hegel from remaining in the emptiness of his pure being is "not a necessity which lies in the concept itself, but rather a necessity which lies in the philosopher and which is imposed upon him by his memory." Hegel tacitly remembers, Schelling argues, that "nature happens to exist," and movement is a part of how one perceives nature.[7] But this unobserved anamnesis, this tacit memory of reality, is not accounted for in Hegel's *Logic*.

Schelling does not criticize Hegel simply for the contradiction of having presuppositions in an allegedly presuppositionless science. If this were the only difficulty, then the presuppositions could simply be removed and the logic would be perfected. The actual problem lies deeper. Hegel has the right presupposition, but he attempts to use it in an incorrect way. He has the right presupposition, that is, for a purely negative philosophy of essence. But this is not the end that Hegel has in sight. At the conclusion of his *Logic,* he thinks that he has accounted for all of the determinate relations in nature and spirit and successfully withdrawn these into his own purified consciousness = absolute knowledge. But Schelling objects: "[H]ow should *true [wirklicher]* spirit be that which cannot move away from the end where it is posited, be that which only has the function of taking up all the preceding moments into itself as that which brings *everything* to an end, but not itself be the beginning and principle of something?" True spirit, according to Schelling, is not merely a final cause. It must be the principal cause of all determinate beings and their relations. Hegel has not attained the positive philosophy that, in Schelling's estimation, he intended to acquire. Instead, he has arrived only at a distorted view of the regulative idea of God in negative philosophy: "For the

6. Ibid., 153, 131, 153.
7. Ibid., 131, 153.

God insofar as He is only the *end,* as He can be in the purely rational philosophy, the God who has no future, who cannot initiate anything, who can
only be as final cause, and in no way a principle . . . , such a God is only
spirit according to . . . essence, thus in fact only substantial spirit, not spirit in
the sense in which piety or normal use of language understands the word."[8]

Schelling grants that Hegel was aware of these problems, which is why he
tried "a further, greater intensification" of the discussion, even "to get to the
idea of a free creation of the world," in the second edition of his *Logic* (1832).
Hegel attempts to reverse the original conclusion of his *Logic,* to transform
his final cause into a first cause, by revising only a few sentences of the book.
This reversal would make the beginning of Hegel's *Logic* roughly equivalent
to the absolute being at the outset of Schelling's identity philosophy. But no
critique of reflective consciousness is forthcoming from Hegel, and Schelling
is left to watch him founder on the futility of reflection attempting to jump
over its own shadow: "[I]f this reversal were possible in the way *Hegel* wishes,
and if he had not just spoken of this reversal but had tried it and really
established it, then he would already himself have put a second philosophy
by the side of his first, the converse of the first, which would have been
roughly what we want under the name of the positive philosophy."[9]

Jacobi (1743–1819) tried a different route to positive philosophy. In his
theosophical period, he appealed to an immediate inner feeling, an "inner
light," by which he claimed to find some grounds for transcending the concept of the impersonal God attained at the conclusion of rational systems of
philosophy. Jacobi's "inner light" took the form of a wish: the desire not to
allow God to be reduced to the status of a regulative idea. And this wish,
Schelling contends, was enough to set him on a potentially fruitful path: "We
cannot declare such an expression to be forbidden, for we ourselves allow a
great importance, at least for the initial determination of concepts in philosophy, to *wanting [Wollen].*" In other words, "[i]t is all very well to say, like
Jacobi: 'I demand a personal God, a highest being to whom a personal relationship is possible, an eternal thou *[ein ewiges Du]* which answers my I, not
a being which is merely in my thought. . . . I demand a transcendent being
which is also something for me outside of my thought.'" This God is also
the one whom Schelling wants to know. However, unlike Jacobi, Schelling
understands the presence of such desire to indicate only the potential beginning of knowledge—not the immediate, fully fledged science of God that

8. Ibid., 155 (Bowie's translation has been modified slightly).
9. Ibid., 157.

Jacobi mistook it to be. Ultimately, Jacobi's fast track to God fails even to provide the critical perspective it set out to yield:

> [T]his philosophy, instead of really attacking the knowledge [of pure reason] which displeases it, *completely* gives way to it, by withdrawing into not-knowing *[Nichtwissen],* with the assurance that only in not-knowing does salvation lie. From this it follows, then, that it considers that merely substantial knowledge which excludes the *actus,* which dominates in rationalism, itself to be the only possible real *[echt]* and true knowledge, not by opposing another *knowledge* to it, but by opposing mere not-knowing to it.[10]

Jacobi was aware of this problem. He tried later to overcome it, Schelling grants, when he attempted to argue in support of the complete rationality of his feeling. This particular attempt to solve the problem was, however, a desperate move: "When Jacobi later substituted reason for feeling in order to make his peace with rationalism, his philosophy also lost the truth which it previously had. Feeling expresses a personal relationship. But now an immediate relationship to the *personal* God was to be attributed to impersonal reason, which is completely unthinkable." Jacobi clearly perceived that systems of negative philosophy do not explain anything in the real world, no more than "geometry really explains anything." Yet he did not see his way clear to a truly positive philosophy. That is to say, he did not develop a philosophy of history but left his thinking to remain ahistorical. Consequently, Schelling complains that Jacobi's remarks about "Christ and Christianity in his later writings are completely in agreement with the views of the most rabid theological rationalism." By relying on feeling, even disguised as "reason," and neglecting to consider the historical determinations of his experiences, Jacobi lost even a proper understanding of the negative ground with which he almost turned to positive philosophy and deprived himself of the means to reach this higher science:

> Every philosophy which does not keep its basis *in* the negative, and which wishes to reach the positive, the divine in an immediate manner, *without* the negative, finally dies of unavoidable spiritual exhaustion. The true character of the Jacobian philosophy is such a scientific haste. For even that aspect of God and divine things he reaches in *his* way reduces itself to so little, is so meager and poor in relation to the fullness and richness of really religious insight *[Erkenntnis],* that one would have to mourn the lot of the human spirit if it were not able to gain greater insight.[11]

10. Ibid., 166, 167.
11. Ibid., 167, 175, 176, 170, 176.

A common problem has come to light in Hegel and Jacobi's approaches to positive philosophy. Both tended to assume that reason's highest activity is found in its ability to rise above historical contingency, that reasoning is essentially an ahistorical activity. But this assumption is precisely the point at issue. And their failures to establish a positive philosophy of existence, working from this assumption, are instructive for Schelling. They reveal to him the weaknesses that must be avoided in his own attempts to articulate a compelling positive philosophy. First, Schelling must not begin by positing a concept of pure being with which his own consciousness could be shown to be identical at the *end* of a reflective system—Hegel's weakness. Second, he must not attempt to evade the problems of the beginning with appeals to mystical illuminations alone—Jacobi's theosophical weakness. Schelling's *Prius* must be an essentially historical concept that accounts for the tensional paradoxes in all attempts to account for the absolute beginning of anything. The beginning of positive philosophy must be none other than the conceivable Beginning of the existing world.

The Positive *Prius* in Schelling's Existential Philosophy

In order to understand Schelling's attempt to transcend what turned out to be only the negative philosophy of Hegel and Jacobi, it will be helpful to consider how the later Schelling tried to surpass that which resembled negative philosophy in his earlier work, his 1804 identity philosophy. Schelling had attempted, before Hegel, to build a system of philosophy that began with the prereflective identity of the All. This beginning allowed him intelligibly to hypothesize the substance of the world as pure being. However, it also came with an inherent weakness. It effectively reduced particular beings only to the status of questionable appearances of the All. Schelling perceived this to be a limitation. Even though his identity philosophy had pure being at the beginning, unlike its concluding position in negative philosophy, it still encountered the same difficulty as the latter. Thus, Schelling's ability to understand existence was not significantly improved when he assumed that the conceptual result of negative philosophy is actually the principle of the world. This move simply shifted the problem, it would seem, from reflective to prereflective types of conceptual deduction without any significant difference in the results. The real world remained a questionable illusion of a static concept even in Schelling's version of the identity philosophy. What is more, his thinking remained largely ahistorical. Its appeal to the identity of thought and being was, with some qualifications, consistent with Eleatic thought in ancient Greece. Schelling himself was able to grant many of these points. But he also came to realize that his early attempt to understand the substantial identity of all things was not simply another type of a priori rationalism. It was the beginning of his account of how a philosopher's knowledge of *a priori* principles is derived from experience. The hypothetical "All" of the identity philosophy was the undifferentiated beginning of what would later become the hypothetically differentiated *Prius* of his positive philosophy of existence.

Plato's writings played a significant role in this transition. Even in the 1804 identity philosophy, Schelling argues, against Kant, that Plato had properly conceived of "ideas" as inherently divine, rather than innately human.[12] It is the Platonic account of ideas that becomes the catalyst for Schelling's development of the *Potenzenlehre,* the existential *Prius* of his positive philosophy.[13] Put differently, the human mind is not the a priori ground in positive philosophy; there are no "innate ideas" to which this type of philosophy can appeal. Rather, it has an existential ground: the manifold of causes, the Platonic "ideas" or Schellingian "potencies," which are said to be united by their substantial divinity. Unlike Plato, however, Schelling claims that the potency of the divine can come to be known best in the light of history. His turn to historical studies amounts to the broadest possible turn toward a posteriori reasoning. This is a necessary step in a philosophy of existence; for "that which *is* can only be understood *a posteriori;* what is understood *a priori* is only what *cannot* be otherwise. Everything *[Es]* does not hang together as smoothly and simply as one thinks, but rather in an emphatically wonderful and, if you like, inconsistent way."[14]

What may be true of the inconsistency of everything *(Es)* is certainly true of Schelling's thought therein. His articulation of the positive philosophy is truly a "wonderful" and sometimes frustrating odyssey. What is potentially

---

12. Cf. *supra,* 62.

13. Cf. Schelling, *Die Weltalter,* in *Werke,* 1.8.289–90.

14. Schelling, *Zur Geschichte der neueren Philosophie,* in *Werke,* 1.10.171–72 (I have modified Bowie's translation). That which *"cannot* be otherwise" is the past. This forms the ground of "God's nature" and human understanding therein. To be sure, the past can be understood otherwise, but it cannot be otherwise than what it was (cf. *Die Weltalter,* in *Werke,* 1.8.259). In the quoted passage, Schelling is relatively unconcerned with logical inconsistencies, because he thinks that the frustration of formal logic, or negative reason *(Vernunft),* is the only way to a truly positive development of the understanding *(Verstand)* (cf. *Werke,* 1.10.174).

confusing about its development is that it appears to have two beginnings, with only the second being the substantial Beginning it wants to establish: First, it "begins" with an empirically dialectical presentation of the *Potenzen-lehre*, which includes an account of that which (is) before being; second, it begins with the assumption that the potencies of the *Potenzenlehre* form the divine unity of the actual world. The first "beginning" starts by reasoning from individual experiences to an account of the absolutely potent beginning of all things in the divine. Schelling knows that this may appear to result in no more than the establishment of an a priori structure of the human mind, the proper result of negative philosophy. But this discussion takes one only to the end of the first "beginning." It must and does progress, in what amounts to a second beginning, to a more broadly historical account of divine priority. In other words, Schelling turns to discuss how the potentiality of the divine has come to be relatively actualized, and likewise known, in the history of mythology and revelation.

This entire process can be described in a different way. The two movements or "beginnings" resemble (in Plato's *Republic*) Socrates' ascent from the "cave" to the "upper region," and his descent back to the city of Athens, where the memory of the transcendent measure of all things is retained as that which causes the order of appearances. Schelling describes the interplay between negative and positive aspects of philosophy in a similar way: "Negative philosophy is only a *philosophia ascendens* (ascending from below), where we can see immediately that it will have only logical significance; and positive philosophy is *philosophia descendens* (descending from above to below). It is therefore only the *ensemble* which achieves the complete circle of philosophy."[15] The "ascents" of Socrates and Schelling may have certain similarities, but that to which they "descend" is quite different, at least in terms of its scope. Socrates descends to the city of Athens in its historical particularity. Schelling, in Christian perspective, descends to the *civitas terrena* in general and must attempt to account for apparent changes in an eternal God's self-revelations throughout the entire history of the world. Positive philosophy does not "descend" merely to a world of relatively true and false appearances. It descends to what cannot be otherwise, to the facticity of chronologically determined events in the historical past. This divine or "theo-thetic" history becomes its true ground.

Schelling insists that this twofold approach is what makes up the unity of

15. Ibid., 1.10.151 n. 1.

philosophy per se. The negative character of the "ascent" is not what grounds the subsequent "descent" of positive philosophy. Rather, the reverse is said to be true: "[N]egative philosophy is founded," properly speaking, "only with [the historical consciousness gained by] positive philosophy; because it is only thanks to the latter that the former becomes certain of its position and that it is placed in a state of resting in itself, equal to itself, and in its natural limits."[16] In other words, the negative "ascent" is properly made only with the consciousness that one's efforts have been, to some degree, prepared by the insights of others in the history of philosophy. This situation, Schelling maintains, will hold true for any attempt to establish a purely negative philosophy of reason. All attempts to purify reason in a transcendental perspective can be valid only if they consciously acknowledge that *purity, transcendence,* and *reason* are terms that have been differentiated historically and continue to form one's "own" consciousness. Schelling attempts to summarize the complexity of this matter when he says that in positive philosophy "the world is in the process of becoming educed or conceptualized *a priori*."[17] Opaque statements such as this have led even serious interpreters to raise complaints about Schelling's general approach: "Unclear, perhaps even in his own mind, as to whether his aim is the empirical verification of *a posteriori* propositions or the graphic exemplification of *a priori* propositions, [Schelling] tries to have it both ways. As a result, he often seems to undercut himself in either endeavor."[18] Edward Beach's apparent frustration is understandable. But Schelling may have a substantial point to make, nonetheless: beyond propositional reasoning, perhaps the order of reality itself does call for an existential logic that allows one to "have it both ways," because that is how the "It-reality" is experienced by humans. If so, then Schelling's admittedly inconsistent articulation of the *Prius* of positive philosophy may hang together in a "wonderful" way.[19]

---

16. Ibid., 1.10.155.

17. In Schelling's words, *"die Folge (die Welt)* a priori *hergeleitet oder begriffen wird"* (*Philosophie der Offenbarung,* in *Werke,* 2.3.130 n. 1).

18. Beach, *Potencies of God(s),* 202.

19. My account of this matter will draw upon a variety of texts from Schelling's *Spätphilosophie,* as I have defined it. This procedure is necessary, I think, in order to achieve optimum clarity with respect to a potentially obscure subject matter. At times, Schelling's attempt to articulate a certain point is clearer in a relatively early text than it is in his later attempts to revisit the same point—and vice versa. At all times, my own account will attempt to remain faithful to Schelling's mature understanding of the existential *Prius* of positive philosophy. Thus, my quotations from earlier texts always have his latest understanding in mind.

Actualization of the Potencies in Individual Experience

Matter (A^1, B)

The positive philosophy begins, in its dialectical mode, with an account of relatively pure "nonbeing," symbolized as the pure potency –A or A^1. As a "potency," it has the potential either to remain relatively pure or to become relatively impure, impotent, or actualized. When this potency becomes relatively actual, it amounts to an initial act of "blind" self-enclosure or "contraction" on the part of something divine, symbolized as the transition from A^1 to B.[20] This primordial contraction, this self-making enclosure of the divine ground, is the beginning of the beginning of positive philosophy. The fact that Schelling begins with a restless negation initially appears to involve him in the same problems he criticized at the beginning of Hegel's *Logic*. But Schelling would insist that this is not the case. Hegel's mistake was to think that his restless negation (pure being = nothing) was a bona fide concept of pure reason. Schelling maintained that it was not. This notion is, in fact, properly derived only from experience. Hegel only tacitly remembered the experience of existence in the formulation of his initiating concept, insisting all the while that no empirical presuppositions entered into his logic. Schelling actively remembers existence and says: "Contraction *[Contraktion]*... marks the beginning of all reality. For this reason, it is the contracting rather than the expanding nature that possesses a primordial and grounding force. Thus the beginning of creation amounts indeed to a *descent* of God [A^o]; He properly descends into the Real [A^1], contracts Himself entirely into the Real [B]."[21] This contraction does not mark the creation of visible matter. It is only the condition of the possibility for beings to exist out of that which is relatively nonbeing. In other words, the primordial contraction "implies a beginning *of* time, though not a beginning *in* time. God himself is not, therefore, being placed in time." But this contraction still means that the manifest world will ultimately be the result of God's initially unconscious self-materialization—and a blind, egotistical principle lies at the base of

20. On the transition from A^1 to B, see Schelling, *Stuttgarter Privatvorlesungen*, in *Werke*, 1.7.429 (here the transition is symbolized as A to B); *Philosophie der Mythologie*, in *Werke*, 2.2.86–87; B is also described at 2.1.391, 1.10.130, and 1.8.215. Schelling equates B with the "Platonic" unlimited, *to apeiron* (2.2.113; see also *Philosophie der Offenbarung*, in *Werke*, 2.3.226).

21. Schelling, *Stuttgarter Privatvorlesungen*, in *Werke*, 1.7.429 (Pfau's translation has been modified slightly, and I have added the bracketed symbols for the emerging potencies).

everything that lives, including the life that is called God. Schelling knows that this notion will be repulsive "to the dogmatic view, which is considered orthodox." The dogmatists Schelling has in mind are negative philosophers who speak of God only as an "entirely self-centered essence, thereby separating Him from all creation." By contrast, Schelling argues that that which is truly "self-centered" in God is relative nonbeing, rather than "essence." The beginning of being, in other words, is beyond being. Schelling defends his prototheology against what has come to be known as ontotheology. He insists that this primordial act "does not imply anything unworthy of God but, in fact, it is this descent that marks the greatest act for God. . . . By contrast, a metaphorically elevated God will benefit neither our minds nor our hearts."[22]

By starting with the primordial contraction of God, Schelling tries to account for revelation in the a posteriori logic of existence. This beginning is based on the existential premise that anything revealed was previously concealed, anything disclosed previously enclosed. Hence, Schelling contends that "that which negates all revelation must be made the basis of revelation."[23] The relative transition from A^1 to B is occasioned by the realization that the existential logic of the beginning requires a certain activity, the relative actualization (B) of the relatively pure potential for unconscious self-hood (A^1).[24]

Consciousness (A^2) and Self-conscious Spirit (A^3)

The actualization of B is relative because it retains its potentiality vis-à-vis the other potencies. As soon as B starts to become actual, as the material

22. Ibid., 430 (Pfau's trans.), 438, 429.

23. Schelling, *Die Weltalter,* in *Werke,* 1.8.223; see also 317–18 (Bolman trans.). This type of thinking is normally associated with Heidegger's later work, specifically the tensions he describes between the concealment-unconcealment, or forgetfulness *(lethe)* and remembrance *(aletheia),* of being. See Martin Heidegger, *Zur Sache des Denkens* (Tübingen: Max Niemeyer Verlag, 1969); *On Time and Being,* 1–24, 55–73. For a brief account of how Heidegger read and transformed Schelling, see Wayne J. Froman, "Schelling's *Treatise on the Essence of Human Freedom* and Heidegger's Thought." Froman interprets the text by Schelling that was most important to Heidegger.

24. That which ultimately causes the transition from A^1 to B, it would seem, is the divine freedom (A^0) beyond the tensions that are coming to light as the potential actualization of matter (B) and spirit (A^2) in the unified life of intelligible nature (A^3). However, Schelling also accords a significant measure of "freedom" and "decision" to B in its purely blind subjectivity. Cf. Schelling, *Die Weltalter,* in *Werke,* 1.8.234 (freedom), 220 and 225 (decision). The different degrees of freedom between A^0 and B are perhaps best described as follows. Because the "*authentic* freedom" of B "does not consist in the power *to be*. . . but in the power not to be" (*Werke,* 2.3.209), then the authentic freedom of A^0 should consist in the greater freedom to be or not to be (cf. *Philosophie der Offenbarung,* in *Werke,* 2.4.353).

antithesis of spirit, its spiritual thesis (A^2) and their synthesis (A^3) are instantaneously implied.[25] The simultaneity of the potencies is also symbolized as $A^1 = B^3$. Schelling explains:

> Where B is yet found in the highest power, A appears necessarily in the lowest power. This ($A^1 = B^3$) is the expression of gravity. In the dynamic process, where the previously mute substance already gives off signs of life, this substance itself is already diminished *as* B, that is, as Nonbeing, by one power. Hence it is $= B^2$, whereas being has been increased by one power, so that the whole formula reads $A^2 = B^2$. Here nonbeing and being are still in a state of equilibrium; hence the dynamic period of nature is that of a struggle, which does not yet result in any solid product.[26]

With these formulations Schelling attempts to account for how differences can appear to be real or, in more technical language, nonbeing can be said to be. He claims that nonbeing (B) is intelligible only in relation to the other potencies, which are properly coming to be in their own rights. It does not become fully actualized in human experience. Put differently, something in "God's nature" always remains hidden, thus accounting for the experience and historical symbolization of the *deus absconditus*. This "negating power [in God's nature] does not cease." Even after an extremely long and complex chain of historical developments leading to experiences of divine revelation, "God cannot become a revealed God from being a hidden one, in such a way that he would cease to be a hidden one." Something divine always remains obscure in God's immanent nature (B). The same holds true for God's transcendent essence (A^0). Even "[t]hat highest spirituality and ineffability of God cannot be changed into intelligibility and comprehensibility, as water was changed into wine at the Galilean wedding."[27] These points are important, at least for scholarly reasons, for they speak against Voegelin's claim

25. Cf. Schelling, *Die Weltalter*, in *Werke*, 1.8.261. The dialectic of antithesis, thesis, synthesis is also suggested when Schelling makes the following symbolic equations: $-A = B$, $+A = A^2$, $\pm A = A^3$ (cf. *Philosophie der Mythologie*, in *Werke*, 2.1.336).

26. Schelling, *Stuttgarter Privatvorlesungen*, in *Werke*, 1.7.451–52 (Pfau's translation). This is a rare passage. Normally, Schelling refers to the process of nature only with the symbols $A^1 = B$, A^2, A^3. That is, when A^2 becomes relatively actual, he normally does not use the symbol B^2 to denote this actuality. Why is this? It would appear that Schelling wants to emphasize the primordially grounding power of B in nature, that matter does not disappear but continues to prevail even after the actualization of the relatively spiritual potencies (A^2 and A^3).

27. Schelling, *Die Weltalter*, in *Werke*, 1.8.245, 256.

that Schelling was a Gnostic intellectual.[28] On the contrary, Schelling argues that the transcendence of the mind into material nature *and* the freedom of its spirit beyond nature are equally obscure.

The potencies of the divine are ostensibly discovered in human experience. They are not offered as pieces of empty speculation. Thus far, Schelling has described only what is experienced when one searches for the beginning of existence. In this search, he contends, the conscious mind (A^2) always encounters its own beginning in obscurity ($A^1 \rightarrow B$).[29] It seems as though something actively resists intellectual penetration. For example, when one begins to reflect on one's own past, let alone its beginning, one discovers that the vast majority of it cannot be remembered. One knows that, in a sense, all of the past was and is still "there." But the majority of experiences hide themselves, so to speak, releasing only fragmentary memories into the relative future that has become one's present. Stated proto-ontologically, this "hiding" is the work of B, the divine self-enclosure, the coming-to-be before being. This beginning is experienced by humans as though it were nothing, as a contrary type of negation *(mē einai)*. But Schelling is careful to stress that the beginning must not be nothing at all, the contradictory type of negation *(ouk einai)*, and he rejects the doctrine of a *creatio ex nihilo* as a misconstrual of these types of negation.[30] He claims: "All finite beings have been created out of [relative] nonbeing yet not out of *nothing*."[31] Nonbeing appears to us "*as* nothing," because it is actually becoming something.[32] The other potencies must experience matter (B) in the same way, according to Schelling, because "matter is nothing but the unconscious aspect of God. . . . [I]n seeking to exclude it from Himself [$A^1 \rightarrow B$], on the one hand, He also strives to integrate it with Himself, on the other hand; He seeks to raise it to form, to transfigure it—although subordinate—into His superior essence and to evoke consciousness *from* this unconscious matter."[33] It is from the divine material ground (B), this unconsciously egotistical, self-loving beginning, that the divine-as-erotic-spirit (A^2) can stand apart from its own ground. Because

28. Cf. *supra*, 28–29.

29. Cf. Schelling, *Die Weltalter*, in *Werke*, 1.8.262.

30. On the two types of negation, see *Philosophie der Mythologie*, in *Werke*, 2.1.288–89, 2.2.32–33.

31. Schelling, *Stuttgarter Privatvorlesungen*, in *Werke*, 1.7.436 (Pfau's trans.); see also *Die Weltalter*, in *Werke*, 1.8.221–22.

32. Cf. Schelling, *Zur Geschichte der neueren Philosophie*, in *Werke*, 1.10.99, 100, 134.

33. Schelling, *Stuttgarter Privatvorlesungen*, in *Werke*, 1.7.435 (Pfau's translation).

the divine is also other-loving (A^2), it can exist from its own material ground
(B) and ultimately become conscious of itself as the intelligible being of existence (A^3).[34]

A complex series of relations results. When B is relatively actual, then A^2
and A^3 are relatively *in potentia;* they are potent for their actuality. When A^2
is relatively actual, the same potential relativity holds for B and A^3. It is likewise the case with the relative actuality of A^3 and the relative potentiality of
B and A^2. This series of relations is fundamentally made up of the systolic tension between B (systole) and A^2 (diastole). But the latter has a limit (= A^3)
to which it can expand. This third term is needed, Schelling argues, in order
to account for nature as a process, for if spirit (A^2) could immediately transform matter (B) into itself, there would be no creative tension between matter and spirit, no generative development or intelligent life in nature (A^3).[35] In
the human soul, the unconscious (B) could be transformed immediately and
completely into consciousness (A^2), if there were no reflective distance—that
is, self-consciousness (A^3)—separating them.

Self-consciousness is the "seed," the product, of the creative tension between conscious and unconscious dimensions of the soul. Schelling describes
this process with an image from visible nature: "A tree, for example, develops
continually from the root [B] to the fruit [A^3], and when it has arrived at the
summit it again throws everything off, reverts to the state of barrenness [A^1],
and again makes itself into a root [$A^1 \rightarrow$ B], only to rise anew. The whole
activity of the plant goes toward the production of seed, only to start afresh
and by a new developmental process produce more seeds, and then begin
over again." As with visible nature, so too with the intelligible process of the
entire universe:

> That original, necessary, and lasting life thus indeed ascends from the low-
> est [A^1] to the highest [A^3], but, having arrived at the latter, it immediately
> returns to the beginning in order to rise from this again. And only here do
> we attain the complete concept of that primal nature (after which all indi-
> vidual concepts [B, A^2, A^3], that had to be posited only in order to attain
> this complete concept, must again be removed)—namely, that primal
> nature is a life eternally revolving in itself, a kind of circle, since the lowest

34. For summary accounts of the relations between these natural potencies, see Schelling,
Stuttgarter Privatvorlesungen, in *Werke,* 1.7.430, 451; *Die Weltalter,* in *Werke,* 1.8.252, 261–62;
and *Philosophie der Mythologie,* in *Werke,* 2.1.336 (where $-A$ = B, $+A$ = A^2, and $\pm A$ = A^3),
391, 2.2.377, 394–99.
  35. Cf. Schelling, *Die Weltalter,* in *Werke,* 1.8.228–29.

always flows into the highest, and the highest again into the lowest.... Of course the distinction of higher and lower again is annulled in this continual circular movement.... Even the concept of beginning and end is again annulled in this rotation.[36]

Once matter and spirit bear fruit, A^3 returns to A^1, and the whole process starts all over again, thus completing the rotary motion of nature.[37] In human experience, the seed of self-consciousness eventually falls into its unconscious ground, specifically when it searches for its origin. To extend the metaphor, when self-consciousness returns to its origin, it decomposes and fertilizes the unconscious. This dissolution of the self is said to create "angst" in the ego ($A^1 \rightarrow B$) and a fervent desire for consciousness (A^2), which ultimately yields higher self-consciousness (A^3) as the human "tree" grows in an individual life.[38] Such growth has a limit, which is reached in the consciousness of this cyclical process itself.

Schelling does not take the self-consciousness attained at the end of his reflections and project it back into the beginning of his discussion in order to found a system with self-consciousness as its ground. This step was, in Schelling's estimation, the essential mistake of Fichte and Hegel. It amounted to a nonempirical flight from the reality of experience in their works. In order to avoid this problem, Schelling remembers the order of experience that brought him to this relative conclusion and realizes that his philosophy of history must begin with the most primordial beginning of all that exists: God's unconsciously egotistical nature, symbolized by the contraction ($A^1 \rightarrow B$), the antithesis of consciousness and self-conscious spirit.

Actualization of the Potencies in World History

Thus far, the only temporal aspect of the *Potenzenlehre* discussed has been that which could be drawn from the "history" of one's individual experiences. Any mature human from known historical periods could understand the analysis of experience involved in the preceding discussion. Indeed, as far as Schelling understood the matter, the level of consciousness developed hitherto is only "pagan" or mythological. It lacks a proper sense of freedom. The

36. Ibid., 231, 229 (Bolman translation).

37. For discussion of this "rotary motion," see ibid., 220, 231, 246; and *Philosophie der Mythologie*, in *Werke*, 2.1.324.

38. Schelling, *Die Weltalter*, in *Werke*, 1.8.336.

potencies are equivalent to (some of the) pagan gods (with the disputable exception of A°), and the cyclical aspect of nature appears to be almost wholly deterministic. But Schelling argues that human consciousness does not develop strictly along natural lines. At discernable points in history, the notion of God's transcendental freedom from nature is revealed to human beings and becomes a constitutive factor in the order of their souls. The extent to which this discovery determines the present order of consciousness comes to light, Schelling maintains, only when the (negative) philosophy of personal experience is expanded to include the entire history of the human race. Thus, in his positive philosophy of history, Schelling seeks to understand how consciousness has risen from its naturally divine ground to a more comprehensive understanding of reality as the interplay of divine necessity *and* freedom. To accomplish his aims, he must attempt to relive no less than the entire past of nature and history in the relative present of his "own" consciousness.

What follows is a summary account of how Schelling understands the divine potencies of nature to manifest themselves in the history of mythology (= nature) and revelation (= the emerging freedom of nature in history). This outline is intended only to fulfill the limited aims of this chapter. It is sufficient to reveal the importance of key themes in Schelling's positive philosophy for comparison with Voegelin's historiography. It is by no means an exhaustive account of his philosophy of historical existence. Schelling developed his positive philosophy over the course of four decades. He produced several volumes of work, published only posthumously, in which its details are elaborated. Even so, despite its extensive size, it will be possible to summarize this work without oversimplification by following Schelling's own two-lecture summary of his entire *Philosophy of Mythology*, which he produces in his *Philosophy of Revelation* (lectures 18 and 21). This summary will guide us through the positive philosophy, except where it does not address specific points of interest to Voegelin in the *Philosophy of Mythology*.

From the perspective of his own historical situation, Schelling understands the order of history to progress from relative monotheism to the absolute monotheism by which history itself will eventually be transcended.[39] This

---

39. Schelling finds this historical drive toward monotheism to be implied already in "the oldest document" of the world, namely, Genesis, where a tenuous unity of God(s), the "Elohim," is found to be in historical tension with the emerging unity of the God "Jehovah." See *Philosophie der Mythologie*, in *Werke*, 2.1.145-ff., 161ff., 174, 2.2.47f.; *Philosophie der Offenbarung*, in *Werke*, 2.3.366–67 n. 1, 2.4.121–23; on the greatest antiquity of Genesis, see also *Die Weltalter*, in *Werke*, 1.8.331.

pattern becomes highly differentiated throughout the *Philosophy of Mythology* and *Philosophy of Revelation.* Its pre- to posthistorical progression develops along three distinguishable types of religion, none of which is a static unity unto itself: mythological religion, revealed religion, and philosophical religion.[40]

Primordial Consciousness *(Urbewußtseyn)* and the Fall

Schelling's historiography begins by hypothesizing the absolute unity of God, which he calls the first notion that presents itself to the spirit.[41] This beginning, a legacy from the identity philosophy, transfers the absolute from the beginning of consciousness to the beginning of all historical differentiation. That which causes the beginning of all differentiations, both in divine nature and in human consciousness, is a cosmic Fall. Before this event, a primordially unified humanity is said to have existed in completely unconscious identity with divine nature, lacking knowledge both of itself and of the divine. In other words, humanity lacked self-consciousness. According to the relevant mythology in Genesis, Adam and Eve did not know that they were "naked" before the Fall.

Schelling's account of the Fall is ambiguous. On the one hand, he says that primordial humanity has its proper guilt *(eigene Schuld)* in the matter. Our ancestors were chased out of Paradise when they chose to renounce their former equality with all of the potencies in order to become like only one of them: the relatively material potential for self-willing (A^1).[42] On the other hand, Schelling knows that by assuming an unconscious identity between primordial humanity and divinity, the former cannot be blamed for "falling." Our ancestors had no knowledge of differences between which they could have chosen freely. They were created, without knowledge *(Wissen)* of their condition, at the center of the deity *(im Zentrum der Gottheit)*. Thus, in order to account for the "*real* divorce" between humanity and its "primordial standpoint," an assumption without which the mythological stage of history becomes unintelligible as an attempt to regain a lost unity, Schelling argues that original sin *(Sündenfall)* must have come about by means of a process that transcended human consciousness and will. He claims:

---

40. On the three types of religion, see Schelling, *Philosophie der Mythologie,* in *Werke,* 2.1.243–52.

41. Schelling, *Philosophie der Mythologie,* in *Werke,* 2.2.24.

42. Cf. ibid., 2.1.142.

> The theogonic process which gives birth to mythology is a *subjective* process insofar as it unfolds itself in *consciousness* and manifests itself by the formation of representations *[Vorstellungen]*. But the causes *[Ursachen]* and, consequently, the objects of these representations are the *real [wirklich]* theogonic powers *[Mächte] themselves,* through which primordial consciousness is [found to be essentially] God-positing *[das Bewußtseyn ursprünglich das Gott = setzende ist]*. The content of the process is not merely *represented* potencies, but the *potencies themselves [die Potenzen selbst]*.

The "subjective" process occurs in the subject of human consciousness in general. This means that the process is not merely subjective in the individual sense; it is "objectively religious," as it pertains to the whole of humanity.[43] Thus, in its second aspect, Schelling does not say that the primordial Fall is caused by a self-consciously human will. The Fall begins to unfold as a process of naturally differentiating potencies. This beginning of the "theogonic process" of history causes humans to perceive a fundamental difference between themselves and the divine, and to represent the latter as something exclusively "outside" of themselves. This representation of the divine is erroneous, according to Schelling, but blame for the error cannot be laid simply upon humans. The Fall is the result not of human freedom, but of a natural process in which human consciousness was completely entwined. It would seem that later humans, with a greater consciousness of historical freedom, could blame God for the Fall after all.

Schelling would not accept this conclusion without qualification. He would likely attempt to solve the problems it creates for piety by saying that God foreknew all of this and caused the Fall as a means to a higher end.[44] Beyond human consciousness, God begins the transformation from A^1 to B. This brings about the initial awareness in human consciousness of the difference between humanity and divinity, self and world, the inner and the outer realms of experience. In mythological terms, Adam and Eve become relatively self-conscious, realizing that they are "naked," as the divine potential for selfhood starts to become actualized. This sense of division yields the condition of the possibility for divine revelation. Without a sense of the difference between humanity and divinity, Schelling argues, the latter could never reveal itself to the former.[45] This difference can come about only by means of

---

43. Ibid., 2.1.205–8; see also *Philosophie der Offenbarung*, in *Werke*, 2.3.378–80.

44. Cf. Schelling, *Philosophie der Offenbarung*, in *Werke*, 2.4.9–10.

45. Schelling, *Philosophie der Mythologie*, in *Werke*, 2.1.179, 2.2.119 ff.; see also *Philosophie der Offenbarung*, in *Werke*, 2.3.188.

God's self-differentiation.[46] It is not primarily a matter of human action, self-consciously understood. Thus, in historical retrospect, the Fall appears to be a felicitous fault, that which ultimately brings humanity from the blind necessity of its divine nature into the consciousness of the "true God" as its essential freedom. To blame or blaspheme either God or humanity for the Fall amounts to an anachronistic error. It tacitly uses the consciousness of freedom, attained only after a long period of historical development, and brings this against either the giver or the recipients of this gift.[47]

The Epoch of Matter (B): Relative Monotheism and Mythological Religion

Beyond laying blame, Schelling contends that the Fall sets in motion the transition from A^1 to B. This transition occurs slowly. At first, it yields the first of the three types of religion, specifically the beginning of "mythological religion," or "relative monotheism."[48] History, properly speaking, has yet to begin. Schelling speculates about the origin of historical consciousness in an absolutely prehistorical *(vorgeschichtliche)* time.[49] The absolute prehistory of consciousness yields the religion of God's blind nature, a period marked by the relative actualization of the first potency: the systole, which immediately begins to imply the relative diastole of the second, and their unity in the third. Yet the plurality of potencies must have been completely unknown to the people of the earliest religion, Schelling supposes, for they knew of only one difference, that which separates the internal and the external, the human and the divine, respectively. This is the age of "Zabism" (astral religion), where a relatively innocuous deity, usually a sky god (for example, Uranus = A^1), is thought to envelop all natural differences within its comprehending presence. Schelling says that this is not the age of mythological "symbolization." The ability to form symbols implies a reflectively conscious distance between

46. Schelling, *Philosophie der Offenbarung*, in *Werke*, 2.4.72.

47. Once again, Schelling himself is not always this clear. The ambiguity between God or humanity as the real cause of the Fall returns when he rejoins this discussion in his *Philosophie der Offenbarung* (2.3.355–60). This ambiguity can be clarified, I suggest, only by focusing on Schelling's central point: the consciousness of freedom (A^3) always has unconscious necessity (B) as its ground.

48. Schelling does not provide specific dates for the periods of history he discusses. He understands them to be relatively different periods along a presupposed line of time.

49. Schelling distinguishes between two terms for what is called *history* in English: *Geschichte* refers to the mere passage of time; *Historie* refers to the increasingly self-conscious description of events (cf. *Philosophie der Mythologie*, in *Werke*, 2.1.235–36).

the symbol and what is symbolized. Zabism is the religion of immediate "inspiration," the tautegorical religion par excellence, where the mythological deity is identical to what it presents itself to be.[50]

The Epoch of Consciousness (A²): Simultaneous Polytheism

Eventually, the consciousness of perceived differences in nature asserts itself to the point where other natural phenomena are suspected as possible equals to the divinity of the Sky. Of particular importance in this period is the emerging consciousness that the principal god, a masculine figure, needs to have a future. This need is expressed, Schelling observes, when the god is worshiped in feminine form: for example, Uranus becomes Urania. Once the masculine god is transformed into or weds a goddess, the immediate future of the gods is ready to be born (namely, A²).[51] This transformation yields an incomplete form of polytheism, which Schelling calls "simultaneous polytheism." This is not the complete form of polytheism, he contends, but merely its nascent stage.[52] Thus far, human life remains relatively tranquil and, most important, unified. Humanity has yet to separate consciously into distinct peoples. However, it has begun to feel ambivalent about its external gods because A² has started its necessary transformation from being the *potency* of nature's spiritual order to being the *principle* of this order. Spirit is starting to bring order out of the relative chaos of material nature—all within human consciousness.

Great violence is portrayed in the mythology of this time. Consequently, Schelling supposes that the emergence of spiritual order was not experienced by humanity as a peaceful transition from its material basis in previous times. Matter (now wholly B) begins forcefully to resist the process of its spiritualization, and humans begin to suffer from not having a god to which they can literally point with the assurance they once felt. In "Greek" mythology (ethnic names being placed in quotes here, as distinct peoples are yet to exist), Uranus becomes Cronos (that is to say, A¹ becomes an angry B that eats its children as soon as they are born) and resists the emerging spiritual order of

---

50. Schelling, *Philosophie der Mythologie,* in *Werke,* 2.2.175–88, 197 ff. (on Zabism), 248–49 (on the distinction between the immediately inspired *[inspirirte]* and the relatively free or reflective character of the truly symbolic *[symbolische]*).

51. Cf. Schelling, *Philosophie der Offenbarung,* in *Werke,* 2.3.389–92.

52. Schelling, *Philosophie der Mythologie,* in *Werke,* 2.1.120–26.

Dionysus (= A^2). In "Babylonian" religion, an unnamed God begins to challenge the supremacy of Mylitta. In "Phoenician" and "Canaanite" religion, Melkart begins to challenge Baal.[53] Schelling understands the names of these deities to be equivalent terms denoting an experienced process throughout human consciousness in general. Anyone from this period could have recognized his or her gods, under different names, in any human society, because humanity is still held together by the weakening primal force that has resisted spiritual differentiation all along—that is, B.

That which causes the differentiation of humanity into peoples is a "spiritual crisis *[geistige Krisis]*." This crisis comes about when an unseen spiritual order (A^2) begins successfully to challenge the visible order of the world (B). It is from this crisis, unfolding "in the ground of human consciousness itself," that humanity divides consciously into different peoples.[54] The result is a proliferation of confusion caused by different languages, laws, and myths— all of which come about from the crisis in consciousness. Schelling grants that there were tribal communities in existence before the emergence of people-constituting myths. But he denies that a collectivity of individuals suffices to account for the self-differentiated entity that constitutes a "people." Tribal societies, he implies, could still recognize one another as part of "humanity," because, before the emergence of spiritual order (A^2), Matter (B) had no serious rival in human consciousness. A "people" is born when spirit challenges matter, hence at the same time as its myths, not before. This point indicates that no myth, properly speaking, can be understood as the creation of an individual or relatively large collectivity, only to be passed on to an already constituted people.[55] Such creativity implies that a self-reflective degree of distance had already been gained from the earliest times of humanity with respect to the difference between a people and its mythology. This implication is simply not allowed, ex hypothesi, in Schelling's speculation on prehistorical societies.

This account of the origin of myths and their peoples begins to clarify how Schelling and Voegelin tend to understand religious and political motivation in general. Notice that the source of fundamental differentiation always comes from "within." Schelling claims:

53. Ibid., 2.2.286–92 ("Greek"), lecture 12 ("Babylonian"), 307 ff. ("Phoenician" and "Canaanite"). For further discussion of these transformations, see Beach, *Potencies of God(s)*, 179–204.
54. Schelling, *Philosophie der Mythologie*, in *Werke*, 2.1.100–101; see also 121, 129, 233, 2.2.172.
55. Ibid., 2.1.62–63.

[A]n *inner,* and therefore irreversible *[unaufhebliche]* separation, as that which exists between peoples, cannot generally be the effect of external causes or natural phenomena. Volcanic eruptions, earthquakes, changes in the levels of the seas, and other such phenomena may suffice to explain the separation of humanity into similar parties but not into dissimilar ones. This latter can be the effect only of *inner* causes, arising from the breast *[Innern]* of homogenous humanity itself *[der homogenen Menschheit selbst],* because only these internal causes would be capable of decomposing a unity into distinct parties, and thus be [truly] natural causes.[56]

This claim requires further attention. Even if one grants Schelling's central point, it is difficult to understand how a single spiritual crisis, which occurs throughout the nature of human consciousness in general, could suffice to cause the division of humanity into different peoples. In other words, how does one crisis cause different reactions? Would not the general nature of this crisis be experienced by all of humanity in the same way, thus causing all humans to welcome the emergence of spiritual order and to agree that their deities were poorly represented in the past? A general change should cause an equally general enlightenment, one would assume, thus sustaining the primordial unity of humanity. Schelling does not appear to have been aware of this difficulty. However, he might have responded by having his readers reconsider the precise nature of this "crisis." It is not caused simply by the appearance of spiritual order (A^2), but by the resistance of Matter (B) to the imposition of order by the emerging Spirit. Matter, according to the *Potenzenlehre,* is inherently self-willing or blindly egotistical. Thus, when the essential nature of Matter becomes actualized, human consciousness responds in kind. Humans become increasingly egotistical; a chain reaction occurs, and the result is a series of apparently different separations of humanity into peoples. These separations are, however, all united by their commonly egotistical nature. This is how one change can cause a series of differences. The division of humanity into peoples does not become radical, with each individual person becoming his or her own "people," because the power of B is always held in check by A^2 (and its emerging A^3).[57] Eventually, however, the sense of separation between peoples does become acute, and individual humans begin to feel that their spiritual gods do not rule in other lands. The

56. Ibid., 2.1.95.

57. Schelling does not think that any potency ever comes to complete dominance, at least in history; if it did, the world would end as it is currently experienced.

former authority of the material deities is challenged in an increasingly open fashion, and people start to become aware of the temporal relativity of the gods and their sovereignty.

It takes another spiritual crisis, this time described as a *katabolē*, or Ground-laying, to restore relative peace between conflicting notions in human consciousness that seek to describe the world's order either as inherently material or as spiritual. This "Ground-laying" is caused by the emergence of A³, the third potency turned principle. Its function is *self-consciously* to maintain the order of nature as subdued matter and vibrant spirit:

> At first, there was only One Potency by which consciousness was exclusively dominated. . . . This first, initially exclusive and tolerating none other beside it, *admits* in turn a *second* potency—that which is destined to surmount the first. This admission is the first victory brought against the exclusivity of B, the first debasement of this to the Ground, the first Groundlaying *[Grundlegung]*, or *katabolē*, as I will call it. The exclusive *domination [Herrschaft]* of the unique principle presented itself in original religion: Zabism. From this point until the moment of the second *katabolē*, where the first principle becomes the object not merely of a possible *[möglichen]*, but of an effective *[wirklichen]* overcoming, . . . we had to do with only two principles. But from now on we come to the effective overcoming *[Ueberwindung*, where B is returned to the potentiality of A¹]. To the extent that the initial principle—which is the cause of the entire tension—is brought back to itself *[in sein An-sich zurückgebracht wird]*, it lives anew in relation . . . to the Highest, which must properly be the third potency, to which it is bound. From now on we have to do with three, that is, with the All *[Allheit]*, the Totality of potencies.[58]

Once again, as with the first spiritual crisis, that which brings the second potency under submission of the third is the appearance of a goddess who will give birth to this future potentiality. When the Phrygian Cybele (= Rhea) is said to marry Cronos, for example, Schelling takes this marriage to indicate a further softening of the principal god, the masculine deity of old. Cybele is even described at times as the transformation of Cronos into a goddess. In any case, this union strengthens the second potency and immediately begins to actualize the third.[59]

58. Schelling, *Philosophie der Offenbarung*, in *Werke*, 2.3.396; see also *Philosophie der Mythologie*, in *Werke*, 2.2.262 (first *katabolē*), 353 (second *katabolē*).
59. Cf. Schelling, *Philosophie der Offenbarung*, in *Werke*, 2.3.399–400.

The Epoch of Self-conscious Spirit (A³): Successive Polytheism and Complete Mythologies

Once the potency of self-conscious spirit (A³) becomes the principal source of order, the time of true or "successive polytheism" has arrived. Successive polytheism, as the name implies, refers to the supremacy of one god, which is succeeded by others in time.[60] This type of polytheism is, according to Schelling, the first manifestation of mythological religion, properly speaking. True polytheism emerges only when humanity begins to feel that all of its "external" representations of the gods are inaccurate. Humanity begins to question the materiality of the divine per se. At this stage, all three potencies are now represented in various world mythologies. And mythologists display an increasing awareness that the gods are limited: they are generated and succeed each other's sovereignty in time. Mythologists attain a considerable distance from their representations. They begin consciously to "symbolize" the gods, in the strict sense of the word, as the absolutely prehistoric *(vorgeschichtliche)* period changes into the relatively prehistoric *(vorhistorische)* period. This is a turbulent time, because the visible gods are, in some cases, completely divested of their divinity. Schelling finds only three "complete" mythologies in this period: the Egyptian, Indian, and Greek. He ranks these, respectively, as the relatively material, the completely spiritual, and the balance between material and spiritual types of order.

Egyptian Mythology

The Egyptians have the greatest difficulty breaking away from the material ground of mythic representations; rather, Horus (A³) has the greatest difficulty subduing Typhon (B), now generally called Seth. Evidence for this claim is found in the fact that the material god retains temples and devotees throughout the high period of Egyptian civilization. As Schelling summarizes the matter, commenting on the general character of Egyptian consciousness, "wherever a church is built to the good God [Horus = A³], the Devil [Typhon = B] builds himself a chapel."[61] Such "chapels" were built to Typhon immediately outside the larger "churches" to other gods. They indicate an Egyptian struggle with spiritual order that is also thought to have

---

60. Schelling, *Philosophie der Mythologie,* in *Werke,* 2.1.120–26.
61. Ibid., 2.2.389.

had its merits. Chiefly, it allowed Egyptian mythologists to remain aware of the material ground of spiritual order, thus to understand the principal gods as forming a unity, "*a* single, enlarged consciousness."[62]

Indian Mythology, Buddhism, and Chinese Atheism

A considerably different style of representation is evident in Indian mythology, according to Schelling, because the Indians understand their gods to be completely spiritual. But this elevated sense of spirit comes with a price: it undermines a good deal of the gods' unity. "In Indian consciousness, the principle of the beginning [Brahma $=$ B], that which is the ground and support of the entire process, has been completely dominated and annihilated by the superior potency [Shiva $=$ A^2]." Without a clear sense of the material ground of all the gods, each divinity acquires its own followers, and they become antagonistic toward one another. In their antagonism, the devotees simply imitate the actions of their gods. Even the highest divinity, whom Schelling takes to be Vishnu (A^3), turns against his predecessors and calls for complete devotion from his followers. Thus, Indian mythology is found to be in a state of confusion: "[I]n place of an authentic mythology, produced in a natural way, we see here a mythology which is truly artificial," one unified only by its thematic sense of destruction. That which is destroyed is the past of the people, and especially the sense that their gods have supported one another in the historical process leading to their dominions. The theme of destruction becomes emphatic in Indian Buddhism. "On the one hand, [Buddhism] is something foreign to authentic India," Schelling claims, and "on the other hand, [it is] the product of a reaction against the mythological process, an antimythological tendency which, from its origins, traverses mythological phenomena." The great enigma here, for Schelling, is that Buddhism appears to be a historical regression in consciousness back to the monism of Parsi religion, where the Mithras appeared as confusions of matter and spirit not long before the first spiritual crisis. One senses some degree of frustration in Schelling's hasty conclusion that "Buddhism, just like mysticism... serves only to render complete the confusion of unfortunate Indian consciousness."[63]

62. Cf. Schelling, *Philosophie der Offenbarung*, in *Werke*, 2.3.401–4; see also *Philosophie der Mythologie*, in *Werke*, 2.2.364–431.

63. Schelling, *Philosophie der Offenbarung*, in *Werke*, 2.3.405.

Buddhists resist the principle of spiritual order (A²) and its final subjuga-
tion (A³) of matter (B → A¹).[64] But the historical manifestation of such
resistance poses a considerable problem for Schelling's account of the natural
or necessary character of mythological development. It should not be able to
occur, given the limited historical stage that natural consciousness has allegedly
attained by this point. However, Buddhists reject traditional religion with a
degree of freedom from mythological symbols that, as we eventually learn,
should be attained only with the historical appearance of Christ.

Conscious resistance to spiritual order among a limited group is not the only
problem that begins to weaken the world-historical dimension of Schelling's
Potenzenlehre. He is also faced with an earlier problem, the appearance of a
stagnation or "standing-still *[Stillstehen]*" in the mythological development
of the Persians. Schelling notes, from remarks by Herodotus, that the Persians were still worshiping their Mithra(s) in the material and cosmological
manner of late Zabism well after the second "spiritual crisis," when other
civilizations had already developed completely differentiated spiritual mythologies. The Persians worshiped the exterior cosmos directly—that is, without
the relative interiority of temples and icons. And they did so at a time when
the Egyptians, Indians, and Greeks had begun to build temples and fashion
icons. With the introduction of such artifacts into religious worship, these
other peoples reveal to Schelling their increasing awareness that the divine is
to be known primarily and specifically in human consciousness, rather than
from the exterior cosmos in general. However, it seems that the Persians remained relatively unaware of this transition from cosmos to consciousness as
the site where divinity is best experienced. Schelling attempts to explain this
problem by saying that a powerful priestly caste was likely responsible for
holding back the Persians from the spiritual advancements already attained
in other civilizations. But he cites no evidence to support this claim; it is
simply a conjecture. And, once again, Persian priests should not have had
the freedom to resist mythological development, nor indeed the ability to
persuade Persians to resist a development that was allegedly irresistible for
other peoples.[65]

The problem of an inconsistent development of mythological religion in
history becomes especially acute when Schelling confronts the "complete
atheism" of China. He discovers, strictly speaking, that the Chinese never

---

64. Schelling, *Philosophie der Mythologie,* in *Werke,* 2.2.lecture 1; see also 431–85 (Indian
mythology), 486–520 (Indian and Buddhist religions contrasted).
65. Ibid., 2.2.208–11.

develop a mythology of their own. They even lack a proper word for God in their earliest language. Confucian, Taoist, and Buddhist elements in their traditions are later developments, which are said to have nothing to do with "the essence of the Chinese." In a state of relative isolation, the Chinese continue well beyond others to think of themselves as humanity per se. They do not become a distinct people, self-consciously "Chinese," making the mythological transition from material to increasingly spiritual symbolizations of divine order. While other civilizations are allegedly developing along the path indicated by the historical *Potenzenlehre,* the Chinese principle of order remains only the material State. These points, apparently evidence of historical stagnation, lead Schelling to speak of the Chinese even as a "second humanity *[eine zweite Menschheit]*"—as a Chinese ecumene.[66]

These anomalies should not have been able to occur, according to Schelling's account of how the natural potencies actualize themselves in the universal history of human consciousness. During the epoch of "mythological religion," human consciousness is still ostensibly dominated by the progressive actualization of natural, which is to say *universal,* potencies. Thus, one should find uniformity among the religious symbolizations of all contemporaries. But such is not the case. Indian Buddhism, Persian religion, and the Chinese ecumene do not follow the historical progression of mythic symbolization that Schelling has, with some difficulty, shown to be unfolding in Occidental cultures. Chinese consciousness, in particular, appears to be inexplicably outside of nature's historical grasp.

When faced with problems such as these, Schelling appeals to the claim that "the exception is what actually confirms the rule *(exceptio firmat regulam).*" He is thus led occasionally to use Chinese consciousness as an exceptional measure against which the mythological progression itself can be defined in the majority of other cultures. It is especially the Chinese exception that seems to persuade Schelling occasionally to qualify the historical dimension of the *Potenzenlehre* as a *hypothetical* account of how the divine comes to be known in consciousness.[67] Nonetheless, he also insists that the need for this qualification does not fundamentally undermine his vision of

---

66. Ibid., 2.2.527, 555; the entire discussion of Chinese civilization is found in lectures 23–24.

67. Ibid., 2.2.236, 558–62, 523. The historical development of the potencies is qualified as "hypothetical" in at least two other places: one with specific reference to the Fall (2.3.360), the other more generally (2.4.8). It is necessary to point out these qualifications, because Schelling is not always mindful of them. Normally, he says unequivocally that history reveals an irrefutable "law" of progress in consciousness (for example, see *Philosophie der Mythologie,* in *Werke,* 2.2.186–87).

order in history per se. His insistence and general confidence in this line of thought is due to what he thinks he has already gained from the vantage point of his own historical position. To wit, Schelling already thinks he *knows* that the mythological process will come to its end in what is eventually described as the only complete type of divine Revelation—namely, that which becomes manifest in Christ's Incarnation. This aspect of Christian Revelation is presupposed as the measure par excellence against which mythological religion itself can be defined and transcended. The philosophy of Revelation seeks to encompass and guide the philosophy of mythology from the outset.[68]

These points bring to mind a fundamental problem in Schelling's historical philosophy, one that he does not sufficiently address. He uses a double standard in his attempts to define mythological religion or natural consciousness as such. On the one hand, the entire *Philosophy of Mythology* attempts to define mythological religion by presupposing the standard of Christian Revelation. This is by far Schelling's main "exception" to the "rule" of natural mythology. On the other hand, from within the *Philosophy of Mythology* itself, early Chinese thought is also occasionally used as a standard, an exception in its own right, against which mythological religion is defined. These standards are antithetical and, as such, ought to produce *different* definitions of mythological religion. The former, on Schelling's account, transcends a strictly mythological order of consciousness when God's self-revelation in Christ creates a definitive, historical break with the mythological or natural order of consciousness in the past. Conversely, the Chinese do not develop a mythological or progressively historical degree of consciousness at all, and they offer a considerable level of resistance to the mythological traditions they encounter. The difference between these standards should prompt Schelling to question the universal scope of the *Potenzenlehre,* at least in its historical dimensions. Either Christian Revelation, with its focus on historical consciousness, is the exceptional standard by which mythological religion is to be defined, or the relatively ahistorical nature of Chinese consciousness is the exceptional standard by which Schelling's historicization of nature is itself called into question. One cannot have it both ways and arrive at the *same* understanding of mythological religion in historical differentiation. But Schelling attempts to have it both ways. He places Chinese and Christian levels of consciousness at opposite points on a scale, between which the mythological consciousness of distinct peoples is understood to progress

---

68. Cf. Schelling, *Philosophie der Offenbarung,* in *Werke,* 2.4.8–9.

toward the completely historical self-consciousness of his Christian present and beyond.

The Chinese remain inexplicably "primitive," whereas mythological cultures "advance" to the point where revelatory consciousness gains the historical grounds by which it can understand itself to be Revelation. The Chinese remain the negative measure compared to which both mythological and revelatory peoples appear to be advanced. At this point, it may appear that only one *positive* standard serves to judge all of the others in history—namely, the standard of Christian Revelation. But this is not so. Recall that Schelling needs to show how consciousness develops with temporal and spatial universality in order for Christian Revelation itself to be grounded in nature and exceptionally true at a certain point in history. The enigma of the Chinese suggests that the nature of consciousness does not change in the history of humanity in general. This is why the Chinese ecumene is available, so to speak, for Schelling to use as a countermeasure to define mythological consciousness. But this use of Chinese thought overlooks a decisive point. It is open to the critique of cultural relativism. If Schelling were to pursue this line of thought consistently, he would have to admit that the Chinese were also justified when they took mythological cultures as a measure against which to declare their own superiority. But no such admission is forthcoming. Schelling does not concede that Providence is not providing him with a universal measure with which to write the history of Christian Revelation as a distinct exception to the rule of advancing mythological consciousness: Providence is not providing him with a consistent view of nature in history. Nor does he face the further problem caused by this weakness in his historiography: the universal God appears not to have universally prepared humanity for Judeo-Christian Revelation. In fact, most of humanity, the Orient, appears to have been left behind in the historical march toward Christian faith. Instead of facing these problems with the seriousness they deserve, Schelling continues his efforts to articulate the history of nature as the universal ground of supernatural Revelation, remaining confident that the end he has in mind will resolve any questions about his procedure. That is to say, he continues to read thematic, historical changes in mythological religions as though they were evidence of a *praeparatio evangelica*.

Greek Mythology and the Mystery Religions

After giving an extensive account of Indian mythology and its antithesis in various forms of Buddhism, Schelling turns to examine what he considers to be the completion of mythological religions: Greek mythology and its perfection in the Mystery religions. In contrast to the violent gods of the Indians, the distinguishing characteristic of the Greek gods is said to be their gentle beauty.

> [T]he Greek gods are born from a consciousness that delivers itself regularly and gently from the violence of the real principle [= B]; they are, therefore, beneficent apparitions or visions in which this—the real principle—disappears, to be sure, but still continues to be in its absence and effacement the type [of principle] which communicates to the nascent forms the reality *[Realität]*, the certainty *[Bestimmtheit]*, by virtue of which the Greek gods are necessary representations, eternal, stable, not merely ephemeral moments (concepts). Greek mythology is the gentle death, the true euthanasia *[die wahre Euthanasie]* of the real principle, which in its expiration and going-under *[Untergehen]* still leaves in its place a world of charming and beautiful apparitions.[69]

That which fundamentally distinguishes the mythological religion of the Greeks is said to be its ability to retain a considerable degree of balance between the material and spiritual principles. The Greeks develop exoteric (= material) and esoteric (= spiritual) forms of their religion, each of which is understood to depend upon the other. In the exoteric sense, the gods are portrayed in physical terms, thus retaining the memory and history of the material principle upon which the other gods are based. In this sense, the Greeks retain what was strongest in Egyptian consciousness: the awareness of the material ground of spiritual order. However, some of the Greeks are also said to have attained the purely spiritual consciousness that characterized the Indians. These were primarily the people who formed the esoteric Mystery religions: both Dionysian and Eleusinian Mysteries dedicated to Demeter.

Schelling discusses the Mysteries in terms of their both exoteric and esoteric aspects. He assumes that an intimate connection held between these. But the esoteric aspect of the Mysteries is most important to him, because it is said to reveal the true beginning of the end of mythological consciousness per se.[70]

---

69. Ibid., 2.3.406.

70. One might justifiably wonder how Schelling can presume to know the content of the esoteric teachings, as this was restricted to initiates. Schelling's account is based largely on three sources: reports by contemporary and nearly contemporary witnesses (for example, Plato, Plutarch, and Pausanias); contemporary scholarship available to him (for instance, by Creuzer, Sainte-Croix, and Warburton); and the assumption that the secret of the Mysteries was not fundamentally a matter of doctrine, but a matter of the internal experience—the dramatic catharsis—that was said to come about as a result of the teachings.

Essentially, Schelling argues that the Mysteries contain "a hidden metaphysic *[eine verhüllte Metaphysik]*" and "a transcendental cosmogony *[eine transcendentale Weltentstehungslehre]*." In effect, "the causes that are known in the Mysteries are none other than the *general* causes that engendered the world."[71] The Mysteries were formed, in other words, because of an increasing awareness that the gods of mythology are the potencies of nature in human consciousness. The initiates of the Greek Mysteries appear to have been first to discover the type of thinking that leads to Schelling's *Potenzenlehre*. This discovery did not cause them to become idealists. Instead, Schelling says, "everything in the Mysteries is fact; all rests on a first event which, as in a tragedy, is pushed until its end. According to the neo-platonists, all is reflection and theorem; to us, all is the thing itself *[die Sache selbst]*." It may seem that the adherents to the Mysteries reverted back to the beginning of mythological consciousness, when "inspirations" of the divine were immediately "tautegorical." But this is not so. In the esoteric religions of Dionysus and Demeter, mythology itself becomes transparent simply as the means by which the potencies of nature express themselves in human consciousness. Accordingly, mythological religion itself is treated with a "free irony" by the initiates.[72] This does not mean that the initiates were enlightened atheists, a clever group of intellectuals who formed secret societies based on the realization that public gods were symbols of merely human experiences. Schelling explicitly rejects this account of the Mysteries, which he found in C. A. Lobeck and J. H. Voß,[73] by turning his focus to the fact that new myths were produced by the initiates for the initiates. The distinctive feature of these myths is said to have been the self-consciousness of their production, that is, under the complete dominion of A³. Yet, unlike the previously mentioned peoples in which A³ became relatively actual, this potency is said to have caused the Greeks to become completely self-conscious, to look both retrospectively at the divine history that brought them to their present state of soul and prospectively toward the future of religion itself.

Retrospectively, the Mysteries taught "none other than the history of religious consciousness, or, to express it in an objective way, the history of God himself *[des Gottes selbst]*, which, existing from his primordial non-spirituality [B], was overcome and transfigured to the point of perfect spiritualization [A³]. In this way, the ultimate content of the Mysteries is assuredly the com-

71. Schelling, *Philosophie der Offenbarung*, in *Werke*, 2.3.491.
72. Ibid., 2.3.500, 512.
73. Ibid., 2.3.457–59, 479–80.

pletely spiritual, and, at the same time, unique God *[einige Gott]*." In other words, the Mysteries taught a version of Schelling's own philosophy of mythology, albeit a historically limited one, where "the history of the gods became the history of God. . . . *[I]nstead* of becoming a fable or being *interpreted* as such, the history of the gods became much more a *verity*. It had its truth mainly in the history of God, which was exposed in the Mysteries. That which appeared on the exterior as the history of the gods was nothing but the interior history of God which had traversed divers moments."[74]

This is a remarkable claim. Once again, Schelling's historicism begins to falter along another line. He seems to forget that the Greeks are supposed to have lacked the historical measure, God's free self-revelation in Christ, by which reflective distance on mythology is allegedly given. How could a select group in Hellenic society have attained, much like Schelling himself, the awareness that mythology is symbolic for experiences of the divine without the principal "exception" to nature, Christian Revelation, by which Schelling has ostensibly attained his own reflective distance on myth? Schelling is aware of this problem and is led, consequently, to attribute a type of revelation to the Greeks. But he is careful to limit it to "the human kind."[75] The specific character of Greek revelation, much like Schelling also finds in the Jews, is limited to a dim awareness of the future of theophany. Even so, his presentation of the theology of the Mysteries begins to look even more like that which he eventually finds in Christian Revelation.

The Mysteries are said to have taught an "interior history," an esoteric theology of history that was essentially monotheistic. What is more, Schelling insists that this monotheism could not have been merely "negative" or ahistorical, as he finds in the subsequent development of Aristotelian theology, because the initiates retained a considerable degree of historical consciousness at the basis of their theological teachings. Rather, "[t]he doctrines of the Mysteries could not have consisted in a purely *negative* monotheism, one which merely excluded polytheism, rather than containing it as surpassed. . . . When monotheism is taught in the Mysteries it is the type which recognizes plurality as a path leading to it and which, because of this, leaves the plurality to subsist." This plurality was not conceived simply on the profane level of history. It subsisted even in the theology; according to Schelling, the monotheism of the Mysteries was also trinitarian: "[T]he principal content of the

74. Ibid., 2.3.494, 502.
75. Ibid., 2.3.525.

Mysteries is assuredly the spiritual God, *one* in his three potencies (once the tension is resolved *[aufgehobener]*) and nonetheless equal to all of these." The triune God of the Mysteries is one whose natural tension *(Spannung)* has been "resolved." This resolution is due to the collective ability of A² and A³ to subdue B, thus restoring its true essence: its *"An-sich"* (= A¹). Schelling takes his example of the one-God-in-three-potencies from the fact that Dionysus was worshiped in three manifestations, each of which was declared to be sovereign over a particular period of time—for example, the Zagreus of the past, the Bacchus of the present, and the Iakchos of the future. Whether one cites this aspect of the Dionysian Mysteries or its counterpart in the Eleusinian Mysteries—where Demeter was worshiped as the Persephone of the past, the Demeter of the present, and the Kore of the future—the end result is still the same, at least for Schelling. "[T]he highest teachings of the Mysteries consisted in this: the causal gods were not united simply in an indissoluble fashion but were one and the same *God*—we can say, leaving itself [B], through itself [A²], and returning to itself [A³]—only as different forms, or rather moments, of this One."[76]

Thus far, the theology of the Mysteries has been described as monotheistic, trinitarian, and historical. Schelling finds the specifically historical aspect of this theology in frequent depictions of the suffering that God is said to endure in the struggle for self-consciousness: "As the whole mythological process rests only on the successive overcoming of the blind being of God *[der successiven Ueberwindung des blind seyenden Gottes]*, or *a fortiori*, of God *as* blind being, these *sufferings* were not the contingent content, but the necessary content of the Mysteries, which . . . could not be anything but the interior, esoteric history of mythology itself." Adherents of the Mysteries understood themselves to be participating in this same suffering, sharing it, and discovering thereby the concrete basis for their ethical teaching. Everything "which human life possesses in pain and surpasses only with difficulty, God has also surpassed." Thus, Schelling interprets, "[w]ho [among the initiates] could still complain about the common accidents in life if he had seen the grand design of all, the inevitable path that God himself had crossed, toward Sovereignty?"[77] Who, indeed! The retrospective teaching of the Mysteries comes to an end with this moral. Once the "grand design" of the past has

76. Ibid., 2.3.502, 500, 513–18, 463. On the similarity between the Dionysian (masculine) and Eleusinian (feminine) trinities, see ibid., 2.3.490.

77. Ibid., 2.3.495, 502–3.

been discovered to lead directly to one's present, it remains only for the future to be divined.

Prospectively, Schelling argues that the Mysteries envisioned a universal religion of the future, one that would reunite all of scattered humanity: "The Greeks *[Hellenen]* themselves did not consider [the Mysteries] as a religion which would be merely their own. Their content was thought to be truly universal, a world religion *[Weltreligion]*. . . . The gods of the Mysteries were recognized . . . as the *universal* and *highest* causes, and consequently as the content of the supreme and truly universal religion." A strong orientation toward the future was evident in the Eleusinian Mysteries, wherein "even the name of *Eleusis* designates that which arrives, that which is to come, or, to use the old festive word, the come *[Kunft]*, the *advent* of God." In the Dionysian Mysteries, the advent of the God in question was that of Kore (A³), or Iakchos (A³), the third and last forms of Demeter and Dionysus, respectively. Schelling pays particular attention to the rites in which Iakchos was depicted as an infant, because they allegedly symbolize the adherents' consciousness of the futurity of the truly universal religion:

> In the processions of Iakchos, a capital role was given to the *mystical winnowing-box [die mystische Wanne]*. . . . It is a known fact that the infant Iakchos was carried in the box, and that Iakchos himself named the box *Diknitēs*. Thus, the box was the *cradle [Wiege]* of God, characterized in this way by the infant. If you ask me why it is a winnowing-box that was chosen as a cradle, I can respond only as follows: By this, Iakchos should be designated as the prince of peace. The box is an image of his pacific works. But by this should also be designated the humble character of his birth, the fact that he had yet to appear as the person whom he would be. And, by an apparently shocking anticipation, but nonetheless from a natural ground, the box is even that which later has become the cradle, in relation to a higher and much holier birth.[78]

These remarks clarify the general approach to the Mysteries that Schelling has been developing. It is Schelling himself who gives a capital role to everything in the Mysteries that looks like nascent Christianity. By the time of the Mysteries, the natural potencies of consciousness have become actualized to the point where humanity will be able to understand Christ as the one God's supreme Revelation in history, but only when the event finally comes. "The

78. Ibid., 2.3.492, 519, 518.

Greek mysteries are effectively the natural transition from paganism to Christianity, *i.e.,* to perfect Revelation."[79] It is as though the history of mythology has provided consciousness with an a priori structure with which to recognize Revelation as such. But no such Revelation comes to the Greeks. At most, their revelation remains imperfect, only a revelation "analogue," Schelling says, which is also found in other mythologies.[80] The mystical cradle of Iakchos was produced only by a "natural" ground. It was not consciously based upon Revelation in the Christian sense of the term. "The ultimate content of the Mysteries was, in a certain sense, a complete surmounting of polytheism, a perfect liberation in this respect, and therefore a monotheism—in *this* sense above, where we indicated it as *future*..., a religion common to all of humanity. The Mysteries could not, to be sure, break through to the true religion itself, but they reached the point where they saw this [religion] as that which is to come."[81] The Mysteries begin to develop in ways that resemble the theology that will unfold in Christianity, but they do so only in a compact way. Even the reality of their exoteric rites does not become equivalent to the self-conscious unity of spirit and matter that Schelling is able to find in Christ. The Incarnation is needed, above all, for the spiritual content of the Mysteries to become completely Real for Schelling. Otherwise said, his Christianity is a Mystery religion for the people.[82]

Greek Philosophy: Plato and Aristotle

Before they become realized in Christ, however, Schelling notes that the Mysteries enter philosophy through Plato. Thus begins what might be described as a process of relative demythologization. It is Plato whom Schelling considers to have been the primary link between the mythological self-consciousness of the Mysteries and the drive toward strictly negative philosophy in Aristotle. It is Plato who writes as the "poet among philosophers" and creates the linguistic tools for subsequent philosophy: the "ideas," the Good beyond being, and the myth of the soul and its passions in dialogical form. Aristotle, in turn, becomes the grammarian among philosophers. He

79. Ibid., 2.3.410.
80. Schelling, *Philosophie der Mythologie,* in *Werke,* 2.1.240.
81. Schelling, *Philosophie der Offenbarung,* in *Werke,* 2.3.524–25.
82. This completes Schelling's account of the natural development in mythological religions. To review this entire process, see the outline of Schelling's summary lectures, which I have translated as the Appendix.

puts the tools to work by setting out to eliminate partiality in his first philosophy or theology. In other words, "Aristotle's metaphysic is a fabric of which the threads belong to Plato."[83]

Plato and Aristotle represent the limit of the possibilities for ancient philosophy. They attain nothing new with respect to the level of consciousness attained in the Mysteries, but they bring this level to the conceptual clarity of philosophy. They encounter the active intellect and then fail to show whence it comes and how it is related to God and the world.[84] They achieve, in the final analysis, the first complete formulations of a truly negative philosophy, reaching the limits of natural revelation and pointing the way beyond themselves to the higher type: the Revelation of Christ's Incarnation. Their failures reveal to Schelling the need for spirit and matter to be completely reunited in Christ. The apparent separation of the soul and God for Revelation to occur is complete by the time of Plato and Aristotle, but no Revelation—in the strict sense of the word—is given to them.

> In Greek consciousness, the mythological process attains its end and its crisis. . . . In mythological religion the primitive relation between consciousness and God was transformed into a real and purely natural relation. On the one hand, it felt like a necessary relation; yet, on the other, it felt provisional, implying the need for a higher relation, destined to replace it and to make it intelligible to itself. Such is the tragic aspect that runs throughout the entire history of paganism. We find already the anticipated sentiment of this exigence, of something to come, of something imminent but not yet recognizable, in certain expressions of Plato, which we can consider seriously, for this reason, as anticipations of Christianity [*Ahndungen des Christenthums*].[85]

Plato prefigures Christian consciousness in "certain expressions." For example, he creates philosophical myths about the intimate community between God and primordial humanity before the Fall.[86] He also appears to accept, by drawing explicitly upon the Mysteries, the punishment of the wicked in Hades and a beatific life among the gods for initiates. Finally, Schelling grants that Plato argued in a *natural* way for the soul's immortality.[87]

---

83. Schelling, *Philosophie der Mythologie,* in *Werke,* 2.1.380–81.

84. Cf. ibid., 2.1.460–61.

85. Ibid., 2.1.256.

86. Schelling, *Philosophie der Offenbarung,* in *Werke,* 2.3.455–59; see also *Philosophie der Mythologie,* in *Werke,* 2.1.463.

87. Schelling, *Philosophie der Offenbarung,* in *Werke,* 2.3.493 (cf. Plato's *Laws* 870d–e), 452–53 (cf. Plato's *Phaedrus* 69c), 493.

Aristotle adds conceptual clarity to Plato's dialogical writings. Schelling is especially surprised to find what he understands to be an account of personal immortality in Aristotle's descriptions of the mind (nous). He claims to find this in Aristotle's call, in the *Nicomachean Ethics,* for philosophers to immortalize themselves *(apathanatizein)* by cultivating the theoretical life.[88] Aristotle's conceptual rationality achieves the perfect end of negative philosophy. It progresses from nature to the singular purity of God beyond the natural world. That which inhibited Aristotle from progressing to a positive philosophy of history, aside from lacking Revelation, was his unwillingness to incorporate the mythic traditions of the past as the ground of his own thinking. Schelling notes that Aristotle was something of a *philomythos,* a lover of myth. But Aristotle's concern for developing a philosophical interpretation of mythic consciousness did not progress, according to Schelling, because he found myths to be of "no use for science." At best, mythic truth was incomplete truth. Even so, in Schelling's account, Aristotle's meager appreciation for myth was enough to touch upon the "analogical succession of principles" in both myth and philosophy.[89] This insight was certainly helpful in Schelling's attempt to develop a philosophical mythology of his own, but one senses that Aristotle's conceptual aridity amounts to a spiritual regression when compared to the livelier teachings of the Mysteries. Specifically, Aristotle's theology envisioned no future of religious consciousness, something that Schelling found to be especially noble in the Mysteries. In their prophetic appeals to the future universality of religion, Schelling claims that the Mystery religions of Greece played much the same historical role as the advent of the Jewish faith.

Jewish Revelation: Law and Prophecy, the Beginning of Revealed Religion

The best of the Greeks were, so to speak, lesser Jews—an outer coating, a shell, hiding something else to be revealed in the future of God's developing nature, for mythology itself is nothing but "an ideal or idyllic shell *[eine ideale oder idealische Hülle]*... that is drawn alongside this history of nature."[90] In a similar fashion, the best of the Jews were, so to speak, natural Chris-

88. Cf. Schelling, *Philosophie der Mythologie,* in *Werke,* 2.1.473–80; see also 557–60. Aristotle's discussion of "immortalizing" *(athanatizein)* is mentioned explicitly at 558 n. 5.

89. Ibid., 2.1.256, 332.

90. Schelling, *Philosophie der Offenbarung,* in *Werke,* 2.3.492.

tians—an outer shell, concealing that which is more substantial for the future of Revelation.

> Judaism, properly speaking, was never anything positive. We can only deter-
> mine it either as a restrained paganism or as a potential, though still hid-
> den Christianity; and it is precisely this middle-position which became the
> cause of its dispersion. Among the Jews, that which is cosmic, the natural,
> that which they had in common with other nations, became the shell
> *[Hülle]* of that which is to come, the supernatural *[Uebernatürlichen];* but
> in fact it was for this that Judaism was itself sanctified.[91]

Both Judaism and Greek mythology are treated as historical means leading toward the fulfillment of Revelation in Christianity. Their historical positions qualify the truth of their religious representations. But the Christians, it seems, benefit from two Old Testaments: one Jewish, the other pagan.

The arrival of Jewish monotheism marks the beginning of consciously historical time *(historische Zeit)*. The absolutely and relatively prehistorical periods are overcome with the special character of Jewish historical consciousness, according to Schelling's historiography. The sanctification of the Jews began quite early, in Abraham's mediated revelation of the "true God." But its full effects took a great deal of time to unfold. The time between Abraham's incomplete revelation and its completion in Christ was marked by the Jews' frequently unsuccessful struggle to keep themselves free from the gods of other nations. Schelling interprets this struggle as a historical progression of the natural potencies. The Jews experience the same potencies of nature, which led to polytheistic mythologies in other nations. But a "superior will" is said to use nature this time around in order to reveal itself among the Jews, thus yielding a relatively stable form of monotheism. This superior will manifests itself for the first time in the story of Abraham's potential sacrifice of Isaac. When God is said to have tempted Abraham to go and offer his beloved son as a holocaust (Gen. 22), Schelling interprets this request as the work of the blind principle of nature (B), the "false God," here represented as the Elohim. This event occurs in the epoch immediately following the first spiritual crisis. Abraham is potentially pagan, as are all of his neighbors, living in the late age of Zabism. But something stops him in the act of carrying out the sacrifice:

91. Ibid., 2.4.148–49.

[A]t the moment when Abraham lifts his hand to kill his son, the angel of Jehovah calls to him and forbids him from bringing his hand against the child. Here, Elohim and the angel of Jehovah . . . are distinguished. . . . That which is named Elohim is the *substance* of consciousness. The angel of Jehovah is nothing substantial, but it is something which can only become in consciousness, can in fact only appear; it is not *substantia,* but is there always only as *actu.*

The true God begins to act upon the consciousness of Abraham, but he does so in a way that recalls the emergence of revelatory consciousness among the pagans: "The true God, in the Old Testament, is also mediated by the false, and is basically tied to the latter. This is the general limit of old-testamental revelation *[der alttestamentlichen Offenbarung].* Insofar as the higher potency, which is the cause of all revelation, surmounts the principle which is opposed to it, it *produces* in the latter the true God as an appearance [in the substance of consciousness]."⁹² It is from this dual consciousness of one God that the Jews take on their middle position in the history of religions.

As restrained pagans, the Jews live under the Mosaic Law. The time of the Law corresponds to the Dionysian period (A²) in Greece. Moses is the representative of spiritual order (A²). More specifically, Schelling finds similarities between the Law and pagan mythology for two reasons. First, as Law, it always has the character of restraining something. It thus has more to do with natural necessity than with the essential freedom proper to divine transcendence. That which is restrained is precisely the dark principle of nature or paganism (B): "All of the Mosaic organization, even its religious code, rests uniquely on the recognition of the *reality* of the principle that we have called the contrary principle, the antidivine." This aspect of Old Testament revelation "presupposes perpetually the tension" caused by this threatening ground of nature. Second, the Mosaic Law does not overcome this natural principle but simply prescribes directives by which the Jews can live with it. For example, the Jews accept a number of pagan practices—circumcision, dietary laws, and sacrifices—but they do so in accordance with their own directives.⁹³

As potential Christians, the Jews begin to live under the expectation of being freed from the Law with the advent of the prophets (A³). The promise of future freedom begins to take shape when Amos, Jeremiah, and Isaiah

92. Ibid., 2.4.129–30, 131–32, 123 (see also 128).
93. Ibid., 2.4.145, 124; cf. 132–42.

speak against the Mosaic sacrifices in the name of Jehovah.[94] The prophets also prophesy the future Messiah, and thereby initiate a tendency that Schelling finds to be characteristic of Old Testament religion in general: the focus on God's name—YHWH—as "he who will be." The particular orientation toward the future in Jewish prophecy leads Schelling to say that "prophetism surpasses the Law; it is to the Law what the Mysteries are to mythology." Even so, despite the advances of their prophets, the Jews are said to achieve no more than "mere revelation." They perceive the spiritual unity and universality of their God, but this revelation does not allow them to conquer their sense of the antidivine ground (= B), which they continue to share with the pagans. Christ is needed for this fundamental overcoming of mythological consciousness and the Law, because "in Christ there is no longer mere revelation *[bloße Offenbarung]*, but its reality *[Realität]*, its effectiveness *[Wirklichkeit]*, the thing itself *[die Sache selbst]*."[95] It is Christ's Incarnation, self-sacrificial death, Resurrection, and Ascension that finally conquer death (= B). These events indicate to Schelling that divine revelation has progressed beyond the mere idea of itself, achieving Revelation in reality, the potencies restored to harmony in an actual life.

The Greeks and Jews were but historical "shells," vessels by which two dimensions of history led to Christ, the only *real* appearance of the mediating potency (A²):

> [T]he universal and personal actions of Christ are neatly distinguished [in history]; but in a moment the two are equally known. The sphere of his universal action (which he does not exercise *as* the Christ) is paganism; his personal action is that which he exercises in Revelation, and this is truly why at the same time he is the personal cause of all revelation. There is, in this sense, a double history of the mediating potency; there is, so to speak, a *historia sacra* and a *historia profana* of his action.

Profane history is found among the pagans, where the Phoenician Melkart, the Egyptian Osiris, the Indian Shiva, and the Greek Dionysus are all revealed, from the perspective of sacred history, to be but ideal manifestations of what becomes real in Christ. The Jews completed their mission when they brought Christ into the world:

---

94. Cf. ibid., 2.4.127 (Amos), 128 (Jeremiah), 145 (Isaiah).
95. Ibid., 2.4.129, 145 (see also 146–47 n. 1), 132.

It had to be that [the Jews] ceased to be a people, that they became dispersed and scattered among the other nations. They were *something* only as carriers of the future *[die Träger der Zukunft]*. So, as the goal was attained, the medium became aimless *[zweckloses]*. Just as the chaff is dispersed by the wind when the living grain it carries in itself is released, so the Jewish people was dispersed by the wind, having no properly independent history since then; it was, in the strict sense, *excluded* from history *[ausgeschlossen von der Geschichte]*.

The Jews may have been sidelined in history, but Schelling finds this to be no cause for what has come to be known as anti-Semitism. He grants that "there will certainly come a day when [the Jewish people] will be reintegrated into the divine economy from which it is currently excluded, as though forgotten. *When* this day will come, *this* will appear as the last developments of Christianity itself. . . . In the meantime, it is noble for the most intelligent no longer to refuse the Jews their necessary rights."[96]

Christian Revelation: Grace and Freedom, the Perfection of Revealed Religion

Schelling's understanding of Christianity, as indicated previously, resembles his understanding of the Greek Mystery religions. He distinguishes both an "interior" or essential aspect of Christianity and an "exterior" one. The interior aspect is found in the sacred-historical teaching that identifies Christ's spirit in pagan mythologies and Jewish revelation, guiding the order of world history ever since its creation. This is the fundamental teaching of esoteric Christianity. The exterior aspect of Christianity concerns the relatively natural development of the three churches: the Petrine (B), Pauline (A^2), and Johannine (A^3). Schelling understands the time of the churches to be equivalent to exoteric or dogmatic Christianity; it falls under the dominion of the natural potencies—albeit guided, once again, by a "superior will." The esoteric aspect of Christianity is most important to Schelling's historiography. Its teachings offer the key to the higher, internal history, which he has been developing all along. Schelling says that he does not care to harmonize his views on essential Christianity with ecclesiastical orthodoxy. Rather, he seeks to attain orthodoxy per se, true opinion for its own sake:

96. Ibid., 2.4.119; cf. 142–43, 150, 151.

It is not important for me to be in accord with . . . ecclesiastical doctrine. I
have no interest in being orthodox, as we say, and it would not be intoler-
able for me to be the contrary. Christianity is simply a phenomenon which
I seek to *explain.* But that which is the sense, the true intention of Christianity must be judged from its authentic documents, exactly as we have
proceeded to determine the meaning of Dionysian doctrine or some other
mythological idea from the most authentic writings.

Christ's Incarnation

Schelling says that the Incarnation is "the most important and most
essential" factor in his entire presentation. But he cautions that it must be
interpreted with great care, as it leads one into the heart of a great mystery:
"that the Son of God should become human appears in general as a *mys-
terium imperscrutabile,* as an absolutely impenetrable secret. Thus, it would
be vain to want to demonstrate the causes: to want to derive some rigorous
conclusion in relation to this would already prove to be pure presumption."
Despite this warning, Schelling spends a great deal of time trying to develop
a detailed account of how the potencies must have changed their relations to
one another during the exceptional events of Christ's worldly existence. He
begins by maintaining that the Incarnation is not the addition of man and
God as separate natures. On the contrary, he argues, in this view "resides
the *prōton pseudos*" of ecclesiastical Christology. It perpetuates the "first error" from Schelling's identity philosophy, and forces one to assume that
God's nature suffers change when Christ becomes human. In order to avoid
this problem, Schelling argues that the change brought about by the Incarnation is not substantial, but only formal: "Here, there is not a passage from
being purely *God* to being man, but only a passage from being *en morphēi
theou* [in the form of God] to being *en morphēi doulou* [in the form of a ser-
vant]. . . . It is not the divine nature itself, but only the personality posited as
outerdivine-divine *[außergöttlich-göttlich]* who, abandoning his outerdivine
majesty [seine außergöttliche Hoheit], manifests himself as a man." Otherwise
said,

> the Incarnation is not an other-becoming *[ein anders-Werden],* but only a
> visible-becoming *[ein sichtbar-Werden].* It is not humanity, as we say habit-
> ually, which is the shell *[Hülle],* but the *morphē theou,* the outerdivine-divine
> being *[das außergöttlich-göttliche Seyn]* which was the concealment of di-
> vinity. . . . This being is, in the Incarnation, deprived of glory, of divinity,

but thereby, it is the *true* glory, the glory of the only begotten Son of the Father which is visible.[97]

Christ is not the Incarnation of God per se.[98] Rather, he is the "visible-becoming" of a divine being, namely, the second potency of nature (A^2). This is why Schelling can say that Christ's Incarnation is not substantially an "other-becoming": this potency has always been in the world. In Christ, however, it reveals itself as the mediating potency par excellence. How does this occur? The Incarnation is primarily the work of the third potency: "It is, in effect, only by *virtue* of the superior potency [A^3] that the antecedent potency can *materialize* itself, can be made the stuff or matter of a birth to come." Schelling argues that one can understand the requisite relational changes among the potencies as follows: "If A^2 becomes matter, that is = first potency, then A^3 becomes = the second, which is to say that the demiurgic function [of the second] passes to the third potency. This is the first formulation, to be sure, of this relatively material, but also relatively immaterial base of the man Jesus. In sum, the man Jesus is brought into the world as all humans, according to the natural course of things." The course of nature changes, however, at the moment of Christ's Baptism. During this event,

> the Spirit is made visible and descends upon [Christ]. This descent of the Spirit at the instant when the Messiah is declared Son of God . . . shows that from this instant the complete divinity is re-established in He who has become man. He is from now on *truly eikōn theou tou aoratou,* visible image of the invisible God. As the Apostle says, the entire divinity lives in him bodily or completely (this is what the word *sōmatikōs* signifies).[99]

Christ's "visibility" is extremely important to Schelling. It is what distinguishes Christian Revelation from the "mere revelation" of the Greeks and Jews. Christ is the ideal God of nature become real. The experience of divine "visibility" in Christ is the fact, the historical content, of Revelation per se. But even this Revelation of divinity progresses throughout several events in Christ's worldly existence. It increases in his death, Resurrection, and Ascension.

97. Ibid., 2.4.201, 153 (on the Incarnation, see 184–85; on God's nature, see 159–60), 163, 165.
98. Cf. ibid., 2.4.164.
99. Ibid., 2.4.84; cf. Col. 1:15, 2:9.

Christ's Death and Resurrection

Schelling understands the Resurrection also to have been the work of the third potency. But this potency is strengthened by the decisive change that Christ's death brings about in the first. The pagans understood that matter, the living principle of death (= B), could be conquered only in an "exterior" way—for example, by conceiving the idea of an afterlife and writing myths about this possible state of existence. Generally speaking, this insight was gained by virtue of the "natural or *equivalently* cosmic potency" (that is, A^3) under the "lower will" of nature. It was precisely due to its natural status that it was unable to conquer death "at its *root*," and this is precisely what is needed for "an interior reconciliation, a reconciliation *with God.*" This is the reconciliation that Christ's death and the Spirit's Resurrection of the Son bring about. The key to this transformation of death, Schelling supposes, is to be found in a particular characteristic of the mediating potency once it has become Christ: "the will toward total submission to God." To be submissive to God, "this signifies precisely only to be submissive to this principle of divine malevolence [= B]. . . . [T]his principle *was* the cause of death. It is precisely in the necessity of death that all of its power and force *[Macht und Gewalt]* is manifested." If the mediating potency wanted to submit completely to "the malevolence of God (to take this upon himself), it had to submit until the *death. Without* this, the submission would not have been perfect; it would have been only a submission with reserve. It is only by advancing *until* death, that *all* resistance was annulled *[aufgehoben].*"[100]

The first potency subsists only by excluding the being of the second: "[T]his principle *is* the malevolent divinity only and in the measure where it excludes the mediating potency. If, therefore, this exclusion is rendered *impossible,* then its force as principle of malevolence *[als Princip des Unwillens]* is deprived and annulled." Schelling thinks that Christ's acceptance of death was completely free, thus causing the first potency to become completely actual and, at the same time, completely impotent. Death is thereby overcome in principle, leaving Christ with the ability to "cover" or protect humanity from death, henceforth, so that "the Father [= B] no longer sees humanity" when believers "put on" Christ, "but only Christ his Son."[101] Once the mediating potency (A^2) has completely surrendered its life, thus

---

100. Ibid., 2.4.194, 202, 202–3.
101. Ibid., 2.4.203, 205.

reducing B to impotence, only the supreme spirit (A^3) is left with the potency to bring life out of death in Christ's Resurrection.

Schelling says that the Resurrection was, in effect, an intensification of the Incarnation. The Holy Spirit also dominates in this event. Christ's natural body is changed, by virtue of the superior potency (A^3), into a spiritual body. Only at this point does Christ become perfectly human: "[T]he *man*, Christ, is *for himself alone* equal to the divine in its *entirety*. It is in this which is found, at the same time, primordial man restored with even more brilliance." Schelling admits that one cannot find an experiential "analogue" for the body of the resurrected Christ and, consequently, that his account of the Resurrection cannot be made completely intelligible. This is an important admission. Clearly, he does not think that perfection is attainable in this life. Accordingly, in an allusion to Georg Hegel and Ludwig Feuerbach, he explicitly rejects all thinkers who attempt to understand themselves as God's equals.[102] But the sobriety in this admission also comes with a price.

By accepting the Resurrection as a historical fact, as he must in order to defend the historical superiority of Christianity to paganism and Judaism, Schelling leaves behind the universal order of experience and focuses on the alleged experiences of others. This means, according to his own understanding of philosophy, that the cornerstone of his "philosophy" of revelation is not based on experience—"mystical empiricism" notwithstanding. If Schelling were to argue that the Resurrection was experienced concretely by some, then he would need to explain the exceptional significance of this extraordinary experience of the divine—beyond, for example, the theophanies ascribed to Roman emperors, Egyptian pharaohs, Indian saints, and so on. In brief, he would have to explain why *vicarious* experiences of Christ's Resurrection can become the guiding focus in his philosophy of revelation. But he makes no attempt to explain this sudden change, apparently failing to notice that the experiences interpreted by his positive philosophy have become relatively idiosyncratic, partial and private in scope. He simply continues to develop his account of the historical meaning of Christianity, now based on beliefs alone.

Christ's Ascension

Among the great events in the life of Christ, there is one about which we have said nothing: his becoming-invisible *[das Unsichtbarwerden Christi]*,

102. Ibid., 2.4.218–19, 220; cf. 164–65.

his elevation from the earth after the Resurrection, that which we call his *Ascension to Heaven [Himmelfahrt]*. We should, therefore, explain ourselves equally on this point. This we could equally do, but we cannot presuppose the required notions to this end, nor begin to develop them here. It would be necessary, *e.g.*, to treat and analyze here the matter of that which we call infinite space, in the same way that we formerly treated, and presented in an entirely new light, the doctrine of infinite time.

After this promising beginning, Schelling chooses not to undertake this analysis, precisely at the place in his *Philosophy of Revelation* where it is needed most. And neither does he address it anywhere else. Instead, he leaves his readers with the impression that they need to keep in mind their perspectival view of space in order to understand Christ's "ascension." He says:

> If, for example, in a particular point of the universe space has become a necessary form of existence, and therefore equally a necessary form of intuition, it is *from this point,* and therefore *relatively* that all the system of the world would appear [to be] in space; but it does not follow that all would be *effectively* in space. And could not the distances which appear to us to be spatial not also be explained from simple relations and different ideas? If it is man who posited and does not cease to posit the outer-divine *[außergöttliche],* and thus the spatial world, one must guard oneself from thinking that this action could be understood otherwise than *relatively* beyond the system [of the world] with which *he* is in connection.

Schelling says that these clues must suffice about the Ascension for the "intelligent auditors *[intelligente Zuhörer]*" of his lectures upon whom he counts.[103] In other words, he leaves his audience to surmise what he wishes to communicate.

Here is a possible interpretation of what he has provided. In the "Ascension," Christ only appeared to ascend into the heavens, that is, from the outer-divine-positing perspective of fallen humanity. In fact, what happened was this: Forty days after the Resurrection, Christ became "invisible," that is to say, he died. Yet he continued to live as the Holy Spirit, and later appeared to descend as such "from above." The "Ascension" of Christ thus causes the beginning of the Church and the *caput mortuum* of paganism. It was necessary for Christ (A^2) to depart, so that that which is superior, the Holy Spirit (A^3), could become further actualized. This claim corresponds to

103. Ibid., 2.4.235, 236.

the "law" that Schelling says has been guiding his reflections all along: "the anterior must *leave, i.e.,* give up its place, in order that the ulterior may *come.*" Christ must continue to live as the Holy Spirit until such time when all of nature will be transfigured into his "spiritual body." It is only at this time that true immortality will be actual, for true immortality is this: "that man, who is internally a purely spiritual being, also becomes as such *externally.*" True immortality is when "the body assumes the nature of a spiritual body, of a *sōmatos pneumatikou.*" Schelling says explicitly that "faith" is required to accept this future transfiguration of humanity in general, of which the Incarnation and Resurrection were only parts.[104]

Faith: Teleological and Hypothetical

In one sense, it would seem that Schelling understands faith to be "the substance of things hoped for and the proof of things unseen" (Heb. 11:1). This is his distinctively Christian acceptance of faith: trust in the future perfection of humanity—intimated with the eschatological index of "philosophical religion"—the "first fruits" of which have been revealed in Christ's Resurrection. This aspect of faith may be called his *teleological* faith. But Schelling continues his discussion. He does not wish to rest in a teleological faith that lacks content. He also grants that a certain type of faith is required at the beginning of philosophical investigations. This faith *trusts in hypotheses* that may or may not lead to the desired "Sabbath rest" of teleological faith. Without the basic trust that something worth knowing may be found, Schelling contends, one would never even begin philosophical inquiries in the first place. Thus, one may speak of Schelling's *hypothetical* faith, his limited acceptance of a properly philosophical type of faith. But there is more. The movement from hypothetical degrees to teleological perfection is said to give faith its true content.[105] Schelling gives no indication that this movement can be completed within this life. Indeed, because the divine author of history has not yet brought about the telos of humanity in general, during the time of "philosophical religion," Schelling expects that philosophical work leading toward this "Sabbath rest" will afford no more than brief periods of rest in this life—for example, in revelations that occur through historiographic studies. He expresses some dissatisfaction with scholars who appeal

---

104. Ibid., 2.4.239 (Ascension as end of paganism), 236–37, 221.
105. Cf. ibid., 2.4.15–16, 13–14.

to faith too quickly, in order to "explain" matters that they would rather not think about seriously; he clearly *wants* to think first and believe later. But his cursory discussion of the Ascension is an important exception to this rule.[106]

It is relatively clear why Schelling avoids serious discussion of the Ascension. Elsewhere, he acknowledges that "in more than one instance" he finds New Testament evangelists "naïvely transcribing" events of which they do not understand the full context: "Their comportment, equivalent partially to mythological consciousness, expresses also that which escapes their understanding. It is in *this* sense that we must conserve, in principle, the concept of inspiration."[107] The Ascension is one of these instances. According to Schelling's historiography, "inspiration" was the proper mode of religious representation during the time of earliest Zabism. Thus, when the evangelists describe Christ's Ascension to the heavens, they regress back to the level of consciousness used to name and worship the Sky god of early Zabism, leaving Schelling with the problem of another historical regression—this time within his paradigmatic tradition—for which he does not provide an account.

To be sure, history neither begins nor ends with the Ascension. Schelling is well aware of this basic fact of life, which is likely one reason for his willingness to set aside problems in the details of his account in order to develop a more significant part of the positive philosophy: his history of the Church.

106. Schelling's Christocentric thinking has been the cause of some apparent embarrassment, even among his most sympathetic interpreters. Although vital to his understanding of positive philosophy, his Christology is politely ignored by Andrew Bowie, who insists that "the best arguments" of the positive philosophy "stand without theology." This claim is perhaps why Bowie's reading of Schelling considers "only certain aspects of the later philosophy in detail" (*Modern European Philosophy*, 129). Of course, Schelling would disagree. The positive philosophy is historical philosophy, and this requires especially the unique difference of Christ's Revelation in order for history to be intelligible as a progression of divine revelations. In a manner that is more faithful to Schelling's project, one scholar has recently attempted to interpret the christological core of the positive philosophy as positive *philosophy*. See Christian Danz, *Die philosophische Christologie F. W. J. Schellings*. Danz's work may be consulted for a more sustained discussion of the topics I have been able only to touch upon here. The central liability in his work, however, is that Danz neglects to address Schelling's difficulty with the doctrine of the Ascension. His account of Schelling's Christology ends with the Resurrection. Paul Tillich briefly mentions Christ's "exaltation" in his books on Schelling's philosophy. But he does so in such a way that Schelling's understanding of this doctrine appears to have been simply orthodox. See Tillich, *Mysticism and Guilt-Consciousness in Schelling's Philosophical Development*, 125; and *The Construction of the History of Religion in Schelling's Positive Philosophy*, 155. Clearly, there is more to Schelling's gloss on the Ascension than a repetition of ecclesiastical orthodoxy.

107. Schelling, *Philosophie der Offenbarung*, in *Werke*, 2.4.177.

He argues that the Church falls prey to the power of the natural potencies, even though Christ had already allegedly overcome them.[108] This claim marks another significant change in Schelling's historiography, one for which he offers no explanation. What the spirit was able to accomplish in one man, Christ, now takes a great deal of time to manifest in the rest of human consciousness. The Church begins a long "external" history, already considered in the introduction to this section and in Voegelin's interpretation of Schelling's eschatology. The history of the Church, we recall, will eventually lead beyond itself to the time of "philosophical religion," when God will finally be known to be "all in all." Schelling states clearly that this time has not yet come; philosophical religion "does not exist."[109] The highest development of consciousness to date is that which can be found in cultures formed by the "interior" history of essential Christianity. Philosophical religion, Schelling implies, will emerge from a culture such as his own: an Occident just waiting to happen.

Summary

Schelling's historical philosophy articulates a discernible order of history progressing through three types of religion. The first type is "mythological religion." It has an absolutely prehistorical *(vorgeschichtliche)* beginning. This is the religion of God's blind "nature" par excellence. At its beginning, it is the religion of unconscious immediacy, where no consciousness of the difference between a material deity and the "one true God" of the spirit is said to exist. Given the dynamic character of nature, however, this phase is said to have an internal progression of its own. It moves from the experience of nature's material order (B) to a relatively spiritual experience of its freedom (A³), as symbols for the dramatis personae who rule in various world mythologies become represented increasingly as spiritual gods. Once Schelling finds the mythologies of Egypt, India, and Greece to have developed symbols for all of the natural potencies (B, A², A³), he says that the relatively prehistoric *(vorhistorische)* period has been reached.

This progression leads mythological religion to an incomplete form of the next religion, the "revealed religion" of the Jews. This stage is, properly speaking, the beginning of consciously historical time *(historische Zeit),* though

---

108. Cf. ibid., 2.4.295–96.

109. Schelling, *Philosophie der Mythologie,* in *Werke,* 2.1.250; *Philosophie der Offenbarung,* in *Werke,* 2.4.333.

particularly among the Jews. But Jewish revelation is incomplete. Early Judaism is said to be plagued with mythic and pagan elements. The revelatory consciousness of the "one true God" beyond nature does not come all at once. Jewish religion must also progress. And it does so by moving from the relatively spiritual necessity of the Mosaic Law (B guided by a "higher will") to the relative freedom from the law proclaimed by the prophets (A³). The prophets prophesy the completion of revealed religion in the future Messiah, whom Schelling takes to be a personal figure. Finally, it is only with Jesus Christ, Schelling argues, that the natural necessity of mythological religion— and its increasingly spiritual counterparts in the Mosaic Law and prophets— comes to its end.

The Incarnation of Christ marks the telos, the end toward which the mythological process and the "mere revelation" of the Jews was headed. At the birth of Christianity, consciousness is elevated to the freedom of a relatively complete historical perspective, although only in Christ and his followers. From the perspective of historical consciousness, the "truths" of the past appear to have been established on merely "natural" grounds. Christ's free unification of God's immanent nature (the Mosaic Law) and transcendent essence (the prophetic freedom from the Law) reveals the perfection of humanity to come. But Christianity is also historicized by Schelling. It simply opens the way to the true religion of freedom, when all will be like Christ. Thus, Christianity must also go through a historical progression, much like the natural development of other religions.[110] It does so by progressing from the legalistic orientation of Petrine Christianity (early Catholicism, dominated by a spiritually elevated B) to the orientation toward grace in the Pauline Christianity of the Reformation (A²).[111]

The beginning of the final age is marked by extreme birth pangs for the culmination of history. This is the time in which Schelling found himself to be living. He realizes that the former types of Christianity offered, so to speak, better news than any of the preceding traditions. But the good news is truly yet to come. The last phase of Christianity, the Johannine (A³), is indistinguishable from the third and last type of religion: "philosophical religion." Schelling's appeal to this phase of religion is an eschatological index. He even wonders whether it is properly called a type of Christianity at all. It does not occur, strictly speaking, within history. Rather, it describes the "absolute monotheism," the absolute identity of the real and the ideal,

110. Cf. Schelling, *Philosophie der Mythologie*, in *Werke*, 2.1.258–59.
111. Cf. Schelling, *Philosophie der Offenbarung*, in *Werke*, 2.4.313–23.

which can come about only when God brings history to an end. In the projected stage of philosophical religion, human consciousness of the divine will be immediate. It will no longer require discursive reasoning, historical consciousness and the like, to bring it to relative immediacy. Everyone will immediately know God to be "all in all."[112]

Much of this presentation may sound Hegelian. Yet, unlike Hegel, Schelling does not leave his interpreters to wonder whether he thinks history has come to its end within his own philosophical reflections. He declares bluntly that philosophical religion "does not exist," for God is not yet known *by all* to be "all in all." At most, Schelling seems to think of himself as a philosophical prophet, one who sees what the "Promised Land" will entail but has not been given the way to enter it. The changes needed in the order of consciousness cannot be brought about by human fiat. They must be actualized by the divine. In contrast to Hegel's negative dialectic of annulment *(Aufhebungsdialektik)*— where a thesis is posited, negated by its antithesis, and finally overcome by their synthesis—Schelling's positive dialectic of generation *(Erzeugungsdialektik)* attempts to have a thesis come to be only by virtue of its antithesis (B). This beginning is intelligible, he argues, only when one focuses on the existential, rather than the formal priority of his antithesis.[113] Rather than "positing" his beginning, Schelling hypothesizes that the divine *Prius* establishes itself in the reality of historical experience and symbolization. Thus, mythological religion is the unconscious or blind antithesis (B) of history, the religion in which the angry or jealous "Father" God is eventually dominant; revealed religion is the relatively conscious thesis of history (A²), the religion in which the "Son" is eventually dominant; philosophical religion will be the fully conscious synthesis of material nature and historical spirit (A³), the religion of the "Spirit," the end of history and an effective re-creation of the world.[114] This is, generally speaking, how the dialectic of the *Potenzenlehre* is said to reveal itself within and beyond the economy of world history.

Within the present order of consciousness, all attempts to conflate either the real or the ideal into one or the other do not yield what Schelling calls "philosophical religion." When vulgar materialists attempt to explain the ideal simply as an epiphenomenon of the real, they regress to a natural or

---

112. Cf. ibid., 2.4.324–33.

113. For discussion of Schelling's *Erzeugungsdialektik*, see Beach, *Potencies of God(s)*, 111–29, 136–47.

114. On Schelling's equation of the potencies with the persons of the Christian Trinity, vis-à-vis creation, see *Philosophie der Offenbarung*, in *Werke*, 2.3.340–45. On their historical significance, see *supra*, 155 n. 67.

mythological state of consciousness, usually unawares. They pretend as though divine transcendence was never experienced or symbolized in history. This type of historical regression is still possible because "God's nature" (matter) continues to appear as though it exists independently from "God's transcendent essence" (freedom). Similarly, when idealists attempt to explain matter simply as a false appearance of the ideal, their thinking tends to become lost in the mystical aspects of revealed religion, and the natural world becomes an illusion. This type of historical regression is still possible because God's transcendent essence continues to appear as though it is substantially different from God's immanent nature. Schelling rejects both materialist and idealist "solutions" to the paradox of consciousness in history.[115] At most, he hopes that the gradual elevation of historical consciousness that can be found in the past will eventually amount to the reconciliation of God's immanent nature and transcendent essence broken by the Fall, or the complete realization that nature's essential freedom is eternal.

Conclusion

Schelling's historical philosophy attempts to account for the evolution of divine and human consciousness within a substantially permanent order of reality. He acknowledges no substantial changes in human nature or the divine in his entire elaboration of this history. When the potencies of "God's nature" become relatively actual at different times in history, nothing changes in the substance of the All, according to Schelling. He discusses only existential

---

115. Schelling would have been displeased with the later attempts, among others, of Engels and Kierkegaard, both of whom were once his students, to understand the history of reality in predominantly material or spiritual terms. Walter Schulz has argued that it was precisely in the perceived failure of Schelling to articulate a coherent positive philosophy that Kierkegaard, Marx, Schopenhauer, and Nietzsche were led to take radically different philosophical stances on the substance of history/reality. Once Schelling's prioritization of the irrational destroyed German idealism, or so it seemed, it left nothing of a persuasive solution to fill the void it created. See Schulz, *Die Vollendung des deutschen Idealismus in der Spätphilosophie Schellings.* In contrast to more conventional interpreters, Schulz argues that Schelling's *Spätphilosophie* forms a consistent whole. Far from destroying German idealism, it provides the historical ground by which it is supported, albeit in the provisional light of history. Thus, Schulz finds it possible to emphasize the negative or quasi-rational achievements of Schelling's later thought. Schulz's attempt to rejoin Schelling's *disjecta membra* resembles Voegelin's. However, Voegelin emphasizes the positive-historical aspect of Schelling's thought, rather than its ability to support neo-Kantian rationalism.

changes that occur in consciousness, when the potencies become principles of material and spiritual order. No substantial change in human nature occurs, for example, in the transition from mythological to revelatory experiences of the world's order. Schelling grants that the same potencies of nature must be presupposed as the constituents of the humanity that undergoes both types of experience. The potencies simply manifest different patterns of actualization in history, thus yielding different accents on nature or its beyond as the true source of order in the discernible epochs of revelation.[116] "Mere revelation" is found among the esoteric Greeks and prophetic Jews, even before Christ becomes "visible" as the "real" principle of the "mediating potency." Thus, Schelling's work effectively begins to weaken the ecclesiastical distinction between natural reason and divine Revelation. For Schelling, the entire order of history is a progression in consciousness from natural revelation to supernatural Revelation. The study of history is, therefore, an inherently theological matter. To be sure, the distinction between reason and Revelation is not explicitly overcome in Schelling's positive philosophy, but it is weakened nonetheless. Finally, the *Potenzenlehre* provides an initial basis for understanding a broad range of religious experiences as symbolic equivalents for one another. But Schelling encounters considerable difficulties in his attempts to demonstrate the *universal* progression of human consciousness in history. Edward Beach has provided an insightful summary of this problem:

> Schelling wants to present his empirical studies as separately grounded and significantly corroborative of his abstract theoretical system. In the actual practice of his "historical-critical method," however, Schelling tends to treat the phenomena of religion more like ciphers to be decoded in terms of a pre-established schema than like fresh data to be analyzed by strictly empirical methods. Modern [that is, contemporary] readers of his work often have the impression that he is trying to mold the material to fit a procrustean bed of aprioristic ideas, instead of proceeding by framing new hypotheses to fit the facts.[117]

This difficulty was also sensed by Voegelin. It accounts for why Schelling's achievement is said to have been "marred" by an "inclination to intellectualize the unconscious and to reduce its movements to the formula of a dialectical process" (*OH*, 3:193). Indeed, in his attempt to see the potencies of nature manifest themselves in a historical succession of world mythologies,

---

116. Cf. Schelling, *Philosophie der Mythologie*, in *Werke*, 2.2.315.
117. Beach, *Potencies of God(s)*, 150.

Schelling does struggle with some traditions more than others. The *Potenzenlehre* is supposed to account for historical change and constancy within God's nature, of which human nature is a part. As such, when God's nature develops, in the transformation from potencies to actualized principles, all world mythologies should be effected in exactly the same way. But the historical data confronted by Schelling do not support this hypothesis conclusively. Stagnations and regressions between peoples—decisive problems with the historical dimension of the *Potenzenlehre*—were found in Persian, Indian, and Buddhist religions; the evangelists' symbolization of Christ's Ascension; and the complete enigma of "Chinese atheism."

In order to articulate a thoroughly empirical philosophy of history, it appears that Schelling's historiography needs to be redone.

CHAPTER THREE

Voegelin's Differentiated Historiography

The origin of things is the Apeiron [Unlimited]. . . .
It is necessary for things to perish into that from which
they were born; for they pay one another penalty for
their injustice according to the ordinance of Time.
—Anaximander, fragments A9, B1

Voegelin attempted to rework Schelling's historiography. He did so in two discernible stages. First, from *The New Science of Politics* (1952) to volume 3 of *Order and History* (1957), he tried another reworking of the *historia sacra* tradition, arguing that the world-transcendent God described in Christian theology providentially determines human experiences of the divine in a progressive series of revelations. This aspect of Voegelin's historical thought is what I shall call his *differentiated* historiography. This term describes the period when he develops the "inner" history of the progressive "differentiation" of consciousness as its pattern and problems were left behind by Schelling. With respect to its problems, Voegelin knows in advance that it will not be possible for him to develop a natural or universal history of spiritual progress; Schelling's historiography has revealed, notwithstanding its intentions, that human consciousness in the Orient as well as in some Occidental peoples simply has not developed with universal conformity. Thus, Voegelin abandons Schelling's attempt to show that changes in the ground of being, marking the discernible epochs of history, are experienced simultaneously throughout human consciousness in general. He turns, instead, to reformulate the main pattern of Schelling's work as an exclusively Western phenomenon. He argues that the developing stages of spiritual consciousness in the West constitute "representative" truth for all of humanity, due to the emergence of universal thinking in Western philosophy and the revelatory religion of the Jews. Voegelin argues consistently throughout this period that the philosophical study of order in sacred history may reveal the meaningful order of history. This contention is formulated in the well-known, programmatic statement by which *Order and History* is introduced: "The order of history emerges from the history of order" (*OH,* 1:ix). In other words, the order *of* history has a discernible *eidos,* or essence, the meaning of which can be found by studying the emergence of spiritual meaning *in* history. For Voegelin, as with Schelling, the essence of history is found to be progressive or "adventitious" until Christ, always with respect to the initiating activity of the "divine ground" in human consciousness. The essence of history is a "process" in consciousness, one that progresses from "compact" to "differentiated" experiences and symbolizations of the divine—from societies in the ancient Near East to Jewish and Christian Revelation, respectively. After Christ, human consciousness either recedes from the "maximal" truth of Christian Revelation, through the growth of "Gnosticism," or retains the "acme" of truth in Christ and early Christianity. Thus, in the period of his *differentiated* historiography, Voegelin uses the level of historical consciousness attained by Christian theologians as a measure to classify, as necessary though subordinate, the levels of consciousness attained during times marked by the predominance of cosmological myth, classical philosophy, and Jewish Revelation. His initial historiography thus identifies fundamental differences between societies ordered by myth, reason, or Revelation—where this triad represents an ascending scale of intellectual clarity with respect to the human condition.

In the period from *Anamnesis* (1966) to volume 5 of *Order and History* (1987), Voegelin becomes aware of ways in which he needs to modify his former historiography, due chiefly to an important discovery. He realizes that the classic philosophers of ancient Greece—especially Plato and Aristotle—understood reason *(noesis)* to be constituted by experiences of divine revelation and, accordingly, begins to argue that the order of consciousness cannot be thought to change as a historical progression from human reason to divine Revelation. The common distinction between "natural reason" and "divine Revelation," used by many postclassical theologians and philosophers alike, is found to be an untenable convention, even a "conceit" formulated by church fathers seeking to gain a monopoly on the concept of Revelation. Accordingly, Voegelin begins to emphasize the experiential "equivalence" of mythic, rational, and revelatory truth in history. I refer to this period of his historical thought, therefore, as his *equivalent* historiography.

These technical terms, the *differentiated* and *equivalent* historiographies, have been introduced in order to account for an accentual change in Voegelin's historical thinking. They adequately reflect Voegelin's own account of how his understanding of order in history appears to change over the course of his mature works (cf. *OH*, 4:1–20). In fact, however, the change that Voegelin announces in his program changes nothing significant in his historiography. Remarkably, his discovery of "equivalent" experiences of revelation in pre-Christian and otherwise "pagan" societies—occasionally extending back as far as Hesiod—is not enough to alter his former conception of history as a meaningful progression toward Christ. The "equivalent" experiences of revelation were not simply equal, he maintains. The revelatory equivalents of classical philosophy and Christian theology are said, once again, to advance on a scale from compact to differentiated levels of truth, respectively. Hence, the initial *progression* in Voegelin's differentiated historiography—from myth, to philosophy, to Revelation—is simply replaced by the *progression* from "noetic" (Greek) to "pneumatic" (Christian) types of revelation. Even in his final analyses, Voegelin's historiography continues to turn, as it did with Schelling, on the Revelation of Christ's Incarnation and Resurrection as the eschatological measure of existential truth in history. Thus, despite possible claims to the contrary, all of which will be analyzed in context, I shall argue that Voegelin's mature historiography remains that of a developmental historicist in the Schellingian style. His later search for order *in* history retains the characteristic features of his former attempt to understand the order *of* history.[1]

1. These points are not generally acknowledged in Voegelin scholarship. Many scholars tend to accept Voegelin's claim that his historiography changes significantly, beginning in *Order and History*, vol. 4. For representative examples, see Glenn Hughes, "Eric Voegelin's View of History as a Drama of Transfiguration"; and Gebhardt, "Toward Universal Mankind." Like Voegelin himself, both Hughes and Gebhardt begin by noting that, strictly speaking, Voegelin does not have an abstract "philosophy of history," but they conclude by reproducing Voegelin's abstract account of the order *of* history nonetheless. John Ranieri is one of few interpreters to notice that Voegelin's historiography does not change significantly in his latest work, but Ranieri does not discuss this point in any detail, as his book is not primarily concerned with interpreting Voegelin's historiography. See Ranieri, *Eric Voegelin and the Good Society*, 215, 233, 236.

To support my thesis will require a good deal of exegetical analysis, constituting the next two chapters of this study, because the thinking involved spans several decades of Voegelin's career, and the points I raise are not generally known to scholarship. Chapters 3 and 4 have been separated to reflect the change that Voegelin announces in his own thinking. Yet they clearly form a thematic unit. The central concern here is to provide a more detailed commentary than is now common on both periods of Voegelin's historiographic thought, focusing on salient points in his adoption and transformation of distinctively Schellingian themes and taking care not to confuse terminological changes with substantial ones. Finally, in order to avoid becoming lost in voluminous details, I have concentrated much of my discussion on Voegelin's lifelong attempt to understand the experiential dynamics of reason and revelation in history.

Voegelin's Knowledge of Schelling's Historiography

The extent to which Voegelin knew of and appreciated Schelling's historiography can be initially determined from relevant passages in his "Last Orientation." Voegelin has brief though high praise for Schelling's ability to understand that historical existence is "the key to [anthropological] speculation." Put simply, Schelling wins this praise by placing a historical and universal spin on the Platonic dictum that appears to find an exact copy of the order of a polis in the individual souls of its members. In Schelling's words, favorably quoted by Voegelin, the order of universal history is thought to be akin to the history of an individual soul writ large: "'There is a light in the darkness,'" Schelling states. "'According to the old and almost outworn saying, man is the world on a small scale. Thus the processes of human life from the utmost depth [A^1] to the highest consummation [A^3] must be in accordance with the processes of universal life. It is certain: anybody who could write the history of his own life from the ground [A^1], would at the same time have concentrated the history of the universe *(Weltall)* in a brief synopsis.'" The proper task of the philosophical historian, therefore, is to recollect how advances in spiritual insight have contributed to the formation of the historian's own order of consciousness in the present. The philosophical historian seeks to know himself, in this case, by recovering as much as possible of the entire development of human consciousness in history. He can do this because his soul is "[d]rawn from the source of things and akin to it," always having within itself the principle for a "'co-knowledge *(Mitwissenschaft)* of creation'" ("LO," 210).² This condition of the soul is what allows it ostensibly to grasp the intelligible order of history.³

The human soul is thought to be a process, with its life substantially identical to the processive life of the universe. Schelling claims, accordingly, that a "double life" of the individual also manifests itself in history. Voegelin interprets: "History thus has a double meaning. It is, first, the actual course of natural and human events in the universe; and this course of events becomes history in the second meaning if it is understood by man as a meaningful unfolding of the universe." Schelling does not claim that the natural potencies experienced in the present order of consciousness have always been actual and therefore known by human beings. The potencies of nature have a history in which they have become actualized in epochs that can be discerned by the trained historian. Specifically, the contemplative historian discovers the second dimension of history, its "inner" meaning, when it is recognized that external changes in symbols reflect initially internal changes in experiences. "This internalization of the course of events, this immersion of the external process into a movement of the soul," Voegelin asserts, "is possible because the internalizing soul is itself part of the stream [of reality and its history]. When the soul gives meaning to the stream, it discovers the stream and its meaning in itself. In this sense the soul is knowledge, and history is a science of the soul." All genuine experiences in history and the symbols by which they are expressed arise from the unconscious depth of the soul. To read the changing trail of symbols in history is to recollect what experiences God has caused to surface in human consciousness. Such a reading begins by the contemplative return, the "anamnesis," to the order of one's own consciousness. The order of consciousness discovered in one's own "history" is then expanded into the order of human history in general ("LO," 211, 212).

For example, the notion that God transcends the world, at least in part, is an experiential discovery that has a history. This discovery was made in what Voegelin and (the latest) Schelling take to be the highest form of historical existence attained thus far, that is, Christian theology and its focus on the

---

2. Voegelin citing Schelling, *Die Weltalter,* in *Werke,* 1.8.207, 200.

3. For the Platonic notion that the large political letters of justice *may* or *may not* be identical to the fine print of justice in the individual soul, see *Republic* 368c–369a (and *NSP,* 61 for Voegelin's later citation). Note the interpretive change that Schelling and Voegelin bring to the Platonic text. Whereas Socrates *questions* whether the large and small letters say the same thing in individual souls, Schelling and Voegelin take him simply to assume that they do. Then, instead of reading the large letters first, as Socrates suggests, they look to the fine print of the individual soul in order to read the large letters of historical order last.

historicity of consciousness. Thus, when a modern philosopher discovers the notion of transcendence to be a living reality in the soul, this notion must be traced back to its historical origin in Judeo-Christian experiences and their symbolizations of the divine in order to be understood in the present. Failure to make this connection will result in a fundamental misuse of the symbol, in this case, "transcendence." Genuine symbols are not made arbitrarily, but surface involuntarily as the divine reveals itself in different ways to successive people and civilizations in history. The ability to make and understand this broader discovery reveals the substantial bond between the present order of consciousness and its past. Thus, what might be called Schelling's open projection psychology is not purely arbitrary—that is to say, in the nihilistic sense where projections are made out of nothing—nor from a purely "immanent" soul cut off in all respects from the divine. Instead, Voegelin argues, "the projection renders results because the materials of human existence in history are manifestations of the same stream of unconscious nature to which the projecting philosopher himself belongs." The proper task of the contemplative historian is, therefore, to construct a dialectical response to what has been given by the divine, not to indulge in the error of thinking that one could construct or project a reality of one's *own* making: "Projection of meaning and stimulation by materials interpenetrate so that the materials receive their meaning from the existence of the interpreter, while they in their turn touch the unconscious and bring to the level of consciousness meanings that otherwise would have remained submerged. History receives meaning from the soul, while the soul discovers the historical meanings as strata in its existence" ("LO," 240).

Schelling's historiography is progressive, but the progression of epochs leading to the present order of consciousness has not been determined by human fiat. He argues, instead, that all progressive changes in epochs reflect relatively new actualizations of divine potencies. History is made by the divine, not by the relatively immanent will of human beings. This point leaves him to describe the intelligible order of history as a "theogonic process" that "unfolds" in the human soul: "Pagan polytheism [dominated by A^1], Hebrew monotheism [eventually dominated by A^2], and Christianity [eventually dominated by A^3] are stages of a theogonic process in which divine revelation and human creation of symbols interpenetrate each other. Myth and revelation are the vessels of divine self-affirmation in the world through man; they are part of the history of the universe just as much as of the history of living forms" ("LO," 211; cf. 226). Evolution, properly speaking, is known not through changes in external phenomena, but by recovering the progressive history of inner experiences of order.[4] Progress in history is substantial, initiated by the divine, and intelligible. It is not to be found in the phenomenal construction of an arbitrary system, based on mundane notions of progress. Rather, it looks primarily toward the past in order to understand the intractable foundation upon which the present has been built. This situation places certain limitations on historical knowledge. Voegelin praises Schelling, against Hegel, for granting that we cannot know the meaning of history as a whole. Schelling is distinguished precisely for his ability to understand that the future can never be brought within the control of a dialectician:

> In Hegel's dialectic, the movement [of the Spirit *(Geist)* in its historical unfolding] has come to its end and philosophy has reached its systematic end with the end of the objective movement; for Schelling the dialectical elaboration of the anamnesis is a work of art that does not prejudice the elaborations of future artists. Hegel's philosophy of history bears still the marks of Enlightenment insofar as the Idea has come to its full, reflective self-understanding in the present; Schelling is beyond Enlightenment insofar as man has become an unexhausted historical existence. For Hegel there is no perspective into a future; for Schelling the unconscious is pregnant with time that has not yet become past. ("LO," 213–14)

Although Voegelin says that the dialectic of Schelling and Hegel is "derived historically" from the same root—the mystical tradition of Jakob Böhme—he also grants that Schelling breaks with Hegel's attempt to objectify what the mystic gains in visionary experiences of the divine: "Schelling insists that 'we do not live in vision *(im Schauen);* our knowledge is piecemeal, and that means it must be produced piece by piece in divisions and stages, and that cannot be done without any reflection.'" This is one of the clearest instances where, as previously noted, Schelling returns behind Hegel to Kant for his understanding of the proper scope and limitations of *reflective* consciousness. This return bears upon Schelling's understanding of historical dialectic. Against Hegel, he maintains that "'the very existence and necessity of dialectic prove that philosophy is not at all yet real science'" ("LO," 214, 213).[5]

---

4. For Voegelin's critique of Darwinian evolution as the work of biological phenomenalists, see "LO," 184–87. Voegelin also draws on Kant's understanding of the limitations of evolutionary thought, specifically from the *Kritik der Urteilskraft* (§§ 80 ff.), when he refers to this text in a public talk from 1977. See Zdravko Planinc, ed., "Structures in Consciousness," *Voegelin Research News* 2:3 (1996), available on-line at http://vax2.concordia.ca/~vorenews; *Conversations,* 146, and "Autobiographical Statement," 117–18.

5. Voegelin citing Schelling, *Die Weltalter,* in *Werke,* 1.8.203, 202.

Schelling continues to understand his age as a time of struggle, though as one that may look cautiously toward a glorious future: "Heralds of [the Golden Age], we do not want to gather its fruit before it is ripe, nor to misunderstand what is already ours. . . . We cannot be narrators [of a completed historical system] but only explorers, weighing the pro and con of each opinion until the right one stands firm, indubitable, rooted forever."[6] In what may seem to be the beginning of an eschatological indulgence, the Voegelin of "Last Orientation" sees "a promise in these words, but not more." He defends Schelling's historicism against possible confusions with Hegel's eschatological Gnosticism. Schelling's "realism" prevents him from indulging in expectations that a perfect realm of peace could be established within the order of human existence, as it is known presently ("LO," 213).

To summarize, Voegelin accepts the following notions in his "Last Orientation" interpretation of Schelling:

- In terms recalling the substantial identity of the human soul and reality, from Schelling's philosophy of consciousness, Voegelin accepts that historical changes in the soul's experiences and symbolizations of the universe reflect changes in the self-determination of being.

- Newly differentiated experiences in history are thought, furthermore, to emerge from the *unconscious* depth of the soul. (These are the "protodialectic experiences" discussed in Chapter 1 of my study.) Accordingly, they cannot be exhaustively interpreted as though they were primarily based on arbitrary or otherwise volitional projections of a completely self-transparent psyche, but should be understood to reflect the mysterious life processes of the universe itself.

- Experiences arising from the soul's depth are best interpreted through *recollective* analysis, or what Schelling calls "anamnesis."

- The order of history reflects the "double life" of individual souls: in the articulation of relatively *meaningless* pragmatic events and in symbolizations of an "inner" *meaning* assigned to these events by the participants in the historical process of reality.

- To know the order of history requires, therefore, a *science* of the human soul, writ large over the general course of historiographic materials.

- Finally, Voegelin praises Schelling for granting, against Hegel, that the future is always pregnant with indeterminate meaning. This point indicates to him that the order of history cannot be known it its entirety, at

6. This is my citation of the complete text that Voegelin alludes to by Schelling, ibid., 1.8.206 (Bolman trans., 91–92).

any point in the present order of existence, by the reflective constructions
of a systematic philosophy of history.

Voegelin accepts these Schellingian notions pertaining to consciousness
and history, just prior to the rearticulation of the historiographic materials
from his *History of Political Ideas* in *The New Science of Politics* and the first
three volumes of *Order and History.*

The Differentiated Historiography:
Developmental History

Voegelin's differentiated historiography is introduced by *The New Science
of Politics.* The opening lines of this work state that human existence in political society "is historical existence." This means that "a theory of politics, if it
penetrates to principles, must at the same time be a theory of history." The
New Science is written, according to the dictum of Richard Hooker in its
epigraph, so that "[p]osterity may know we have not loosely through silence
permitted things to pass away as in a dream." This quote signals more than
the basic point that good lessons in politics ought not to be forgotten, especially in light of the fact that Voegelin was writing shortly after World War II.
It suggests that Voegelin will attempt to use the historical principles underlying his politics in order to defy Anaximander's claim that all things must
pass away, "according to the ordinance of Time."

This point is not immediately obvious. After all, in the concluding chapter of *The New Science,* Voegelin agrees with the author of Ecclesiastes when
he declares that all things have "a time to be born and a time to die," and
that the deeds of God "from the beginning to the end" cannot be fathomed
by the human mind (Eccles. 3:2, 11). Voegelin contends: "What comes into
being will have an end, and the mystery of this stream of being is impenetrable. These are the two great principles governing existence" (*NSP,* 166,
167).[7] Is this realistic thinking not in agreement with Anaximander's dictum?
Perhaps the author of Ecclesiastes would agree that it is, but it is not strictly
an equivalent statement for Voegelin. Notice that he says these principles

---

7. This is one of Voegelin's clearest statements on the mystery of being. For discussion, see
Glenn Hughes, *Mystery and Myth in the Philosophy of Eric Voegelin.* Hughes emphasizes the
sobriety in Voegelin's discussion of the "elemental mysteries" of human life, thus eliminating
some of the mystification caused by Voegelin's technical language.

govern "existence." This term indicates that what comes into being will have an existential end. But what of its substantial end? Do all personal human traits pass away after all, both existentially and substantially? Likely not, according to Voegelin. He will argue that spiritual consciousness has developed in history to the point where expectations of depersonalization after death reveal such thinking to be determined by the compact or "cosmological" order of being. In more conventional language, Anaximander and the Preacher of Ecclesiastes lived before the historical revelation of personal immortality in Christ's Resurrection. It was therefore natural for them to think that life ends in depersonalization. But Voegelin was living in the era of Christ. Thus, if he were to accept the thinking of pre-Christian realists without qualification, his thinking would be anachronistic. To avoid this problem, he attempts to preserve the level of consciousness gained in Christianity, arguing that it constitutes a philosophically defensible advance in the history of experience and symbolization. Voegelin understands historiographic work to be an immortalizing quest for God, whether the historiographer knows it or not. The divine is the first and last cause of history's order and the conscious emergence of this order in the soul of the historian. The proper task of the philosophical historian is to preserve the line of meaning in history that leads from and back again to God.

Voegelin's differentiated historiography is potentially confusing, because it equivocates on whether a discernible order *of* history can be found. On the one hand, Voegelin explicitly criticizes progressive historicism. He states bluntly that history has no *eidos,* no essential meaning or knowable form. There is no general meaning *of* history, he claims. There is only meaning *in* history. "The problem of an eidos in history... arises only when Christian transcendental fulfilment becomes immanentized," when secular progressivists grow tired of waiting for the Second Coming of Christ or the transcendental perfection of their humanity only after death. "The course of history as a whole is no object of experience; history has no eidos, because the course of history extends into the unknown future. The meaning of history, thus, is an illusion; and this illusory eidos is created by treating a symbol of faith as if it were a proposition concerning an object of immanent experience." On the other hand, Voegelin does claim to know something about the *eidos* of history. He notes that "the substance of history consists in the experiences in which man gains the understanding of his humanity and together with it the understanding of its limits." He even says that this "gain" is progressive. It advances through three types of truth in history: "The first of these types is the truth represented by the early empires [namely, the Egyptian, Babylonian, Assyrian, Persian, and Chinese]; it shall be designated as 'cosmological truth.' The second type of truth appears in the political culture of Athens and specifically in tragedy; it shall be called 'anthropological truth.' ... The third type of truth that appears with Christianity shall be called 'soteriological truth'" (*NSP,* 120, 78, 76–77).[8] The specific differences between these types of truth will be discussed in the sections that follow. For now it is sufficient to note that Voegelin has suggested a threefold account of history's order, that is, an order *of* history, rather than simply an account of various types of order *in* history. He claims that the differentiated order of history is a meaningful progression from cosmological (pagan) to soteriological (Christian) types of truth. This point recalls Schelling's account of the threefold progression of religions. But how is one to account for this apparent contradiction in Voegelin's work? "History," it seems, is both meaningful and meaningless, progressive and static, ordered and chaotic. Eventually, Voegelin reveals the presupposition that allows him to speak of history in this double sense. To wit: he accepts the division of historiography into "sacred" and "profane" dimensions.

Sacred and Profane Historiographies: Voegelin's Historical Survey

Voegelin takes the distinction between sacred and profane historiographies from Saint Augustine and from Karl Löwith's twentieth-century reinterpretation of the Christian symbolism.[9] Augustine, it seems, found the key to the meaning of history:

> History no longer moved in cycles, as it did with Plato and Aristotle, but acquired direction and destination. Beyond Jewish messianism in the strict sense the specifically Christian conception of history had, then, advanced toward the understanding of the end as a transcendental fulfilment. In his elaboration of this theoretical insight St. Augustine distinguished between a profane sphere of history in which empires rise and fall and a sacred history

---

8. This triad is reproduced in the first volume of *Order and History* (*OH,* 1:56). Though this volume was the first to be published, it was written after volumes 2 and 3. See Ellis Sandoz, "Voegelin's Philosophy of History and Human Affairs." This point alone suggests the legitimacy of using these categories to interpret the developmental historiography as a progressive account of truth.

9. Voegelin refers to Karl Löwith's *Meaning in History* (Chicago: University of Chicago Press, 1949) for the philosopher's distinction between the unknowable order *of* history and knowable experiences of order *in* history.

> which culminates in the appearance of Christ and the establishment of the
> church. . . . Only transcendental [sacred] history, including the earthly pil-
> grimage of the church, has direction toward its eschatological fulfilment.
> Profane [immanent] history, on the other hand, has no such direction; it is
> a waiting for the end; its present mode of being is that of a *saeculum senescens,*
> of an age that grows old. (*NSP,* 118)

It is profane history that has no *eidos,* or essence; it is meaningless. Sacred
history has a meaningful essence, the progressing types of truth mentioned
above. This distinction explains Voegelin's equivocal use of the term *history.*
His account of meaning in history is guided by the assumption that a sacred
meaning of history can be discerned, a point that also agrees with Schelling's
distinction between "interior" (sacred) and "exterior" (profane) historiographies. This is an important clarification. Although Voegelin's terminology
changes in later works, this distinction is retained throughout all of his latest
historiography.

The need for a new sacred history is addressed explicitly in the first and
second volumes of *Order and History.* The model for interpreting the "effective
past in relation to the historical present" was "set by St. Paul in Romans,"
wherein Christian faith and grace succeed the natural order of the Gentiles
and the Law of the Jews:

> The historical present was understood by St. Paul as the life under the
> divine revelation through Christ, while the effective past surrounding the
> new society was furnished by Jews and Gentiles. All three of the commu-
> nities—Christians, Jews, and Gentiles—belonged to one mankind as they
> all participated in divine order; but the order had been revealed to them in
> different degrees of clarity, increasing in chronological succession. . . . His-
> tory and its order, thus, were established by the measure in which various
> societies approached to the maximal clarity of divine revelation [that is, in
> Christ].

Voegelin refers to Paul's writing as "a masterful creation of historical order."
It was limited only by the relatively scant knowledge that Paul had of other
cultures. "Obviously," Voegelin grants, "the construction could not be ultimate but would have to be amended with changes and enlargements of the
empirical horizon" (*OH,* 1:131).

The first amendments to receive attention by Voegelin are "the *Civitas
Dei* of St. Augustine and the parallel *History against the Pagans* of Orosius."
These attempts to relate the horizons of Greek and Roman culture to Chris-
tianity, though taken to be theoretically sound, are rejected by Voegelin as

"premature generalizations from the phenomena known at the time." His rejection is based on later revisions from greater expansions of the "empirical horizon." To be sure, the Augustinian conception was a great success. It was transmitted through what became known as the Middle Ages and still served as the basic model when Jacques-Bénigne Bossuet "brought it up to date for the last time, in his *Discourse on Universal History* of 1681." However, after Bossuet the distinction between sacred and profane history began to suffer from apparently irreparable flaws. Voegelin explains:

> The construction had always suffered under the difficulty that the events of Israelite history, as far as they were known through the Biblical narrative, followed by the appearance of Christ and the history of the Church, had been elevated, under the title of an *historia sacra,* to the rank of the representative history of mankind, while the history of the cosmological empires, Hellas and Rome, had been reduced to a byplay of profane history, uneasily connected with the representative history through such categories as the *praeparatio evangelica.* . . . In this respect the Augustinian construction was heir to the defects of the Pauline method of historical interpretation. Even in late antiquity the construction had required a generous overlooking of obstreperous phenomena, such as the existence of a Sassanian by the side of the Roman empire; during the Middle Ages, when the Roman organization of the Mediterranean area had collapsed and given way to the centrifugal, parallel organizations of the Byzantine-Orthodox, Arabic-Islamic, and Western-Christian civilizations, the conflict with reality had worsened; and by the eighteenth century, with the rise of Russia to great-power rank and the beginning familiarity with the size and civilizational rank of China, it had become unbearable. (*OH,* 2:14–15)

It would seem that the *historia sacra* of Christian theology has become empirically untenable, specifically with regard to its claim to representative universality. The empirical horizon has expanded to the point where parallel histories are known from various civilizations—each claiming superiority over the others, and none transcending the parochial nature of the enterprise itself. This is how the matter appeared to Voltaire, at least, in his critical work *Essay on General History* (1756). Voegelin notes that it was comparatively easy for Voltaire to show that "a europocentric, unilinear construction of history" was untenable because it "had to omit such phenomena as China, Russia, and the Arab world." Voegelin is sympathetic to the need for considering problems that arise for developmental history when the empirical horizon expands. But he remains unpersuaded by the level of Voltaire's remarks. His "attack," Voegelin complains, was conducted "primarily on the phenomenal level," and its lack of philosophical substance is revealing: "the blow was no sooner delivered than it was clear that even a defective construction [that is, the Augustinian], which had at least a grip on the problem, was better than the dilettantic smartness of phenomenal argument" (*OH*, 2:15).

In terms recalling the style of analysis from the "Last Orientation," Voegelin contends that Voltaire was a historical phenomenalist. He criticized others while retaining an unexamined historical faith of his own, the faith in "progress toward the reason of the eighteenth-century bourgeoisie." This faith in the progressive character of rationality could serve Voltaire as a substitute for Augustine's *historia sacra,* however, "only under the condition that nobody would raise the fundamental question where and how the symbolism of an historical mankind had originated." When this question is raised in light of the expanding horizon of historical knowledge, Voegelin discovers that "mankind is not constituted through a survey of phenomena by even the most erudite historian, but through the experience of order in the present under God." The notion of a historical progress of reason or spirit, assumed by Voltaire, is itself a Christian discovery. Thus, considered historically, Voltaire retained the style of thinking that originates in Christian historicism, despite his best efforts to free himself from the tradition. Voltaire's attack "did not resolve any problems—it could only bring them into the open" (*OH*, 2:16).

Others attempted to rectify this problem. Oswald Spengler and the early Arnold Toynbee (in the first six volumes of his *Study of History*) attempted to understand historical order "in radical isolation against the *historia sacra.*" They found history to reveal a meaningless rise and fall of empires on the profane level. They eliminated the Christian meaning of "mankind and its history" in the process, however, and are said to have reached "the impasse of self-annihilation" (*OH*, 2:16). Voegelin diagnoses the central "defect" in their efforts with a distinctively Schellingian notion, without mentioning Schelling as the source of his critical orientation. First, he says that Spengler and Toynbee show a complete disregard for meaningful history as an "inner form."[10] Voegelin alludes to "many factors" that have contributed to this problem, but the greatest is said to be this: both Spengler and the early Toynbee, unlike Schelling, fail to emerge from the crisis of their historical situation; they fail to interpret the meaning of history in light of the *philosophia perennis,* remaining "burdened with the remnants of certain humanistic traditions, more specifically in their late liberal-bourgeois form, according to which civilizations

10. For more descriptions of historical meaning as an "inner" form, see *OH*, 1:125, 126, 355, 409–10, 2:7; and *Anam.,* 158.

are mystical entities producing cultural phenomena such as myths and religions, arts and sciences" (*OH,* 1:125–26). Unlike Schelling, they think that civilizations produce myths and other spiritual artifacts, that reality is socially constructed.

Voegelin attempts to transcend their efforts by accepting the converse "principle," arguing that societies are in fact produced by concrete experiences of transcultural reality. He protests: "Neither of the two thinkers has accepted the [Schellingian] principle that experiences of order, as well as their symbolic expressions, are not products of a civilization but its constitutive forms" (*OH,* 1:126). In Schellingian terms, a "people" is born simultaneously with its myths. A self-conscious, preexistent culture does not produce its myths; rather, mythic or revelatory experiences of the divine produce the self-understanding of a people. Two decades earlier, in his *Race and State* (1933), Voegelin openly praised this insight as distinctively Schellingian. He described it as "the first profound insight into the religious nature, in the broadest sense, of all community formation" (*CW,* 2:150–51). In the first volume of *Order and History,* however, Voegelin retains this notion without calling attention to its source.

Hegel attempted to construct a different philosophy of history, Voegelin grants, this time "from the side of the *historia sacra.*" He thought that a representatively human history could be "expanded beyond the Judaeo-Christian sacred history by demonstrating the participation of all human societies in the unfolding of the Logos [spiritual order] in time." Voegelin has considerable praise for Hegel's attempt. He says that its success was "remarkable," given the state of historical knowledge in nineteenth-century Germany. However, Voegelin also notes a "serious defect" in the attempt, the cause of its "ultimate failure." In order to make his progressive history work, Hegel had to transform and overcome the self-consciousness of ancient Greek philosophers and Christian saints, specifically with regard to the general notion of human finitude that persists to this day. He needed to attempt a reduction of "the Logos of revelation to the logos of philosophy, and the logos of philosophy to the dialectics of consciousness. Philosophy *(Liebe zum Wissen)* was supposed to advance toward Gnosis *(wirkliches Wissen)*—and that could be done only through anaesthetizing the philosopher's sensitiveness for the borderline between the knowable and the unknowable." The mystery described formerly in symbols such as "transcendent being" had to be brought fully within the "immanent" grasp of the dialectician. The effort was futile. "The superbly skilful manipulation of the Gnostic symbolism could, of course, not abolish the mystery—either of the order of being, or of an historical mankind—but the sheer massiveness of the dialectical work, the vast expansion of the Gnostic *opus* to the limits of the phenomenal world, could push the mystery so far out of sight that the impossible at least appeared to have become possible" (*OH,* 2:16–18).

Finally, a third revision of traditional historiography was attempted by Karl Jaspers and the later Toynbee. In his work *Vom Ursprung und Ziel der Geschichte,* Jaspers grants that "philosophy of history has its roots in Christian faith." But precisely for this reason, he argues that it cannot be valid for those who do not accept the specific points of the faith. The religion that requires *faith* in its ability to attain universality cannot produce a universal philosophy of history. He thus seeks to find an empirical axis of world history that yields a defensible sense of meaning for all of humanity, including Christians, an epochal time that would be equally convincing to people from the Orient and Occident alike. He finds this epoch "in the spiritual processes which take place in China and India, in Iran, Israel, and Hellas, between 800 and 200 B.C., with a concentration about 500 B.C. when Confucius, Laotse, the Buddha, Deutero-Isaiah, Pythagoras, and Heraclitus were members of the same generation." This period refers to Jaspers's well-known "axis-time." It was allegedly during this period of history when all of the basic thought categories were symbolized that most people continue to presuppose today.

In his later work *A Study of History* (volumes 7–10), Arnold Toynbee accepts the basic presuppositions of Jaspers's axis historiography, but he seeks to correct some of its details. First, he argues that the axis time should be expanded considerably in order to include "the coexistence of the four higher religions—Mahayana Buddhism, Hinduism, Christianity, and Islam." Second, he rejects the concentration on the year 500 B.C., for Buddha, Confucius, and Pythagoras were only chronological contemporaries; they did not attain the same level of spiritual insight into reality and its order. Toynbee's latest work thus turns to examine the "progress of religion" as the progress of history proper. Voegelin applauds this change. It signals the overcoming of historical nihilism in Spengler's work and a return "to the Augustinian *historia sacra*—though with the recognition of four 'higher religions' of equal dignity" (*OH,* 2:19, 20, 21).

Both Jaspers and the later Toynbee transcend modern progressivism in their historiographies. They do not fall prey to the blinding conceit that their epoch is self-evidently the best and only continues to improve. However, Voegelin notes considerable limitations in both thinkers that help to clarify what his own historiography must avoid. Toynbee was unable to include Judaism in his "higher religions," and Jaspers excluded Christianity altogether. Moreover, both failed to discuss the significance of Moses, and both continued to show signs of embarrassment with respect to the Western style of analysis in their works. These defects signal to Voegelin that "willfulness" and "a profound misconception of history and its structure" still weakened their historiographies (*OH*, 2:22).

To address the first problem, Voegelin includes a lengthy discussion of Jewish symbols in the first volume of *Order and History* and a plan for two volumes on specifically Christian problems. To address the second problem, he reflects on "the hard fact that philosophy of history has indeed arisen in the West and nowhere *but* in the West. There is no such thing as a non-Western philosophy of history. For a philosophy of history can arise only where mankind has become [consciously] historical through existence in the present under God." The uniquely Western insight into the historicity of consciousness is valid for all of humanity, one might say, just as the discovery of a medicine in the West may be used to cure physical diseases elsewhere. The medicine that Voegelin attempts to bring to a wide range of civilizations is the philosophy of history. And the disease he attempts to cure is nothing less than human mortality.[11] Although knowledgeable of Oriental cultures, most of the research for Voegelin's philosophy of history focuses on developments in Western societies. But he would not flinch from charges that his work suffers from "Europocentrism." He argues that the historicity and rationality of consciousness are fundamental constituents of humanity per se, so it need not concern him greatly that these notions were discovered only in the West. People from the Orient might have some misgivings, however, as the superiority of Western spirituality is said to entail "assimilation" for the societies that have not broken through to consciously historical existence "in Western historical form" (*OH*, 2:22, 23, 22). Before the assimilation can properly take place, more work needs to be done by Western historians, Voegelin grants, because the "earth-wide, imperial expansion of Western civilization since the sixteenth century A.D." has created the aforementioned confusions among historians. The West is no longer conscious of its own historiographic superiority, due to the massive influx of newly discovered materials.

---

11. This point is evident, among other places, in the Augustinian epigraph with which each volume of *Order and History* is opened: "In the study of creature one should not exercise a vain and perishing curiosity, but ascend toward what is immortal and everlasting." The immortalizing feature of historiographic study comes to the fore in the fourth volume of *Order and History*, which I analyze at length in the next chapter.

Civilizations which formerly were to us only dimly known, or entirely unknown, now fill the horizon massively; and archaeological discoveries have added to their number a past of mankind that had been lost to memory. This enormous expansion of the spatial and temporal horizon has burdened our age with the task of relating an ever more comprehensive past of mankind to our own historical form of maximal clarity, which is the Christian. It is a work that has barely begun. (*OH,* 1:132)

Voegelin accepts the "burden" of the "task," and undertakes to write a new sacred or developmental history, this time in the Augustinian-Schellingian style. Thus, when he says that history has no *eidos,* he is speaking only of profane history.

Faith and Philosophical Historiography: The Historical Progression of Truth

One equivocation has been clarified, but another one rises to take its place, for Voegelin is unclear about the cognitive dimension of his developmental history. Is its notion of advancing truth ultimately supported by classical philosophy, Christian faith, or perhaps some defensible combination of the two? At times, he suggests that historical advances in existential truth can be proved by philosophical analysis. He argues that there is an "intelligible order of history," and this "must be sought through a theoretical analysis of institutions and experiences of order, as well as of the form that results from their interpretation." That is to say, the source of "historical objectivity... must be sought in historical form itself; and conversely, if there is a suspicion of subjectivity, it must attach again to the form." Historical form, he continues, will appear to suffer from undue bias only if "faith is misinterpreted as a 'subjective' experience." If faith is properly understood as an experienced event in which God has entered the human soul at particular times and distinctive ways in history, then the "historical form" is revealed to be "an ontologically real event in history." This is the end to which Voegelin's philosophy of history attempts to lead. Faith, he continues, "must be understood as an event of this nature, as long as we base our conception of history on a critical analysis of the literary sources which report the event and do not introduce subjectivity ourselves by arbitrary, ideological surmising." The philosophical explication of faith symbols, therefore, "will cast an ordering ray of objective truth over the field of history in which the event objectively occurred." It seems that, in accordance with the distinction I made in the previous chapter,[12] teleological faith is apparently unnecessary to accept Voegelin's "theoretical analysis" of history's "intelligible order," for history is said to be an "intricate dialectical process," an "objective reality" with a "causal mechanism of differentiation" (*OH,* 1:62–63, 130, 128, 129). Accordingly, one should be able to interpret history's order with the impartiality of philosophical science. But this is not Voegelin's last word on faith and philosophical historiography.

Like Schelling, Voegelin speaks of "objective" advances in truth when he interprets the order of history before its climax in Christ. Yet once he reaches the point where Christian symbols need to be interpreted, Voegelin begins to speak about faith in a different way—without calling attention to the change in meaning. He describes faith as a *sacrificium intellectus,* a sacrifice of the intellect, and says that such faith is needed in order to accept the superiority of Christian historiography.[13] When Voegelin emphasizes this need, his understanding of faith is typically taken from a verse in the Letter to the Hebrews (11:1), in which faith is described as "the substance of things hoped for and the proof of things unseen." Voegelin interprets: "Ontologically, the substance of things hoped for is nowhere to be found but in faith itself; and, epistemologically, there is no proof for things unseen but again this very faith." Voegelin admits that this circularity creates a "tenuous bond" with respect to the "communication" between human beings and "the world-transcendent God." This bond may "snap easily," because "[u]ncertainty is the very essence of Christianity" (*NSP,* 122). Nonetheless, this is the bond that is needed, Voegelin maintains, in order to understand the superiority of Christian truth in historical differentiation. Without such faith, the order of history will appear to be an "abysmal mystery," an "instrument of divine revelation for ultimate purposes that are unknown equally to the men of all ages" (*OH,* 1:129).

Voegelin's use of a teleological understanding of faith to contend that human cognition is limited comes with a price: it tends to reduce what drives

12. Cf. *supra,* 175–76.

13. Voegelin to Alfred Schütz, January 1, 1953, in *The Philosophy of Order,* 451. Voegelin does not want to suggest that the "sacrifice" amounts simply to a capitulation to dogmatism: "In the 19th-century atmosphere of liberal editorializing, the sacrifice of the intellect was understood as an abdication of reason through the acceptance of dogma. But this is not how it was understood from Athanasius to Kant. For Athanasius *sacrificium intellectus* signifies the obligation not to operate with the human intellect in regions inaccessible to it, i.e., in the regions of faith" (ibid.). But, of course, what remains "inaccessible" is precisely the question at issue. One need not be a liberal editorialist to raise it.

his historiography toward further determinations to the level of ironic or tacit knowledge. It should not be confused, for example, with Socrates' appeals to the limitations of human knowledge. Unlike Socrates, Voegelin's faith is the *"cognitio fidei"* of church fathers, the trust behind which cognition of a historically determinate sort is implied. The specific *cognitio* of Voegelin's *fides* is found in his claim that "[f]aith is the anticipation of a supernatural perfection of man," that the "destiny of man lies not in the future but in eternity" (*NSP,* 124, 157; *OH,* 2:4). Voegelin does not explain why this cognition is superior to the unambiguously agnostic conclusions that result from Socrates' hypothetical lines of reasoning—why the Christian belief in the "supernatural perfection of man" is superior to the knowledge that such anticipations describe only one possibility of what the mystery of death might entail.[14] The ironic type of cognition implied by Voegelin's understanding of Christian faith needs to be kept in mind. As in Schelling, his understanding of faith is primarily teleological.[15] This is the type of faith that guides his entire historiography, even though his discussions of the matter clearly wish to suggest that he has not left philosophical reasoning behind in order to construct a Christian theology of history.

This ambiguity in Voegelin's appeals to faith has caused an accentual divide between his interpreters. German readers tend to emphasize what I have called the hypothetical type of faith in Voegelin's work, thus leading them to interpret Voegelin as a *philosophical* historian and political *scientist.* North American readers tend to emphasize the teleological type of faith, thus leading them to interpret Voegelin as a *Christian* historian who draws upon classical philosophy as the handmaiden to his theology.[16] As I have indicated, both

14. A point to which I return in Chapter 4.

15. In his later work, Voegelin continues to speak of faith in the sense of Heb. 11:1. See, for example, "Immortality" (1967), 52; and *OH* (1974), 4:329.

16. For representative examples of German and North American interpreters, see Helmut Kuhn, "Das Problem einer philosophischen Historiographie: Zum Werke von Eric Voegelin"; English versions of the Germanic reading may be found in Gebhardt, "Toward Universal Mankind" and "The Vocation of the Scholar." For a North American reading that stresses Voegelin's faith, see Michael P. Morrissey, *Consciousness and Transcendence: The Theology of Eric Voegelin.* Frederick G. Lawrence has noticed a similar problem among Voegelin scholars, specifically between Jürgen Gebhardt and Paul Caringella. See Lawrence, "The Problem of Eric Voegelin, Mystic Philosopher and Scientist." Lawrence attempts to bridge the accentual divide between rational scholarship and meditative faith by highlighting "Voegelin's Augustinian approach." This approach, Lawrence contends, "leads [Voegelin] to avoid rationalism, while restoring reason to its classic status" (58). Lawrence is certainly correct to say that Voegelin avoided the unpersuasive reduction of reason to modern "rationalism," but his reliance upon Augustine is partly what calls into question whether Voegelin has indeed understood reason in its "classic status."

types of faith are evident in Voegelin's writings, and the teleological type out-weighs the hypothetical trust in presuppositions that Voegelin inherits from classical philosophy. To support this thesis, his account of the historical progression of truth needs to be examined in greater detail.

"Cosmological Truth": Mythic Order in the Ancient Near East

Voegelin's term for the earliest type of religious representation is *cosmological truth*. Its symbolic form is myth. Voegelin's designation of this period in history corresponds, I suggest, to the period and methods of interpretation that were found in Schelling's account of "mythological religion." For Voegelin, as with Schelling, the cosmological style of truth represents the gods as identical to eminent things in the cosmos. The people in cosmological societies ostensibly had no consciousness of a world-transcendent divinity. Their myths remained "compact" or intracosmic. But Voegelin does not refer to "cosmological truth" as a type of experience and symbolization that vanished with the societies in which it first appeared. He grants that its symbols are still evident today as expressions of the "primary experience of the cosmos." For example, in the wake of Schelling's historiography, Voegelin says that Chinese civilizations remained "cosmological" up to the twentieth century (*OH*, 1:61), even though other civilizations in the West "advanced" beyond this symbolic form. Despite this qualification, however, Voegelin argues that a temporal progression of truth can be discerned by interpreting Mesopotamian, Achaemenian (Persian), and Egyptian mythologies, the principal representatives of the cosmological style of truth.

Voegelin's placement of the aforementioned societies in a historical line of advancing truth resembles Schelling's account of how the potencies of nature become actualized during the time of "mythological religion." His interpretation of Mesopotamian mythology is equivalent to Schelling's account of the emergence of the first potency (B), his interpretation of Persian mythology resembles Schelling's account of A^2, and his reading of Egyptian mythology resembles Schelling's account of A^3. Mesopotamian society is said to have produced the most compact—that is, tautegorical—symbols of the societies under consideration. The gods of the *Enuma elish,* a cosmogonic epic (ca. 1500 B.C.E.), are found to have been identical to the world: "The gods *are* the world," Voegelin asserts, "and the progressive structural differentiation of the universe is, therefore, a story of the creation of the gods. The cosmogony is at the same time a theogony." The Egyptians are said to have come closest to a genuine consciousness of divine transcendence, thus indicating that all of the potencies have become relatively actual. However, despite these similarities, on the basis of this text alone it cannot be established with certainty that a Schellingian progression of natural potencies guides Voegelin's historiography. His five and one-half pages on the Achaemenian empire allow one to see the establishment of a dualistic theology, but it is not clear that he understands this theology to indicate the emergence of Schelling's second potency (A^2). What is more, when Voegelin turns to discuss the triad of Egyptian gods (Amon, Re, and Ptah), he says that there is "no hidden meaning in the number three." Rather, the triadic symbolism is said to have been motivated by political circumstances: "[I]t might as well have been four or five gods, if the political situation had required them," that is, to sustain the unity of the empire (*OH,* 1:41, 46–51, 87).

These points suggest that Voegelin has left behind the natural or universal dimension of Schelling's *Potenzenlehre.* If he were developing a strictly Schellingian reading of these societies, he would ascribe motivation for their symbols of spiritual order to the worldwide actualization of divine potencies in the human soul. Instead, he turns curiously to suggest that pragmatic events motivated the sacred symbolism of the Egyptians. This suggestion is uncommon in Voegelin's historiography and requires interpretation. In the Introduction, I cited Voegelin's agreement with Schelling's claim that a people is constituted by its "inner" experiences of divine order, whether its mythologists know it or not.[17] Voegelin often remains true to this claim. For instance, when he interprets the spiritual motivation of Jewish symbols, he warns against the "positivistic trap" that may tempt one to substitute "more probable pragmatic events for the legendary ones" in Israelite historiography (*OH,* 1:126, 385). In other words, he argues that philosophical historians must not "demythologize" the mythic traditions of order they study as, for example, Rudolf Bultmann would have had them do. Their primary task, rather, is to understand the ancient authors on their own terms. Demythologization obscures the sense in which spiritual truth might be found to advance in history by distorting, anachronistically, the experiences under consideration by the philosophical historian.[18] When Voegelin interprets the

---

17. Cf. *supra,* 20–21.

18. For Voegelin's critique of Bultmann's demythologization *(Entmythologisierung)* of ancient texts, see his essay "History and Gnosis," in *The Old Testament and Christian Faith,* ed. Bernhard W. Anderson (New York: Herder and Herder, 1969), 64–89.

Egyptians, however, he appears to be quite willing to fall into this "positivistic trap," even though he is certainly no positivist.

This methodological lapse can be explained as part of Voegelin's attempt to defend the superiority of Christian symbolism in his differentiated historiography. This explanation is suggested by a pattern in his use and neglect of his empirical method of interpretation. On the one hand, when he is faced with interpreting Egyptian symbols that resemble later developments in Christian theology—for example, the trinitarian theology in the aforementioned Amon Hymns, and a similar conception that Egyptologists have identified in the "Memphite Theology"—Voegelin tends to diminish these similarities by appealing to their motivation in political events. On the other hand, when he is faced with interpreting symbols that clearly differ from later Christian developments—for example, the importance of divine kingship and the symbolization of gods in animal form—he explains the symbolism with an appeal to its "compactness" (*OH*, 1:86–87, 88–95, 72–74). In more conventional language, he allows the Egyptians to be primitive but hesitates to accord full weight to their spiritual sensitivity.

Voegelin says that the distinguishing feature of all societies ordered by the cosmological myth is the "consubstantiality"—or "compactness"—between humanity and the divine cosmos evident in their symbols.[19] This point makes it nearly impossible for Voegelin's contemporaries to interpret ancient symbols, due to the fact that we presuppose the differentiation of immanent and transcendent aspects of reality as a habit of thought. Accordingly, when he turns to consider the Egyptian "Memphite Theology" (ca. 3100 B.C.E.), he says that the "substantial oneness of events on the various levels of existence cannot be communicated by an analysis at all; we must let the text speak for itself." But Voegelin offers an analysis, nonetheless. The gods of the Memphite Theology, it seems, are symbols for mundane experiences, mainly political events culminating in the divinity of the pharaoh (*OH*, 1:89–90). An attempt to defend this point is made, even though he grants that a number of features in Egyptian theology resemble later developments normally associated with Christianity: for example, the authors of the Memphite Theology "must have had a rather detached [or differentiated] attitude toward their own product" because they "could intersperse their myth of the creation with 'footnotes,' relating the principles which they used in constructing it"; they were "apparently . . . aware of the problem of a creation *ex*

19. Cf. *OH*, 1:16, 78, 84, 86–87, 89, 92, 95, 100, 106.

nihilo"; the highest god, Amon, was occasionally described as "a hidden, invisible god, whose name is unknown"; and the authors of Egyptian mortuary texts (ca. 2050 B.C.E.) sensed that "their souls open to the peace of the god" only "in the beyond." These points seem to indicate that a differentiated level of consciousness was experienced and symbolized by the members of this "cosmological" society. Despite this indication, however, Voegelin maintains that no experience of divine transcendence ever truly occurred in Egypt (*OH*, 1:93, 91, 86, 101; cf. 98–101). "The cosmological culture of Egypt never was broken effectively by anthropological or soteriological developments." Like Schelling, he says that the Egyptians proved "tenaciously resistant to differentiating experiences and a reorientation of human existence toward transcendent divinity" (*OH*, 1:57, 74; cf. 82). They resisted, in Schellingian terms, the advance of the completely spiritual principle (A³) and clung tenaciously to the material ground (B) of divinity.

To be sure, Voegelin shows some appreciation for the cosmological type of truth. He acknowledges that the cosmological myth "holds together the blocs [of immanent and transcendent dimensions of reality] which in later history not only will be distinguished, but also are liable to fall apart." The myth guards against "the extremes of a radically other-worldly faith and of an agnostic metaphysics.... Differentiation, one would have to say, is not an unqualified good; it is fraught with the dangers of radically dissociating the experiential blocs held together by the myth, as well as of losing the experience of consubstantiality in the process" (*OH*, 1:84). This is a rare admission, but it is also relatively inconsequential to Voegelin's philosophy of history. Though qualified periodically by generous statements such as this, Voegelin's historiography retains its character as a subtle drive toward the eschatological consciousness of Christian historicism.

The historical discovery of divine transcendence allegedly requires the experience of a "leap in being," Voegelin's equivalent phrase for the "spiritual crisis" that was found in Schelling's historiography. This "leap" is what constitutes the decisive epochal change in the history of consciousness. It is "the epochal event that breaks the compactness of the early cosmological myth and establishes the order of man in his immediacy under [the world-transcendent] God." The leap occurs twice in the history of humanity, though roughly at the same time, in ancient Israel and Hellas. But it has different effects on the people in these civilizations:

> The two occurrences, while they run parallel in time and have in common their opposition to the Myth, are independent of each other; and the two

experiences differ so profoundly in content that they become articulate in the two different symbolisms of Revelation and Philosophy. . . . Leaps in being, to be sure, have occurred elsewhere; but a Chinese personal existence under the cosmic *tao,* or an Indian personal existence in acosmistic illumination, is not an Israelite or Christian existence under God. While the Chinese and Indian societies have certainly gained the consciousness of universal humanity, only the Judaeo-Christian response to revelation has achieved historical consciousness. (*OH,* 2:1, 22)

Like Schelling, and certainly many others, Voegelin emphasizes the differences between Revelation and philosophy in the differentiated period of his historiography. The "leap in being" lies at the core of this distinction. It prepares the way for Christian historians eventually to look upon the symbolic forms of Greek philosophy and Jewish Revelation as the twin "Old Testaments of Christianity" (*OH,* 2:24).[20] As with Schelling's account of the "spiritual crisis" that distinguishes advancing epochs of spiritual truth in history, Voegelin's account of the "leap in being" is a significant factor in his reading of world-historical developments as a *praeparatio evangelica.*

"Anthropological Truth": Tragedy and Philosophy in Ancient Greece

"Anthropological truth" first appears in the political culture of Athens and specifically in tragedy. Voegelin uses this phrase "with the understanding that [it] covers the whole range of problems connected with the psyche as the sensorium of transcendence" (*NSP,* 77). His appeal to the "whole range" of problems beyond tragedy is an allusion to the specific insights of the "mystic philosophers," mainly Plato and Aristotle, who discover the transcendent nature of the divine and the immanent nature of the soul as the site or "sensorium" where this aspect of divinity is experienced. The Greek tragedians and philosophers discover the soul, differentiate its structure, and begin to suppose that the divine transcends all things human and cosmological: "[T]he psyche itself is found as a new center in man at which he experiences himself as open toward transcendental reality. Moreover, this center is not found as if it were an object that had been present all the time and only escaped

20. Voegelin refers to Clement of Alexandria (*Stromateis,* bk. 6) for the notion that Christianity has two Old Testaments. Schelling knew the *Stromateis* (cf. *Philosophie der Mythologie,* in *Werke,* 2.2.187). He quoted it often but did not explicitly use the theme mentioned by Voegelin.

notice." The philosophers do not discover an a priori structure of the mind, which has always been the condition for humans to experience transcendence, merely unawares. Rather, it seems that Voegelin is presupposing, at this point, that a Schellingian potency has become historically actualized in the philosophers' leap in being: "The psyche as the region in which transcendence is experienced must be differentiated [actualized] out of a more compact [potential] structure of the soul; it must be developed and named." This is not a natural actualization of potentials in human nature, one that would occur throughout humanity. It is a historical actualization, which is specific to the West. It is, however, one that Voegelin takes to be "representative" for all of humanity. But how do the philosophers come to this condition of openness with respect to the divine? Is the soul opened by God, or do they open it themselves? Voegelin equivocates in his answer to these questions. He says, at times, that this opening "is as much action as it is passion." At other times, he is more clear: the Hellenic leap in being is not based on divine Revelation. When Plato describes the erotic "mystical ascent" toward the beautiful itself, in his *Symposium,* he arrives only at "the border of transcendence" (*NSP,* 67, 66). This claim is important, because Voegelin thinks that Plato is distinct among Greek philosophers: his theological philosophy bears the greatest resemblance to the insights gained in Judeo-Christian Revelation.

Voegelin's clearest account of Platonic philosophy is found in a letter to Leo Strauss, written while preparing the lectures that were eventually published as *The New Science of Politics.* Voegelin states:

> I would say that the problem of the Platonic myth and dialogue has a close connection to the question of revelation. Plato propounds no truth that had been revealed to him; he appears not to have had the experience of a prophetic address from God. Therefore no direct announcement. The myth of Plato seems to be an intermediate form—no longer the polytheistic myth that, because of the concentration of his soul, had become impossible; but it is not yet the free diagnosis of the divine source of the knowledge of order.[21]

Like Schelling, Voegelin interprets Plato as one of the Greek mystics who stood on the historical border between the compactness of cosmological myth and the superior differentiation of divine transcendence and revelatory grace in Judeo-Christian theology. Plato was able to transcend the cognitive limitations of myth, but he could not understand the revelatory constitution

---

21. Voegelin to Strauss, April 22, 1951, in *Faith and Political Philosophy,* 87.

of order with complete freedom. Why was this so? A second Schellingian notion, retained in the previously cited quotation, will help to answer this question. Notice that Voegelin appeals to the "concentration" of Plato's soul. This term refers to the need for humanity and divinity to separate completely, for consciousness to be concentrated or contracted in its immanence under a transcendent mystery, in order for Revelation to occur. Like Schelling, Voegelin says that "Revelation in the Jewish and Christian sense seems possible only when man historically developed a consciousness of his humanness, which clearly separates him from transcendence. Such consciousness is, for example, not yet given in Homer's polytheism or with Hesiod. Divine and human are still interconnected." Voegelin continues this same line of thought by presupposing another point from Schelling's critical study of mythology, namely, the rejection of "anthropomorphic" explanations of mythology:

> This fact is veiled through the unfortunate theory of "anthropomorphism" in polytheistic cultures. So far as the Greek gods are concerned there is no anthropomorphic representation of the divine, but rather a theomorphic symbolization of the contents of the human soul. The development of the soul . . . appears to me to be the process in which man dedivinized himself and realized the humanity of his spiritual life. Only with this spiritual concentration will it be possible to experience oneself as being addressed by a world-transcendent God.[22]

The reason Plato received no "direct announcement" is that the conscious separation of humanity and divinity remained incomplete in his soul. This was not a failing of Plato's personal ability to symbolize the divine; it was occasioned by his historical position. In the dialogues,

> God does not speak unmediated, but only as mediated through Socrates-Plato. Insofar as the place of God as the addresser is taken by Socrates-Plato, as the speaker in the dialogue, the fullest expression of "theomorphic" polytheism seems to be the final reason for the dialogue form; the divine and the human are not yet completely separated. . . . Plato seems to have been aware of this problem of his divinity in the polytheistic sense.[23]

Like Schelling, Voegelin grants only that Plato "prefigured" the superior understanding of divine-human reality that was gained by the appearance of Christianity: "The leap in being, toward the transcendent source of order, is

22. Ibid., 82.
23. Ibid., 87.

real in Plato," and later ages have "recognized rightly" his account of the paradigmatic polis in heaven[24] as "a prefiguration of St. Augustine's conception
of the *civitas Dei*. Nevertheless, a prefiguration is not the figuration itself.
Plato is not a Christian" (*OH,* 3:92; see also 226, 366).[25]

Neither does Voegelin find revelatory experience or consciousness in Aristotle's writings during the differentiated period of his historiography. He refers
to Aristotle's account of the impossibility of friendship *(philia)* between gods
and humans, due to their radical inequality, as proof of this point (*NSP,*
77).[26] Even more, the same point is generalized beyond Aristotle:

> The impossibility of *philia* between God and man may be considered typ-
> ical for the whole range of anthropological truth. The experiences that were
> explicated into a theory of man by the mystic philosophers had in com-
> mon the accent on the human side of the orientation of the soul toward
> divinity. The soul orients itself toward a God who rests in his immovable
> transcendence; it reaches out toward divine reality, but it does not meet an
> answering movement from beyond. (*NSP,* 77–78)[27]

The experience of an "answering movement" appears only with the historical
advent of Judeo-Christian Revelation.

"Soteriological Truth": Salvation History in Jewish and Christian Revelation

The anthropological truth of the Greek philosophers prepares the way for
Christians eventually to attempt a rational account of their faith. Hellenistic
philosophy allows Justin, Origen, Clement of Alexandria, and Augustine,

---

24. Cf. *Republic* 592b.

25. Geoffrey L. Price has recently traced the development of what I have called Voegelin's
differentiated historiography from the *History of Political Ideas* to the first three volumes of
Order and History. See "Critical History after Augustine and Orosius: Voegelin's Return to
Plato." While offering insightful comparisons between two massive bodies of text, the suggested importance of Plato in Voegelin's historiographic method is called into question by
Plato's limited status as a representative of "anthropological truth," and by the continuing importance of Augustine that emerges more clearly in Voegelin's later work.

26. Cf. Aristotle, *Nicomachean Ethics* 1158b29–1159a13. In making this claim, Voegelin
overlooks another passage from the *Ethics* that contradicts him. At one point, Aristotle says
that one who pursues intellectual activity *(noun energōn)* is "beloved of the gods *[theo-
philestatos]*" (1179a23–32).

27. This understanding of Aristotle in particular, and of the Greeks generally, is elaborated
in the third volume of *Order and History* (cf. *OH,* 3:362–66).

among other church fathers, to offer a reasoned account of how God is both transcendent and yet intelligibly related to the human soul's experiences. Jewish Revelation, the second "Old Testament" in Voegelin's historiography, prepares Christianity for its Messiah and allows Paul to understand history as a progression from the natural and divine law of the pagans and Jews to God's full Revelation in Christ. Soteriological truth, therefore, has its immediate beginning in Judaism.

Jewish Revelation. Voegelin's most substantial account of Jewish symbols and experience is found in *Israel and Revelation,* the first volume of *Order and History.*[28] The volume opens with the word *God* and concludes with the word *Jesus.* This appears to be no accident. Like Schelling, Voegelin tends to favor Jewish experiences of Revelation that allude to the future of theophany in the Messiah later identified by Christians. He praises messianic prophets, and criticizes others who dwell on the perfection of the Law or imply that the fulfillment of human nature can take place within this life. Voegelin's account of Jewish Revelation begins by suggesting a fundamental limitation in cosmological symbolism. He contends that societies ordered by the cosmological myth sensed "the lasting of cosmic and the passing of social order," but this observation "did not penetrate the soul decisively and, consequently, did not lead to new insights concerning the true order of being and existence." These "new insights" began to unfold when the transcendent God began to liberate humanity from cosmological bondage, at some time in the second millennium B.C.E.: "In Genesis 15 the decisive step of liberation occurs, when Yahweh makes his berith [covenant] with Abram." On this occasion, "the peculiar nature of a berith with Yahweh reveals itself. In the mundane situation of Abram . . . nothing has changed. The new domain of Yahweh is not yet the political order of a people in Canaan." God's newly created presence in history is limited to "the soul of Abram." It yields an order that originates "through the inrush of divine reality into his soul and from this point of origin expands into a social body in history. At the time of its inception it is no more than the life of a man who trusts in God; but this new existence, founded on the leap in being, is pregnant with future" (*OH,* 1:111, 194).

Voegelin's appeal to the novelty of Abram's experience is questionable in a philosophical study of order. To be sure, Abram's experience of the divine

---

28. For further discussion of the significance and limitations of this volume, from the perspective of a biblical scholar, see Bernhard W. Anderson, "Revisiting Voegelin's *Israel and Revelation* after Twenty-five Years."

may be new with respect to the historical records. But Voegelin's philosophy of history takes this novelty, the beginning of the "leap in being" in Israelite Revelation, to indicate more than a change in the surviving records of human experience. The novelty ostensibly indicates that "a change in being" has occurred, "with consequences for the order of existence" (*OH,* 1:11). Thus, Voegelin's claim about Abram's novelty is not simply historical in the conventional sense of the word; it is an ontological claim based on Schelling's process theology. But Schelling's guidance is not acknowledged in the first volume of *Order and History.* Voegelin equates historical existence and the order of being without explaining how this equation can be justified philosophically. In other words, it is not clear why an apparent change in the experience of an individual human also reflects a change in the order of being itself. Earlier, in the "Last Orientation," Voegelin addressed this problem with the help of Schelling's philosophy of the unconscious. The link between existence and being was accounted for in the presupposition that genuine symbols arise through "protodialectic experiences." These were described as genuine "irruptions" of being that emerge from the soul's unconscious depth because it is substantially identical to the ground of being itself. By presupposing the substantial identity of the soul and divine ground, the history of experience and symbolization could be read as the history of being revealed through the changing record of protodialectic experiences. But Schelling's philosophy of the unconscious is not mentioned by Voegelin in the first volume of *Order and History.* What is more, there are few clear references to the conception of substantial identity here, as discussed previously in Chapter 1, that would help us to understand Voegelin's presuppositions about the historical unfolding of being. However, these presuppositions are clarified—with a direct reference to Schelling—in a contemporary letter that Voegelin wrote to his friend Robert Heilman:

> [I]t is peculiar to the nature of man that it unfolds its potentialities historically. Not that historically anything "new" comes up—human nature is always wholly present—but there are modes of clarity and degrees of comprehensiveness in man's understanding of himself and his position in the world. . . . What I have just adumbrated (most inadequately, to be sure) is the basis of historical interpretation since Herder and Baader and Schelling. History is the unfolding of the human Psyche; historiography is the reconstruction of the unfolding through the psyche of the historian. The basis of historical interpretation is the identity of substance (the psyche) in the object and the subject of interpretation; and its purpose is participation in

the great dialogue that goes through the centuries among men about their nature and destiny.[29]

These comments reveal that Voegelin continues to accept the basic presuppositions in Schelling's philosophy of consciousness and history, namely, his notions of substantial identity and the unfolding of the "potentialities" of human nature in history. This conception of history's order and the position of consciousness therein may allow one to organize historical records based on concrete experiences rather than abstract ideas, but the central problem for a philosophy of historical advances in truth remains unresolved. Without knowledge of human experiences predating the emergence of written records, it remains impossible to say whether any "modes of clarity" or "degrees of comprehensiveness" are new to the order of being, rather than simply to the small part of experience glimpsed through historical records. "Being" may have "irrupted" in similar ways a countless number of times in the unknown past—simply without being recorded.

This problem was not unknown to Aristotle. Nor was it unknown to Voegelin. He quotes decisive passages from Aristotle's works, all of which indicate that important discoveries may have occurred an indefinite number of times in the past, but draws no conclusions from them for his philosophy of history (*OH*, 3:289–91).[30] Voegelin's frequent appeals to the mystery of historical order tend to overlook this insight with respect to the unknowable past; they tend only to acknowledge the unknowable future.[31] In fact, however, it is not clear that any experience is ontologically new in the historical past. And without being able to establish ontological novelty, Voegelin and Schelling are unable to read even the "inner" history of experience as a history of being, changing self-revelations of the divine, and so on. This is a considerable problem. Voegelin clearly glimpsed it—to judge by his citations of Aristotle—but he set it aside, nonetheless, in order to elaborate a progressive account of spiritual truth in history.

The "new domain of Yahweh" is said to expand considerably from the

---

29. Voegelin to Heilman, August 22, 1956 (*CW,* 19:29; Voegelin's parenthetical additions).

30. The Aristotelian passages in question are *Meterologica* 1.3, *Metaphysics* 1074b, and *Politics* 1329a40–1329b35.

31. The knowable past and unknowable future are historiographic themes that Voegelin takes from Schelling's account of the ontohistorical dimensions of anamnesis (cf. "LO," 212–13). These themes continue throughout Voegelin's later work (cf. *NSP,* 120; *OH,* 1:ix, 2:2; *Anam.,* 116; and *CW,* 12:96).

individual soul of Abram when a great leader emerges among the society of Hebrews under Egyptian rule. "At the time when the Egyptians themselves strained their cosmological symbolism to the limits without being able to break the bonds of its compactness, Moses [13th century B.C.E.] led his people from bondage under Pharaoh to freedom under God." The Exodus started to become the quintessential symbol for historical meaning in strictly spiritual terms. It was animated by "a new spirit"—Voegelin's equivalent term for Schelling's "higher will"—which also potentially revealed the beginning of a historical journey from death to life: "Egypt was the realm of the dead, the Sheol, in more than one sense. From death and its cult man had to wrest the life of the spirit." However, instead of ushering in the spiritual life, the Exodus immediately yielded nothing but "the desert of indecision." The Hebrews remained caught between "the equally unpalatable forms of nomad existence and life in a high-civilization." This situation was not a specific impasse only for them. It signaled, according to Voegelin, "the eternal impasse of historical existence in the 'world,' that is, in the cosmos in which empires rise and fall with no more meaning than a tree growing and dying, as waves in the stream of eternal recurrence." The Hebrews left behind one civilization and entered "the world," a place where they too would succumb to the danger of becoming one more civilization that rises and falls without meaning. At times, Voegelin's interpretation of this defection from the spirit reaches sermonic proportions: "By attunement with cosmic order the fugitives from the house of bondage could not find the life that they sought. When the spirit bloweth, society in cosmological form becomes Sheol, the realm of death; but when we undertake the Exodus and wander into the world, in order to found a new society elsewhere, we discover the world as the Desert. The flight leads nowhere, until we stop in order to find our bearings beyond the world" (*OH*, 1:112, 113).

The Hebrews did not stop to find their spiritual bearings, according to Voegelin. They took the world of Canaan in exchange for the emerging life of the spirit. And the central point of the Exodus was obscured: "[H]istory," Voegelin says, "is the Exodus from civilizations." History is the Exodus from "the world," all of its civilizations, which represent only the realm of death. Israel never truly recovered from its penchant to prefer cosmos over spirit: "On its pragmatic wandering through the centuries Israel did not escape the realm of the dead. In a symbolic countermovement to the Exodus under the leadership of Moses, the last defenders of Jerusalem, carrying Jeremiah with them against his will, returned to the Sheol of Egypt to die." Again, Voegelin interprets the spiritual meaning of this alleged defection with distinctively

Christian imagery: "The promised land can be reached only by moving through history, but it cannot be conquered within history. The Kingdom of God lives in men who live in the world, but it is not of this world. The ambiguity of Canaan has ever since affected the structure not of Israelite history only but of the course of history in general" (*OH,* 1:133, 114).

As the Chosen People turned increasingly toward the cosmo-political realm, preferring human kings to God, it turned toward death and set in motion a pattern that repeats itself, according to Voegelin, throughout the political history of Western civilizations. The consequences of this worldly orientation become significant for the understanding of human destiny. Safety is sought in numbers: "[T]he spirit of God, the *ruach* of Yahweh, is present with the community and with individuals in their capacity as representatives of the community, but it is not present as the ordering force in the soul of every man." Only the community survives. The individual has no destiny beyond death. And it is precisely this lack of self-consciousness in the individual that indicates to Voegelin the principal reason that philosophy did not develop among the Israelite tribes: "Only when man, while living with his fellow men in the community of the spirit, has a personal destiny in relation to God can the spiritual eroticism of the soul achieve the self-interpretation which Plato called philosophy. In Israelite history a comparable development was impossible," that is, due to its communitarian mediation of the divine. The turn toward death in the cosmo-political realm also affected adversely the extent to which the Revelation of God could be understood. Even a "revelation of the world-transcendent divinity as personal and intense as the Mosaic (more personal and intense than ever befell a Hellenic philosopher)" is "blunted by the intramundane compactness of the tribe" (*OH,* 1:240; cf. 235–42). The worldly choices of the Chosen People obscure the truly spiritual process of history, as Exodus from the world, and the movement from death to life begins to reverse itself in the pragmatic course of events.

A remnant of the spiritual Exodus movement emerges, however, as the prophetic tradition. With the emergence of the prophets, Voegelin sees the third and last phase of Exodus that is glimpsed by Israelite Revelation. The first phase was Abram's emigration from Ur of the Chaldeans, thus beginning the "Exodus from imperial civilization." The second phase began when Yahweh and Moses led the emerging people of Israel out of Egypt; it ended when they reached "the form of a people's theopolitical existence in rivalry with the cosmological form." The final phase began when the prophets Isaiah (eighth century B.C.E.) and Jeremiah (seventh century B.C.E.) turned away from "the concrete Israel" in order to face "the anguish of the third procreative act

of divine order in history: The Exodus of Israel from itself." The unknown
author of Deutero-Isaiah experienced this anguish most acutely, around the
middle of the sixth century.[32] Like Schelling, Voegelin finds the central function of the prophets to lie in their attempts to call Israel back to the spirit of
Yahweh, to resist pagan elements in the Law, and eventually to proclaim the
need for a future Messiah: "The Yahwism of the Prophets still appears to be
the best recognizable 'contribution' of Israel to the civilization of mankind,
whereas the symbols concerning organized existence [the Deuteronomic Torah]
seem so closely related to the cosmological myth of the time that the specific
Israelite difference is difficult to determine." The task of the prophets was
properly spiritual and universal, in contrast to the "worldly" and parochial aims
of the nation. They struggled "against the Law" in an attempt "to disengage
the existential [that is, spiritual] from the normative issues" (*OH,* 1:491, 186,
447 n. 1). Curiously, however, Voegelin criticizes one of the most spiritual of
the prophets, Isaiah, when he counseled King Ahaz of Judah to stay out of
the world's battles. This matter needs to be considered in some detail, for it
bears on Voegelin's later interpretation of Christian eschatological symbols.

The Kingdom of Judah was threatened with conquest by two enemies:
first by the alliance between Israel and Syria, then by the Assyrian empire. If
Judah refused to join Israel and Syria in battle against the Assyrians, it would
be destroyed by them; this was the more immediate threat. If Judah later
refused to pay tribute to the Assyrians, it would be destroyed by the larger
empire. On both occasions, the prophet Isaiah offered similar advice to King
Ahaz: Do not fight, but trust in the Holy One. "If you do not trust, you will
not last." Do not seek protection from Assyria against Israel and Syria; do
not seek protection from Egypt against Assyria. Your strength lies in "returning and resting," in "sitting still and confidence" (Isa. 7:4–9, 30:15, 31:1–3).
Isaiah seems to have been a gentle pacifist. But such is not the case, according
to Voegelin: "Isaiah's counsel does not originate in an ethics of nonviolence;
it is not calculated to lose the war in order to gain something more important than earthly victory." Isaiah had no hopes in personal immortality; he
was not a Christian pacifist. On the contrary, his counsel was offered in an
attempt "to win the war by means more certain than an army" (*OH,* 1:451).
Voegelin's interpretation is sound. Later, in view of the Assyrian threat,
Isaiah said: "Turn to him [Yahweh] from whom you have deeply revolted. . . .
'And the Assyrian shall fall by a sword, not of man; and a sword, not of man,
shall devour him; and he shall flee from the sword, and his young men shall

---

32. For the dates of Isaiah, Jeremiah, and Deutero-Isaiah, see *OH,* 1:437, 482.

be put to forced labor. His rock shall pass away in terror, and his officers desert the standard in panic,' says the Lord, whose fire is in Zion, and whose furnace is in Jerusalem" (Isa. 31:6–9). Isaiah counseled trust in the "sword" of Yahweh as a spiritual means toward an intraworldly end. The trust has a "utilitarian component," Voegelin says, a notion he borrows from Gerhard von Rad. Worldly prosperity is thought to be "the reward of faith." And this point "has something to do with magic in so far as it can be understood either as a spiritualized magic or as a faith that has sunk to the magic level" (*OH,* 1:450).

Voegelin criticizes Isaiah's magical inclination—his supposition that the order of the world can be changed simply by faith—as a metastasis. "The constitution of being is what it is, and cannot be affected by human fancies. Hence, the metastatic denial of the order of mundane existence is neither a true proposition in philosophy, nor a program of action that could be executed." This faith indicates a problem with the human will, the will in defiance of God: "The will to transform reality into something which by essence it is not is the rebellion against the nature of things as ordained by God. And while the rebellion has become sublime in Isaiah's trust that God himself will change the order of the world and let Judah win its victories without battle, the danger of derailment in various directions is obvious." The divine ordination of the world remains what it is, "even when the one world-transcendent God is revealed as the ultimate source of order in the world, as well as in man, society, and history." The "leap in being is not a leap out of existence." But this confusion is implied by Isaiah's metastasis. "Isaiah, we may say, has tried the impossible." He has tried to leap into "a divinely trans-figured world beyond the laws of mundane existence. The cultic restoration of cosmic divine order becomes the transfiguration of the world in history when carried into the historical form of existence. . . . A gulf opens between the world as it is and the world as it will be when it has been transfigured" (*OH,* 1:453, 452). Isaiah attempted to bring the spiritual perfection of human-ity into this world and failed to see the historical process of spiritual Exodus as a transfiguring movement—the possible fulfillment of which could lie only beyond death.

Voegelin does not criticize Isaiah exclusively on his own terms. Another standard is brought in to formulate his critique. Voegelin's principal guide to the interpretation of political reality is not the philosophical politics of Plato and Aristotle; rather, it derives from the historicospiritual politics of Augus-tine and Schelling. Isaiah's counsel is thought to be dangerous because it was nostalgic and anachronistic. It hearkened back to a time when the Chosen

People could have chosen to live under the spirit of Yahweh, but chose instead to go the way of the nations, competing against them for worldly power. Thus, a central point escaped the attention of Isaiah: it was already too late for Judah. It had a human king, thus breaking the *berith* with Yahweh. It had taken a decisive stake in the world, with all the political consequences that followed from this choice. Judah was not even in a position where it could remain relatively ambivalent to the exigencies of worldly government—for example, as was Jesus with respect to Roman taxation policies (Matt. 22:15–22). Isaiah's call for a general "return" was futile. "The present under God" had become "a suicidal impasse," Voegelin asserts, when the Chosen People became "a small people in opposition to empires." In this situation, only a metastatic faith would make the call for return seem plausible. Voegelin commends King Ahaz for not capitulating to this semblance of piety (*OH,* 1:356, 483; *AR,* 68). He is consistently critical of prophets who claimed or implied that an intra-worldly fulfillment of human nature was possible. To be sure, he grants, the prophets knew that the transformation of reality they desired could not be brought about through human action; it would have to come about through God's decisive intervention. But this qualification was not enough to curtail their hopes for an immanent transfiguration of reality. Thus, Voegelin also rejects Hosea's apocalyptic vision of a transfigured future within historical time as "metastatic yearning." Such yearning cannot hold out, remaining unchallenged indefinitely, for the order of reality patiently resists the extreme measures of its impatient creatures: "[T]he consciousness of passing, the presence of death in life, is the great corrective for futuristic dreams [of the metastatic variety]—though it may require a strong personality to break such dreams, once they have become a social power in the form of accepted creeds" (*OH,* 1:456, 482–83).

Voegelin finds this strength of personality in Jeremiah. He says: "Jeremiah indeed returned from the metastatic vision of the future to the experience of the untransfigured present." Moreover, his return did not have to break completely with Isaiah, according to Voegelin's dialectical reading of the Isaianic writings. Jeremiah accepted and expanded one of the lessons he learned from his predecessor: "[T]he order of society in history is reconstituted in fact through the men who challenge the disorder of the surrounding society with the order they experience as living in themselves." At last, Voegelin finds the consciousness of a break with collective existence "contracted into the existence of the Jeremiah who enacted the fate of the people while carrying the burden of the Anointed." At last, "[t]he great motive that had animated the prophetic criticism of conduct and commendation of the virtues" is "traced to its source in the concern with the order of personal existence under God" (*OH*, 1:483, 484, 485).[33]

With the clear differentiation of his soul as a personal existence under God, however, Jeremiah became neither a philosopher nor a Protestant individualist. Instead, he inaugurated what Voegelin calls the last or "existential" phase in the prophetic concern with a future Messiah. Jeremiah inherited the symbol of the Messiah from his predecessors but changed it significantly, based on the "new" order of his personal existence. Amos (ca. 750) and Hosea (ca. 745–735) had sought the Messiah in the restoration of institutional order, Isaiah in a metastasis of reality itself.[34] In its third and final phase, what Voegelin calls the "Messianic problem" is reduced by Jeremiah to the representative existence of one man who will rise from the House of David. Deutero-Isaiah resumes the symbolic work of Isaiah and Jeremiah, and prophesies the future Messiah as a Suffering Servant.[35] But it takes the better part of five centuries before a small band of Jews finds this Servant in Jesus (*OH*, 1:474–75, 482, 491ff., 515).[36]

Christian Revelation. Voegelin does not develop a substantial account of Christian eschatological symbols in the period of his differentiated historiography, even though they inform his entire notion of historical progress. At most, one finds brief statements contrasting the soteriological truth of Christianity with the anthropological truth of Greek philosophy. The specific difference between the Greeks and Christians is said to lie in the symbolization of grace, wherein God is experienced by Christians as one who "bends" toward the human soul. Voegelin argues: "The experience of mutuality in the relation with God, of the *amicitia* in the Thomistic sense, of the grace which imposes a supernatural form on the nature of man, is the specific difference of Christian truth. The revelation of this grace in history, through

33. For further discussion, see Geoffrey L. Price, "Recovery from Metastatic Consciousness: Voegelin and Jeremiah."

34. For the dates of Amos, Hosea, and Isaiah, see *OH*, 1:312.

35. "Deutero-Isaiah" is a modern convention that Voegelin accepts to designate the unknown author of Isa. 40–55. The author is thought to have flourished in the middle of the sixth century B.C.E. (*OH*, 1:491, 482).

36. For a Jewish perspective on Voegelin's understanding of the theology and historical consciousness evident in the Hebrew scriptures examined in *OH*, vol. 1, see Moshe Idel, "Voegelin's *Israel and Revelation*: Some Observations." Idel's essay culminates in a call for *Israel and Revelation* to be rewritten with help from Voegelin's terms and questions from the perspective of rabbinic Judaism.

the incarnation of the Logos in Christ, intelligibly fulfilled the adventitious movement of the spirit in the mystic philosophers." The insights of the philosophers, relying only on the "unseen measure" of right conduct, were "confirmed" and "fulfilled" with the Incarnation of Christ, the Revelation of "the measure itself." In this sense, Voegelin says cryptically, "the fact of revelation is its content" (*NSP,* 78). This statement appears to mean that the historical fact of Revelation is its new content: the experience of grace through Christ.

Voegelin himself does not explain this phrase. Instead, he says that this conception of Revelation "as well as . . . its function in a philosophy of history" is more fully elaborated in H. Richard Niebuhr's *Meaning of Revelation.* Surprisingly, however, Niebuhr does not use this language in any of the passages cited by Voegelin. But Schelling does. At several places in his *Philosophy of Revelation,* Schelling speaks of the historical "fact" and "content" of the "visible" measure of truth, the Incarnation of Christ.[37] Moreover, as discussed previously, Schelling also thinks that Christ has the same "function" in a philosophy of history. But Voegelin has comparatively little to say about what constitutes Christian truth as "the maximum of differentiation." He says only that "Christianity has concentrated [Hellenistic] demonism into the permanent danger of a fall from the spirit—that is man's only by the grace of God—into the autonomy of his own self, from the *amor Dei* into the *amor sui.*" Christians gain the insight that "mere humanity, without the *fides caritate formata* [formative faith of God's love], is demonic nothingness" (*NSP,* 78 n. 5, 78–79, 79).

The proper order of loves in an individual life is found in one who progresses from the predominance of self-love to the love of God. But this transformation is only the beginning of the salvation from nothingness promised by Christian symbolists, whose focus on salvation leads Voegelin to characterize their type of truth as "soteriological." Ultimately, the historical "function" of Christianity is to reveal that the human desire for salvation "will find fulfillment in transfiguration through Grace in death" (*OH,* 3:364). Now, to understand this notion properly in a philosophy of history would require an account of how Christ's Incarnation, Resurrection, and Ascension can be understood potentially to redeem all of humanity. But Voegelin remains silent on these points during the period of his differentiated historiography, that is, for nearly two decades. Instead, he *assumes* the superior truth of Christian

---

37. Cf. Schelling, *Philosophie der Offenbarung,* in *Werke,* 2.3.185, 196–97, 377.

soteriology and begins to elaborate some of its consequences for his philosophy of history.

Voegelin argues that Christianity has endowed Western thinkers with a properly philosophical understanding of the historicity of human consciousness:

> There is a strict correlation between the theory of human existence and the
> historical differentiation of experiences in which this existence has gained
> its self-understanding. Neither is the theorist permitted to disregard any
> part of this experience for one reason or another; nor can he take his posi-
> tion at an Archimedean point outside the substance of history. Theory is
> bound by history in the sense of the differentiating experiences. (*NSP,* 79)

In historical existence, "reflective analysis, responding to the pressure of
experience, will render symbols increasingly more adequate to their task.
Compact blocks of the knowable will be differentiated into their component
parts and the knowable itself will gradually come to be distinguished from
the essentially unknowable. Thus, the history of symbolization is a progression from compact to differentiated experiences and symbols" (*OH*, 1:5).[38]
Christian theology lifts historical studies "to the ultimate border of clarity
which by tradition is called revelation." It was not simply the symbols that
changed with the advent of Christianity. Rather, even the "complex of experiences" in pagan mythology and philosophy "was enlarged by Christianity
in a decisive point," namely, the point of grace or friendship with God (*NSP,*
79, 77).[39]

This is an important summary. The notion of a historical progression from
"compact" to "differentiated" symbols remains a constant feature throughout all of Voegelin's later work. It constitutes the basis for his claim that
"soteriological truth" is superior to, though cannot do without, its anthropo-

38. This quote offers one indication of the *progressive* character of Voegelin's "compact"
and "differentiated" symbols in history. Terry Barker and Lawrence Schmidt have attempted
to criticize Zdravko Planinc for claiming that Voegelin's notion of compact and differentiated
symbols is progressive—at one point even citing this quote (390), but failing to notice the
progression mentioned by Voegelin himself. See Barker and Schmidt, "'Voegelin Not Mysterious': A Response to Zdravko Planinc's 'The Significance of Plato's *Timaeus* and *Critias* in Eric
Voegelin's Philosophy'"; Planinc's essay is found in the same volume.

39. Voegelin's claim that *experiences* change in history, not just their symbols, is another
point that Barker and Schmidt criticize Planinc for making, allegedly taking Voegelin out of
context. But this textual reference in addition to the previous one from *OH*, vol. 1 (and from
the latest historiography, *OH*, 4:305), lend further support to the claim made by Planinc (see
"'Voegelin Not Mysterious,'" 383).

logical and cosmological predecessors. The language of "compact" (potential) to "differentiated" (actualized) truth in history is also one of the distinctively Schellingian themes in Voegelin's historiography. This is certainly not an obvious claim. Thus far, Voegelin has not mentioned Schelling in a favorable light. His differentiated historiography is written during the time when he is most critical of Schelling.[40] However, once again in a private correspondence from this period, Voegelin acknowledges that his historical philosophy is guided by Schelling. In a little-known letter to Alfred Schütz, Voegelin says that "the differentiation of these experiences [of transcendence] . . . is a historical process—the theogony in the sense of Schelling."[41] The notions of compact and differentiated symbols, history as the "process" in which this transfiguration of reality occurs, and Christ as the cornerstone of historical meaning are Schellingian features that one finds in all of Voegelin's historiography.

The importance of Christian symbols to Voegelin's historiography, and their lack of substantive analysis, during the period I have called his differentiated historiography, prompted Schütz to complain that Voegelin takes his stand "wholly on Christian doctrine." This, at least, is how the matter appeared to Schütz after reading *The New Science of Politics*. He summarizes his interpretation as follows: "Every fall from the Christian faith involves gnosis of either the intellectual or the emotional form or of that voluntaristic form that you subsequently discuss so very instructively and skilfully."[42] Voegelin responds to Schütz sympathetically: "I agree that my position concerning Christianity is too sketchily presented and that the formulations might give rise to misunderstandings such as, for example, that I am trying to defend Christianity and that I condemn all that is not Christian." Voegelin even attempts to convince Schütz that his concern with Christianity "has no religious grounds at all."[43] Rather, he maintains that his concern is motivated by the simple fact that philosophical historians have tended to overlook, inadmissibly, the fifteen hundred years of Christian thought between antiquity and the rise of modernity. "Whatever one may think of Christianity," Voegelin claims, "it cannot be treated as negligible. A general history of

40. Cf. *supra.*, 24–44.

41. Voegelin to Schütz, November 7, 1949, quoted in Helmut R. Wagner, "Agreement in Discord: Alfred Schütz and Eric Voegelin," 85. Voegelin also mentions the Schellingian theogony in *From Enlightenment to Revolution* (1975), though without specific reference to the language of compact and differentiated experiences in history (*FER,* 12).

42. Schütz to Voegelin, November 1952, in *The Philosophy of Order,* 443.

43. Voegelin to Schütz, January 1, 1953, in ibid., 449.

ideas must be capable of treating the phenomenon of Christianity with no less theoretical care than that devoted to Plato or Hegel." It would appear that Voegelin's concern with Christianity is based uniquely on his desire to understand the order of history in a manner acceptable to philosophical scientists. Responsible historians must interpret the vast field of Christian symbols, rather than simply overlooking it due to anti-Christian biases. Voegelin expresses appreciation for the intellectual gains that come with Christian thought, especially its emphasis on historical "degrees in the differentiation of experiences." This point even allows him to formulate "a principle of philosophizing": Philosophers must include in their interpretations of history "the maximally differentiated experiences," so long as they wish to be "operating rationally." They do not "have a right" to base their interpretations on more "compact types of experience while ignoring differentiation, no matter for what reason. . . . Now with Christianity a decisive differentiation has occurred," the revelatory experience of God's grace.[44]

Voegelin elucidates the Christian experience of grace by contrasting it with Plato's parable of the cave (*Republic,* bk. 7). Plato, it seems, did not know who "forced" his prisoner to turn around *(periagoge)* in order to be "dragged" up to the cave entrance and the light of the sun. "It is this 'forcing' that in essence is differentiated in Christian 'revelation' or grace as the experienced intrusion of transcendence into human life. . . . This is new."[45] Furthermore, Voegelin praises the Christian distinction between spiritual and political realms,[46] and explains in greater detail why, "as a philosopher," he is "not inclined to throw Christianity overboard." He distinguishes between "essential Christianity" and "the gnosis of historical eschatology" in "certain texts in Paul" and the Book of Revelation, anticipating that "[n]ot everybody will like this distinction. The sectarian movements and certain trends within Protestantism insist that eschatological Christianity is the essential one, while what I call essential Christianity is for them the corruption of Christianity by the tradition of the Catholic church." Voegelin's "essential Christianity" is based on two "Pauline compromises." First, with the later Paul, it

---

44. Ibid., 449–50.

45. Ibid., 450. A similar understanding of the parable is reproduced in *Plato and Aristotle.* "To be sure," Voegelin states, "the Platonic *periagoge* has the overtones of conversion; but no more than the overtones." "[T]he philosopher's authority. . . will be superseded by the revelation of spiritual order through Christ. The order 'by nature,' thus, is a stage in the history of order; and a theory of order in the Platonic sense requires for its systematic completion a philosophy of history" (*OH,* 3:115, 96).

46. Voegelin to Schütz, January 1, 1953, in *The Philosophy of Order,* 451.

does not proclaim "that the world will end tomorrow and that social order is therefore entirely irrelevant." Second, essential Christianity understands "the faithful living in eschatological expectation [to be] the historical *corpus Christi mysticum*."[47] The essence of Voegelin's Christianity is therefore mystical. It seeks a "critical clean-up" through the process of "radical symbolization" that begins with Meister Eckhart and leads through "the great mystics up to Cusanus." Voegelin appreciates this movement and, as in Schelling's dismissal of orthodoxy, shows no concern that his thoughts are "untenable from the Catholic standpoint and would have to be classified as a variant of that Modernism which has been condemned as a heresy."[48]

This private correspondence contains Voegelin's clearest and most detailed account of Christian symbols from the period of his differentiated historiography. It reveals the source of the ambiguities encountered thus far. In private, Voegelin is a Christian mystic, like Schelling, whose thought is beyond the religion of the churches. His account of "essential" Christianity resembles Schelling's distinction between "esoteric" Christianity, with its "inner" history, and the exoteric teaching of the churches. In his published works, however, Voegelin attempts to write "a philosophical inquiry concerning the order of human existence in society and history" (*OH*, 1:xiv; see also 2:ix). This tension between the historical mysticism of Christianity and the empirical mysticism of classical philosophy accounts for his curious treatment of "cosmological" societies and his hesitation to decide between classical philosophy or Christian faith as the best account of spiritual order.

Although acknowledging his "sketchy" treatment of Christian symbols in *The New Science,* Voegelin could not interpret them further in the early vol-

---

47. Ibid., 452, 453.

48. Ibid., 456, 457. Voegelin also discusses four specific points in Christian doctrine, which he takes to be historical advances over cosmological myth and Jewish Revelation. I can only mention these here: Christology "reduced to its essence and made humanly universal" the "experience of divine help," which was "symbolized in all pre-Christian civilizations polytheistically and in national pluralism" (454); the doctrine of the Trinity properly transformed Christianity from monotheism to "trinitarianism," thus allowing it to account for divine transcendence, divine "intervention reaching into 'nature,' the superimposition of a *forma supernaturalis* in human nature upon the Aristotelian *forma naturalis,*" and the presence of the spirit in the Church (454–55); the Mariological dogmas of *Maria co-redemptrix* and *Maria mediatrix omnium gratiarum* stress the need for human "participation in the work of salvation" (455); and Dionysius Areopagita and Thomas Aquinas attain a "critical understanding of theological speculation and its meaning," which culminates in the insight that theological language rests on an "*analogia entis,* i.e. the recognition that theological judgments are not judgments in the sense of statements about the content of the world," but are simply analogous to these (455–56).

umes of *Order and History* without breaking the chronological order of his historiography. The original plan for his great work was to progress in the following manner: First, an analysis of ancient Near Eastern civilizations, ordered by the "cosmological myth," was to serve as "background" material for understanding the emergence of the world's first consciously historical civilization: the constitution of ancient Israel in representative experiences of transcendental Revelation. Second, an analysis of ancient Greece, with its mythic and tragic forms of order, was to serve as background material for the emergence of transcendental philosophy in Plato and Aristotle. Third, the ecumenic expansion of Near Eastern empires was to be analyzed with a view toward understanding the rise of Christianity and its flowering in medieval civilization. Finally, a second volume on specifically Christian types of order was to analyze the Protestant Reformation with a view toward understanding the contemporary crisis of Western civilization, namely, the breakdown of Christianity as a public cult and the forgotten historiography that once supported the supremacy of its truth. Six volumes were planned in total for *Order and History* (see *OH*, 1:x–xi). However, the two volumes concerned specifically with Christian symbolism never appeared. Voegelin published the first three volumes, leading up to his treatment of Christianity, and then publication stopped on this project. It took seventeen years before the fourth volume of *Order and History* appeared, announcing the need for a change in historiography.

CHAPTER FOUR

Voegelin's Equivalent Historiography

The origin of things is the Apeiron [Unlimited]. . . .
It is necessary for things to perish into that from which
they were born; for they pay one another penalty for
their injustice according to the ordinance of Time.
—Anaximander, fragments A9, B1

The Anamnetic Transition to Historical Equivalences: Remembering Plato and Aristotle

Anamnesis (1966) is the most important work that Voegelin
published between the third and fourth volumes of *Order and History*. It is a
transitional work, leading toward the equivalent historiography that begins
to emerge in his latest period of thought. In *Anamnesis,* Voegelin begins to
elaborate three of the most important changes in his understanding of history
and consciousness. First, he realizes that genuinely historical consciousness
does not begin with its experience and symbolization in ancient Israel. Historiogenesis, Voegelin's term for the unilinear construction of historical order
from a divine-cosmic origin to an author's present, is also found in the earlier
societies of Mesopotamia and Egypt. Voegelin continues to claim that these

societies were ordered by the "compact" myths of the cosmos, but he realizes the need to abandon the conventional account of their "cyclical" historiographies. For example, in the Sumerian King List (ca. 2050 B.C.E.), a text that Voegelin had examined before (cf. *OH*, 1:21–27), he now finds the author tracing a line of order from the first king, the god Enlil, to the human king of the author's present. This movement from divine to human order greatly resembles that which is found among Israelite historiographers. Thus, considered in light of his philosophy of history, the Israelite effort no longer appears to Voegelin as a completely novel form of historical consciousness; it continues and adapts the earlier historiogenesis that it also found among its neighbors (*Anam. Ger.,* 79–116). The second change conveyed by *Anamnesis* breaks another convention that Voegelin had presupposed in his earlier work: the distinction between "natural reason" in classical philosophy and "divine Revelation" in Judeo-Christian religions. Voegelin discovers that Plato and Aristotle, among others, understood *noesis* (contemplative reason) to be constituted by experiences of divine revelation, and he even grants that they described their experiences of the divine with equivalent terms for what Christians call Grace. Finally, this notion of symbolic and experiential "equivalents" is the third change in Voegelin's thought introduced by *Anamnesis*. In addition to the breakdown of the reason-Revelation distinction, it gives Voegelin the intellectual means effectively to abandon his earlier distinction between anthropological and soteriological types of truth. These modes of symbolization become experiential "equivalents" that Voegelin must rework into his later historiography. His attempt to rethink the process of history takes the general form of critical comparisons between classical philosophy and Christian theology. Accordingly, the following chapter will focus on how Voegelin relates the "equivalents" of classic philosophy and Christian theology to his account of history as a spiritual progression of two revelatory types of truth.

In *Anamnesis,* Voegelin describes the *Symposium* as the locus classicus for Plato's awareness that reason is constituted by experiences of divine revelation. Voegelin's focus on the *Symposium* is new. He did not interpret this dialogue in the "Plato" section in the third volume of *Order and History,* and it was mentioned only briefly in *The New Science.* Now Voegelin interprets at least part of the dialogue, the concluding speech on eros that Socrates relates from Diotima, and discovers the awareness of revelatory consciousness in this representative text of classical philosophy. When Socrates describes eros as "a very powerful spirit," one of several mediating between *(metaxy)* the human and the divine,[1] Voegelin takes this description to indicate the experience of mutuality between humanity and divinity—precisely the mutuality that he formerly acknowledged only in Judeo-Christian experiences and symbolizations of the human-divine encounter. He also claims to find a historical component in Plato's symbolization of eros. It reveals to him, and ostensibly to Plato as well, a historical sequence in levels of consciousness moving through three dispositions of order in the human soul: the mortal *(thnetos)* of the Homeric past, the spiritual man *(daimonios aner)* of the present, and the "complacent ignoramus" *(amathes)* or spiritual dullard who resists the representatively human degree of "philosophical experience" in Socrates. Voegelin notes:

> As we reflect about the sequence of the three types, there emerges the field of history which is constituted by the event of philosophy. For the man who through philosophical experience enters into the tension of differentiated knowledge about the order of being recognizes, not only himself as the new type of the *diamonios aner,* but also the man who still lives compactly in the cosmic primary experience, as the historically older type. Further, once the humanly representative level of differentiating experience has been attained [in Plato-Socrates], no way leads back to the more compact levels. *(Anam.,* 128, 129)

Plato allegedly knows that the emergence of erotic philosophy in Socrates constitutes a before and after *in history* from which there is no return to the level of consciousness attained, for example, in Homer's compact understanding of humanity as "mortal." Platonic eros, in Voegelin's account of the matter, is an experience of immortalizing "tension" toward the divine—the fulfillment of which lies only implicitly beyond death *(Anam.,* 130).

From this brief characterization, it appears as though Plato were an Augustine *in potentia*. Voegelin clearly has Augustine in mind, though he does not make the connection explicitly. He interprets Platonic eros as an immortalizing practice of dying with intimations of historical consciousness, and implies that what was lacking in Plato can be found in Augustine. He concludes the chapter with what he calls "the great principle of a material [that is, general] philosophy of history *[das große Prinzip einer materialen Geschichts-philosophie]* that we owe to an insight of Augustine":

> He begins to leave who begins to love [the *daimonios aner*]
> Many the leaving who know it not [the *thnetos* & *amathes*],

---

1. Cf. Plato, *Symposium* 202e–203a.

for the feet of those leaving are affections *[erotes]* of the heart:
and yet, they are leaving Babylon [the world and death].
(*Anam.,* 140; *Anam. Ger.,* 279–80)[2]

Voegelin commends Augustine for beginning to generalize the "affections of the heart" beyond Plato's allegedly restricted focus on Socrates' particular experiences in Athens. Augustine is said effectively to broaden individual experiences of affection for the divine and to reinterpret them as the spiritual Exodus of faithful humanity from the world (Babylon). He properly understands "the historical processes of exodus, exile, and return as figurations of the tension in being between time and eternity" (*Anam.,* 140). Augustine's generalized account of the meaning of love in historical differentiation was limited, according to Voegelin, only by the horizon of historical materials available to him at the time. This means that the details of Augustine's historiography can no longer be followed, due to the expansion of historical knowledge in recent centuries, but the principle he discovered remains valid for Voegelin. It becomes the principle that equates historical study with the search for immortality in spiritual Exodus from "the world" and death. This principle may have guided Voegelin's earlier interpretation of the Exodus in Israelite symbolization; it is certainly part of what guides all of his later historiography.

Voegelin does not make the connection more explicit between Plato's eros and Augustine's "affections of the heart" because he still thinks that Plato's consciousness was more compact than Augustine's. He says that Plato's historical consciousness remained bound to his particular circumstances. Plato did not generalize the Socratic experience of eros in order to become a philosopher of world history, even though the potential for such generalization can be found in his work: "The inklings of a material philosophy of history, which are in principle present in Plato's work, did not immediately lead to further attempts to explore and survey the field of history as a whole." Plato lacked "critically validated comparative materials" from older cultures in the Middle East and Far Eastern contemporaries. Unlike Voegelin, Plato did not feel the need to develop "philosophical concepts" for the "theoretical mastery of such materials," because he simply did not have them. Thus, unlike Voegelin, he could not see the generally human presence of eros as the spiritual mode of Exodus, the immortalizing salvation of humanity from the world and death. Voegelin suspects that Plato could have become a philosopher of

2. Voegelin quotes from Augustine's *Enarrationes in Psalmos* (64.2). This passage also appears as a guiding principle for historiographic interpretation in Voegelin's unpublished "Configurations of History" (1968), in *CW,* 12:105–6; and *The Ecumenic Age,* in *OH,* 4:178.

world history if he had access to the historical materials available to Voegelin himself, for such an "unfolding" of history's order "would have been possible at any given time." But Plato's thinking remained bound to the concrete Athenian struggle between philosophy and sophistry.[3] To be sure, Voegelin does not describe Plato's struggle with sophistry as an idiosyncratic problem. He maintains that the desire for intellectual clarity receives its dynamism "always from contemporary situations of struggle." Augustine also struggled with Manichaeans, Aquinas with Muslims, and Voegelin continues to struggle with modern philosophies of history attempting to make an "immanent" reason or will the impetus of historical progress (*Anam.*, 137–38). Nonetheless, an important implication remains in Voegelin's treatment of Plato and Augustine: some rise above their struggles better than others. For Voegelin, Augustine rose above his contemporary crises better than did Plato. Perhaps this is why the central figure in *Anamnesis*—Voegelin's only book with a distinctively Platonic title—is Aristotle.

Voegelin's earliest reassessment of Aristotelian *noesis* is found in "The Consciousness of the Ground," the first chapter of the larger essay titled "What Is Political Reality?" (*Anam.*, 147–74; *Anam. Ger.*, 287–315). Within the context of the larger essay, "The Consciousness of the Ground" attempts to recount the classic experience of the "noetic interpretation" of the soul's own structure. It is, above all, a chapter on the nature of reason. Although the Aristotelian *nous* (mind) is not translated as "reason" in this essay, it is evident that Voegelin's concern with *noesis* should be considered as an account of reason. In a contemporary discussion, he says: "The ground of existence, in Platonic and Aristotelian philosophy—but especially in Aristotelian—is the *nous:* reason or spirit or intellect. . . . Here the model is man and his experience of such a ground, hence reason is the ground of existence for man" (*Conversations,* 4). In *Anamnesis,* Voegelin's nearly exclusive focus on Aristotle should

---

3. Voegelin is certainly correct when he says that Plato did not become a philosopher of history in the Christian style. The reasons for this will be discussed when I interpret his account of Plato's historical consciousness in *The Ecumenic Age.* However, the supposition that Plato's understanding of eros remained bound exclusively to Socrates' experience is simply false. One reason for this mistake may be found in Voegelin's misinterpretation of an important Platonic myth on the subject: that which is conventionally called the "myth of Er" at the end of the *Republic.* In his earlier interpretation of the myth (*OH,* 3:54–62, 129–34), Voegelin correctly notes that the protagonist of the tale, Er, is described as a "Pamphylian." This means that he represents the man "of all tribes"; he is "an Everyman." But Voegelin fails to notice that in Plato's Greek, the protagonist's name is not Er, as most English translations have it, but Eros (cf. *Republic* 614b). Accordingly, the myth attempts to articulate what everyone desires to know about the human soul in matters of life and death.

come as somewhat of a surprise. Aristotle was singled out in his earlier work as the chief representative of "anthropological truth." Voegelin interpreted Aristotle as one who gained an impressive understanding of order in human existence, both in its personal and social dimensions. But Aristotle, among others, was found to be lacking in soteriological consciousness; he did not know how humanity could be saved from the world's disorder and death, and he even declared that friendship *(philia)* between humans and the divine is impossible. Furthermore, elsewhere Voegelin charged Aristotle with curiously transforming the Platonic experience of transcendence with an "intellectual thinning-out" of the "fullness of experience which Plato expressed in the richness of his myth" *(OH,* 3:276). Aristotle lacked the degree of spiritual sensitivity needed for a proper interpretation of Plato's philosophical myths. Why does Voegelin now turn favorably to Aristotle? It would seem that Aristotle's *Metaphysics,* a text that Voegelin had not analyzed in volume 3 of *Order and History,* now provides him with a suitably subtle terminology with which to begin his own analysis of *noesis* in historical perspective.

Voegelin's textual analysis focuses on the experiential beginning of noetic insights: "In the experience and language of Aristotle, man finds himself in a condition of ignorance *(agnoia, amathia)* with regard to the ground of order *(aition, arche)* of his existence." Aristotle knows, furthermore, that one would not be able to perceive one's own ignorance in this way if one were not already "in the throes of a restless urge to escape from ignorance *(pheugein ten agnoian)* in order to seek knowledge *(episteme)*." That is to say, "whoever is perplexed *(aporon)* and wonders *(thaumazon)* is conscious *(oetai)* of being ignorant *(agnoein)*."[4] It is the recognition of one's restless ignorance that breaks forth into questions concerning the "where-from?" and "where-to?" of all that exists. These are the questions that guide the philosopher's search *(zetesis)* for the ground of existence. The search is not completely blind, therefore, but carries with it the knowledge of ignorance. It is a "knowing questioning and questioning knowledge *[wissendes Fragen und fragendes Wissen].*" Otherwise said, in order to ask a question, one must already have some sense of the direction or goal to which the question is leading. One's questioning "still may miss its goal *(telos)* or be satisfied with a false one," but help is found in the realization that "[t]hat which gives direction to the desire and thus imparts content to it is the ground itself *[der Grund selbst],* insofar as it moves man by attraction *(kinetai)*" *(Anam.,* 148–49; *Anam. Ger.,* 289). The philosopher's initially dim awareness of a transcendent reality is

4. Voegelin quotes Aristotle from *Metaphysics* 982b18.

what initiates the restlessness in the soul and guides the search. The "answer" to the search is then symbolized by the "divine ground." It would seem that the mind is restless until it rests in God. Indeed, the Aristotelian experience of *noesis* is found to begin and end with the divine ground moving the entire process in the philosopher's questioning consciousness.

Voegelin cautions that the experience of noetic tension toward the ground "may be interpreted but not analyzed into parts." He then interprets the entire experience retrospectively: "Without the *kinesis* of being attracted by the ground, there would be no desire for it; without the desire, no questioning in confusion; without questioning in confusion, no awareness of ignorance. There could be no ignorant anxiety, from which rises the question about the ground, if the anxiety itself were not already man's knowledge of his existence from a ground of being that is not man himself." Voegelin's reference to the divine ground as that which moves the soul "by attraction" indicates that he now acknowledges mutuality in Aristotle's experience of *noesis* as a divine-human encounter. "Aristotle adds *[überhaut]* to the exegesis of the noetic desire for the ground and the attraction by the ground the symbol of mutual participation *(metalepsis)* of two entities called *nous* (1072b20ss)" (*Anam.,* 149; *Anam. Ger.,* 290). Aristotle adds this symbol, *metalepsis,* to the efforts of pre-Socratic thinkers, and mutual participation between divine and human reality becomes one of the distinguishing features of Platonic-Aristotelian philosophy, according to Voegelin.[5]

Such intimacy seems to indicate that the line between humanity and divinity, mortals and immortals, has become significantly blurred, if not erased outright. Voegelin addresses this problem. He says that it originates in a terminological ambiguity from Aristotle's text. In his various usages of the term *nous,* Aristotle "understands both the human capacity for knowing questioning about the ground and also the ground of being itself *[den Seinsgrund selbst],*" often without indicating clearly which sense of the term he has in mind (*Anam.,* 149; *Anam. Ger.,* 290).[6] Here is the source of the difficulty. Voegelin

5. Voegelin equates the Platonic and Aristotelian terms for *participation*—*methexis* and *metalepsis,* respectively. See "Immortality" (1965), 89; and "Reason: The Classic Experience" (1974), in *Anam.,* 103.

6. Voegelin's *"Seinsgrund selbst"* is clearly a reference to Aristotle's Unmoved Mover, that "which moves without being moved *[ho ou kinoumenon kinei].*" In one of his more Platonic moments, Aristotle responds clearly to the question of how the Prime Mover can move the human soul without being in motion itself: "[I]t causes motion as being the object of love [or the beloved, *erōmenon*], whereas all other things cause motion because they are themselves in motion" (*Metaphysics* 1072a25, 1072b4).

attempts to solve the problem by recalling its historical context. Aristotle gives the divine and human *nous* the same name, he argues, because "synonymity of expression means equality of genus by genesis" in his thinking. The phrase "by genesis" is decisive for understanding Aristotle properly, for Aristotle's thinking is still said to be in the process of detaching itself from mythic symbolizations of order. Be that as it may, it is not altogether clear whether Voegelin understands Aristotle to be leaving behind Homer's myth of the cosmos or Plato's myth of the soul. The former possibility seems more plausible, however, because the genesis of human *nous* from divine *Nous* closely parallels the demiurgic fashioning of *nous*-in-*psyche*-in-*soma* (mind-in-soul-in-body) in Plato's *Timaeus* (*Anam.*, 149, 206, 68).[7]

Voegelin cites two passages from the *Metaphysics* in order to substantiate his point: "Each thing *(ousia)* will be created through that which is of the same name"; and "[t]he thing which communicates the synonymity of the other things is comparatively the highest thing of this type" (*Anam. Ger.*, 290).[8] Voegelin refers to these passages in order to reveal the continuing importance of mythic symbols even after Aristotle's *noesis* has afforded consciousness the ability to articulate its own structure. Thus, "synonymity," "genesis," and "mutual participation" are interpreted as mythic symbols, which Aristotle allows to enter his exegesis of noetic consciousness. Mythic symbolization "ingresses into the noetic exegesis because the noesis egresses from the myth, as it interprets its logos [structure, inherent order]." The continuing presence of mythic symbols does not signal a "methodological derailment" on the part of Aristotle, Voegelin maintains. Rather, it reveals simply "the residue of prenoetic knowledge of order and the background without which the noetic knowledge of order would have no function" (*Anam.*, 152, 151). Even after noetic insight into the order of consciousness has differentiated the rationality of consciousness as being moved by, and tending openly toward, the divine ground, "[o]ur knowledge of order remains primarily mythical." *Noesis* functions as a "differentiating correction" to the "preknowledge of man and his order that stems from the compact primary experience of the cosmos, with its expression in the myth." It differentiates the intracosmic understanding of "the relations between the ground of being and man, ground of being and world, man and world, as well as the relations between things

7. Cf. Plato, *Timaeus* 30b, 37a.
8. Aristotle, *Metaphysics* 1070a4ff., 993b20ff. Voegelin makes his own translations of Aristotle's Greek. I have translated Voegelin's German, and thereby broken with Gerhard Niemeyer's English translation of *Anamnesis*, because Niemeyer ignores Voegelin's German translations of Aristotle's Greek (cf. *Anam.*, 149).

in the world, so that the reality-image of being replaces the reality-image of the cosmic primary experience." *Noesis* cannot simply replace the mythic truth of order. It "does not discover objects that until then were unknown, but it discovers relations of order in a reality that was also known to the primary experience of the cosmos" (*Anam.*, 150, 206, 134).

Voegelin does not credit Schelling with helping him to understand why philosophers should not depreciate mythic thought. Instead, he turns to a parenthetical remark in the *Metaphysics,* the same passage that my foregoing analysis found interpreted by Schelling,[9] and credits Aristotle with recognizing that the prephilosophic lover of myth, "the *philomythos,*" was also something of a lover of wisdom, a *philosophos,* for myth and philosophy are both expressions of the "wondering" *(thaumazein)* by which "[a]ll people are equally excited" (*Anam.*, 157).[10] All people, even the most ancient mythologists, participate in the same movements of consciousness when they search for the "where-from?" and "where-to?" of their existence. "When Homer and Hesiod trace the origin of the gods and all things back to Ouranos [Heaven], Gaia [Earth], and Okeanos [Ocean], they express themselves in the medium of theogonic speculation, but they are engaged in the same search of the ground as Aristotle himself."[11] The experience and symbolization of noetic consciousness do not change the substantial order of human consciousness, Voegelin suggests, but make it more explicit as participation in the divine ground. *Noesis* lifts the reality of participation "into the light of consciousness." But such participation is still a reality "even when it is not fully conscious of its own character, i.e., even when it is not knowledge about knowledge."

---

9. Cf. *supra,* 165.

10. Aristotle, *Metaphysics* 982b18 ff. Voegelin's "all people" translates the opening words of the *Metaphysics.* Aristotle says: "All humans naturally desire knowledge. An indication of this is our esteem for the senses; for apart from their use we esteem them for their own sake" (980a22ff.; cf. *Anam.*, 183). In the last volume of *Order and History,* Voegelin interprets this statement as opening "the great reflective study of consciousness, the act of remembering its range from sense perception to its participation in the divine *Nous.*" Clearly, "[i]f this sentence were torn out of its noetic context," he continues, "it could be ridiculed as an empirically false statement; for quite a few men obviously do not desire to know but are engaged in the construction of Second Realities [that is, ideologies]. . . . If, however, we do not literalize the sentence and thereby destroy its noetic validity, it will express a thinker's conscious openness toward the paradox of existential consciousness; and it will furthermore symbolize this openness as the potential of 'all men,' even though the potential be deformed through acts of oblivion by all too many" (*OH,* 5:47).

11. Cf. Aristotle, *Metaphysics* 983b28 ff.

The desire for knowledge is not the experiential motivation of philosophers alone, "but of every experience of participation. . . . It is always man's existential transcending toward the ground, even when the ground does not become conscious [to one in search of order] as the transcendent pole of the desire" (*Anam.*, 93, 183).

Despite this high praise, Voegelin knows that Aristotle did not have an unqualified love of myth. The classic philosopher accepted some of the wonders of myth but rejected others. He accepted the opinions of the fathers *(patrios doxa)*—for example, that the heavenly bodies are divine—while he rejected the notion of the gods' human or animal form as an invention to help ordinary people speak of gods, but which should now be abandoned.[12] "The philosopher thus eliminates the *thaumasia* [wonders] of the polytheistic myth but retains the knowledge of the *philomythoi* [lover of myths] about the divinity of the ground. He clearly grasps the difference of the grades of truth between the primary experience of a cosmos full of gods and the noetic experience for which the divine is the ground of the cosmos and of man" (*Anam.*, 158).

This is an important insight for Voegelin. He takes it to be "the first steps toward a theory of equivalent symbols and experiences" in history ("EESH," 125–26). That is to say, Aristotle takes the first steps toward a philosophy of history that does not have to reject the cosmological myth of the past as completely false, but receives it as a limited though necessary step toward the truth of his present. Voegelin knows that "Aristotle's name does not conjure up in our time the figure of a philosopher of history." But he stresses that "his analysis of the temporal flow in consciousness as the dimension in which noesis recognizes itself as the presence of truth and, at the same time, the myth as the past, is a philosophical accomplishment about history that has not been surpassed until today." Aristotle knows, Voegelin implies, that profane history is meaningless—and that meaningful history is to be found only in "the inner dimension of consciousness of desire and search after the ground." What is more, because all people are said to experience this inner dimension of desire, "the field of history is always universally human, even if only a relatively small sector of the philosophers' position would be materially [that is, generally] known. The human universality of the desiring and searching participation in the ground results further in the equivalence of the symbolisms in which the consciousness of the ground is expressed." By

---

12. Cf. ibid., 1071b1–15.

"equivalence," Voegelin means to say that "all experiences of the ground are in like manner experiences of participation [in the universal structure of reality], even though they may considerably differ from each other on the scales of compactness and differentiation, of finding and missing the ground." The notion of "equivalents" should not be misunderstood to suggest the uncritical *equality* of symbols. Rather, one might say that Homeric myth and Platonic-Aristotelian philosophy are equivalents only in a categorical sense: within the homogeneous medium of reality, they both express a relatively common search for the ground. They are equal in kind, even though they differ considerably in the degree of clarity attained with respect to the relations of order symbolized. Yet their differences are not sufficient to allow later generations to become proud of their historically superior insights: "The equivalence of the symbols thrown up in the stream of participation . . . leads to the loving turning back to the symbols belonging to the past, since they express phases of that same consciousness in the presence of which the thinker finds himself."[13] Aristotle catches sight of the universally human desire for the ground that, according to Voegelin, Plato tended to overlook due to his distracting focus on the refutation of sophists. But Voegelin does not proceed with his analysis by discussing the reasons Aristotle also neglected to develop a universal philosophy of history. Instead, he turns to determine the point at which he must diverge from Aristotle "in the historical situation of our time" (*Anam.*, 158–59).

The central difficulty that Voegelin finds in Aristotle's noetic philosophy is his lack of concern for clarifying the distinction between humanity and divinity. This distinction is said to become "fuzzy," especially in Aristotle's description of enthusiastic experiences of "mutual participation." Voegelin translates the central text for this problem as follows: "Thought *(nous)* thinks *(noei)* itself through participation *(metalepsis)* in that which is thought *(noeton);* for it *(i.e.,* thought, *nous)* becomes that which is thought, as it grasps *(thigganon)* and thinks *(noon),* so that thought and that which is thought are

---

13. For Voegelin's elaboration of the notion of equivalences of experience and symbolization in history, see "EESH," 115–33. Schelling also uses a notion of equivalent experiences to interpret different versions of the Egyptian symbols for Isis, Osiris, and Typhon. He says that the inner experience is where one may find the similarity that underlies the different external representations of these figures (cf. *Philosophie der Mythologie,* in *Werke,* 2.2.369–71). But Schelling does not develop this insight explicitly as a theory of "equivalents," perhaps because it is already presupposed in his account of natural potencies differentiating in the successive periods of history.

the same. Thought *(nous)* is that which can grasp *(dektikon)* reality *(ousia)*, or that which is thought" *(Anam., 167; Anam. Ger., 308)*.[14] As revealed by his parenthetical remarks, Voegelin understands this passage to describe the human *nous* in search of the divine as its *noeton*. He criticizes Aristotle for his ambiguous description of *metalepsis* and finds it to be "no accident" that Georg Hegel could use this statement "as the great peroration of the *Encyclopedia*" — a "gnostic-dialectical speculation" that attempts to reveal the reflective identity of the human and divine Spirit *(Anam., 167–68)*.[15] Aristotle, it seems, did not anticipate the radical, incarnational thinking of a Hegel. He thus left his noetic philosophy open to the abuse of later thinkers.

Despite this difficulty, Voegelin's return to classical philosophy has afforded him a number of important insights for his own historiography. First, he finds the consciousness of revelatory experience to have been the constitutive feature of classical *noesis*. This discovery allows him to bring the classical philoso-

---

14. Aristotle, *Metaphysics* 1072b20–2. Once again I have translated Voegelin's German, including his parenthetical remarks, which the English translator has ignored. Voegelin states: "Das Denken *(nous)* denkt *(noei)* sich selbst durch Teilnahme *(metalepsis)* am Gedachten *(noeton)*; denn Gedachtes wird es (sc. das Denken, *nous*), indem es ergreift *(thigganon)* und denkt *(noon)*, so daß dasselbe sind Denken und Gedachtes. Denn das, was Gedachtes oder Realität *(ousia)* ergreifen kann *(dektikon)*, ist das Denken *(nous)*." This translates Aristotle's Greek: *"auton de noei ho nous katametalēpsin tou noētou. Noētos har hihnetai thigganōn kai noōn, hōste tauton nous kai noēton."* In the Aristotelian text, it is not at all clear that the symbol *nous* refers to the human mind. On the contrary, because this remark occurs in a section in which Aristotle is attempting to describe the perfect activity of the divine mind, which humans enjoy only occasionally, the *nous* may indeed be the God and the human mind its "object of thought" *(noeton)*. This suggestion makes better sense of the context: Aristotle is clearly attempting to describe the priority of the divine to the human mind.

15. Voegelin's reading of the Aristotelian passage improves when he returns to address it in his later essay "Reason: The Classic Experience" (1974). He notes: "When read in the Aristotelian context, the sentence articulates the dynamics of sameness and difference of the knower and the known in the act of noetic participation, the joy of momentary sameness with the divine notwithstanding. When read in the context of the *Encyclopaedie*, the sentence expresses the beginnings of a philosophical enterprise that has been brought to its successful conclusion by Hegel. For in the Hegelian conception, philosophy begins as the 'love of wisdom' in the classic sense and moves from this imperfect state toward its consummation as 'real knowledge' *(wirkliches Wissen)* in the System. From the classic participation in the divine *nous* it advances through the dialectical progress of the *Geist* [Spirit] in history, to identification with the *nous* in self-reflective consciousness." This work, however, Voegelin considers to be merely an "eristic" trick of "speculative magic" by which Hegel reveals himself to be in revolt against reality *(Anam., 108–9; CW, 12:284–85)*. For Voegelin's elaboration of his Hegel critique, see "On Hegel," in *CW,* 12:213–55.

phers into the orbit of what Schelling calls "revealed religion." Schelling also grants, we recall, that reason in Plato and Aristotle—and the level of consciousness attained in the Mysteries—could be understood as a revelation analogue. But Voegelin appears to go even further here. He summarizes the discovery in terms suggesting the equivalence of classical *noesis* and Christian experiences of divine Grace: "Out of a comprehensive complex of knowledge, the classical noesis differentiates the consciousness of the ground by way of love of God, of being moved by grace of the ground to the point of feeling compelled to 'turn around' [Plato's *periagoge*] from being lost in the world toward inclination to the ground." Voegelin emphasizes that this differentiation affords "knowledge," not simply opinion or belief. Hence, the knowledge that comes from such concrete experiences of "love" is said to yield a *"cognitiones fides,"* a faith based on cognition gained in the experience. The movement away from being lost in the world and death is symbolized by the relative immortality of Plato's "spiritual man" *(daimonios aner),* knowing himself consciously to exist in the mortal-immortal middle ground of the *metaxy.* This middle ground of consciousness becomes the site in which Voegelin finds history itself to be constituted as an immortalizing process of the divine ground in human consciousness (*Anam.,* 184; cf. 124, 132–33).

Shortly after the publication of *Anamnesis,* Voegelin begins to acknowledge that Aristotle also spoke of *noesis* as an immortalizing activity. He takes Aristotle's symbol for "immortalizing" *(athanatizein)* from a passage in the *Nicomachean Ethics,* which he translates as follows:

> The life of the intellect *(nous)* is higher than the human level; not by virtue of his humanity will a man achieve it, but by virtue of something within him that is divine. . . . Nor ought we to obey those who enjoin that a man should have man's thoughts and a mortal the thoughts of mortality, but we ought to immortalize *(athanatizein)* as much as possible and do everything toward a life in accordance with the highest thing in man. ("Immortality," 87–88)[16]

Both Plato and Aristotle discover that human consciousness is not simply mortal, as Homer had allegedly thought. It is not just slipping back into what Anaximander called the Unlimited *(Apeiron)* but exists in a state of tension between mortality and immortality, time and eternity. This tension,

---

16. Aristotle, *Nicomachean Ethics* 1177b30–1178a. This is the passage that I found footnoted by Schelling, cf. *supra,* 165 n. 88.

and especially its accent on the immortalizing pull on consciousness, becomes the central focus in Voegelin's latest historiography.

The Equivalent Historiography:
Developmental History Revisited

In light of the considerable changes in Voegelin's reassessment of certain experiences in classical philosophy, one would expect his historiography to change considerably. *The Ecumenic Age,* volume four of *Order and History* (1974), announces a "break" in his general conception of the project. His description of this change is potentially confusing, however. On the one hand, he says that nothing was inherently wrong with the way the project was originally conceived. There were indeed advancing insights into divine and human reality, "leaps in being," that marked epochal changes in human consciousness and civilizational order. On the other hand, he says that something was quite wrong with the original program: "When I devised the program I was still laboring under the conventional belief that the conception of history as a meaningful course of events on a straight line of time was the great achievement of Israelites and Christians who were favored in its creation by the revelatory events, while the pagans, deprived as they were of revelation, could never rise above the conception of a cyclical time." Voegelin acknowledges, for the first time to his English readers, that the "cyclical" convention "had to be abandoned" when he discovered historiogenesis in other civilizations. Historiogenetic speculation is now said to be "a millennial constant in continuity from its origins in the Sumerian and Egyptian societies, through its cultivation by Israelites and Christians, right into the 'philosophies of history' of the nineteenth century A.D." (*OH,* 4:1, 2, 7). The original project also had to be abandoned due to the discovery of revelatory experiences articulated by classical philosophers. In *The Ecumenic Age,* Voegelin becomes even more explicit with respect to the revelatory nature of classical *noesis:*

> The openness, in all directions, of consciousness toward the reality of which it is a part . . . is the joyous willingness to apperceive a reality that is informed by the same Nous as the psyche—that is all.
> But that is considerably more than is conventionally realized. Under the title of "reason," or the theologically condescending title of "natural reason," this constitution of the psyche once achieved is so much taken for granted that its origin in a theophanic event has passed from public con-

sciousness. Substantially, this oblivion has been caused by the theologians'
eagerness to monopolize the symbol "revelation" for Israelite, Jewish, and
Christian theophanies. (*OH,* 4:236)

To correct this mistaken convention, Voegelin emphasizes that the life of
reason in classical philosophy is "firmly rooted in a revelation." He complains that this point is "conventionally anesthetized" by philosophical historians who report only "the philosophers' 'ideas' without touching the
experiences that have motivated them." This practice must not be allowed in
a philosophical study of order, Voegelin now contends. The "philosophers'
theophanies must be taken seriously. The questions which the revelatory
experiences impose must not be dodged, they must be made explicit: Who is
this God who moves the philosophers in their search? What does he reveal
to them? And how is he related to the God who revealed himself to Israelites,
Jews, and Christians?" Voegelin now grants that "[u]nless we want to indulge
in extraordinary theological assumptions," the God of classical philosophy is
identical to the God of Judeo-Christian theology (*OH,* 4:228–29).

Clearly, a substantial revision of the historiography is in order, and Voegelin
knows it. He begins to emphasize his earlier point, from *The New Science of
Politics,* that the order of history has no philosophically discernible meaning
or essence—no *eidos.* He reproduces the dictum of Karl Löwith that he first
mentions in *The New Science:* there is no abstract meaning *of* history, but
only meaning *in* history. And he complains that the "final answer to the
meaning of history has been given not once but several times too often."
Consequently, "[t]here would be no sense in adding one more 'meaning of
history' to the more than enough that we have, pretending that the new one
at last will be the right one." He even sympathizes with the critical points
against "philosophies of history" that were raised by Jacob Burckhardt in his
1868 lectures *On the Study of History.* Burckhardt criticizes progressivist constructions of history's order that prevailed in his time. He maintains that the
construction of a philosophy of history reveals only "'our profound and
most ridiculous selfishness.'" The truth of this claim will be understood,
Burckhardt continues, when it is acknowledged that "'[e]verybody considers
his own time to be, not one of the many passing waves, but the fulfillment
of time.'" Voegelin commends Burckhardt as "one of the rare modern historians who has faced the issue and analyzed it." Voegelin also praises Immanuel
Kant for a similar observation. Kant had noticed, in the eighteenth century,
that progressivist histories reduce people of the past to the status of mere "contributors" to the glorious present; he also realized that progressivists unwit-

tingly reduce themselves to the status of being mere contributors to some other mistakenly glorious present in the future (*OH,* 4:214, 193, 325–26, 224; see also 2:4).[17]

In light of these acknowledgments, it would seem that, recalling the programmatic statement with which *Order and History* was introduced, Voegelin no longer thinks that the "order of history" will emerge from critical studies on the "history of order." He seems to have arrived at a considerably different understanding of what historical studies can achieve: "The process of history, and such order as can be discerned in it, is not a story to be told from the beginning to its happy, or unhappy, end; it is a mystery in process of revelation" (*OH,* 4:6). In fact, however, this is not Voegelin's last word on the order *of* history. Appearances notwithstanding, he still claims to know a great deal about history's order; he even concludes his study by attempting to add one more meaning of history to the "more than enough" that he says we already have. Despite his clear awareness of some of the problems involved in such constructions, he begins to formulate what amounts to a new version of the old historiography.

He does so, first, by distinguishing between two dimensions of history. These dimensions are called "History I" and "History II." This procedure reflects the old distinction between profane and sacred dimensions of history, respectively. History I is described as a society's self-interpretation. It is the account of a society's greatness that usually draws upon historiogenetic speculation in order to reveal the divine legitimation of its present order. This self-interested history "is greatly cherished by the members of a society." It is typically used by imperialists who seek to establish a perfect realm of peace in the historical existence of an empire with ecumenic aspirations.

---

17. Voegelin does not mention the text from which he takes this account of Kant's understanding of historical progress. However, his reference to the "cosmopolitan" realm of reason (*OH,* 2:4), toward which Kant thought the order of history to be progressing, indicates that he has in mind Kant's *Idee zu einer allgemeinen Geschichte in weltbürgerlicher Absicht,* wherein Kant asserts: "It remains strange that the earlier generations appear to carry through their toilsome labor only for the sake of the later, to prepare for them a foundation on which the later generations could erect the higher edifice which was Nature's goal, and yet that only the latest of the generations should have the good fortune to inhabit the building on which a long line of their ancestors had (unintentionally) labored without being permitted to partake of the fortune that they had prepared" (Prussian Academy edition of Kant's *Works,* Berlin, 1900–1955, 8:20). I have followed L. W. Beck's translation of this text, "Idea for a Universal History from a Cosmopolitan Point of View," in *On History,* by Kant, ed. and trans. L. W. Beck (Indianapolis: Bobbs-Merrill, 1963), 14. For an overview of this area of Kant's thought, see Fackenheim, "Kant's Concept of History," in *God Within,* 34–49.

The imperial attempt to find meaning in life, finally, is said to take the form of a "concupiscential exodus" toward worldly greatness (*OH,* 4:173, 197). Thus, Voegelin's "History I" accounts for the dimension of worldly or profane existence described by Augustine as the concerns of the *civitas terrena.* Likewise, Voegelin's "History II" accounts for the dimension of spiritual existence symbolized by Augustine's *civitas Dei.* He says that History II is typically shunned by worldly societies. History II symbolizes the experiences that recall to one's attention the broader spiritual context of life and death, "the never quite repressible knowledge that all things that come into being will come to an end." The awareness of History II can be acknowledged either reluctantly or with joy. In the former sense, it can be expressed as one's "tragic consciousness" that civilizations exist only as parts of the greater whole in which empires rise and fall without permanent meaning. For example, on occasion of the Roman conquest of Carthage (146 B.C.D.), a proud moment for Romans on the level of History I, Polybius relates how general Scipio Aemilianus was seized by a moment of horror when he realized that someday the same doom might befall his own people (*OH,* 4:173, 182, 132). The broader context of History II emerges in the consciousness of Scipio, and this realization is experienced as tragic by the imperial conqueror who would make all histories lead to Rome. Scipio suffers from having placed his trust in the self-interpretation of Roman society's greatness (History I) while knowing this interpretation, on some level, to be limited by the spiritual order of reality of which Rome is only a part. His suffering is an indication that he has begun to leave "the world" of conventional greatness, as he turns sadly to face the order that does not submit to human conquerors.

The emergence of History II need not be experienced as tragic, Voegelin argues. It may be embraced by those who learn to replace the "concupiscential exodus" of ecumenic conquerors with the "spiritual exodus" of philosophers, prophets, and saints. That is to say, the search for imperial meaning, human unity, and permanence in the world may be transformed by the expectation that human life can be perfected, and universal humanity united, only by God beyond death. Voegelin claims that the emergence of this expectation sheds some light upon the general course of history, insofar as it yields a pattern in which "concupiscential exodus" (History I) is increasingly replaced by "spiritual exodus" (History II). He devotes considerable attention to explaining how this expectation initially comes about, and suggests that it constitutes the only meaningful sense of advance that can be sustained by philosophers of history. Accordingly, it needs to be examined in some detail.

"History I": Expansion of the Spatial Horizon of Humanity—Profane History

In *The Ecumenic Age,* Voegelin focuses on the fact that the "spiritual outbursts" analyzed in previous volumes of *Order and History,* the "leaps in being" in Hellas and Israel, occur during times of great civilizational crisis, more specifically, when the Persian, Macedonian, and Roman empires successively compete to dominate the one ecumene of humanity. Voegelin calls this time of imperial expansion the "Ecumenic Age," a period of history extending roughly from the rise of the Persian to the fall of the Roman empires. It was during this time, he argues, that the spatial horizon of humanity was pushed significantly close to its limits to reveal *for the first time* that the true boundary surrounding all of humanity is a spiritual horizon, namely, death, that cannot be crossed, explored, or conquered in this life. The suffering caused by the ecumenic wars becomes a significant factor in the discovery of divine transcendence and the notion that human perfection might lie beyond the universal horizon of death. These insights are found to emerge in the works of ancient historiographers who reflect on the meaning of their suffering. Thus, by drawing on their works, Voegelin formulates a general order of history, a "triadic unit of experience" that looks distinctively Schellingian: the concupiscential expansion of empires (B) gives rise to spiritual outbursts (A²) that are eventually synthesized by historiographers (A³) who attempt to construct a meaningful account of conquests and spiritual outbursts in the historical contexts known to them at the time. This "triadic unit" attempts to account for the unfolding of consciousness—still in a *progression* from "compact" to "differentiated" degrees of clarity—during the Ecumenic Age and beyond (*OH,* 4:114, 308, 314).

Voegelin's discussion of this development begins with a "compact" symbolism predating the onset of the greatest imperial expansions. He focuses on the changing meaning of the symbolic pair *oikoumene-okeanos* (habitation-horizon) in order to discuss this general transformation. "*Oikoumene* and *okeanos* belong together as integral parts of a symbolism which, as a whole, expresses a compact experience of man's existence in the cosmos." The word *oikoumene (ecumene)* symbolizes the habitat of human life in the cosmos. This habitat is defined by its horizon, symbolized by the word *okeanos,* the "great encircling" of the *oikoumene.* In its oldest-known usage, Voegelin observes that the word *okeanos* does not refer to the ocean as a body of water surrounding the inhabited land. Rather, it is a mythical symbol for the widest possible horizon that encircles the habitat of humanity: *okeanos* symbolizes the encircling horizon of death. In the Mesopotamian epic of Gilgamesh, for example, "Gilgamesh is not yet the differentiated discoverer or conqueror in pursuit of the ocean as a spatial horizon, but still the mythical hero in pursuit of life beyond death. The waters he has to cross, in Tablet X, are not the Ocean . . . in the sense of a border of the ecumene but the waters of death beyond the world of this life" (*OH,* 4:202, 203–4 n. 16). These horizon-forming "waters" of death are also symbolized in Egyptian myths dating from the middle of the second millennium B.C.E., and this is still the "compact" meaning of the word *okeanos* when it is used in Homer's epics (eighth century B.C.E.). In Homeric usage, the *okeanos*

> marks the horizon where Odysseus finds the Cimmerians and the entrance to the underworld of the dead (*Odyssey,* XI); it is the border of the *oik-oumene* beyond which lie the Islands of the Blessed (IV, 56 ff.). In the epics, thus, the *oikoumene* is not yet a territory to be conquered together with its population. The experience of the "horizon" as the boundary between the visible expanse of the *oikoumene* and the divine mystery of its being is still fully alive; and the integral symbolism of *oikoumene-okeanos* still expresses the In-Between reality of the cosmos as a Whole. (*OH,* 4:203)

Voegelin notices that the meanings of the symbols change drastically by the fifth century B.C.E. In Herodotus, he observes that the river Okeanos has become "the ocean-sea that surrounds the land mass of the ecumene and the mankind inhabiting it." The enlightened Herodotus, in his *Histories,* complains that he is unable to find the Ocean and "pours his scorn on the older conception: 'For my part I know of no river called Ocean, and I think that Homer, or one of the earlier poets, invented the name' (II, 23)." Herodotus even laughs at those who continue to draw maps of a round earth completely surrounded by this imperceivable ocean-stream (4.36) (*OH,* 4:204). The Ocean has thus become a fictional horizon, the ocean-sea a literal thing that can be crossed, and the ecumene a spatial land that can be conquered. The imperial search for the Isles of the Blessed, as a place on earth where humanity attempts to regain its lost unity through military conquest, is well under way.

Voegelin interprets the outcome of the ecumenic wars in a curious way. On the one hand, he criticizes the entire process as "concupiscential." The pursuit of ecumenic domination reveals itself to be a misdirection of eros, a fatuous attempt to attain the permanence of immortality in this life and to conquer the order of reality in which everything must die. Voegelin knows that this drive to conquer the ecumene was not exhausted by the failures to establish a world empire during the Ecumenic Age. It was simply restrained by "spiritual outbursts" in people who emphasized the impenetrable nature of the human horizon (= death). But the spiritual restraints of mystics could not hold out against the worldly desires of imperial pragmatists. These latter eventually circumnavigate the globe in their attempts to conquer the ecumenic horizon and reach paradise in this life, but their attempts were always bound to fail:

> If one tries [in spatio-temporal existence] to reach the *okeanos,* with its Islands of the Blessed and its entrance to the underworld, one returns to the point from which one started. The superb irony of the ecumene having the shape of a sphere that brings the concupiscential explorer of reality back home to himself, and of this sphere being situated in a cosmic horizon of infinite extension and duration, has hardly yet entered the consciousness of a mankind that is reluctant to admit concupiscential defeat. (*OH,* 4:210)

The concupiscential drive continues to this day, "and since it has become a bit silly to chase around the earth, one must engineer round trips to the moon." One must even imagine "extra-ecumenes" to conquer in the infinite universe: "Hence, we live in the age of other worlds than our own, of invasions from Mars, and of flying saucers. Anything will do, as long as it puts off the confrontation with the divine mystery of existence." Voegelin argues that these and other more serious diversions from the reality of death are now more inexcusable than ever. Some cardinal lessons have been learned from the Ecumenic Age: "No imperial expansion can reach the receding horizon; no exodus from bondage is an exodus from the *condicio humana;* no turning away from the Apeiron, or turning against it, can prevent the return to it through death" (*OH,* 4:211, 215). In other words, space is not "the final frontier," as the authors of *Star Trek* would have it. The exploration of space is simply the latest manifestation of the "concupiscential exodus" that created the great suffering of the Ecumenic Age. The only difference between ancient and modern imperialism, Voegelin contends, is that moderns should know better.

Voegelin criticizes imperial expansions after the Ecumenic Age. However, he thinks that his ability to criticize them is *determined* by the fact that he lives in the time after ecumenic conquests failed to achieve human unity and permanence by crossing the *okeanos* only on this side of death. His critique of postecumenic imperialism is, therefore, historically relative, and this point tends to undermine his ability to criticize imperialist expansions during the

Ecumenic Age itself. The critique that he does provide is weakened by his supposition that the lust for domination needed to be exercized during the Ecumenic Age in order to reveal the spiritual nature of humanity's ultimate horizon. The sufferings of the Ecumenic Age reveal to Voegelin that "the concupiscence of conquest cannot reach the horizon beyond which lies the divine source of human universality, [and] from this very failure emerge mankind and its habitat as the site where the universality of man has to be realized in personal, social, and historical existence." Voegelin stops just short of being thankful for the human misery and mass murder of conquest during the Ecumenic Age. He says that it offers a "spectacle of meaningful advances," albeit a "nauseating" one, to later historians of the spirit. Indeed, the redemptive meaning that he attempts to take from this period is the discovery of world history itself. More specifically, developmental history eventually becomes the properly spiritual horizon *(okeanos)* that one must begin to cross in this life, through "spiritual Exodus," in order to anticipate one's salvation through Grace in death. It is in the Ecumenic Age when the perfection of humanity is allegedly first sought beyond death. And a great deal of death was apparently necessary for this discovery, because "history as the horizon of divine mystery that surrounds the spatially open ecumene can hardly emerge unless the [spatial] ecumene actually opens under the impact of concupiscential expansion, and the expansion is no more than a senseless rise and fall of peoples and their rulers unless the consciousness of the historians can relate the events to the truth of existence that emerges in the spiritual outbursts" (*OH,* 4:208, 215, 313). Developmental historians, albeit on a spiritual level, become the saviors of meaning during great periods of civilizational crisis. They attempt to rise above the fray and pull some measure of order and peace out of the seemingly hopeless manifestations of chaos and destruction all around them.

In fact, however, the muted self-congratulation of developmental historians is one thing, but the meaning they attempt to derive from periods of senseless suffering is quite another, at least for philosophers. Voegelin's hesitation to criticize ecumenic expansions seriously is curious. Perceptive readers will have already noticed from the foregoing analysis that his own account of the "compact" symbol *okeanos* reveals that the horizon of humanity was already properly understood to be death, by Mesopotamian and early Egyptian symbolists, even before the period of ecumenic conquests. The failure of these conquests was not needed after all to induce the spiritual awareness of death as the true horizon of the *condicio humana.* The inescapable suffering caused by natural death and limited warfare appears to have been quite enough. Of course, Voegelin's common sense would agree with these basic points. But his agreement would likely be dialectical, and therefore ambiguous.

This matter has been sensed by a recent interpreter of *The Ecumenic Age*. On the one hand, John Ranieri notes that, for Voegelin, "'phenomenal' [that is, pragmatic] events do not 'cause' differentiations of consciousness. Imperial expansion does not serve as an efficient cause, generating differentiations of consciousness." Nonetheless, he continues,

> [i]f not the cause of differentiations, pragmatic events would seem to be [for Voegelin] at least a significant catalyst in their emergence. Voegelin acknowledged that certain levels of social, political, and economic achievement are more favorable to differentiation than others, but he did not develop this theme much beyond this observation. . . . We are left with an acknowledgment that there is some connection between pragmatic conditions and the development of [spiritual] consciousness, but the stratification of reality reflective of the "double constitution of history" with which we have to contend makes it difficult to articulate what that connection might be.[18]

It is true, Voegelin does not want to say that spiritual discoveries of divine transcendence were simply *caused* by the suffering from imperial wars of expansion. However, he does say that they were "induced" by these conquests (*OH*, 4:197). In addition, he clearly thinks that ecumenic expansion was necessary for later historians to realize that humanity's ultimate horizon is death. This is an important and surprising equivocation that needs to be faced by interpreters of Voegelin's latest historiography. Unfortunately, it is more frequently overlooked.[19]

Despite the ambiguity, there is a clear accent in Voegelin's thought. He implies that the conquests actually confirmed what was only dimly known before by the "compact" symbolists of the ancient Near East. After all, their understanding of spiritual reality was insufficient to restrain the mad lust for

18. Ranieri, *Voegelin and Good Society,* 234–35.

19. See, for example, the otherwise thoughtful study by Stephen A. McKnight, *"Order and History* as a Response to the Theoretical and Methodological Problems Confronting Historians in the Twentieth Century." McKnight begins by saying that Voegelin understands "spiritual outbursts" (or "leaps in being") to have *preceded* the pragmatic breakdown of the cosmological style of truth during the imperial expansions of the Ecumenic Age (270, 273); then he reverses this claim without explanation (274), only to return to the primacy of spiritual over pragmatic events (278). The strength of McKnight's essay lies in his ability to emphasize the scientific character (or impartial scope) that Voegelin's historiography at least seeks to attain.

conquest that emerged from their societies in the first place. Was it not? But this objection is weak, for neither did the "differentiated" understanding of spiritual reality in the twentieth century C.E. prove sufficient to restrain similar lusts for domination. World wars, genetic engineering in the search for immortality, and the expansion of the ecumene toward outer space all served to indicate that no progress has been gained if it cannot be known in advance that *Star Wars* is not needed to reveal death as the true horizon of all things in the universe. Of course, it is possible to know this point in advance, but it is also possible to know that this knowledge is not new. It does not come from a *new* self-revelation of being or the "beyond being" of God. Rather, it stands in continuity with the oldest knowledge of human existence, clearly known to the most perceptive symbolists in the earliest periods of history. For example, another author whom Voegelin discusses, also predating the Ecumenic Age, has formulated the same insight without the benefit of ecumenic suffering. Thus, Anaximander (ca. 560 B.C.E.): "The origin *(arche)* of all things is the Apeiron [boundless]. . . . It is necessary for things to perish into that from which they were born; for they pay one another penalty for their injustice *(adikia)* according to the ordinance of Time" (*OH,* 4:174). Voegelin's partial agreement with this basic truth has already been noted. But now one must consider the reason he ultimately ignores it and turns to develop a philosophy of history that seeks to avoid the perishing of "all things."

Voegelin continues to place Anaximander in the "compact" period of human consciousness. Anaximander's symbolization of the *Apeiron* allegedly reveals that he lacked a properly differentiated consciousness of the symbolizing mind, not to mention its place in history: "What actually had to be differentiated from the earlier [Anaximandrian] experience" by later thinkers "was the noetic consciousness implied in the compact dictum" (*OH,* 4:185).[20] Anaximander's understanding of the *Apeiron,* it seems, is insufficiently tensional or dialectical. More specifically, his extant writings reveal no consciousness of life as a tensional existence between the pulls of mortality and immortality. He appears to think that humans, in addition to everything else in existence, rise mysteriously from the *Apeiron* and perish back into that

20. Voegelin makes this statement even though he knows that Anaximander's work exists only in fragments. This suggests a general problem in his account of "compact" thinkers. It is not clear how he can suggest that the earliest thinkers had a compact understanding of spiritual reality when their works have survived only in fragments. Yet, despite this difficulty, Voegelin would likely wish to insist that the real problem lies deeper.

from which they were born. That is all. Voegelin is not content to rest with Anaximander's dictum, because he knows that experiences of "immortalizing" also arise in the Ecumenic Age. These experiences of "spiritual Exodus" within reality, of life lived in conscious tension toward the divine Beyond, begin to counter the concupiscential drive that tries mistakenly to realize one of the strongest human desires within this life: the desire for personal immortality.

"History II": The Horizon Retracted and Mythically Crossed—Sacred History

Although History I (concupiscential exodus) and History II (spiritual exodus) have been separated for purposes of analysis, Voegelin argues that they are closely related in the Ecumenic Age. As the attempt to unify the ecumene through imperial conquest reveals itself increasingly to be ill-conceived, the spiritual outbursts "induced" by the suffering gradually gain social momentum. The notion of a transcendental fulfillment of human desires gradually becomes a more persuasive alternative to the failed attempts at achieving perfection in military campaigns. Eventually, "concupiscential exodus has to retract into the embarrassing consciousness of a non-ecumenic ecumene, of a limited unlimited." Empire clashes with empire, fails to conquer the foe, causes more suffering than it alleviates, and increasingly resigns to live with the knowledge that its jurisdiction does not surround all of the known world. "The experience of this untenable result prepares the situation in which the ecumenic rulers become ready to associate their empire with an ecumenic religion, in order to channel the meaning of a spiritual exodus into a concupiscential expansion that has become flagrantly nonsensical" (*OH,* 4:197–98).

Voegelin suggests that spiritual outbursts follow the failures of imperial conquests to cross the universal horizon that defines humanity in this life. Outbursts of the spirit allow the later prophets of Israel, Plato, Aristotle, and others to begin crossing the horizon of death mythically. Deutero-Isaiah and Daniel have visions of a divinely transfigured reality in which life will ultimately be saved from perishing. Plato realizes that human existence is structured in between *(metaxy)* the immortalizing pull of the divine *Nous* and the mortalizing counterpulls of the bodily passions. Aristotle realizes that *noesis* is the experience that best describes the consciousness of divine-human participation *(metalepsis)* in the immortalizing *(athanatizein)* nature of the mind itself. Finally, Aristotle also realizes that experiences of mutual participation between divine and human reality have long been present, though perhaps unawares, in the experienced wonders described by mythologists. This realization allows him to interpret the mythological past with a measured degree of respect. Voegelin appreciates all of these insights. He even grants that they were precipitated by genuine theophanies. But they also remained compact, he argues. They lacked the freedom conveyed by later visions of a transfigured life in the Beyond, and remained bound to the necessity of life-and-death rhythms in the cosmos. With respect to the Greeks: "Man can immortalize only when he accepts the apeirontic burden of mortality. The balance of consciousness between the height and the depth, between Nous and Apeiron, becomes the balance of immortality and mortality in the [Aristotelian] *bios theoretikos,* in the life of reason in this world" (*OH,* 4:237). One might suspect that this level of articulate consciousness suffices to account for all generally human experiences of the superlative reality under consideration. Theophanies can be understood mythically, rationally, or through the "philosopher's myth." But Voegelin is not ultimately content with the insights gained by classical philosophy. He continues to think that, within his present epoch of consciousness, the supreme understanding of the immortalizing pull is still to be found in experiences of Christ's Resurrection. This is the event in the Ecumenic Age that crosses the human horizon emphatically—this time, so to speak, from the side of divinity. This event is of singular importance to Voegelin. It guides the vision of traditional historiographers, in whose wake he continues to think and write; it constitutes the apex of differentiated historiographies, yielding their Before-and-After division par excellence; and it makes historiography itself a contemplative exercize of the spirit. Surprisingly, however, Voegelin does not discuss the historical event constituted by those who claim to have witnessed Christ's bodily Resurrection. Instead, he writes a perhaps intentionally esoteric chapter on Paul's vision of "the Resurrected."

Voegelin's relatively narrow focus on Paul's spiritual experiences elicited passionate complaints from some of his Christian supporters,[21] while it found support from other interpreters sympathetic to the general aims of Christian theology.[22] Of this latter group it is Michael P. Morrissey, in *Consciousness and Transcendence,* who goes to the greatest lengths to excuse Voegelin for

21. For discussion, see Michael P. Federici, "Voegelin's Christian Critics"; and James M. Rhodes, "Voegelin and Christian Faith."

22. For representative examples, see Morrissey, *Consciousness and Transcendence,* 101–6; Morrissey, "Voegelin, Religious Experience, and Immortality"; Geoffrey L. Price, "The Epiphany of Universal Humanity"; and Eugene Webb, "Eric Voegelin's Theory of Revelation."

neglecting to discuss the Gospel accounts of the Resurrection. Morrissey contends that Voegelin's "hermeneutical method" seeks to interpret experiences from literary texts written by the subjects of the experiences themselves: "Paul left writings that expressed his own experience; Jesus comes to us only through the mediating interpretations of other writers." Thus, Voegelin interprets Paul on "the Resurrected" but ignores the resurrected Christ of the Gospels. Morrissey points to precedents in Voegelin's interpretation of notable Greeks to substantiate his claim about Voegelin's method: Voegelin also ignored Pythagoras for a similar reason—he is known only through the writings of others—and focused on the fragmentary writings of Xenophanes, Parmenides, and Heraclitus. It appears, therefore, that Voegelin can be easily excused for his curious choice of texts, regarding the Resurrection appearances. But Morrissey's point is weak, because there are other precedents in Voegelin's works that contradict it. For example, Voegelin did interpret a great deal of Jesus' sayings from other writers in an earlier essay, "The Gospel and Culture" (1971), in which he also avoids any discussion of the Resurrection appearances (see *CW*, 12:172–212). If he wanted to apply his hermeneutical method consistently, Voegelin could have interpreted the allegedly firsthand accounts of the bodily Resurrection experiences that are given in the Gospels, as it is impossible to prove that these writings are not genuine reports by eyewitnesses: one Gospel author even shows some level of concern for conveying a truthful account of these matters (see Luke 1:1–4). The author of Luke, in the Book of Acts, also claims to relate Paul's own words from his experience of the *bodily* Resurrection of Christ, but Voegelin neglects to interpret these passages—without explaining how he could know that Paul's experiences have not been accurately conveyed. Thus, if Voegelin had a hermeneutical method, he did not apply it consistently. And this point leaves interpreters to suspect that he wants to avoid the Gospel accounts of the Resurrection for another reason. Morrissey offers a second suggestion: "Revelation, Voegelin claims, does not tender information about the world." Consequently, he suggests, "[t]hose who seek to locate revelation in miraculous events Voegelin would consider spiritually obtuse."[23] These words may ring true for Voegelin's general distrust of metastatic miracles, but Morrissey's line of defense has an apologetic tone, attempting to shame questioners for being obtuse, that easily leads one to disregard a crucial point in this discussion. The question is certainly not the symbolic "location" of Revelation, but its substantial content. It would seem that Paul's experience differed in content from those described

---

23. Morrissey, *Consciousness and Transcendence*, 282 n. 67.

in the Gospels. And Voegelin remains silent as to how or why. Thus, Morrissey's defense needs to be questioned with a closer look at Voegelin's writings than he provides. His first line of defense is open to refutation on textual grounds; his second one, which amounts to an evasion of serious questions about the Resurrection, will be questioned further once Voegelin has been shown to attempt the same.

Voegelin discusses only the spiritual or "pneumatic" aspect of Paul's experiences. He does not discuss the empty tomb and bodily Resurrection stories in the Gospel narratives, nor the extent to which Paul himself struggles to account for the salvation of the body—presumably in accordance with the content of his vision. Instead, his peculiar focus on Paul attempts to provide a philosophically persuasive interpretation of the Resurrection as a historical advance in theophanic visions and their symbolic interpretations. He states that "if any event in the Metaxy has constituted meaning in history, it is Paul's vision of the Resurrected." Be that as it may, the fundamental point in Voegelin's reading of Paul needs to be emphasized. He takes Paul's vision to yield only a spiritual insight into God's creation, albeit the preeminent one in history. The vision does not change anything in the general order of reality. Rather, it begins to "transfigure" human consciousness by making Paul representatively aware of an immortalizing process in reality that was only dimly known by his "equivalent" predecessors: Deutero-Isaiah, Daniel, Plato, and Aristotle, among others. In Paul, the immortalizing process in reality has a distinctively personal character. Unlike the "immortalizing" of the Greeks and Jews, Paul claims to witness the transfigured perfection of an individual. His vision thus becomes representative for the personal immortality of all who are open to the divine spirit in the same manner as Paul himself. Voegelin interprets a passage from Paul's Letter to the Romans to support this point: "'If the spirit *(pneuma)* of him who raised Jesus from the dead dwells in you, then the God who raised Jesus Christ from the dead will also give new life to mortal bodies by means of the spirit indwelling in you' (8: 11). Faith in Christ means," Voegelin interprets, "responsive participation in the same divine *pneuma* that was active in the Jesus who appeared in the vision as the Resurrected." This immortalizing *pneuma* is itself not new to the order of reality, he grants. But the "divine irruption" in Paul is said to constitute a "new existential consciousness" (*OH,* 4:243, 242, 246). Its novelty is found only on the level of human consciousness, but this is sufficient to drive Voegelin's historiography.

> In Paul's myth [of death and Resurrection], God emerges victorious, because
> his protagonist is man. He is the creature in whom God can incarnate

himself with the fullness *(pleroma)* of his divinity, transfiguring man into the God-man (Col. 2:9). The whole creation that is groaning can be redeemed, because at one point, in man, the sonship of God is possible (Rom. 8:22–23). The [immortalizing] movement in reality, that has become luminous to itself in noetic consciousness, has indeed unfolded its full meaning in the Pauline vision and its exegesis through the myth. The symbolism of the man who can achieve freedom from cosmic Ananke [Necessity], who can enter into the freedom of God, redeemed by the loving grace of the God who is himself free of the cosmos, consistently differentiates the truth of existence that has become visible in the philosophers' experience of *athanatizein* [immortalizing]. (*OH*, 4:251)

Clearly, a distinctively Christian vision still provides the "maximum of differentiation" to which Voegelin alluded in his earlier historiography (cf. *NSP,* 79; *OH*, 1:132). But now he elaborates the matter in more detail. He describes three points to the "hard structure of truth" that come upon the historical scene in the "mythopoetic genius of Paul." These points are thought to reveal the extent to which Paul's vision of "the Resurrected" transcends the "noetic revelation" of classic philosophy. First, Paul experiences the presence of the God who creates in radical freedom from the cosmos. Paul's God is therefore beyond the creative demiurge described by Plato in the *Timaeus,* not limited by cosmological Necessity *(Ananke)* in the creative process. Second, Paul's vision is said to reveal that reality itself is engaged in a process of immortalizing "transfiguration." The vision takes Paul beyond the tensions of life and death in the cosmos and allows him to differentiate "the experience of the directional movement [in reality] by articulating its goal, its *teleion,* as the state of *aphtharsia* [immortality or non-perishing] beyond man's involvement in the Anaximandrian mystery of Apeiron and Time." Finally, and most important for Voegelin, Paul becomes conscious of the progressive, developmental character of history and articulates the new order in human consciousness where the transfiguration of reality "becomes luminous in its actual occurrence." To Paul, "[t]he vision of the Resurrected is . . . more than a theophanic event in the Metaxy; it is the beginning of transfiguration itself." Paul interprets his vision historically. He develops what Voegelin calls a "mythical" account of God's history with the Chosen People, and "a new accent falls on the area of 'history' and its rank in the whole of reality" (*OH*, 4:250, 250–51, 248, 251). These points call for critical reflection.

First, Paul's experience of God is said to have transcended the relatively compact theology of Plato. According to Voegelin's reading of the *Timaeus,* Plato attempted to write only a limited work, an *alethinos logos,* a "true story," of the Demiurgic presence of God in man, society, history, and the cosmos. This philosopher's myth is carefully devised so as to make the tale of divine presence in reality compatible with the existential truth of man's tension toward the divine ground. . . . Even the Platonic myth, however, is not yet fully differentiated; for Plato, though he established the truth of existence as the criterion for the truth of the myth, refrained from developing the criterion completely.

Plato seems to have been aware of an aspect of divinity beyond the Demiurge, Voegelin grants at times, but he "surrounded" this further experience of divinity with "deliberate uncertainties." Accordingly, the "true story" in the *Timaeus* "did not go beyond the figure of a Demiurge whose noetic efforts remained limited by Ananke," the Necessity that resists a completely intelligible ordering of the world (*OH,* 4:249–50). The central implication is this: Plato wrote cautiously of the unknown God, but revealed little to Voegelin that could be used in a philosophy of history. Thus, Voegelin's account of Plato's historical consciousness is quite brief. He claims that Plato was inclined to develop a progressive account of history's spiritual order, but failed to do so because he lacked Paul's experience of the unknown God revealed in Christ.

Voegelin's account of Plato's historical consciousness is based on a fusion of two Platonic myths from separate dialogues: the myth of the age of Cronos and the myth of the age of Nous.[24] When taken together, these myths suggest to Voegelin the familiar theme in a *differentiated* historiography: the age of the god Cronos is superceded by the age of the god Zeus, which is finally understood by the age of the god Nous (Intelligence) (*OH,* 4:226–27). This construction is questionable, however, because it is contradicted by other points made by the characters who tell the myths in Plato's dialogues, and it is not clear that any of these represents the historical consciousness of Plato himself.[25] Both myths are told in separate dialogues by characters named "Stranger." Voegelin uncritically equates their speeches with Plato's incomplete philosophy of history and ignores the passages contradicting his reading. To take an example from *Laws* 4, the speech during the age of Nous hearkens back fondly to the age of Cronos, when humans were ruled by daimons instead of other humans. It does not suggest that a new age of differentiated

24. Plato, *Statesman* 271d–272b; *Laws* bk. 4.

25. The caution against constructing "Plato's philosophy" from particular claims made by any of his main characters is argued persuasively by Planinc, drawing upon the prudential good sense of Gadamer's hermeneutics and several colleagues and students of Leo Strauss. See Zdravko Planinc, *Plato's Political Philosophy: Prudence in the "Republic" and the "Laws,"* 12–19.

consciousness has dawned in which the compact past has been rationally transcended. Quite to the contrary, the Stranger does not claim that his experiences of Nous are *new*. He knows that the remote past is unknowable, and this knowledge qualifies all claims to novelty in his present. The myth pertaining to the origin of cities makes this point clearly. The Athenian Stranger says that "tens upon tens of thousands of cities" have come into being during the "infinite length of time" preceding the mythical account he sets out to develop, so he does not suspect that his account of the origin of cities improves upon anything else from the past. Indeed, he summarizes his apparent lack of concern for historical progressions with an appeal to his inability to know the remote past: "What pertains to the ancients should be left alone and bid good-bye, and spoken of in whatever way is pleasing to the gods; but what pertains to our new and wise men must be accused, insofar as it is responsible for bad things."[26] The ancients can neither be accused nor excused, for the remote past is unknowable; it is precisely for this reason that a historical philosophy of being—such as Voegelin and Schelling attempt to develop—lacks persuasive grounds for its beginning. Despite Voegelin's construction of a three-phase philosophy of history from parts of some of the Platonic dialogues, Plato's Athenian Stranger seems in fact to have been uninterested in historiography as a *philosophical* source of order.

Paul, on the contrary, claims that the unknown God has been revealed to him in Christ (cf. Acts 17:22–31), and he says a good deal about the historical implications of the event. He thereby continues the historiogenetic type of thinking that Voegelin criticizes in others but inexplicably supports in Paul. To be sure, Voegelin does not accept the truth of this theophany uncritically. He takes it to be a historical advance, but he also claims that it created a "turbulence" in Paul—as does any theophany—which, however, left him particularly open to a rather serious distortion of the reality of experience. Paul's vision of "the Resurrected," according to Voegelin's reading, caused him to expect that reality itself would be transfigured within his own lifetime, that Christ would return soon in the Second Coming and redeem all of the faithful from their mortality. Voegelin criticizes this expectation as "metastatic," and he commends Plato for not permitting such "enthusiastic expectations to distort the human condition" (*OH*, 4:252, 241, 239). Curiously, however, Voegelin does not criticize Paul for interpreting his theophany as a *Christophany*. Paul's vision of an immortalized human—something that clearly violates the order of experience even more so than Isaiah's question-

26. Plato, *Laws* 713a–714b, 676a–c, 886d.

able trust in God's military aid—is not criticized as a metastasis of reality in the soul of the visionary.

Voegelin is generally protective of Paul's vision, perhaps surrounding it with some "deliberate uncertainties" of his own. He goes so far as even to construct what amounts to a prohibition of questions surrounding the event:

> The vision emerges as a symbol from the Metaxy, and the symbol is both divine and human. Any attempt to break up the mystery of divine-human participation, as it occurs in a theophanic event, is fatuous. On the subjective side, one cannot "explain" the divine presence in the vision by a psychology of Paul. And on the objective side, "critical doubts" about the vision of the Resurrected would mean that the critic knows how God has a right to let himself be seen. (*OH,* 4:243)

Voegelin's rejection of subjective psychologies is well taken. Appropriately, he will not have anything to do with unphilosophical speculation from those who would, for example, presume an intimate knowledge of Paul's psychic life and attempt to "explain" his vision as the result of a fit of epilepsy or the like. But to shield the vision from "critical doubts" in what claims to be a philosophical study of order is disturbing. It resembles the "prohibition of the question" concerning the premises of an argument for which Voegelin frequently criticized Auguste Comte and Karl Marx—in particular.[27] What is more, Voegelin does not interpret Paul completely on his own terms. He acknowledges that, for Paul, the vision is "more than a theophanic event in the Metaxy," but his interpretation limits it to the Metaxy nonetheless, a term not used by Paul; furthermore, his decision to avoid discussion of the bodily Resurrection appearances is clearly another manifestation of the same problem. What may be Voegelin's own "critical doubts" or "deliberate uncertainties" pass by almost imperceptibly (*OH,* 4:248, 243). This observation can be made without assuming to know "how God has a right to let himself be seen," for this claim amounts simply to a non sequitur that obscures a more fundamental problem.

Hitherto, Voegelin's philosophy of history concentrated on experiences of a generally human character. He frequently appealed to the common wellspring of experience, symbolized by Heraclitus's notion that the Logos is common *(xynon)* to all humans, making them like-minded *(homonoia),* and enabling the mature *(spoudaioi)* to discuss reality's order (cf. *NSP,* 28, 66, 77,

---

27. Cf. *FER,* 258–63; *NSP,* 24, 140; *Science, Politics, and Gnosticism,* 20–49; *Anam.,* 3–4; and *OH,* 4:330.

64). But Paul's experience of "the Resurrected" obviously breaks with the common order of experience interpreted by philosophers, and Voegelin's acceptance of its historical significance tends to make his account of history's order philosophically unempirical. That is to say, Paul's experience of "the Resurrected" is relatively idiosyncratic or private. And Voegelin encounters the same problems as Schelling when he attempts to use it as the basis for a universal philosophy of history. One cannot sympathetically recollect the "spiritual body" of the Resurrected Christ as a blinding-light experience in one's own past. One is not even expected to be able to do so by Christian teachings. Rather, one is expected to trust *vicariously* in the experiences that God has allegedly given to others. "Blessed are those who have not seen and yet believe," the Risen Jesus reportedly says to the doubting Thomas (John 20:29). If these words may be taken as normative for Christian faith, notwithstanding the accentual differences that denominational theologies may give them, then it becomes clear that the lot of humans who would be Christian needs to accept the truth of the Resurrection—perhaps the defining experience of Christianity—vicariously. But there can be no such appeal to vicarious experiences in the Platonic-Aristotelian philosophy that Voegelin also attempts to espouse. This point calls to mind a fundamental difference in the meaning of theophanic experience for philosophers and Christian theologians. Christian faith cannot be based on the simple trust in God's *ability* to raise the dead. Rather, it needs to trust that this power has already become manifest to a few select people in the Resurrection of Christ. Now, to place one's trust in this manifestation of God's Grace necessarily forces one to leave behind the common order of human experience, in which bodily resurrections of the dead do not occur, and to base one's understanding of God's dealings with humanity on the relatively idiosyncratic experiences of the apostles. Such faith breaks with the universal order of human experience commonly interpreted and trusted by the classical and empirical philosophers whom Voegelin commends, and it leads one to suspect that *Christian* and *philosopher* might be, after all, mutually exclusive terms.[28] Clearly, the stakes

---

28. The different understanding of what constitutes trustworthy experience to which I have called attention in the foregoing analysis speaks against the repeated assertions of Barker and Schmidt that Voegelin's attempts to blend "Classic and Christian" elements in his historiography were largely successful (cf. Barker and Schmidt, "'Voegelin Not Mysterious,'" 377, 381, 385, 393, 405). Barker and Schmidt are correct to argue that Voegelin may have *wanted* to articulate a "Classic *and* Christian" philosophy of history. But the fundamental questions that arise from his works are whether he was successful and, beyond this, whether the enterprise itself is tenable.

are quite high in this discussion. Voegelin is to be commended for articulating a complex vision of historical order that allows it to emerge. But his apparent acceptance of a teaching of Christian faith at this point in his historiography tends to undermine the empirical basis of the historical *philosophy* he clearly wants to write. In order to make his historiography philosophically convincing, he would have had to call attention to and explain this change in the meaning and scope of experience, addressing why vicarious experiences of the Resurrection should be trusted beyond the theophanies open to any and all human beings in the broad light of day.

Voegelin would likely wish to disagree. He does attempt to bring the substance of Christian faith into the range of philosophical intelligibility as a common experience. He states, in a rare autobiographical moment: "When reading the First Letter to the Corinthians, I have always the feeling of traveling, with Paul, from *phthora* [perishing] to *aphtharsia* [immortality] in a homogeneous medium of reality, from existence in the Metaxy as a way station to immortality as a goal, with death as a minor incident on the road. Death is indeed reduced to 'the twinkling of an eye' in which reality switches from imperfection to perfection" (*OH*, 4:247). Voegelin may have felt that he was "traveling" while reading the letters of the saint, but the relevant question in a philosophical study of history is whether or not he truly travels with *Paul*.

Voegelin's reenactment of the experience does not resemble the miraculous events described by Paul, but clearly attempts to suggest that there is something universal in Paul's vision, which has philosophical relevance. To "travel" with Paul from perishing to immortality is to follow his interpretation of the experience as a saving "Tale." Paul's Tale is, according to Voegelin, a "myth" that recounts the developmental history of death and resurrection "to its end." It is, therefore, chiefly due to the historical consciousness that Paul uses to tell his Tale, I argue, that Voegelin is led to disregard what he calls "uncritical encumbrances" in the letters of the saint and to formulate what amounts to a second programmatic statement for *Order and History*: "The truth of existence emerges from the theophanic events in history." Yet this is substantially the same principle with which Voegelin opens his great work. Note how the two statements can be easily blended: "The truth [order] of existence [history] emerges from the theophanic events [order] in history" (*OH*, 4:251; cf. 1:ix). Despite all of the critical observations he continues to make with respect to there not being an "order *of* history" discernible to philosophers, Voegelin continues to construct a developmental account of history's order just the same. The only change between the early and later historiographies is his increasing appreciation for the complexity involved in

such constructions. But he does not reach the point where the entire enterprise is discarded. Instead he "travels"—ostensibly with Paul.

It is Paul who tells the sacred-historical Tale of salvation that Voegelin
attempts to recount. In his vision of "the Resurrected," Paul realizes that the
transfiguration of mortal reality begins in history and points to its transhistori-
cal realization. This is the "spiritual Exodus" that Voegelin has been defending against the concupiscential exodus of ecumenic conquerors:

> This understanding of the vision . . . is possible only if the experience of a
> reality which paradoxically moves toward the divine Beyond of its struc-
> ture, if the movement of the psyche toward the divine depth, is pursued to
> the point at which existence under the conditions of *genesis* [birth] and
> *phthora* [perishing] is revealed as an event in the history of the divine Be-
> yond. The Resurrection can be the beginning of transfiguration because it
> is revealed to Paul as an event in the tale of death he has to tell: "For as
> through one man came death, so now through one man comes the resur-
> rection of the dead. For as in Adam all men die, so in Christ all men shall
> be made alive" (I Cor. 15:22–23). (*OH*, 4:248)

Voegelin understands the "homogeneous medium of reality" in which he feels
Paul traveling toward immortality to be "the same medium of the myth in
which the Fall of Adam occurs." Paul sets up the dramatis personae in his myth,
Adam and Christ, and recounts the history of salvation from Adam's death
to Christ's perfected life in the Resurrection. Paul's Tale progresses as follows:

> In a first act *(aparche)*, Christ is raised from the dead; then, when the
> *parousia* [Second Coming] has occurred, those who belong to Christ will
> be raised; then comes the end *(telos)*, with Christ handing over his kingdom
> to God the Father after he has destroyed the principalities *(arche)*, author-
> ities *(exousia)*, and powers *(dynamis)*; "and the last of the enemies to be
> destroyed is Death *(thanatos)*" (I Cor. 15:26). All things having been sub-
> jected to Christ, then, the Son himself will be subjected to God, "so that
> God may be all in all" (28). The war with the rebellious cosmic forces ends
> with the victory of God. (*OH*, 4:248)

Voegelin accepts the basic content of Paul's vision, as well as the historiographic principle that Paul uses in its interpretation. The vision reveals to
Voegelin the order *of* history, consciousness, and reality itself. Despite his
numerous warnings against placing one's trust in the "hypostasis" or reification
of abstract concepts derived from experience, he reaches a number of abstract
conclusions of his own in this historiography. First, he says that "conscious-

ness is not a constant but a process advancing from compactness to differentiation." In other words, it has a history in which it unfolds. Second, because the differentiating events in which it unfolds "are experienced as immortalizing movements, history is discovered as the process in which reality becomes luminous for the movement beyond its own structure; the structure of history is eschatological." Third, reality itself is said to have an "eschatological structure," and human consciousness is described as "the site of [its] transfiguration" (*OH*, 4:305, 304, 312). Finally, Voegelin suggests that consciousness, history, and reality have not ceased to unfold historically. They continue to bloom and may lead to the time of "universal humanity." The unity of humanity that was sought erroneously by imperial conquerors in the Ecumenic Age, and more recently by utopian revolutionaries, will arrive only when God removes the horizon of death that no human efforts can abolish: "Universal mankind is not a society existing in the world, but a symbol which indicates man's consciousness of participating, in his earthly existence, in the mystery of a reality that moves toward its transfiguration. Universal mankind is an eschatological index." This vision of the immortal eschaton tends to unbalance Voegelin's thought in much the same way that it did Paul's. It would seem that Voegelin has obtained a similar "assurance of immortalizing transfiguration" from his historiographic studies, for he hesitates only briefly with respect to the other possibility that death might entail. That is to say: "One could imagine a philosopher to create the symbol of a *perditio in nihilo* as the countersymbol to the *creatio ex nihilo*. But philosophers hesitate to let the *nihil* of the beginning become the *nihil* of the end, though there are exceptions" (*OH*, 4:305, 256, 271). Voegelin mentions none of these exceptions by name, though one is readily found in Plato's Socrates.

In the *Apology*, Socrates provides a more balanced account of the possible meaning of death. He says that death can be either one of two things: some type of immortality, whether personal or impersonal, or a dreamless sleep. What is more, he goes to some length to argue that neither of these possibilities will result in something bad for a good human being.[29] Voegelin overlooks Socrates' account of death as a "dreamless sleep" in his reading of the *Apology* (cf. *OH*, 3:7–14). Consequently, he interprets Plato as a seeker of

---

29. Plato, *Apology* 39e–42a. The possibility that death might result in the end of one's personal existence is even mentioned seriously in the *Phaedo,* during Socrates' exuberant attempt to charm the fear of death out of Simmias and Kebes (91b; on Socrates as a fear charmer, see 77e). The *Phaedo* is frequently cited for proof that Plato "believed" in the immortality of the soul. But this claim overlooks the pedagogical nature of Socrates' last conversation with his young friends and the balanced thanatology he develops with adults at the Athenian court.

personal immortality and goes to even greater lengths to explain why the pull of death cannot be thought to lead toward depersonalization:

> The obvious reason is the fact that we have an "experience of reality" but no experience of the *nihil* other than the creative divine ground of reality or the fall into non-being as the sanction on non-participation in the divinely grounded and ordered reality. The movement that draws man into existential participation is a movement toward a more eminent degree of reality, not toward perdition; it is experienced as the *athanatizein* of the philosophers or the *aphtharsia* of Paul. The experience of reality, one might say, has a built-in bias toward more reality; the symbolism of a cessation of reality would be in conflict with the experience of the movement as an exodus within reality. (*OH*, 4:271)

As indicated by my comments on the *Apology,* the "bias" toward *personal* immortality described in the preceding quote seems to be Voegelin's, not that of Plato or Aristotle, for it is not to be found so clearly in what has come to light of the philosophers' "immortalizing."[30] Voegelin's comments about the "experience of reality" are also open to question. To say that it is impossible to experience "the *nihil*" is too restrictive. For example, recalling one of Socrates' basic points in the *Apology,* everyone can remember the relative nothingness of a dreamless sleep. And this, it seems, is neither an experience of the "creative divine ground" nor a punitive "fall into non-being." It is something else for which Voegelin does not give an account. Instead, he focuses on the "immortalizing" nature of historiographic studies and chooses Paul as the most differentiated thinker to arise in the Ecumenic Age.

Voegelin's discussion of Paul reveals a number of problems in his historiographic method. Strictly speaking, he does not interpret Paul on his own

---

30. The supposition that Voegelin's comments are motivated by his desire for personal immortality is based on textual evidence. In an earlier work, he expresses an autobiographical sense of horror at "the nothing that makes us shudder with anxiety from the bottom of existence." He suggests that this horror is not based on a simplistic fear of death, understood as biological extinction; "it is the profounder horror of losing, with the passing of existence, the slender foothold in the partnership of being that we experience as ours while existence lasts" (*OH*, 1:4, 5). Voegelin seems to provide a more balanced thanatology in his 1967 essay "Immortality: Experience and Symbol," where he emphasizes the *metaxic* character of consciousness: "[T]he life structured by death is neither the life of the mortals, nor the lasting of the gods, but the life experienced in the tension of existence. It is the life lived in the flow of [human-divine] presence.... [T]hat is all." But he concludes by sympathizing with "the more robust" who will not care about this "anemic immortality." He appears to want more, and says that this desire is "quite healthy" ("Immortality," 91).

terms; he transforms part of his thought and uses it in the construction of a philosophy of history. He turns Paul into a mythologist, first of all, and Plato into an incomplete philosopher of history, thus obscuring the historical consciousness of both. He brings Paul closer to the "knowing myth" of Platonic philosophy and Plato closer to the developmental history of Pauline theology than the textual records will allow. Voegelin does not acknowledge this problem. Instead, he attempts to argue that the difference between Platonic-Aristotelian philosophy and Pauline theology is only accentual. Classic philosophy concentrates on the epiphany of order in the cosmos that includes the mystery of death, whereas Pauline theology concentrates on the epiphany of salvation from this cosmos. The difference between the classic and Christian theophanies and the types of salvation they may entail is "not contradictory," Voegelin maintains; it "does not compel a choice between alternatives. On the contrary, the two conceptions together act out, in the luminosity of consciousness, the paradox of a reality that moves beyond its structure." The efforts of both classic philosophy and Pauline theology are welcomed as categorical "equivalents." They are said to differ only in the decisive "accent" that Paul's vision of immortality brings to the analysis (*OH*, 4:258, 246, 241). But the implicit conclusion is clear: classical philosophers understand how best to live with respect for divinity in the *civitas terrena,* whereas Paul is granted the superior cognition of faith in the *civitas Dei*—into which the faithful are ostensibly being transfigured. These claims call for a closer look at the texts that Voegelin uses in his construction. Because his historiography turns decisively on Paul, the following remarks shall be limited to a brief consideration of Voegelin's New Testament exegesis.

Upon closer inspection, it is not clear that Paul has a *mythical* understanding of his vision, even in Voegelin's sense of the term, nor of the theophanic history that he constructs to proclaim its superiority.[31] Paul, unlike Plato's Socrates, does not use the word *myth (mythos)* to describe his experiences, neither with respect to the first nor to the second Adam. He seems to interpret these men as historical figures. The word *mythos* is used only five times in all of the New Testament writings—each time critically, and never in any of the letters known to be from Paul's hand. For example, in 1 Timothy (4:7; see also 1:4), the author contrasts "godless and silly myths *[mythoi]*" with a

---

31. For an attempt to develop Voegelin's mythological reading of Paul, which also draws upon the understanding of myth in Claude Lévi-Strauss, see Hendrikus Boers, "Interpreting Paul: Demythologizing in Reverse."

proper training in godliness *(eusebeia),* without suggesting that his readers could have recourse to any such thing as a godly, true, or pious myth. In 2 Timothy (4:4), myths are said to be directly opposed to truth *(aletheia).* In Titus (1:14), readers are warned to stay away from Jewish myths told by men who reject the truth of Christ. Finally, 2 Peter (1:16) summarizes the point at issue. The author declares: "We did not follow sophistically devised myths *[sophizo mythoi]* when we made known to you the power *[dynamis]* and presence *[parousia]* of our Lord Jesus Christ, but we were eyewitnesses *[epoptes]* of his majesty." Clearly, the New Testament authors have a general distrust of myths, and Paul appears to share their distrust by not consciously constructing any myths of his own. He does not even avail himself regularly of the closest parallel to mythic speech in the New Testament, namely, the parable; parabolic writing is used only in two parenthetical remarks of one Epistle, which is not known conclusively to be of Pauline origin (Heb. 9:9, 11:19). Consequently, Paul seems not to have distinguished between mythic and prosaic accounts of experience. A further indication of this point is suggested by the way that one of his contemporaries responded to his account of the Resurrection. After hearing Paul's account of his vision, in the presence of King Agrippa, Festus retorted: "Paul, you are mad *[Maine];* your great learning is turning you mad." Paul insists that he is not mad; he is "speaking the sober truth" (Acts 26:24–25).

Voegelin appears to have distorted Paul's writings by interpreting them as myths.[32] What is more, this problem is complicated further when he attempts to blend Paul's visions with those of the other disciples. Paul is said to have been a man who "knew something about visions" and "classified [the other

---

32. Michael Morrissey would likely wish to disagree. In a recent essay, he states his complete agreement with Voegelin's mythic account of Paul's experiences of "the Resurrected," without mentioning any of the problems to which I have just pointed: "[W]hat is needed today in Christian faith and theology is a 'remythologizing' agenda in order to make alive once again the gospel story, deadened by centuries of hypostatized literalism, dogmatism and rationalism." If we are to follow Voegelin's guidance, he continues, "the Bultmannian project of demythologization—translating the mythic symbols of the New Testament (unseemly to us moderns) into their 'real' existentialist meaning—must today yield to the metaleptic project of participation in the myth as myth, which alone can make transparent the truth of the theophany it seeks to illuminate." See Morrissey, "Eric Voegelin and the New Testament: Developments, Problems, and Challenges," 498. Morrissey seems to be unaware that Voegelin's reading of Paul, in particular, is open to criticism that need not rely on the practices of authors he criticizes for being "spiritually obtuse" (once again), antiquarian, positivist, and anti-Christian. My analysis attempts to demonstrate that Voegelin can be criticized on his own terms, without relying on any of these questionable biases.

visions] as of the same type as his own (I Cor. 15:3–8)" (*OH*, 4:244). When one turns to the cited text, however, one discovers no such classification made by Paul. He lists several appearances of the Resurrected Christ without saying that they were similar or dissimilar. The assumption of a homogeneous classification of Resurrection appearances is clearly Voegelin's. Finally, it is not clear that Paul himself thought of the Resurrection only as a spiritual experience. He repeatedly refers to the bodily aspect of Christ's Resurrection, even in some of the passages quoted by Voegelin (Rom. 8:22–23, 11; cf. *OH*, 4:240, 242), while struggling to make sense of this aspect of his experience with the notion of a "spiritual body" *(sōma pneumatikon)* (1 Cor. 15:44, 55; cf. *OH*, 4:241). If Paul's experience of "the Resurrected" was only a spiritual insight, then it becomes unclear why he would wrestle with the awkward symbolism of a "spiritual body" in the first place. What has become clear is that Voegelin downplays the bodily miracle that the early Christians took to be the Resurrection, seemingly in his attempt to make an esoteric historiography more palatable to what Friedrich Schleiermacher calls the "cultured despisers" of Christianity in modern times. Voegelin's reading of the New Testament has a distinctively apologetic feel, a feature that is most disappointing in a philosophical study of order and comes as something of a surprise. Voegelin is normally careful to recover the self-understanding of the authors he interprets. His historiographic thought attempts to understand their respective levels of consciousness in order to describe advancing epochs in history. But his interpretation of Paul is uncommonly incautious in this respect, as it ascribes a mythological consciousness to him that is lacking in the texts. This problem is serious. It tends to undermine the cornerstone of his entire philosophy of history: if Voegelin cannot interpret Paul on his own terms, then he loses the historical basis for his claim that reality has an "eschatological structure" revealed by the experiences of this important Christian visionary.

Conclusion

Chapters 3 and 4 have provided a detailed account of Voegelin's differentiated and equivalent historiographies, respectively. I conclude by reflecting on the different periods that Voegelin distinguishes in his historical thought, reserving concluding remarks on the Schellingian character of his historiography for the general conclusion to this study.

Voegelin's differentiated historiography distinguishes epochs of experience and symbolization, allegedly rising to the maximal differentiation of consciousness in Christian Revelation. However, once he discovers revelatory experiences in some of the Greek philosophers, he begins to speak of the "equivalence" of Christian theology and Greek philosophy. One would expect this discovery to change his understanding of historical progress significantly, but no such change is evident in his equivalent historiography. He begins to use different terminology, speaking of the "noetic" revelation of Greeks and the "pneumatic" revelation of Christians, but the notion of a historical progress of existential truth is retained. These terms continue to distinguish the Greeks and Christians, respectively, on the ascending scale described by his earliest historiography. Voegelin attempts to defend the notion of spiritual progress in his latest work by calling attention to the superior historical consciousness said to be evident in Paul's "mythology," contrasting it with the "deliberate uncertainties" that limited Plato's. But in doing so, he ascribes a questionable acceptance of myth to Paul and a questionable concern for history to Plato. These are the central exegetical problems that call Voegelin's historical philosophy into question.

Some theoretical problems have also come to light. In its latest version, Voegelin's historiography still presupposes too much knowledge about the remote past. At one point, he asserts: "The great noetic and pneumatic differentiations do not occur among paleolithic hunters and fishers, but in ages of cities and empires." Yet this point is precisely what he cannot know about the remote past. A Socrates, Jesus, or someone better *may* have arisen many times in the prehistorical consciousness of humanity—without having a Plato or an Evangelist to give him cultural immortality through writing. In addition, there may have been women within consciously historical times who achieved equal or better accounts of human-divine order, but were not deemed worthy of cultural immortality by literate men. This point should not be mistaken for an attempt on my part to be *en vogue*. Rather, it simply calls attention to a significant feature of empirical reality, hypothetically speaking, that shall forever elude the philosopher of history, thus making it impossible to establish a persuasive beginning for his or her enterprise: the experiences of most women and illiterate men, by far the majority of humanity, remain inaccessible to the philosophical historian's grasp. Voegelin overlooks these problems. He claims that "[t]here are no Greek insights into the structure of reality apart from those of the philosophers in whose psyches the noetic theophany occurred; nor are there Israelite, Jewish, and Christian insights into the dynamics of transfiguration apart from the prophets, apostles, and above all Jesus, in whose psyche the pneumatic revelations occurred" (*OH,* 4:306, 270). To be sure, this point is certainly true of the extant historical records, but it becomes questionable when considered as part of a general philosophy of history. It overlooks the facts that most people in a civilization are not writers, the work of most writers does not survive, and all of these people have consciousness and articulate experiences that would be relevant to a philosophy of history if they could be known. When Voegelin constructs his philosophy of history, it is as though such problems do not exist. His historical thought is "monumental" in Friedrich Nietzsche's sense of the term.[33] It interprets famous authors in history and assumes a great deal about the rest of human consciousness in its attempt to fill in the blanks.

Several difficulties with Voegelin's attempt to legitimate this procedure in a philosophical study of order have been indicated. But at no point was it necessary to suggest that a fundamental break with his thinking is needed. Instead, my critical remarks have drawn upon the philosophical principles of order that Voegelin himself thankfully worked to recover in his philosophy of consciousness—especially his repeated emphasis that there is no vantage point, whether sacred or profane, outside of reality from which the whole could be known conclusively. His arguments in the philosophy of consciousness supporting this point are generally persuasive, but he tends to forget his own better judgment when he turns to construct his progressive account of history's order. If one returns to the concrete principles of his philosophy of consciousness, it appears that Voegelin's philosophy of history is perishing— "according to the ordinance of Time" and the empirical order of *Nous.*

---

33. Cf. Nietzsche, "On the Uses and Disadvantages of History for Life."

PART THREE

Order

Historiography

Conclusion

CHAPTER FIVE

Voegelin's Participation in the "Schelling Renaissance"

Voegelin studied Schelling in graduate school, under the supervision of Schellingian scholar Othmar Spann. These studies left their mark on Voegelin, but it did not appear immediately. Voegelin quotes Schelling only as one authority among others in his German works from the 1930s, and he produces some four thousand pages of his *History of Political Ideas* before returning to Schelling and realizing that the entire project is theoretically flawed. After this rereading of Schelling compels him to rework his *History,* Voegelin begins to depreciate Schelling's significance in the majority of his published writings. This study has argued, however, that Schelling continued to be a primary guide for Voegelin's philosophical orientation throughout his career, by drawing attention to substantial agreements between their works and supporting these with references to letters that Voegelin sent to colleagues during the time when he was most critical of Schelling. Thus, despite the appearance created by Voegelin's published criticisms of Schelling, substantial agreements between their conceptions of order and history have been found to remain.

Order

Schelling's identity philosophy is a substantial basis for Voegelin's philosophy of order. Schelling argues that the order of human consciousness is constituted by its unconscious, luminous depth (= B). He claims that this depth is substantially identical to the divine substance of the universe—"the All." In accordance with this supposition, he argues that the phenomenal truths perceived in reflective types of philosophy and the natural sciences cannot be taken as exhaustive accounts of the structure of reality. They are relatively partial and incomplete when compared to the substantial impartiality gained by contemplative philosophers. Such minds realize that thought and the substance of the universe are identical *before reflection* and are thereby able to know the only "objective" truth available to human consciousness—the law of identity (A = A). This knowledge provides the universal measure in thought with which Schelling is able to dismiss particular claims either to matter *or* spirit as the fundamental substance of the universe. He does not have to choose between what these terms represent in order to discuss the fundamental substance of reality, as both are thought to be substantially identical in the living process of the All.

Voegelin's description of the world as a "charmed community" in which all the "partners in being" are substantially identical (or "consubstantial") suggests that the Schellingian identity philosophy he supported in his 1943 letter to Alfred Schütz continues to guide his anthropological thinking in *Order and History.* Nothing in Voegelin's later work perpetuates the *proton pseudos* criticized by Schelling's identity philosophy. Voegelin does not assume, at least in his philosophy of consciousness, that phenomenal differences between things in the world reflect substantial differences in reality. Textual evidence has been provided to reveal precisely how he accepts this claim. But it is further supported by the following facts: Voegelin never retracts his published acceptance of Schelling's "ontology," the *Potenzenlehre* described as "process theology" in the German *Anamnesis,* and his latest critique of ego-based identity philosophy *(Identitätsphilosophie)* cannot be said to have the mature Schelling in mind as one of its targets. Schelling's ontology seems to have been chiefly responsible for allowing Voegelin to understand, criticize, and transcend the "phenomenalism" that passed for philosophy among many of his contemporaries.

Historiography

Schelling's account of how the divine substance of the All unfolds in human consciousness is a substantial basis for Voegelin's developmental conception of history's order. Schelling's historical philosophy argues that all of the divine potencies of nature become actualized in human consciousness throughout successive periods of history. They do so within a *substantially* permanent order of reality. He acknowledges no substantial changes in human nature or the divine throughout the entire process of history. He discusses only formal changes that occur in reflective consciousness. The same potencies are presupposed as the constituents of the humanity that undergoes both mythological and revelatory types of experiences. The potencies simply manifest different patterns of actualization, thus yielding different accents on nature or its Beyond as the source of order in the discernible epochs of God's self-revelation to humanity in history. Schelling finds "mere revelation" among the initiates of the Mystery religions in ancient Greece and among the prophets of Israel even before Christ becomes "visible" as the "real" principle of the "mediating potency." His historical philosophy effectively begins to weaken the ecclesiastical distinction between natural reason and divine Revelation. The order of history manifests itself, he argues, in a progression from natural to supernatural types of revelation, symbolized by the transition from mythological to revealed types of *religion*. To be sure, the distinction between reason and Revelation is not explicitly overcome by Schelling, but it is weakened nonetheless. The extent to which his historical philosophy draws upon his *Potenzenlehre* is greatly responsible for this. Its focus on the *substantial* identity of human-divine reality provides an initial basis for understanding a broad range of religious experiences as symbolic equivalents for one another. Accordingly, one could interpret his historical thought by accenting its different elements, yielding either a differentiated or an equivalent historiography. But its central weaknesses are not easily resolved by the skills of an interpreter.

Schelling encounters considerable problems in his attempt to demonstrate the universal progression of human consciousness throughout history. He presupposes that the divine potencies should become actualized simultaneously throughout the entire nature of human consciousness, that when "God's nature" unfolds all world mythologies should be affected in the same way, thus producing equivalent symbols for substantially equivalent experiences of the divine. But his examination of the textual evidence does not support this hypothesis conclusively. He finds evidence of historical stagnations and regressions in Persian, Indian, and Buddhist religions, and the Evangelists' description of Christ's Ascension. Furthermore, the lack of development in China is such that he attempts to use China's "complete atheism" as a countermeasure against which developments in the West can be understood as progressions toward the more complete understanding of existential order gained by Christians. He begins by presupposing that God shows no partiality, but his analysis of the historical records of experience leaves him to confront the problem that universal truths seem to emerge in particular people, times, and places.

Voegelin attempts to solve this problem by facing it directly. He constructs a differentiated historiography predicated on the claim that historical consciousness is a Western discovery, arising in what he eventually calls the Ecumenic Age and having universal bearing on how the general nature of human consciousness is best understood. However, aside from granting that universal truths emerge in particular circumstances, his developmental account of history's order retains many of the points that are distinctive to Schelling's work. In a private correspondence, Voegelin tells Schütz that he understands the historical progression of mythology in terms of Schelling's "theogony." That is to say, his account of "compact" or "cosmological" myth is equivalent to Schelling's account of "mythological religion." His account of "anthropological" and "soteriological" types of truth is equivalent to Schelling's account of "revealed religion," and his eventual appeal to the "eschatological structure" of history—leading toward the "universal humanity" in his latest historiography—is equivalent to Schelling's account of "philosophical religion" as an eschatological index. Voegelin also retains the notion of "leaps in being" as an equivalent for Schelling's account of the epoch-making "spiritual crises." And he finds the most "differentiated" level of experience and symbolization in an esoteric reading of Christian saints, notably Paul and Augustine. None of these points is dropped in Voegelin's account of the change that ostensibly comes about in his latest historiography. In fact, no substantial change is evident between the two historiographies he describes. His latest work recasts the historical progression of spiritual truth as a development from "noetic" to "pneumatic" types of revelation. But because Schelling also granted a certain type of revelation to select members of pre-Christian societies, this change in Voegelin's terminology constitutes no fundamental break with Schelling. His latest historical thought continues to be oriented by the Schellingian principles he acknowledges in a private letter to Robert Heilman in 1956. Guided by Schelling's mystical variety of Christian historicism, Voegelin identifies history and being in a "self-interpretive" process theology of history, leading from compact experiences and symbolizations of cosmological order to the differentiated claim that reality itself has an eschatological structure—from which salvation lies only through "grace in death."

Voegelin's claim that the historical process of differentiating consciousness appears to be leading toward the unity of universal humanity has caused his historical thought to be confused with Georg Hegel's. But it has become clear in this study, to the contrary, that the prereflective understanding of such unity in Schelling's identity philosophy best explains how Voegelin can construct a historical philosophy of reflective differentiations without falling prey to the Gnosticism of Hegel's brand of historicism. Voegelin's understanding of the process of historical differentiations synthesizes for reflective consciousness only what is always already united in the divine substance of the universe. He does not attempt to produce or construct the identity of humanity and divinity at the end of a reflective system, but attempts to remember the forgotten identity that has always been substantially real. He summarizes this point succinctly in *The Ecumenic Age:* "Things do not happen in the astrophysical universe; the universe, together with all things founded in it, happens in God" (*OH,* 4:334).

The Break with Schelling

Voegelin does not frequently call attention to the Schellingian orientation in his thought. Instead, he appeals to others for insights that are more distinctively Schellingian. For example, he replaces Schelling's claim that the substance of the All is known through intellectual intuition—prereflective or "protodialectic" experiences of contemplative reason—with praiseworthy references to William James's concept of "immediate experience" (see "EESH," 131). He replaces Schelling's concept of absolute identity with the concept of "consubstantiality," a term he takes from the Oriental Institute at the University of Chicago (see *Conversations,* 46–47). He refers to Karl Löwith for the dictum that there is no meaning *of* history, only meaning *in* history, but he does not dwell on the fact that he once found the same point in Schelling's *Ages of the World* (see "LO," 212).[1] Finally, instead of appealing to Schelling's "open soul" (or liberality) as a principal guide through the "creed communi-

---

1. Regrettably, it will be difficult for most readers to corroborate this point, due to a typographical error in the recently published version of "Last Orientation." In the Hoover Institution typescript of this text, Voegelin states that in Schelling, "the source of 'meaning' is *now* clearly circumscribed as the anamnetic dialogue that is going on in the soul" (Hoover Institution, Eric Voegelin Archives, box 59, folder 7, 184; emphasis added). But in the published text it says: "the source of 'meaning' is *not* clearly circumscribed as the anamnetic dialogue…" ("LO," 212; emphasis added). The point that Voegelin takes from Schelling is the open-ended character of the future. Schelling's "anamnesis is neither completed nor will it be completed soon, and we do not know, therefore, the meaning of history as a whole" (ibid.).

ties" of modernity, he refers to Henri Bergson's *"l'âme ouverte"* as the primary symbol for a spiritual realist's openness toward reality.[2]

Clearly, Voegelin found it necessary to restrict his own participation in the Schelling Renaissance to the "undercurrent" level he found in others. Why he did so remains to be considered. Perhaps the main reason lies, after all, in Schelling's alleged Gnosticism. My work has indicated that Voegelin's published accounts of this problem are insufficient to explain why he was so reticent to acknowledge being guided by Schelling during the greatest part of his publishing career. Quite simply, with the help of Voegelin's own account of Schelling's philosophy in "Last Orientation," strong indications have been found to suggest that Schelling was no more of a Gnostic intellectual than Voegelin himself. Both thinkers were critical realists who occasionally set aside their empirical insights from the philosophy of consciousness to speculate on an abstract order of history, determined in large part by characteristic features borrowed from Christian faith. But the "Last Orientation" also reveals that Voegelin's understanding was not based solely on his own reading of Schelling. Rather, it defers at significant points to the guidance of some prominent scholars at the time. Consider, for example, how Voegelin summarizes his discussion of Schelling's anthropology:

> The idea of the grace that falls in as a ray of divine love but still is grasped from the bottom of the eternal unconscious reveals the non-Christian character of the Promethean experience [that ostensibly orders the soul of Schelling]. The tension between creaturely finiteness and infinity, the tension between life and death, is solved in the Christian experience by grace that grasps man from above and annihilates him into the happiness beyond; the Promethean grace [of Schelling] is grasped by man and releases the tension of life and death in a flash of immanent happiness. ("LO," 222)

Two points from these lines require special attention. First, it is odd that Voegelin's summary should turn to relatively early texts—mainly, *Of Human Freedom* and the *System of Philosophy in General*—in order to emphasize the non-Christian character of Schelling's understanding of faith and Grace. Schelling's latest accounts of these experiences are far more sympathetic to the aims of Christian theology than the early Voegelin leads one to believe in the quoted passage. Voegelin knows the later texts well, but he ignores them

---

2. Bergson is one of several thinkers whom Voegelin mentions as a participant in the "undercurrent influence" of the "Schelling Renaissance." Cf. *supra*, 10, 43; "LO," 241; and *FER*, 117.

in his account of Schelling's anthropology. Second, it is odd that he should describe the experience of Grace as "immanent." Schelling does not tend to describe it in this way, and Voegelin is usually careful to emphasize why: no experience can be purely immanent in Schelling's anthropology, because human existence is structured by the universal tension between *God's* immanent nature (potencies A^1, A^2, and A^3) and transcendent freedom (A^0). Fortunately, a footnote attached to the quoted passage helps to explain why Voegelin's exegesis turns in these odd ways. A secondary reference cited therein reveals that his understanding of Schelling's "Promethean" anthropology is guided by Hans Urs von Balthasar's interpretation of the same.[3]

Balthasar's reading of Schelling focuses only on early texts. He says that it is unnecessary to interpret Schelling's latest work, the voluminous *Philosophy of Mythology* and *Philosophy of Revelation*, as it "no longer exerts a living influence on contemporary history."[4] Balthasar claims to find a "Prometheus Principle," a non-Christian type of rebellion, that characterizes the recent history of German idealism. His focus on early works by Schelling in the discussion of this principle leads him to interpret Schelling as one among several "Promethean" idealists—in a list that includes Johann Fichte, Novalis, Johann Hölderlin, and Friedrich Schiller. Most significantly, however, Balthasar's reading is best summarized by his claim that "Schelling's anthropology is indistinguishable from his gnostic theology."[5]

In his *Autobiographical Reflections,* Voegelin says that he first learned of modern Gnosticism from Balthasar's *Prometheus* (1937). He then discovered accounts of Schelling's Gnosticism in Balthasar's *Apokalypse der deutschen Seele* and Ferdinand Christian Baur's *Die christliche Gnosis* (1835) (see *AR,* 65–66). These are the principal books that seem to guide his decision to dismiss Schelling as a Gnostic intellectual in the majority of his published works. Considered pragmatically, this decision must have had a certain appeal for Voegelin. It saved him the trouble of overturning an established convention in German scholarship on Schelling and from entering a debate that may have made it more difficult to gain a hearing for his own work. But the decision

---

3. See "LO," 222 n. 47; and Balthasar, *Apokalypse der deutschen Seele,* vol. 1, *Der deutsche Idealismus* (1937). Voegelin also mentions this work earlier in his "Last Orientation." He refers to it as "perhaps [the] most important" secondary work considered by him, and as an "excellent chapter" on Schelling ("LO," 199 n. 2).

4. Balthasar, *Apokalypse der deutschen Seele,* 246 n. 2.

5. Ibid., 223. The theme of Gnosticism appears at other places in the text as well (cf. ibid., 209, 210, 238, 246, 247). Balthasar also discusses Schelling's accounts of the "double life" (229) and "melancholy" (248–49).

to follow Baur and Balthasar remains curious on another level. The central weakness in their studies could not have escaped Voegelin. Both men interpret only relatively early works by Schelling. They focus on a time in his philosophical development when Christian symbols were less important than they became in his latest period, when his identity philosophy was easily mistaken for the reflective identity systems of Fichte and Hegel, and the central theme of his latest work—the historicity of consciousness—had yet to be developed. But Voegelin knew the later works well, and understood them far better than Balthasar. His ability to identify several participants in a Schelling Renaissance bears witness to this point. Unlike Balthasar, Voegelin does maintain that Schelling's latest work continues to exert a living influence on contemporary history, the "undercurrent influence" of Schellingian realism he finds in Arthur Schopenhauer, Søren Kierkegaard, Friedrich Nietzsche, and Sigmund Freud, among others (see "LO," 241). He devotes considerably more attention to Schelling's latest thought than do any of the critics he acknowledges as authorities in print. As a consequence, he gains a better understanding than most of the core of Schelling's philosophical anthropology. But his early nod to prominent scholarship in his field created the lasting tensions in his accounts of Schelling's significance, resulting in the subject matter of this book.

Had Voegelin remained consistently true to the insights gained in his Schellingian philosophy of consciousness, had he then undertaken a thorough rewriting of his historiography—facing all of the metastatic aspects of biblical religions seriously—and had he been able to publish at least some of his results by the late 1960s, then the Schelling Renaissance might have become a far better response to phenomenology and related strains of modern thought than what we have inherited in its place—namely, existentialism and its variant forms in deconstruction and postmodernism. Too much to ask of the past, perhaps. But all is not lost, for the future still hangs in the balance for the serious recovery of philosophy that Voegelin and Schelling were able to envision.

Translation of Schelling's Outline for the Philosophy of Mythology in His *Philosophy of Revelation* (Lectures 18 and 21)

[Lecture 18]

I. Primordial Consciousness *(Urbewußtseyn)*
   Primordial humanity, enclosed within the three potencies, to which it is equal.

II. Transition to Process [= Fall]
   Man turns himself exclusively toward one principle (B), and falls under its control.

III. Process
   A: *First Epoch.* Exclusive reign of the *real* principle (= B) in consciousness. Complete being-out-of-self *(Völliges Außersichseyn)*. Transition to following moment: astral religion—*Uranus*—Zabism, religion of absolutely prehistorical humanity. [Relative Monotheism]

[Emergence of First Spiritual Crisis]———————————————

   B: *Second Epoch.* The *real* principle = B renders itself accessible, surmountable by the superior [principle], becomes the matter (mother) of the latter—: Moment of *Urania* and of the first appearance of the superior potency, of *Dionysus: Persian, Babylonian, Arabian.* [Simultaneous Polytheism]

C: *Third Epoch.* Effective combat, which itself passes through several moments.

AA: *First Moment.* The *real* principle still restrains the superior in complete subordination, allowing it no part in being—form of servant *(Knechtsgestalt),* in which the superior potency appears—the *Phoenician Herakles* (Melkart). The opposing god—*Cronos* the Father.

[Emergence of Second Spiritual Crisis]——————————————

BB: *Second Moment.* Repeated softening [of first principle]—becoming—wife of Cronos—*Cybele* (mother of the gods [= Rhea])—*Phrygian* race.

CC: *Third Moment.* Effective surmounting [of first principle]. Progressive rise to superiority of third potency (to the extent that the first is surmounted). Complete mythologies, yielding another threefold distinction. [Successive Polytheism]

[Egypt]

1) The *real* principle (Typhon) still continues to fight for its existence: *Egyptian* mythology. The *three* potencies, *Typhon, Osiris, Horus* (Horus as infant—Isis).

[India]

2) The *real* principle is completely out of the battle (subjugated); but without this the unity would again be reformed; this is posed only in an ideal manner; the potencies, in effect, are in a state of complete separation from themselves *[Außereinanderseyn]: Indian* mythology—*Brahma* = B, *Shiva* = second, *Vishnu* = third potency.

[Greece]

3) Reestablishment of unity: the *real* principle returns to its latency and is conserved as the *ground* of religious consciousness; the second principle becomes effective in the surmounting of the first; the two together posit the third as the end of the entire process: *Greek* mythology.

a) *Exoteric* aspect: the material gods (causes, merely epiphenomenal), origin of the disintegration *(Zergehen)* of the *real* principle: the *world of the gods* in common consciousness.

[Lecture 21]

　　b) *Esoteric* aspect: The potencies as *primordial causes [verur-sachenden]* in the proper sense of the term; the secret of all the process: *doctrines of the Mysteries,* where the content is the *One* God, not as abstract but passing through the three potencies, and which

　　　　aa) as *real,* but subjugated by the second potency (Dionysus) becomes itself = Dionysus—*Dionysus of the first potency* (the oldest), Zagreus = Dionysus of the past—*from* which—,

　　　　bb) in his achieved effectivity, as dominator *[Ueberwinder]* of the first potency, he is *Dionysus of the second potency,* Bacchus = Dionysus of the present—*through* which—,

　　　　cc) as posited through the two others (he who properly should be), [he is] *Dionysus of the third potency,* Iakchos = Dionysus of the future—*in* which are all the gods.

　　Corresponding to these three divinities, as their common consciousness—Demeter.[1]

　　1. Schelling, *Philosophie der Offenbarung,* in *Werke,* 2.3.xvii–xviii, xix–xx. This is how Schelling presents the philosophy of mythology in the context of his *Philosophy of Revelation.* The shorter account of mythological religion in the latter text could not be followed exclusively in my own sketch of these "philosophies," because Schelling cleans up the historiography in the latter text by completely ignoring the problems of historical "stagnation" in China and Persia.

BIBLIOGRAPHY

Classical Texts and Translations

All translations from German, French, and Greek are my own, unless otherwise indicated. I have used the Loeb Classical Library (Harvard University Press) for the Greek texts. I have also frequently consulted the translations listed below. The *Revised Standard Version* of the Bible has been used for biblical quotations cited without Greek analysis.

Selected Works by F. W. J. Schelling

The Ages of the World. Trans. and ed. Frederick de Wolfe Bolman Jr. New York: Columbia University Press, 1942.

Ideas for a Philosophy of Nature. Trans. and ed. E. Harris and P. Heath. Cambridge: Cambridge University Press, 1988.

Le monothéisme. Trans. and notes by Alain Pernet. Paris: Librairie Philosophique J. Vrin, 1992.

Of Human Freedom. Trans. J. Gutman. Chicago: Open Court Press, 1936.

On the History of Modern Philosophy. Trans. Andrew Bowie. Cambridge: Cambridge University Press, 1994.

Philosophie de la mythologie. Trans. Alain Pernet. Grenoble, France: J. Millon Krisis, 1994.

Philosophie de la révélation, Livre Premier: Introduction à la Philosophie de la Révélation. Trans. Jean-François Marquet and Jean-François Courtine. Paris: Presses Universitaires de France, 1994.

Sämmtliche Werke (in a new arrangement). Ed. Manfred Schröter. 12 vols. Munich: Beck, 1927–1954. *Sämmtliche Werke.* Ed. Karl Friedrich Anton

Schelling. 14 vols. Stuttgart and Augsburg: J. G. Cotta'scher Verlag, 1856–1861.

"Schelling's Aphorisms of 1805." *Idealistic Studies* 14 (1984): 237–58.

Stuttgarter Privatvorlesungen. Ed. Miklos Vetö. Turin: Bottega d'Erasmo, 1976. *Stuttgart Seminars.* In *Idealism and the Endgame of Theory: Three Essays by F. W. J. Schelling,* trans. Thomas Pfau, 195–268. Albany: State University of New York Press, 1994.

System der gesamten Philosophie und der Naturphilosophie insbesondere. In *Sämmtliche Werke,* pt. 1, vol. 6. *System of Philosophy in General and of the Philosophy of Nature in Particular.* In *Idealism and the Endgame of Theory: Three Essays by F. W. J. Schelling,* trans. Thomas Pfau, 139–94. Albany: State University of New York Press, 1994.

System of Transcendental Idealism. Trans. Peter Heath. Charlottesville: University Press of Virginia, 1978.

Selected Works by Eric Voegelin

Anamnesis. Trans. and ed. Gerhart Niemeyer. Columbia: University of Missouri Press, 1990.

Anamnesis: Zur Theorie der Geschichte und Politik. Munich: R. Piper and Co. Verlag, 1966.

Autobiographical Reflections. Ed. Ellis Sandoz. Baton Rouge: Louisiana State University Press, 1989.

"Autobiographical Statement at Age Eighty-two," "Consciousness and Order: Foreword to 'Anamnesis' (1966)," "The Meditative Origin of the Philosophical Knowledge of Order" (1981), and "Responses at the Panel Discussion of 'The Beginning of the Beginning.'" In *The Beginning and the Beyond: Papers from the Gadamer and Voegelin Conferences,* ed. Frederick Lawrence. Supplementary issue of *Lonergan Workshop,* vol. 4. Chico, Calif.: Scholars Press, 1984.

The Collected Works of Eric Voegelin. Ed. Paul Caringella, Jürgen Gebhardt, Thomas A. Hollweck, and Ellis Sandoz. 34 vols. Columbia: University of Missouri Press, 1990–2000.

Conversations with Eric Voegelin. Ed. E. O'Connor. Montreal: Thomas More Institute, 1980.

Faith and Political Philosophy: The Correspondence between Leo Strauss and Eric Voegelin, 1934–1964. Trans. and ed. Peter Emberley and Barry Cooper. University Park: Pennsylvania State University Press, 1993.

From Enlightenment to Revolution. Ed. J. H. Hallowell. Durham: Duke University Press, 1975.

"Industrial Society in Search of Reason." In *World Technology and Human Destiny,* ed. R. Aron, 31–46. Ann Arbor: University of Michigan Press, 1963.

"Liberalism and Its History." *Review of Politics* 36:4 (1974): 504–20. Originally published as "Der Liberalismus und seine Geschichte." In *Christentum und Liberalismus: Studien und Bericht der Katholischen Akademie in Bayern,* ed. Karl Forster, 13–42. Munich: Zink, 1960.

The New Science of Politics: An Introduction. Chicago: University of Chicago Press, 1987.

On the Form of the American Mind. Vol. 1 of *The Collected Works of Eric Voegelin.* Trans. Ruth Hein. Ed. Jürgen Gebhardt and Barry Cooper. Baton Rouge: Louisiana State University Press, 1995.

Order and History. Columbia: University of Missouri Press, 1999–2000. Vol. 1, *Israel and Revelation* (1956). Vol. 2, *The World of the Polis* (1957). Vol. 3, *Plato and Aristotle* (1957). Vol. 4, *The Ecumenic Age* (1974). Vol. 5, *In Search of Order* (1987).

"Plato's Egyptian Myth." *Journal of Politics* 9:3 (August 1947): 307–24.

Political Religions. Trans. T. J. DiNapoli and E. S. Easterly III. Lewiston, N.Y.: Edwin Mellen Press, 1986.

Published Essays, 1966–1985. Vol. 12 of *The Collected Works of Eric Voegelin.* Ed. Ellis Sandoz. Baton Rouge: Louisiana State University Press, 1990.

Race and State. Vol. 2 of *The Collected Works of Eric Voegelin.* Ed. Klaus Vondung. Trans. Ruth Hein. Baton Rouge: Louisiana State University Press, 1997.

"Religionsersatz: Die gnostischen Massenbewegungen unserer Zeit." *Wort und Wahrheit* 15:1 (1960): 5–18.

Science, Politics, and Gnosticism. Trans. William J. Fitzpatrick. Washington, D.C.: Regnery Gateway, 1990.

"Structures in Consciousness." Public talk from 1977. Transcribed and ed. Zdravko Planinc. *Voegelin Research News* 2:3 (1996). Available on-line at http://vax2.concordia.ca/~vorenews.

"Symposium Contributions." In *The Question as Commitment: A Symposium.* Ed. Elaine Cahn and Cathleen Going. Thomas More Institute Papers, vol. 77. Montreal: Associates of the Thomas More Institute, 1979.

"What Is History?" and Other Late Unpublished Writings. Vol. 28 of *The Collected Works of Eric Voegelin.* Ed. Thomas A. Hollweck and Paul Caringella. Baton Rouge: Louisiana State University Press, 1990.

Wissenschaft, Politik, und Gnosis. Munich: Kösel-Verlag, 1959.

Other Sources

Abrams, M. H. *Natural Supernaturalism: Tradition and Revolution in Romantic Literature.* New York: Norton, 1971.

Aland, Kurt, Matthew Black, Carlo M. Martini, Bruce M. Metzger, and Allen Wikgren, eds. *The Greek New Testament.* 3d ed. Stuttgart: United Bible Societies, 1983.

Anastaplo, George. "On How Eric Voegelin Has Read Plato and Aristotle." *Independent Journal of Philosophy* 5:6 (1988): 85–91.

Anderson, Bernhard W. "Revisiting Voegelin's *Israel and Revelation* after Twenty-five Years." In *Politics, Order, and History: Essays on the Work of Eric Voegelin,* ed. Glenn Hughes, Stephen A. McKnight, and Geoffrey L. Price, 284–98. Sheffield, England: Sheffield Academic Press, 2001.

Aristotle. *Metaphysics.* Vols. 1–9, trans. H. Tredennick. Vols. 10–14, trans. H. Tredennick and G. Cyril Armstrong. Cambridge: Harvard University Press, 1933, 1935.

———. *Nicomachean Ethics.* Trans. H. Rackham. Cambridge: Harvard University Press, 1934.

———. *The Politics.* Trans. Carnes Lord. Chicago: University of Chicago Press, 1985.

Augustine. *City of God.* Trans. G. G. Walsh, D. B. Zema, G. Monahan, and D. J. Honan. New York: Doubleday, Image Books, 1958.

———. *Confessions.* Trans. Henry Chadwick. Oxford: Oxford University Press, 1992.

Balthasar, Hans Urs von. *Apokalypse der deutschen Seele.* Vol. 1, *Der deutsche Idealismus.* Salzburg and Leipzig: A. Pustet, 1937.

Barker, Terry, and Lawrence Schmidt. "'Voegelin Not Mysterious': A Response to Zdravko Planinc's 'The Significance of Plato's *Timaeus* and *Critias* in Eric Voegelin's Philosophy.'" In *Politics, Order, and History: Essays on the Work of Eric Voegelin,* ed. Glenn Hughes, Stephen A. McKnight, and Geoffrey L. Price, 376–409. Sheffield, England: Sheffield Academic Press, 2001.

Beach, Edward Allen. *The Potencies of God(s): Schelling's Philosophy of Mythology.* Albany: State University of New York Press, 1994.

Boers, Hendrikus. "Interpreting Paul: Demythologizing in Reverse." In *The Philosophy of Order,* ed. Peter J. Opitz and Gregor Sebba, 153–72. Stuttgart: Ernst Klett, 1981.

Bowie, A. *Schelling and Modern European Philosophy.* London: Routledge, 1993.

————, trans. Introduction to *On the History of Modern Philosophy.* Cambridge: Cambridge University Press, 1994.

Caringella, Paul. "Voegelin: Philosopher of Divine Presence." In *Eric Voegelin's Significance for the Modern Mind,* ed. Ellis Sandoz, 174–206. Baton Rouge: Louisiana State University Press, 1991.

Cooper, Barry. *Action into Nature: An Essay on the Meaning of Technology.* Notre Dame: University of Notre Dame Press, 1991.

————. *Eric Voegelin and the Foundations of Modern Political Science.* Columbia: University of Missouri Press, 1999.

————. Introduction to *Political Religions,* by Eric Voegelin, v–xxvi. Lewiston, N.Y.: Edwin Mellen Press, 1986.

Danz, Christian. *Die philosophische Christologie F. W. J. Schellings.* Vol. 9, *Schellingiana.* Stuttgart–Bad Cannstatt: Frommann-Holzboog, 1996.

Derrida, Jacques. *Margins of Philosophy.* Trans. Alan Bass. Chicago: University of Chicago Press, 1986.

Dussort, Henri. *L'École de Marbourg.* Paris: Presses Universitaires de France, 1963.

Fackenheim, Emil L. *The God Within: Kant, Schelling, and Historicity.* Ed. John Burbidge. Toronto: University of Toronto Press, 1996.

Federici, Michael P. "Voegelin's Christian Critics." *Modern Age* 36 (1994): 331–40.

Frank, Manfred. *Eine Einführung in Schellings Philosophie.* Frankfurt: Suhrkamp, 1985.

Franz, Michael G. *Eric Voegelin and the Politics of Spiritual Revolt.* Baton Rouge: Louisiana State University Press, 1993.

Froman, Wayne J. "Schelling's *Treatise on the Essence of Human Freedom* and Heidegger's Thought." *International Philosophical Quarterly* 30:4 (December 1990): 465–80.

Gadamer, Hans-Georg. *Truth and Method.* Trans. Joel Weinsheimer and Donald G. Marshall. 2d ed. New York: Crossroad, 1992.

Gebhardt, Jürgen. "Erfahrung und Wirklichkeit—Anmerkungen zur Politischen Wissenschaft des spirituellen Realismus." In *The Philosophy of Order: Essays on History, Consciousness, and Politics,* ed. Peter J. Opitz and Gregor Sebba, 332–44. Stuttgart: Klett-Cotta, 1981.

————. Introduction to *The Collected Works of Eric Voegelin,* ed. Jürgen Gebhardt and Thomas A. Hollweck, 25:1–34. Columbia: University of Missouri Press, 1999.

————. "Die Suche nach dem Grund—Eine zivilizationsgeschichtliche Konstante?" In *Symbol und Ordnungsformen im Zivilizationsvergleich,* ed.

Akademie für Politische Bildung. Tutzing: Akademie für Politische Bildung, 1990.

———. "Toward the Process of Universal Mankind: The Formation of Voegelin's Philosophy of History." In *Eric Voegelin's Thought: A Critical Appraisal,* ed. Ellis Sandoz, 67–86. Durham: Duke University Press, 1982.

———. "The Vocation of the Scholar." In *International and Interdisciplinary Perspectives on Eric Voegelin,* ed. Stephen A. McKnight and Geoffrey L. Price, 10–34. Columbia: University of Missouri Press, 1997.

Germino, Dante. *Beyond Ideology.* Chicago: University of Chicago Press, 1976.

Gottfried, Paul Edward. *The Search for Historical Meaning: Hegel and the Postwar American Right.* DeKalb: Northern Illinois University Press, 1986.

Hayes, Victor C. "Schelling: Persistent Legends, Improving Image." *Southwestern Journal of Philosophy* 3 (1972): 63–73.

Hegel, G. W. F. *The Phenomenology of Mind.* Trans. J. B. Baillie. New York: Harper and Row, 1967.

Heidegger, Martin. *On Time and Being.* Trans. Joan Stambaugh. New York: Harper Torchbooks, 1972.

Hughes, Glenn. "Eric Voegelin's View of History as a Drama of Transfiguration." *International Philosophical Quarterly* 30 (1990): 449–464.

———. *Mystery and Myth in the Philosophy of Eric Voegelin.* Columbia: University of Missouri Press, 1993.

———, ed. *The Politics of the Soul: Eric Voegelin on Religious Experience.* Lanham: Rowman and Littlefield, 1999.

Hughes, Glenn, Stephen A. McKnight, and Geoffrey L. Price, eds. *Politics, Order, and History: Essays on the Work of Eric Voegelin.* Sheffield, England: Sheffield Academic Press, 2001.

Husserl, Edmund. *Cartesian Meditations.* Trans. Dorion Cairns. Dordrecht: Kluwer Academic Publishers, 1993.

Idel, Moshe. "Voegelin's *Israel and Revelation:* Some Observations." In *Politics, Order, and History: Essays on the Work of Eric Voegelin,* ed. Glenn Hughes, Stephen A. McKnight, and Geoffrey L. Price, 299–326. Sheffield, England: Sheffield Academic Press, 2001.

"Journalism and Joachim's Children," *Time* (March 9, 1953): 57–61.

Kant, Immanuel. *Critique of Pure Reason.* Trans. Norman Kemp Smith. New York: Macmillan, St. Martin's Press, 1965.

Keulman, Kenneth. *The Balance of Consciousness: Eric Voegelin's Political Theory.* University Park: Pennsylvania State University Press, 1990.

Kuhn, Helmut. "Das Problem einer philosophischen Historiographie: Zum Werke von Eric Voegelin." *Zeitschrift für Politik* 28 (1981): 116–29.

Kuhn, Thomas S. *The Copernican Revolution.* Cambridge: Harvard University Press, 1957.

Lawrence, Frederick. "The Problem of Eric Voegelin, Mystic Philosopher and Scientist." In *International and Interdisciplinary Perspectives on Eric Voegelin,* ed. Stephen A. McKnight and Geoffrey L. Price, 35–58. Columbia: University of Missouri Press, 1997.

———, ed. *The Beginning and the Beyond: Papers from the Gadamer and Lonergan Conferences.* In supplementary issue of *Lonergan Workshop,* vol. 4. Chico, Calif.: Scholars Press, 1984.

Levinas, Emmanuel. *Totality and Infinity: An Essay on Exteriority.* Trans. Alphonso Lingis. Pittsburgh: Duquesne University Press, 1992.

McKnight, Stephen A. "The Evolution of Voegelin's Theory of Politics and History, 1944–1975." In *Eric Voegelin's Search for Order in History,* ed. Stephen A. McKnight, 26–45. Baton Rouge: Louisiana State University Press, 1978; New York: University Press of America, 1987.

———. "*Order and History* as a Response to the Theoretical and Methodological Problems Confronting Historians in the Twentieth Century." In *Politics, Order, and History: Essays on the Work of Eric Voegelin,* ed. Glenn Hughes, Stephen A. McKnight, and Geoffrey L. Price, 259–81. Sheffield, England: Sheffield Academic Press, 2001.

McKnight, Stephen A., and Geoffrey L. Price, eds. *International and Interdisciplinary Perspectives on Eric Voegelin.* Columbia: University of Missouri Press, 1997.

Morrissey, Michael P. *Consciousness and Transcendence: The Theology of Eric Voegelin.* Notre Dame: University of Notre Dame Press, 1994.

———. "Eric Voegelin and the New Testament: Developments, Problems, and Challenges." In *Politics, Order, and History: Essays on the Work of Eric Voegelin,* ed. Glenn Hughes, Stephen A. McKnight, and Geoffrey L. Price, 462–500. Sheffield, England: Sheffield Academic Press, 2001.

———. "Voegelin, Religious Experience, and Immortality." In *The Politics of the Soul,* ed. Glenn Hughes, 11–31. Lanham: Rowman and Littlefield, 1999.

Moulakis, Athanasios. "Political Reality and History in the Work of Eric Voegelin." In *The Promise of History: Essays in Political Philosophy,* ed. Athanasios Moulakis, 120–34. London and New York: Walter de Gruyter, 1985.

Nash, George. *The Conservative Intellectual Movement in America since* 1945. New York: Basic Books, 1976.

Nieli, Russell. "Eric Voegelin: An Eschatological Direction to History?" *Fides et Historia* 22 (1990): 3–15.

Niemeyer, Gerhart. "Are There Intelligible Parts of History?" In *The Philosophy of Order: Essays on History, Consciousness, and Politics,* ed. Peter J. Opitz and Gregor Sebba, 302–15. Stuttgart: Klett-Cotta, 1981.

———. "Christian Faith and Religion in Eric Voegelin's Work." *Review of Politics* 57:1 (1995): 91–104.

———. "Conservatism and the New Political Theory." *Modern Age* 23 (1979): 115–22.

Nietzsche, Friedrich. "On the Uses and Disadvantages of History for Life." In *Untimely Meditations,* ed. Daniel Breazeale, trans. R. J. Hollingdale, 57–123. Cambridge: Cambridge University Press, 1997.

Opitz, Peter J., and Gregor Sebba, eds. *The Philosophy of Order.* Stuttgart: Ernst Klett, 1981.

Petropulos, William. "Eric Voegelin and German Sociology." Ed. Peter Halfpenny. *Manchester Sociology Occasional Papers* 50 (February 1998): 1–21.

———. "Social Science and Salvation: Notes on One Branch of German Sociology." Paper presented at the annual meeting of the American Political Science Association, Washington, D.C., September 1, 2000.

Pfau, Thomas, trans. and ed. *Idealism and the Endgame of Theory: Three Essays by F. W. J. Schelling.* Albany: State University of New York Press, 1994.

Planinc, Zdravko. "Homeric Imagery in Plato's *Phaedrus*." In *Politics, Philosophy, Writing: Plato's Art of Caring for Souls,* ed. Zdravko Planinc, 122–59. Columbia: University of Missouri Press, 2001.

———. *Plato's Political Philosophy: Prudence in the "Republic" and the "Laws."* Columbia: University of Missouri Press, 1991.

———. "The Significance of Plato's *Timaeus* and *Critias* in Eric Voegelin's Philosophy." In *Politics, Order, and History: Essays on the Work of Eric Voegelin,* ed. Glenn Hughes, Stephen A. McKnight, and Geoffrey L. Price, 327–75. Sheffield, England: Sheffield Academic Press, 2001.

———. "The Uses of Plato in Voegelin's Philosophy of Consciousness: Reflections Prompted by Voegelin's Lecture, 'Structures of Consciousness.'" *Voegelin—Research News* 2:3 (1996). Available on-line at http://vax2.concordia.ca/~vorenews.

Plato. *Gorgias.* Trans. W. C. Helmbold. New York: Macmillan, 1952.

———. *Laws.* Trans. Thomas L. Pangle. Chicago: University of Chicago Press, 1988.

————. *Phaedo.* Trans. Harold North Fowler. Cambridge: Harvard University Press, 1990.

————. *Republic.* Trans. Paul Shorey. Vols. 1–2. Cambridge: Harvard University Press, 1982, 1987.

————. *Theaetetus.* Trans. H. N. Fowler. Cambridge: Harvard University Press, 1987.

————. *Timaeus.* Trans. R. G. Bury. Cambridge: Harvard University Press, 1961.

Price, Geoffrey L. "Augustine and Vico in Voegelin's Philosophy of History." Paper presented at the annual meeting of the American Political Science Association, San Francisco, August 31, 1996.

————. "Critical History after Augustine and Orosius: Voegelin's Return to Plato." In *International and Interdisciplinary Perspectives on Eric Voegelin,* ed. Stephen A. McKnight and Geoffrey L. Price, 84–116. Columbia: University of Missouri Press, 1997.

————. "The Epiphany of Universal Humanity." In *The Politics of the Soul,* ed. Glenn Hughes, 65–83. Lanham: Rowman and Littlefield, 1999.

————. "Eric Voegelin: A Classified Bibliography." *Bulletin of the John Rylands University Library of Manchester* 76:2 (summer 1994), and subsequent updates from *Voegelin—Research News,* available on-line at http://vax2.concordia.ca/~vorenews.

————. "Recovery from Metastatic Consciousness: Voegelin and Jeremiah." In *Politics, Order, and History: Essays on the Work of Eric Voegelin,* ed. Glenn Hughes, Stephen A. McKnight, and Geoffrey L. Price, 185–207. Sheffield, England: Sheffield Academic Press, 2001.

Ranieri, John. *Eric Voegelin and the Good Society.* Columbia: University of Missouri Press, 1995.

Reardon, Bernard M. G. "Schelling's Critique of Hegel." *Religious Studies* 20 (1984): 543–57.

Rhodes, James M. "On Voegelin: His Collected Works and His Significance." *Review of Politics* 54 (1992): 621–47.

————. "Philosophy, Revelation, and Political Theory: Leo Strauss and Eric Voegelin." *Journal of Politics* 49:4 (1987): 1036–60.

————. "Voegelin and Christian Faith." *Center Journal* 2 (summer 1983): 55–105.

Saltzman, Judy Deane. *Paul Natorp's Philosophy of Religion within the Marburg Neo-Kantian Tradition.* New York: Georg Olms Verlag Hildesheim, 1981.

Sandoz, Ellis. "Medieval Rationalism or Mystic Philosophy? Reflections on the Strauss-Voegelin Correspondence." In *Faith and Political Philosophy: The*

    Correspondence between Leo Strauss and Eric Voegelin, 1934–1964, trans.
    and ed. Peter Emberley and Barry Cooper, 297–319. University Park:
    Pennsylvania State University Press, 1993.

————. "Truth and the Experience of Epoch in History: A Voegelinian Per-
    spective." *Modern Age* 38 (1995): 7–21.

————. *The Voegelinian Revolution: A Biographical Introduction.* Baton
    Rouge: Louisiana State University Press, 1981.

————. "Voegelin's Philosophy of History and Human Affairs." Paper pre-
    sented at the annual meeting of the American Political Science Associa-
    tion, San Francisco, August 31, 1996.

————, ed. *Eric Voegelin's Significance for the Modern Mind.* Baton Rouge:
    Louisiana State University Press, 1991.

————. *Eric Voegelin's Thought: A Critical Appraisal.* Durham: Duke Uni-
    versity Press, 1982.

Schulz, Walter. *Die Vollendung des deutschen Idealismus in der Spätphilosophie
    Schellings.* 2d ed. 1955. Reprint, Pfullingen, Germany: Neske, 1975.

Sedlar, Jean W. *India in the Mind of Germany: Schelling, Schopenhauer, and
    Their Times.* Washington, D.C.: University Press of America, 1982.

Shankman, Steven. *In Search of the Classic: Reconsidering the Greco-Roman
    Tradition, Homer to Valery and Beyond.* University Park: Pennsylvania
    State University Press, 1994.

Simmons, William P. "The Platonic *Metaxy* in the Writings of Eric Voegelin
    and Simone Weil." Paper presented at the annual meeting of the Amer-
    ican Political Science Association, Chicago, September 2, 1995.

Snow, Dale E. *Schelling and the End of Idealism.* Albany: State University of
    New York Press, 1996.

Spann, Othmar. *Religionsphilosophie: Auf Geschichtlicher Grundlage.* Vienna:
    Gallus-Verlag, 1947.

Srigley, Ronald D. *Eric Voegelin's Platonic Theology: Philosophy of Consciousness
    and Symbolization in a New Perspective.* Lewiston, N.Y.: Edwin Mellen
    Press, 1991.

Tillich, Paul. *The Construction of the History of Religion in Schelling's Positive
    Philosophy.* Trans. Victor Nuovo. Lewisburg, Pa.: Bucknell University
    Press, 1974.

————. *Mysticism and Guilt-Consciousness in Schelling's Philosophical Devel-
    opment.* Trans. Victor Nuovo. Lewisburg, Pa.: Bucknell University Press,
    1974.

Tilliette, X. *Schelling: Une philosophie en devenir.* Paris: Vrin, 1970.

Wagner, Helmut R. "Agreement in Discord: Alfred Schütz and Eric Voegelin." In *The Philosophy of Order,* ed. Peter J. Opitz and Gregor Sebba. Stuttgart: Ernst Klett, 1981.

———. *Alfred Schütz: An Intellectual Biography.* Chicago: University of Chicago Press, 1983.

Webb, Eugene. *Eric Voegelin: Philosopher of History.* Seattle: University of Washington Press, 1981.

———. "Eric Voegelin's Theory of Revelation." *Thomist* 42 (1978): 95–110. Reprinted in Ellis Sandoz, ed. *Eric Voegelin's Thought: A Critical Appraisal.* Durham: Duke University Press, 1982.

———. *Philosophers of Consciousness: Polanyi, Lonergan, Voegelin, Ricoeur, Girard, Kierkegaard.* Seattle: University of Washington Press, 1988.

Weiss, Gilbert. "Political Reality and the Life-World: The Correspondence between Eric Voegelin and Alfred Schütz, 1938–59." In *Politics, Order, and History: Essays on the Work of Eric Voegelin,* ed. Glenn Hughes, Stephen A. McKnight, and Geoffrey L. Price, 125–42. Sheffield, England: Sheffield Academic Press, 2001.

———. *Theorie, Relevanz, und Wahrheit: Eine Rekonstruktion des Briefwechsels zwischen Eric Voegelin und Alfred Schütz (1938–1959).* Munich: Wilhelm Fink Verlag, 2000.

Wiser, James L. "Reason and Revelation as Search and Response: A Comparison of Eric Voegelin and Leo Strauss." In *Faith and Political Philosophy: The Correspondence between Leo Strauss and Eric Voegelin, 1934–1964,* trans. and ed. Peter Emberley and Barry Cooper, 237–48. University Park: Pennsylvania State University Press, 1993.

Žižek, Slavoj. *The Abyss of Freedom.* Ann Arbor: University of Michigan Press, 1997.

———. *The Indivisible Remainder: An Essay on Schelling and Related Matters.* New York: Verso, 1996.

INDEX

Abraham/Abram: and Isaac, 166–67;
  experience of transcendence, 211–12;
  mentioned, 214
Abrams, M. H., 48
Æschylus, 73, 75n49
Ahaz, King of Judah, 216–17, 218
Amor Dei (love of God), 220, 238
Amor sui (self-love), 220
Amos, 167, 168n94, 219, 219n34
Analogia entis, 37, 224n48
Anamnesis (recollection): in Voegelin, 23,
  79, 187, 189, 190; in Schelling, 62, 62n16,
  118; mentioned, 49, 118, 131
Anaximander, 183, 191, 192, 238, 248,
  248n20, 253
Anschluss, 2
Apeiron, 138n20, 183, 238, 245, 248, 250, 253
Aquinas, Thomas, 8, 19, 37, 41n58, 83n57,
  230; *amicitia*, 219; *analogia entis*, 224n48
Aristotle:
—Schelling on, 64, 65, 65n26, 163–65
—Voegelin on: 74n45, 94n65, 107; reason,
  184, 230–39; historical consciousness/
  position of, 193, 213, 233–34, 235–36, 252;
  and Revelation, 210, 227, 237–38; *zetesis*
  of, 231–32; Unmoved Mover of, 232n6;
  and myth, 233–35, 250; *bios theoretikos*,
  250; mentioned, 120, 207, 210nn26,27
—Works: *Nicomachean Ethics*, 165, 210,
  210n26, 238, 238n16; *Meterologica*, 213n30;
  Metaphysics, 213n30, 231–37, 232n6, 233n8,
  234n10, 237nn14,15; *Politics*, 213n30

Athanasius, 201n13
Augustine (Saint), 8, 19, 100, 217; historiography of, 193–94, 195, 228–30; *saeculum
  senescens*, 194; *civitas Dei*, 210, 242, 262;
  civitas terrena, 242, 262

Baal, 149
Bacchus: and Dionysus, 161, 279
Bakunin, Mikhail, 44
Balthasar, Hans Urs von, 275–76,
  275nn3,4,5
Barker, Terry, 221nn38,39, 257n28
Basilides, 38
Baur, Ferdinand Christian, 31–32, 275–76
Beach, Edward Allen, 48n64, 73n43, 137,
  149n53, 179n113, 181
Berdyaev, Nikolai, 10
Bergson, Henri-Louis, 10, 43, 274, 274n2
Böhme, Jakob, 26n35, 31, 189
Bolman Jr., Frederick de Wolfe, 48n64
Bossuet, Jacques-Bénigne, 195
Bowie, Andrew, 22n31, 48n64, 64n21, 130n4,
  176n106
Brahma, 153, 278
Brentano, Franz, 80
Broerson, Theo, 34, 34n48
Bruno, Giordano, 17, 96–98, 102
Bultmann, Rudolf, 204, 204n18, 263n32
Burckhardt, Jacob, 240

Caringella, Paul, 48, 202n16
Cassirer, Ernst, 21